To  Judith
with love

'The doves weep because there is no peace.'

Anon.

ONE

When the bus was diverted for the fourth time that morning because of bomb damage, Lyndsey MacLaren jumped off the slowly moving vehicle, a tall, leggy girl with finely boned features whose concern at that moment was to get to the Centre, where mothers and children were to be evacuated. She had promised to be there at half past eight and it was now twenty past.

She had cut through several side streets when she stopped, feeling suddenly disorientated. She knew the district yet everything seemed strange. There was no damage here, not even a cracked windowpane. Then, as she felt herself trembling, she leaned against the wall of one of the houses.

How stupid! Of course there was no damage, there had been no bombs dropped on this part. Why was she not thinking clearly? Lyndsey mentally shook herself. It could be tiredness, she had been up all night helping those who had been bombed out and injured. She closed her eyes, momentarily reliving the horrifying scenes she had witnessed. Then a voice brought her back to the present.

'Are you all right, miss?' A middle-aged woman was coming across the road. 'Saw you from the window. Been in the bombing, have you?'

5

'Yes – but I'm not hurt. I think I was running too fast. I'm on my way to the Centre to help with the evacuation and I'm late.'

'There'll be a lot more wanting to be evacuated after last night,' the woman said grimly. 'We were lucky here, but for how long now that the bombers have got further into the city? They promised they wouldn't. Promises, promises, that's all we ever hear. I remember – '

'I must go,' Lyndsey said and moved away.

The woman called after her. 'Why rush? You could be dead tomorrow!'

Lyndsey did not run this time, not because of the woman's prophecy of doom but because she knew she had to slow up or she would be no use doing her job. As she walked she became aware that although there had been no fires here the pungent smell of charred wood was still strong in her nostrils. Would she ever be rid of it?

Minutes later the Centre came into view. Before Lyndsey reached it she could hear the rise and fall of voices. The hall was full and there seemed to be more adults this morning. Some mothers would be going with their children into the country, some would go as far as the station, and others would say their goodbyes at the Centre. Whenever mothers and children parted there were always harrowing scenes.

The younger children were usually subdued, the older ones boisterous, seeing the evacuation as a big adventure. Usually the conversation among the adults covered many subjects, but as Lyndsey edged her way through the crowd the topic this morning seemed to be centred on the previous night's raid.

One woman proclaimed loudly, 'When the poor bloody Eastenders were being pounded night and day you said, "Ain't it a shame," but now the bombs are close to your own doorstep you start moaning.'

'I wasn't moaning,' a small woman replied mildly. 'I

6

was simply saying we should be supplied with bigger and better shelters.'

Lyndsey caught snatches after this: 'All ten in the family wiped out' . . . 'My mam who lives in Poplar has been bombed out three times and she says, you gotta keep cheerful, Maggie' . . .

This last remark reminded Lyndsey of an incident the night before when an elderly woman had had most of her clothes blown off in a bomb blast. She had said with a toothless grin, 'Good job I was left with me vest and bloomers on, gal, weren't it? Saved the blushes of them poor rescue fellers!'

It was this kind of attitude, Lyndsey thought, that helped to win wars, not prophecies of doom.

She had reached the back of the hall when Ann Matley, the girl she had been on her way to visit the day before, came hurrying up. 'Are you all right, Lyndsey? I was so worried, were you caught in the raid?'

Before Lyndsey could reply a small wiry woman came bustling up. 'Come along, girls, no time for gossiping. Lyndsey, would you attend to that child over there.' She pointed to where two small girls were isolated against the dark green distempered walls. 'The youngest one has wet her knickers. The mother came with them but she seems to have disappeared.'

Lyndsey pulled off her gloves. 'I'll get her changed right away.'

'I doubt whether there'll be time for that, the coaches will be here soon to take them to the station. Just talk to her, tell her that her mother will be back any minute. I don't want the poor little thing to start wailing and perhaps set some of the other children off. Ann, you come with me.'

The smallest child, her thumb in her mouth, had big tears rolling slowly down her cheeks. The older girl, pale-faced, stood close to her, her gaze towards the door. Lyndsey, thinking of the child sitting cold and wet on the coach, then on the train journey, went straight to the

7

kitchen and came out with a bowl of warm water, a towel and a newspaper. Going to the children she dropped to her knees and smiled from one to the other.

'Now then, let me see who you are.' The labels pinned to their coats announced them as being Connie and Janie Howard. When Janie gave a hiccuping sob Lyndsey drew her into her arms. Although she had been with the organization for some time she could not get used to the misery of the younger children, some who had never been any further than their own front streets and who were now to be uprooted and live with strangers.

'It's all right, pet,' she soothed. 'Your Mam will be back soon. I'm going to get you changed and then you'll be warm and comfortable. Connie, I'm sure you'll both have a change of knicks in your holdall?'

The older child nodded, 'Me Mam went to look for me grandad, he was going to see us off.' Her lips trembled. 'But she hasn't come back. We both have new knickers, I'll get a pair out.'

By the time Lyndsey had washed and dried the skinny little limbs and pulled on a pair of navy blue fleecy-lined knickers, a woman came hurrying up. She gave a cry of dismay. 'Oh, Janie – you haven't – ?'

Lyndsey grinned. 'Only wet them, worse things happen at sea. I've changed her and wrapped the others in a newspaper. Perhaps you can take charge now, I can hear someone calling me.'

'Yes, yes, of course. I was looking for my father, he might have gone straight to the station.'

Lyndsey was about to leave when she paused. 'Are you going with the children, Mrs Howard?'

'Only to the station. I have a sick husband, but I have spoken to one of the helpers who's agreed to take over from me on the platform.'

'Oh, good. Connie and Janie will be well looked after, don't worry.'

This incident was only one of several that Lyndsey had

to deal with during the next few minutes. Two children and one of the mothers were sick, then through some horseplay among the older boys she had to deal with a bloodied nose, a twisted ankle and some scratches that drew blood.

A man then called through a megaphone that the coaches had arrived and everyone was to behave in an orderly manner. He warned if the children did not behave themselves they would be left behind.

At this a woman shouted, 'Not if I know it! Let some other bugger look after mine, I've had a bellyful.' Which brought a burst of laughter.

At last the coaches were filled and on their way to the station. To Lyndsey, the parting at the station was always the worst, with some children sobbing and mothers weeping. Some women tried to snatch their children from the carriages at the last minute, declaring it was far better for them to be killed by bombs than to die of misery with strangers.

Ann and Lyndsey sat together on the back seat, with Ann talking about the raid. 'It was so unexpected, wasn't it? We had all got so used to the East End getting the heavy bombing that I think we began to feel that we were immune. Not that *we* suffered any damage, or the streets around us.'

'I'm glad,' Lyndsey said quietly, not wanting to talk about the raid.

'Mother and I went into the shelter of course when we saw wave after wave of planes coming over,' Ann went on, 'and it wasn't until we were in the shelter that Mother reminded me that you would be on your way to us and could have been caught in the thick of it. Were you?'

Lyndsey told her she had taken cover. Ann said, 'Good,' and went on to talk about the new boyfriend she had met, describing him and where they had met. Lyndsey, who had been determined to close her mind to the previous night's raid, tried hard to concentrate on what she was saying, but images kept rising . . . the stranger grabbing her arm and running her to a shelter as bombs fell around them . . . the overcrowded shelter, being jammed against the chemical closets, four of them to serve a mass of people. She experienced again the nausea at the stench . . .

Then someone had shouted down to ask for volunteers and she had gone up with a number of people . . . and had been shocked at the devastation, the cries of those injured . . .

Ann's voice impinged on the images. 'I tell you what staggered us when at last we came out of the shelter, the number of fires, and the hundreds of places that were burning! I know it was terrible but it was magnificent to watch, the colours of the flames! I don't think any artist could capture such beauty.'

Beauty? Lyndsey closed her eyes trying not to see the two people who had come running out of a house, their clothes ablaze . . . The smell in her nostrils now was not of charred timbers but clothes burning, flesh . . .

Lyndsey sat up. 'I wonder where we are bound for today?'

Ann shrugged. 'Who knows? I think it's daft keeping it a secret from us, and I also think it's stupid removing names from signposts and railway stations. If the Germans drop spies by parachute they would have maps and soon find out where they were.'

A woman in front turned her head. 'They wouldn't. It's difficult to identify places. What's more, if removing place names saves lives, especially *my* kids' lives, then I'm all for it!'

Ann grinned at Lyndsey, then leaning forward she said in a serious tone, 'You're right, of course, I'm being stupid.'

Lyndsey found it difficult to weigh up this small sandy-haired girl, but then they had known one another for just a short time. Ann had come to help at the Centre two weeks before and possibly because she and Lyndsey were the the youngest of the volunteers they had been drawn together.

Ann's mother had invited her to tea the day before and Lyndsey was sorry she had not been able to go.

Ann began saying how she would like to buy a new dress and talked clothes until they reached the station.

Fortunately the partings were made easier this time by a group of soldiers who talked and joked with the children, plus two lively porters and a cheery, informative train driver.

Lyndsey who had looked for Connie and Janie saw one of the helpers, a plump motherly woman, take over from Mrs Howard and was satisfied they would be all right.

During the journey there was some discussion where they were making for. The same woman who had spoken earlier about the signs disclosed they were in Kent – she recognized landmarks. It made no difference to Lyndsey where she was going, all she wanted was to see the children settled. At least the system was better than at the beginning of the war. Then, when the mass evacuation took place, the children were taken to a hall where those fostering them came and chose the child, or children, they wanted, which was a terrible, humiliating experience for those left until last. Now villagers were allotted their evacuees and billeting officers dealt with them, delivering those mothers and children who could not be collected.

Lyndsey had sympathy for the people who were forced to take evacuees if they had room and angry with those who had facilities but made excuses. They had grandparents coming to stay, parents, cousins, uncles and aunts – coming any day now.

There was a lot of friction in some homes. Many children had come from tenements, were lousy, flea-ridden, tough – but others were lovingly accepted, treated as family.

When the evacuation was done through schools, teachers travelled with them and some stayed the whole time. But there were a number of voluntary organizations run by various districts and it was to one of these that Lyndsey belonged. On a long journey arrangements would be made for the helpers to stay overnight, on short journeys they often returned once the children had been handed over. Lyndsey liked staying over, for there was no one to rush back to, not like Ann who had a family and, invariably it seemed, a boyfriend to meet.

Lyndsey thought with a sudden longing of when she had lived at Echo Cove. How carefree her life was then, how fun-loving she had been. There was no shortage of boyfriends then. Some of the boys were those she had known since childhood, the others were summer visitors; they had swum, sailed, had beach parties, danced in barns . . .

Then had come the double tragedy when she had lost both parents and grandparents and her Uncle Richard had brought her to London to live with him and his wife Marian. They were kind enough to her in their own way, but they were dedicated to their work, and when they did entertain it was people of their own generation with the talk always of war situations.

The September day was fine and sunny and when they arrived at their destination the novelty of being in the countryside, plus being welcomed at the village hall where tables were laid with bread and jam and scones and jugs of lemonade, there was a lightening of spirits among most of the party. But some of the smaller children still had the bewildered look that never failed to pull at Lyndsey's heartstrings.

When the meal was over billeting officers started going round with their lists, getting people organized. A few of the evacuees had been collected by villagers living near. Lyndsey, who had caught sight of little Connie and Janie sitting with a stranger, was on her way over to have a word with them when someone caught hold of her arm. It was a woman with twin boys who had travelled with them. She begged Lyndsey's help and looked so pale and distraught Lyndsey felt alarmed.

'What's wrong, Mrs Frear? Where are the children?'

'They're all right. We went to our billet, it's just down

the street. Our landlady is very nice. She was going shopping and took the boys with her. She told me she would only be about half an hour and said to make myself comfortable.' The woman swayed and Lyndsey made to take her to a seat. She protested gently.

'No, I need to lie down. I have a terrible migraine come on and it's the only way.' The woman paused. 'The only thing is I feel I can't go upstairs and lie down in a stranger's house. Would you come with me?'

Lyndsey agreed and after she had explained the position to a billeting officer they left.

By the time they reached the house the woman was so ill Lyndsey had to help to undress her and get her into bed. She drew the curtains and after telling her she would stay until her landlady returned she went downstairs.

The kitchen had a cosy air; the chintz-covered armchair was so inviting that Lyndsey sank into it and closed her eyes. What a lot had happened since the day before. She was glad she had been able to find a phone to leave a message for Marian to let her know she was all right. Marian was a stickler for things like order, punctuality . . .

Lyndsey roused to hear voices. Heavens, she had fallen asleep! She sat up, and found a small, plump woman smiling at her. 'Hello, you are the young woman who brought Mrs Frear home. Your friend Ann has just told me. She said to tell you she's catching the next train back to London. She'll phone you this evening.'

Lyndsey got up. 'Oh – thanks. I'm sorry I fell asleep, I've never done that before.'

'Don't apologize, I know you were all up very early. Would you like a cup of tea? I'll soon make one.'

'It's very kind of you, but I must get back to the hall.'

'Well, don't you worry about Mrs Frear and the boys. I'll look after them, I'm delighted to have their company. I've been a widow for the past ten years and my family all live away.'

This was one of the cases that Lyndsey felt would turn

out well. Heart-warming for a mother and sons to have such a welcome. Some people took the evacuees in for the money then half starved them. There were others who tried to treat them as paid servants. On the other hand there were women evacuated who expected to be waited on hand and foot. Lyndsey wondered on her way back to the hall if everything had gone smoothly.

She was met a few minutes later by a worried-looking billeting officer called George. 'It's Lyndsey, isn't it?' he said. 'I've come up against a problem and everyone seems suddenly to have disappeared. Perhaps you can help.' He held out a list.

'There seems to be a slip-up. A Mr Wright and his sister who run a small farm agreed to take two older boys to help with the animals, but all I'm left with are two little lasses, and they're too young to do any farm work! They're called Howard, Connie and Janie. Perhaps you know them?'

'Yes, I do, I met them this morning. Where are they?'

'In the car. Trouble is there's no place else to take them. I don't live here, I came over from Frinley to help.'

As they walked to the car Lyndsey suggested that the family at the farm might take the girls until other accommodation could be found. And George agreed.

The two children were sat close together in the back of the car. 'Hello,' Lyndsey said softly, 'we meet again.' Connie looked at her hopefully and Janie gave her a faint tremulous smile. Lyndsey got into the car. 'I'm going with you, we're taking you to a farm.' She sat between the children and put an arm around each.

George grinned and got into the car. 'Glad you've agreed to come. Judging by the map the farm is about a mile away.'

The children were silent. Lyndsey asked them if their grandfather had come to see them off at the station and they both nodded. She asked if they had seen the sheep and the cows from the train and they nodded again. She

14

presumed that the woman who had taken charge of them in the train had returned to London.

George talked about the evacuation saying how smoothly everything had gone until this, his last 'assignment' for the day. He added, 'Perhaps we'll be lucky, perhaps they love little girls.' His tone belied the hope.

When the farm came into view Lyndsey was about to say it looked a bit bleak, but quickly changed it to, 'It looks solid.' It was stone-built with outhouses on the right. The only sign of life was a cat washing itself in front of the house.

As they drew closer however, there was the brightness of a fire to be seen through one of the windows. In answer to their knock on the weatherbeaten door a big woman with tousled grey hair appeared. She wiped her hands on her coarse sacking apron as she demanded to know what they wanted.

When George explained, she said, 'We don't want no kids.' He studied the list and reminded her that they had agreed to take two boys. To this she replied, 'Well, me and me brother changed our minds, didn't we? We ain't got no convenience. No lavatory, just two holes in the ground, out back, behind those bushes. You can take a look if you like.'

Lyndsey stared at her. 'Two holes in the ground? Yes, we *would* like to take a look.' She marched away and George hurried after her.

'I say, Lyndsey, there's something wrong here. It says earth-closet. I can't imagine any billeting officer accepting two holes outside.'

'And neither can I. That's why I want to take a look.'

They found the holes behind the group of bushes, looking as if they had been recently dug. Lyndsey looked about her then pointed to a short distance away where there was a concrete slab with a large bucket on it covered by some creosoted planks of wood.

'There's your earth-closet,' she said, fuming. 'They've actually pulled it down, knowing that no one would allow

15

them to have children under these conditions. Come on, I shall have something to say to Miss Wright *and*, I hope, her brother.'

Brother and sister were standing side by side at the back door when Lyndsey came up to them. Neither showed any expression.

She looked from one to the other. 'I can't believe it. I can't believe that two mature people would go to the trouble of pulling down an earth-closet to avoid taking two poor kids who've been bombed out of their home! All I can say is, may you simmer in your own stinking slime!' With that she marched away with George once more hurrying after her.

'Oh, Lyndsey, I don't know what the people at the hall are going to say. You were a bit strong, weren't you?'

'Strong? I only wish I had said a lot more!'

George began to laugh. 'You got through to the woman. Did you see her face, it was puce. But her brother didn't turn a hair.' He suddenly sobered. 'The trouble is, there's nowhere else to take the little lasses. The village has been combed for accommodation.'

'I'll find somewhere if it takes till midnight. Someone, somewhere, with a heart, will take pity on the poor mites.'

The children, who had waited patiently in the car, showed no surprise when Lyndsey told them that the farm was not quite suitable for them to stay.

When they went back to the hall and described what had happened at the farm they were all furious. The billeting officer who had dealt with the Wrights said, 'I don't like the people, but they did have a good fire on and they were eating well when I visited them. After all, we don't expect Buckingham Palace for the children, just some comforts. But I wouldn't have allowed even older boys to have stayed under their present conditions. What some people will do!'

Over cups of tea George laughingly told them all what Lyndsey had said to the Wrights. The majority laughed, thought it was a good comment, but one of the older women scolded Lyndsey, told her that no matter what happened she must never lose her temper. It was part of the job.

Lyndsey said she would try and be more circumspect in future yet knew deep down she would have difficulty in controlling her tongue if a similar incident occurred. She drained her cup and got up. 'Well, I'm on my way to tour the village for accommodation. I promise you I'll come back with somewhere comfortable for Connie and Janie to stay.'

But after tramping around for an hour Lyndsey was forced to accept that she might meet defeat. She was walking towards some small shops when someone hailed her. 'Miss MacLaren – Miss MacLaren, wait, please . . .'

Lyndsey turned to find a red-haired woman hurrying towards her. She was flamboyantly dressed, her eyelashes heavily mascaraed, her cheeks rouged and her lips ruby red. She came up, beaming, breathless.

'I've been dying to meet you – I've heard all about your meeting with the farmer and his sister.'

Lyndsey felt alarmed. 'Heavens! News certainly travels around here, I'll be losing my job if this gets much further afield.'

'No you won't, you did quite right. Oh, I loved what you said to them. "May you simmer in your own stinking slime!" Such rich words to roll around one's tongue.'

She leaned forward and added in a confidential way, 'I may look like a tart, dear, most people in this village think I am, but actually I was on the boards. My husband and I did a double act. My stage name is Bette Bascony.' She gave a deep-throated laugh. 'My maiden name was Lizzie Fish! Do you wonder that I was glad to change it? Still, I'm not here to talk about me – it's the children –'

'You'll take them?' Although Bette Bascony might not be a billeting officer's dream of the right person to mother children, Lyndsey knew she would have no hesitation in letting Connie and Janie Howard stay with her. There was a great warmth in this woman.

'Yes, I will,' Bette said. 'I didn't offer to take any children before because I was expecting to go back to London to live, then a nephew of my husband wanted to come for a visit so I postponed it. But there – that's another story. Come and see the house, it's just down here.'

It was a large, three-storey brick-built house with a chestnut tree on one side and a small copse on the other. Lyndsey found herself thinking that when the weather was warmer it would be an ideal place for children to play.

They went into a living room that was as flamboyant as Bette herself. In most homes the black-out curtains were just that, but Bette's, which covered the whole of one wall, were richly appliquéd with pieces of velvet and brocade in reds, greens, blues, purples and golds. There was also a looped pelmet that was heavily fringed with gold braid. Another wall was decorated with photographs of music hall artistes. From the ceiling hung a large bowl in which five or six goldfish swam lazily. There were two budgies in a cage, a black and white cat stretched out on a fur rug in front of the fire and at the side of the fireplace were four black kittens curled up in a box. A children's paradise!

To complete the picture, apart from two comfortable-looking chairs were two massive floor cushions with Eastern-looking coverings and three exotic lamps with cherry-coloured shades.

'It's lovely, Mrs Bascony,' Lyndsey enthused. 'What better place can there be for children than this?'

Bette beamed. 'I'm so glad you like it, and for heaven's sake call me Bette, everyone else does. And your name, I know, is Lyndsey. Look, you go and fetch the children, I'll get a meal ready and make up a bed. What about you? Are you staying overnight? If so I would love to have you stay here.'

Lyndsey had no hesitation in saying that she would like nothing better.

She was back in no time and was touched by the way Bette hugged each child in turn saying softly, 'Come to Aunt Bette, my little darlings. Here, let me have your hats and coats.'

The gazes of the children were everywhere and when Janie saw the kittens her whole face lighted up. She shyly asked their names and when Bette said, 'Eeny, Meenie, Miny and Mo,' both children laughed. The ice was broken and although neither Connie nor Janie had much to say Lyndsey felt sure it would not be long before they would be chattering away.

Later, when the children were fast asleep in a plump feather bed, Bette and Lyndsey settled down beside the fire for a chat, Bette smoking a cigarette in a long cigarette holder. Lyndsey, not wanting to talk about her own life, asked Bette about her life in the theatre.

'It was a lovely life, darling, peopled with some wonderful characters. Oh, there was some bitchiness, there were tragedies, but there was also a lot of fun and laughter. I wouldn't have missed it for worlds.'

Bette went on to say that she came from a long line of stage people. Her parents were music hall stars and she had been born in the theatre. She had done a song and tap dance routine from the age of four. Then when she was sixteen she met and fell in love with Rupert Bascony, a magician. With her parents' consent they married and Bette became her husband's assistant.

'He was a wonderful man, everyone liked Rupert.' Bette paused. 'Then six months ago he became ill. He was in hospital for a while and before they were going to release him the doctor told me I should get him into country air. I rented this house, had it all done up, but – he died before he even saw it. Rupert had begged me not to grieve if anything happened to him because we had had such a wonderful life together and I tried not to. I didn't even tell any of them in the village. But lately I've realized I can't go on living here. I want to go back to London.'

19

'Is that wise?' Lyndsey asked gently. 'With all the bombing.'

'I need to be active, I've been on the go all my life. Now I'm simply stagnating here.'

Lyndsey hesitated a moment then said, 'You seem to have quite a few rooms here, why don't you offer to take some servicemen, those who've been on active duty and although not wounded need somewhere to recuperate. Some need only a few days, it's peace and quiet they want.'

Bette was immediately interested. She sat up, took the stub of the cigarette from the holder and threw it in the fire. 'I didn't know about that. I wouldn't mind taking on such a job, I would feel I was doing something worthwhile. Where would I apply?'

'I don't know, but I can ask my Uncle Richard's wife. Marian seems to know everything about that kind of thing.'

'You sound as if you don't like her,' Bette said, eyebrows raised.

Lyndsey felt dismayed. 'I'm sorry if I gave you that impression. I admire her tremendously. She's so efficient and an indefatigable worker. She's with the Ministry of Defence and my uncle is with the Ministry of Supplies. He's often away and Marian goes away too at times, in connection with her work. I think the trouble is I've hardly had a chance to get to know her.'

'It sounds as if you live with them?'

'I do. Uncle Richard is my guardian. My parents and my grandparents are dead. They were on holiday in Italy and were caught in a freak storm while touring. They were buried under a mountain fall.'

'Oh, Lyndsey, how awful. I wouldn't have mentioned it had I known.'

'It's all right. I realize I have to talk about them. It happened over a year ago, yet somehow I still feel raw about it.'

'Of course you do.'

Once Lyndsey had talked about the tragedy she felt she

must explain about Richard and Marian. 'Uncle Richard was my grandparents' only son. They left him the house in Mayfair. He was a globe-trotter but after the accident he told me he was home to stay and he was going to bring me to London to live with him. Not long after this he married Marian and sometimes I think he married her to try and give me a proper home.'

'You could be wrong,' Bette said gently.

'Yes, I could be. I must try to get to know her better. Now tell me more about your stage life, that is, if you can bear to talk about it.'

'Darling, I like nothing better. My trouble is that I never know when to stop. What shall I tell you?'

For the next half hour Bette took Lyndsey into a world unknown to her, of artistes not only doing two performances in an evening, and matinées, but working at two theatres at the same time, madly taxi-ing from one to the other.

'You did this,' Bette said, 'whether you had pains in your belly, a splitting headache or a streaming cold. *And* you smiled.'

She went on from there to talk about digs and landladies, the good and the bad, those who would put you in damp beds and half starve you and the real troupers who would welcome you with a good meal and have the beds ready warmed.

'There were times, of course, when you had no choice, all the good places were filled up.' A pensive look came into Bette's eyes. 'Rupert and I had decided that when we retired we would start a theatrical boarding house. But it was not to be.' She jumped up. 'Come and see our photographs. Oh, don't worry, I'm not going to tell you who everyone is on this wall, it would take until the early hours!' Bette pointed to a group of photographs in the middle. 'These are the ones I like the best, when I became Rupert's assistant in his act. Don't you think he was handsome?'

Lyndsey saw a tall, slender man with fair hair and an

endearing smile. In every photograph he was in evening dress with a cape draped over one shoulder. 'Very attractive,' Lyndsey said, 'and *you* are saucy.' Bette was wearing a short, bouncy-skirted dress, her shoulders bare, frilled net around her wrists and ribbon bows in her hair.

She laughed. 'That was what Rupert used to say. Oh, I want you to compare two photographs. Just a minute.' She went to the mantelpiece, took a photograph from an envelope and came over with it. 'Now this is Rupert's nephew who is coming this weekend to stay. Compare it with this photograph of my husband when he was twenty-four. Don't you think they look alike?'

The one taken from the envelope was of a man in air force uniform, a pilot-officer. Lyndsey said they could be twins and Bette nodded. 'That's exactly what I thought when I saw it. I got such a surprise when I heard that Andrew was in England. His family emigrated to New Zealand when he was a baby. It'll be lovely to see him. Come along, let's have a drink. It's not often I have anyone to drink with and I hate drinking on my own.'

They sat down with a glass of sherry each then Bette began talking about how she would like to start a concert party and go round the camps.

'I know ENSA does it, but there's room for more and there are quite a few splinter groups I've heard of.' Bette laughed. 'If I get one going I'll rope you in. The men need some glamour.'

Lyndsey stared at her. 'A concert party? I can't sing, I can't act, I would be no good.'

'Yes, you would, you could dance, you have the body and legs for it. You could have been one of the Windmill girls. I bet you can kick your height without any effort.'

Lyndsey said she had done so fooling around when she was at school, but not since. Then getting up she laughed and added, 'But if you want a demonstration – blame it on the sherry.' She did a double kick that brought applause from Bette.

'Marvellous! You're in.'

'Bette, don't take this seriously, I'm hoping to join the Wrens in six months' time.'

'*That* is six months away, darling!' Bette sat up again. 'Lyndsey, would you come to stay for the weekend when Andrew is here? It would help. I've never met him before and although I'm not exactly the shy type' – she grinned – 'it would be so nice to have someone younger here.'

When Lyndsey hesitated Bette said, 'I will have the children to look after,' Lyndsey laughed and called her a schemer, then told her she would like to come for the weekend.

It was after midnight when they went to bed and Lyndsey lay in bed in the country quiet her mind turning over the events of the day, arriving late at the Centre, meeting little Connie and Janie, going to the awful farm, meeting Bette Bascony. Lyndsey felt a warmth thinking of Bette, knowing she had made a new friend.

She thought of Marian, brisk, so organized, not attractive, yet having a personality. Had she misjudged her? Was it jealousy that Marian was living in her grand-parents' house where she had spent so many happy holidays? Perhaps it was this that made her seem such a stranger. They had been such a closely-knit family.

An image of all the photographs covering one wall of the room downstairs came into Lyndsey's mind then. Bette had pointed out various people and told her stories about them, the juggling family, the circus clown she had once been in love with, the acrobatic trio, the tap dancers, the stand-up comics . . . so many different turns. What a colourful life Bette had led. And she had loved – and been loved.

Under her eyelids Lyndsey saw a tall, fair-haired man in RAF uniform, a man with an endearing smile. Would he be as attractive as his Uncle Rupert? In another five days she would know.

It was her last thought before she slept.

TWO

When Lyndsey arrived back the following morning she was surprised to find Marian at home. 'Hello,' she said, 'is something wrong? It's unusual to find you here at this hour.'

Marian, who was sorting through some papers, looked up.

'Oh, there you are, Lyndsey. I'm glad you left a message for me. I was worried knowing you could be in the bombing area. I have to go away in connection with my work and I could be away for a month or more.' She gathered up some papers and put them in her brief-case. 'Under the circumstances I think it would be wise for you to stay with some friends of mine in Cornwall. I have spoken to them and they would be delighted to have you.'

'No,' Lyndsey said sharply, 'I want to stay in London. I also have a job to do. Mrs Grey will be here.'

'No, she won't. She's taking the opportunity of visiting her daughter.' Marian shook her head with an impatient gesture. 'Be reasonable, Lyndsey, I can't leave you on your own, not now that the raids are spreading to other districts.'

'Then I shall stay with friends of my own. Ann Matley offered to put me up whenever I wanted and so did a friend in Kent. I know it would mean train travelling but I wouldn't mind that.'

'Well – I suppose it will be all right, it's just that I don't want you to be on your own.' Marian picked up a coat from the back of a chair and put it on, then she frowned. 'I don't remember you mentioning having friends in Kent.'

Lyndsey, not wanting to go into details, said, 'It's a safe part, the evacuees are there. When are you leaving?'

'Not until six o'clock. I came home to pack and to wait until you arrived, but now that you're here I shall go back to the office. Richard isn't expected home for several weeks. If he should come home before I'm back he can sleep here and eat at his club.'

Lyndsey said, before she could stop herself, 'Why did you and Uncle Richard marry?'

'Why?' Marian looked at her in surprise. 'Because we fell in love. Isn't that the usual reason?' A faint smile touched her lips.

'But you're not – '

'Demonstrative? Not in public, no. Richard and I would like to be together all the time, we would like to have children, but there's a war on, and as we are needed, and in different sectors . . .'

Lyndsey, who found it impossible to think of her globe-trotting uncle and this small efficient woman as parents, found herself staring. Marian, who seemed unaware of it, began pulling on her gloves.

'Let me know when you've decided which friends you will be staying with. Send your letters to the office, they will forward them on to me. If there is any bombing in the area at all do go into the basement shelter. I hope you will be sensible about it.'

Lyndsey wondered what Marian would say if she knew about the raid she had been involved in two days before. Marian came over and kissed her on the cheek. 'Take care of yourself, Lyndsey.'

'And you. Give Uncle Richard my love when you write to him.'

'I'll do that. 'Bye.'

Lyndsey watched the small, neat figure from the

drawing-room window, watched her hailing a cruising taxi and thought what an enigma this woman was. She seemed to have no warmth yet spoke of Richard and herself being in love and wanting children. Although Lyndsey had seen very little of her uncle over the years she loved him because he had always been so kind to her as a child, had talked to her as an equal about the foreign places he had visited. He had brought her presents, unusual presents from the countries he visited. He had been so gentle with her when she lost her parents and grandparents and later he talked to her about his own grief that he had spent so much of his life away from his own parents.

And yet in spite of this she never felt she really knew him. Did Marian? Once she said that she had met Richard in Paris, and only once had she spoken about her parents when she mentioned that her father had been a dominant man and had refused to allow her to follow a business career. She added that both she and her mother had felt freed when he died. Perhaps it was because of her father that Marian had learned to keep a tight control over her emotions.

Lyndsey, who had come from a warm, closely-knit family, felt a sudden longing to feel arms around her holding her close, to be wanted, loved.

A phone call to Bette saying she was free to come and stay with her brought such a gleeful response that Lyndsey's despondency vanished. Bette urged her to get on a train and come right away but Lyndsey explained it would have to be the weekend, . . . she was looking forward to seeing them all.

Mrs Grey, who had been housekeeper to Marian and Richard since they were married, came in to see what Lyndsey wanted for lunch. She was an efficient but taciturn woman who spoke disparagingly of what she called the 'idle rich'. When Lyndsey asked her one day why she worked for them when she despised them so much, Mrs Grey snapped, 'You mind your own business, it has

26

nothing to do with you.' After that Lyndsey took care to avoid her whenever possible.

Now, not wanting to cause any fuss, she said, 'A snack will do, Mrs Grey, a sandwich even, I shall be going out this afternoon.'

'Gallivanting again, I suppose. I heard about you being out all night. It's time you did something useful, like going into a factory!'

Lyndsey bridled. 'The night before last, Mrs Grey, I had no sleep, I was putting out incendiaries, helping those injured in the bombing. There were people without arms, without legs, and I saw a body without a head. I don't call that gallivanting, Mrs Grey! Yesterday I went with the evacuees into the country and this afternoon I'm going to the Centre to help care for those who were made home-less. Tomorrow I'm – '.

'I didn't know,' the woman mumbled.

'You should ask, Mrs Grey, you're a difficult woman to talk to.'

'You're a different class to me and mine!' she retorted.

'I'm no different. When I was putting out incendiaries there was a titled woman helping me. She didn't tell me, someone else did. When planes are up there the enemy doesn't say, you mustn't shoot that one down the pilot is the son of a lord!'

'I'll get your meal.' Mrs Grey shuffled out.

Lyndsey's anger drained away. Why did she always fly off the handle when someone said something that annoyed her? Mrs Grey had daughters working in munitions – one of them had been injured in an explosion. No doubt she was thinking of that and was resentful that another girl was living in luxury and, to her mind, 'gallivanting'.

In the afternoon Lyndsey went to the Centre where there was always a job to do. Every volunteer had agreed to do twenty hours a week as they did in the WVS, but many, like Lyndsey, did a lot more. There were clothes to be sorted for the homeless, and although they were secondhand they were good quality, the public had been generous. There were mattress covers to be filled with straw, cups of tea to be made for the pallid-faced people whose misery was heartbreaking to see, especially the older people who had lost everything they owned, little houses they had lived in all their married lives.

But always, in every group or crowd there were always those who would cheer the others up. 'Come on, snap out of it! We ain't going to let that rotten Hitler beat us, are we?' At this there would be a concerted cry of 'No!' even if some of the voices were weak. Someone else would remind them of the Tommy Handley comedy show and add, 'We'll see what Funf is up to this week.' The *ITMA* show was one of the highlights of the week, the other was the nine o'clock news and every night at nine o'clock people would be glued to their wirelesses.

And when Churchill was speaking the whole country listened in. His stirring speeches inspired them to be confident that Britain could not fail to win, 'not while every one was working and fighting to that end!' There were often cheers after these speeches.

The first time Ann came to the Centre since they had been to Kent she said, 'Sorry I rushed away, I had my boyfriend to meet, he does shift work. Actually, I went off him that evening, but I've met someone else who is a *positive dream.*'

Ann talked about him as she worked, but it did not hold her up. It was one of the things Lyndsey admired her for, her dedication to the job and her liking for children. Although she had rushed away the day of the evacuation she would not have left unless there were people to take over the job.

Lyndsey told her about going to stay with Bette Bascony for a while but made no mention about meeting an attractive flying officer. Ann was already at the next stage of her story about the new boyfriend.

By the time Saturday morning came Lyndsey was not

only looking forward to seeing Bette and the children and meeting Andrew but to the country quiet to enjoy a good night's sleep. The sirens had been going day and night and although there had been no bombing in their area the constant gunfire had made her relive the night of the raid when she had seen so many people killed and injured. She had spoken about it to Ann when she had remarked that Lyndsey looked 'jaded' and was given the advice, 'Put it right out of your mind, you can if you're determined to do so. If you don't it'll become an obsession with you and it could make you ill.'

Lyndsey knew it was sensible advice and only hoped the weekend would clear her mind of the horrors. A good omen was the fact that she began to feel excited during the train journey on the Saturday morning and her excitement was heightened when she arrived at her destination to see a tall man in air force uniform waiting with Bette and the children.

Bette, a cerise flimsy scarf tied around her forehead, with flowing ends, gave her an exuberant welcome. 'Lyndsey, darling, how lovely to see you again. We missed you, the children have never stopped talking about you. Oh, we're going to have a lovely time. Connie, Janie, give your Auntie Lyndsey a kiss.' With shy smiles the children held up their arms and Lyndsey hugged them. Then Bette was saying, 'And now you must meet my dear nephew.' To Andrew she added, 'Andrew, this is our very lovely Lyndsey MacLaren.'

Lyndsey found herself looking into deep blue eyes, eyes that held a roguish twinkle. His handclasp was firm as he said, 'Bette had you billed in glowing lights as THE PERFECT GIRL! If you had not turned up this morning those lights would have dimmed considerably for me.'

Lyndsey laughed softly. 'They'll soom dim when you get to know me. I have faults as long as your arm.'

'I prefer to believe Bette, who is a most discerning person.'

Oh, that engaging smile. Lyndsey felt a tremor go through her. What charm he had. Any girl could fall for a man like this. She must beware and not let herself get carried away. She said on a teasing note, 'And what does Bette have to say about *you*?'

'She knows that I work hard and play hard.' He grinned. 'I told her so. Not that there is much opportunity for playing hard on a sheep farm in New Zealand. To be honest I really lead quite a monastic life.'

'Oh yes?' They all laughed and Bette said, 'Come along, we'll walk home and have a cup of coffee, then we're going for a ride in Andrew's car. He has only enough petrol for this one jaunt.'

Andrew explained that the car had been lent to him by a friend, who had also been generous enough to give him his petrol ration. As they went out of the station Andrew swung Janie up into his arms and took hold of Connie's hand, as though he were used to handling children. Perhaps he was, perhaps he was married and had a young family of his own. Lyndsey would not allow herself to dwell on such a possibility.

Janie, thumb in mouth, finger hooked over her nose, was eyeing Andrew in an old-fashioned, speculative way as though trying to weigh up how he fitted into the party. Connie, after Lyndsey had taken her other hand, gave a jump and said, 'We saw some hens yesterday and chickens.'

This set Janie off to inform Lyndsey that they had had eggs for breakfast that morning, brown ones, which the hens had laid. And after that they chatted away about all they had seen and done. They had nursed the kittens, taught the budgies to say their names, fed the goldfish, seen the sheep and the cows.

Bette laughed. 'We've never had a dull moment. They've even made friends with my neighbours. One of them, Mrs Petrie, has offered to come and sit with them if we want to go out this evening. We'll see.'

While Bette made the coffee the children went out into the back garden to play with shuttlecocks and battledores. Lyndsey said, 'You're good with children. Have you a family of your own?'

'I have two sisters and two brothers with twelve children between them. When I saw Connie and Janie this morning it felt like a little bit of home.'

The wistfulness in his voice was something Lyndsey had heard in the voices of other servicemen and understood only too well that dreadful longing, the awful ache for home – and family.

'Bette tells me that *you* are splendid with children, Lyndsey, and work with evacuees. She also said that you are planning to join the Wrens in time. Why not the Waafs?' he teased.

'Because I've lived by the sea all my life and love it.'

Andrew asked her where she had lived and when Lyndsey told him a small fishing village on the north-east coast called Echo Cove, Andrew gave a shout.

'I know it! Or should I say, I know *of* it. A cousin of mine who came on a visit to England about three years ago stayed at a place called Caister. He mentioned Echo Cove and how the cliffs echo voices and sounds at full tide. Well, isn't that a coincidence! Tell me more about it.'

Lyndsey hesitated a moment then explained how her parents had run a pottery business there. At this Andrew gave another shout.

'My cousin brought back pottery pieces as presents from Echo Cove! They were displayed in a café with wonderful murals painted on the walls. Could these be pottery pieces your parents had made? Or is that *too* much of a coincidence?'

'No,' Lyndsey said quietly. 'Their work was displayed in the café. My father painted the murals. Ivy, who ran the café, was an old and very dear friend of the family.'

Bette, who had come in with a tray, said worriedly, 'Andrew, I think it might be best not to pursue the subject.

31

You see, Lyndsey's parents and grandparents were killed in a tragic accident.'

Andrew was so contrite that Lyndsey said quickly, 'It's all right. I think it's best to talk about them; for a long time I couldn't. Here, Bette, let me help you.' Lyndsey laid out the cups and saucers and when the coffee was poured they talked about their suggested run-out in the car that afternoon.

'There's a farm about three miles away where they have ducks on the pond,' Bette said, 'and they have cattle, geese and turkeys. I thought the children would love it.' She laughed suddenly. 'I must be mad. Here is poor Andrew wanting to get away from sheep and I'm suggesting going to a farm. What would you like to see, Andrew?'

'The ducks on the pond,' he answered promptly, a twinkle in his eyes. 'Actually, it would be interesting to talk to an English farmer. I'm also interested in visiting some of my father's side of the family.'

Bette explained to Lyndsey that Andrew's father and her husband Rupert, who were brothers, had been adopted by different families when their widowed mother died, Rupert by people connected with show business and his brother by a couple who emigrated to New Zealand.

'And it was only recently that Dad learned who his real parents were,' Andrew said. 'So, when he knew my mind was set on coming to England to join the RAF he asked me to look them up. Bette was first on my list.' He smiled from Bette to Lyndsey. 'And aren't I glad she was.'

The children came running in saying they were cold. The late September morning had been sunny but now it had clouded over. Bette took off their coats and hats and scarves and while Lyndsey warmed Janie's hands in hers Andrew clasped Connie's hands. To Lyndsey there was a lovely close feeling of being with a family again.

After lunch they wrapped up and clambered into the Austin car. It was old but seemed efficient. The sun had come out again but the air was perceptibly colder than

32

that of the morning. The children, excited at this treat, chattered away wanting to know what noises ducks and turkeys and geese made. Andrew did a passable imitation of the quacking, the gobble-gobbling and hissing that brought a laughing comment from Bette that she must have him in her concert party. To this Andrew grinned and asked if it was a promise or a threat!

There was a happy, carefree atmosphere as they drove along a low-hedged lane, then Connie said, 'Look, Auntie Bette, there's a man with a big umbrella up in the sky.'

There was a sudden silence. Andrew brought the car to a halt. He got out followed by Lyndsey and Bette, with Bette telling the children quietly to stay where they were.

The parachutist had jumped from a Messerschmitt, which even now was completing its screaming dive out of the sky. It crashed behind a belt of trees and black smoke rose. Flames followed the smoke, then, as the parachutist landed, came the exploding of ammunition.

In a seemingly deserted countryside people came running from all directions. A woman from a nearby cottage waved a rolling pin. Then a farm worker appeared carrying a pitchfork and yelling, 'I'll stick this into that German's guts. He'll pay for my lad!'

A police car came into view, bell clanging. It turned right at the road junction ahead. Bette shuddered. 'I hope they get there before anyone has a chance to kill the pilot. He's some mother's son, God help him.' Andrew said he would go and see what he could do. He vaulted a nearby gate and sprinted across the field.

The children were silent, looking from Bette to Lyndsey with rounded eyes, obviously sensing the drama of the man with the 'umbrella' in the sky. Bette said, 'It's all right, my lovelies, we shall all go to the farm when Uncle Andrew comes back.' To Lyndsey she added in a low voice, 'We must, we can't spoil their pleasure.'

Andrew, who was not long away came back with the information that the German pilot, as well as being wounded before he jumped, had two broken legs, a gash in his forehead and a fractured elbow. He smiled a little grimly, 'And believe it or not, the man who was waving the pitchfork was as gentle as a lamb with him, trying to ease him until the ambulance arrived.'

'And the woman with the rolling pin?' Lyndsey asked.

'Oh, she went to a nearby cottage to get a cup of tea for him. That's life, isn't it? If the airman had been an arrogant young Nazi he might have had the pitchfork in his guts. But come along, we'll get these children to the farm.'

It turned out to be a pleasurable afternoon, especially for the children, who were in their element with the animals. The farmer's wife sat them down to a tea of home-made cakes and scones that reminded Lyndsey of the teas that Ivy used to serve in her tea-room at Echo Cove, which brought a sudden ache for the days that had gone. Ivy had died the year after Andrew's cousin had been in England. With a determination not to dwell in the past Lyndsey made an effort to join in the conversation.

By the time they returned, the children were sleepy after their adventurous afternoon and when Bette told them later it was time for bed they made no protest. When they were settled she suggested that Andrew and Lyndsey might like to go to the pictures. 'I don't know what's on,' she said, 'but I can look it up in the papers.' A lengthy discussion ended up with them all agreeing it would be nicer to stay in and have a lazy evening than split up.

It was an evening Lyndsey felt she would always remember. Bette reclined on the divan smoking a cigarette in a long holder and looking like one of the vamps in a film, but without the hot sultry look; Andrew smoked a pipe, sitting sideways in the armchair, his long legs over the arm, while Lyndsey curled up on a pile of cushions. They talked on all sorts of subjects, their childhood, growing up, their families, the war and its effect on people's lives. The odd thing was that although they were discussing the war Lyndsey felt remote from it, as though she were in a different world. Even the incident of the afternoon seemed like part of a dream. She put it down to the cosiness of the room, the close involvement with people, caring people.

When for a moment there was a companionable silence she said, 'Bette, I'm so glad you took Connie and Janie to live with you. Children need affection. It must be terrible for some of the evacuees who go to homes where they are fed and housed but given no love.'

Andrew swung his legs to the floor. 'But it could give them character. I remember my father once saying that when his widowed mother died it seemed the end of the world for him. She had indulged him and his brother Rupert, given in to their every whim. His adoptive parents changed all that. Dad said he hated them at first, but eventually came to respect them and to know that although they were not demonstrative they did their best to care for him and see he had a decent education.'

Bette sat up. 'And, you know, Lyndsey, there's the other side of it. There are a lot of evacuees who come from big, poverty-stricken families who don't know what it is to get a kiss or a cuddle and who find themselves billeted with loving people.'

'Yes, I know.' Lyndsey sighed. 'It's such a topsy-turvy world. But I still think that discipline should be tempered with love.'

Andrew tapped the dottle out from his pipe. 'I agree there should be discipline, especially with women. Women definitely need to be disciplined.'

Lyndsey flared. 'Who do you think you are, laying down the law? No man disciplines me!'

Bette gave a low chuckle. 'Can't you see he's teasing you?'

Andrew was by now grinning broadly. Lyndsey picked up a cushion and threw it at him. He jumped up. 'Want a fight do you?' He rolled her over the floor tickling her and she squealed and kicked out, then lay giggling helplessly.

35

'That's enough, you two,' Bette said laughing. 'You'll wake the kids. How about a drink of sherry? Or perhaps you would prefer a beer, Andrew?'

He said, 'I tell you what I would like to do and that is stretch my legs and have a beer when I come back. Who wants some fresh air?'

'Ask Lyndsey,' Bette said.

Lyndsey agreed and Andrew went to get her coat. He held it out.

'Get it on quick before you change your mind. Making arrangements in this house is a bigger problem than planning a campaign.'

She slipped her arms into the coat and Andrew quickly buttoned it up. A small tremor went through her. The attention was almost like a caress. Seeing her cream beret in her pocket, he plucked it out and pulled it on, bringing it down over her eyes. 'You won't be able to see in the blackout anyway, but you can lean on me. I eat carrots and can see in the dark!'

Lyndsey answered him in a monotone. 'I can see in the dark and I don't eat carrots!' She pushed up the beret and grinned.

Andrew laughed. He touched the tip of her nose with his finger 'Lyndsey MacLaren, you are a girl after my own heart.' To Bette he added, 'If we're not back before the early hours don't call us, we'll call you.'

'You'll have that girl back by eleven o'clock, or else . . . Come on the pair of you. I'll go first and put out the light then you can open the door. And when you get outside stand a moment until your eyes get accustomed to the blackout.'

'Yes, ma'am,' Andrew said. 'Any further instructions, ma'am?'

'Don't cheek the air-raid warden if you meet him or he might lock you both up.'

'In one cell? Lovely.'

Bette laughed. 'Out – and mind what you're doing. I'm going to switch off the light.'

When they were outside they stood a few moments in silence then Andrew said softly, 'You really are a lovely person, Lyndsey, great fun.'

She felt her heartbeats quicken. It was a long time since anyone had said that to her. It was good to be able to laugh, to indulge in horseplay . . . although this could have its dangers. Andrew linked his arm through hers. 'Well, off we go. If we fall, we fall together!' He took a deep breath. 'Mm, that air smells good.'

'It does. I missed the fresh sea air when I came to London, still do. Not that I regret coming to London. I had to get away from Echo Cove, and more important still I needed to be occupied.'

'I think you ought to go back home while these raids are so heavy,' Andrew said gently.

A few houses loomed up out of the darkness and they passed them before Lyndsey replied, 'I'll go back some day, but not yet. I feel I'm doing something towards the war effort.' She looked up at him. 'Tell me, Andrew, do you feel scared when you have to go up on a mission?'

'Yes, I do, and so do the other men, but they, like me, say that once the action begins they forget everything else but the job in hand. I had done quite a lot of flying at home – I had my own plane, in fact – and a group of us did a lot of acrobatic flying, which helped enormously.'

Lyndsey gave a shudder. 'It must be awful going up, knowing you are going to kill. I would hate it. Yes, I know it's war, but I hate everything about it, even the blackout. It's so strange not being able to see a light anywhere.'

'I know that moonlight is more romantic,' Andrew said quietly, 'but – '

'I used to enjoy a walk in the moonlight, but since the phrase "Bomber's Moon" came into being, it's taken all the romance away.'

'Nothing can take romance away between two people if

they're in love,' Andrew said gently. 'Whoops! You nearly led me into that group of trees!'

'*You* are supposed to be leading me,' Lyndsey protested. 'You are the one who's eating carrots to give you better night vision. I wonder who launched *that* idea?'

'The growers of carrots, of course,' Andrew answered laughing. 'It's a load of cod's wallop, but people believe it because they want to believe it. Ah, some small houses ahead, don't walk me into them. Some more trees further on but with white bands round their trunks, which is sensible. Do you know I walked into a tree when I was in London, one they had forgotten to put a white band on. I had a bump on my forehead the size of an egg. Mind you, I hadn't started to eat carrots then.'

They both laughed and Andrew squeezed her arm against him. 'This is nice, Lyndsey. It's fun.'

They passed the small shops then turned right at the crossroads into a high-hedged lane. There were trees in the fields on either side and their branches met overhead to create a tunnel which at first sight appeared to have no end, but as their eyes became accustomed to the blackness they could make out a field gate, where beyond they could see a windmill, the sails still.

Andrew said, 'One of our neighbours at home is a Dutchman whose father was a miller. He used to tell me about the working of the mill when I was a boy and once he told me how, during the first world war, the sails were used to signal to other people when the enemy was in the vicinity.'

They stood in silence for a while then Andrew turned to her. 'Lyndsey, would you write to me? Letters mean a lot. I get them from home but to have one from you would mean a great deal.' He tilted her face towards him. 'I've never been so taken by a girl before. We seem to be on the same wavelength.'

Lyndsey had never been attracted to a man so much before either. But was it just their loneliness that was drawing them together? She put the thought aside. She said, 'Of course I'll write to you, Andrew, and I'm sure that Bette will too. She's a great person.'

'She certainly is. Such a lovely warm character. And so are you, Lyndsey.' Andrew leaned towards her but then he drew back and said, 'I think we had better walk on,' and the unsteadiness in his voice told Lyndsey his feelings. She also knew that if he had kissed her she would have responded.

After that Andrew began to talk brightly of taking Bette and Lyndsey out to dinner and a show in London on his next leave. 'I don't know when it will be and the trouble is you can get a pass, then have it cancelled at the last minute. But we *will* have that evening out sometime, I promise.'

Lyndsey felt a sudden depression, knowing that it would not be only a cancelled pass that could stop him from keeping his promise. But she forced herself to say lightly, 'That would be lovely, Andrew. It will be something to look forward to.'

Andrew was due to return to his station the following morning early and when they returned from their walk he stopped outside Bette's door and cupped Lyndsey's face between his palms. 'We better say goodbye now. No, not goodbye, just au revoir, we'll meet again.' He kissed her gently, then putting his arm around her he drew her close and she could feel the wild thudding of his heart against her breast.

Lyndsey, suddenly recalling the words of Vera Lynn's song, 'We'll meet again, don't know where, don't know when . . .' felt a sudden anguish. Would they ever meet again?

'Take care of yourself, Andrew,' she whispered.

'Will do.' There was the unsteadiness again in his voice and when he kissed her a second time they clung together.

It was the steady tread of footsteps coming along the

road that made them draw apart. A man's voice boomed, 'Is that you, Mrs Bascony?'

A man wearing a tin hat came into view. Andrew said, 'No, it's her nephew and – my – girlfriend.'

'Oh, yes, she told me you were coming. In the Air Force, aren't you? Shoot a few of them planes down for me.' He gave a laugh. 'I'll leave you to say good night, but don't linger too long, there's rain on the way.' He went tramping off.

Suddenly Bette opened the front door.

'Hello, you two. I heard voices.'

'We met your warden,' Andrew said. 'And do you know what, I forgot to cheek him. An opportunity missed! But there's always the next time.'

He touched Lyndsey's cheek lightly and although she could see he was smiling, she felt she wanted to cry.

THREE

Although Andrew had been in the house for such a short time he was missed greatly on the Sunday morning. The children kept asking about him, wanting to know when he would be coming back. 'Soon,' Bette said. 'As soon as he can get some more leave, but he does have aeroplanes to fly.'

'Is he up there now?' Connie asked with a worried frown. 'He won't have to come down with one of those big umbrellas, will he?'

Bette and Lyndsey exchanged glances. Bette said, 'No, darling, of course not. Now then, after we've tidied up we're going to go for a walk. In the meantime you and Janie can feed the goldfish and the budgies. I'll give you the seed.'

With this done the children went out into the garden to play. Bette went up to make the beds while Lyndsey washed up.

She had just dried a bowl and put it on the shelf when, from the window, she saw Janie sitting by a bush in the garden, head bowed. She went out.

'Janie?' The child looked up, her eyes full of tears.

'Oh, my love, what's wrong?' Lyndsey picked her up. 'Have you a pain?'

Connie said from behind them, 'She wants to see me Mam and Dad, and I told her she can't because we're evac – evacu-eed.' Connie was near to tears now and

Lyndsey, aching for their homesickness, bent down and put an arm around her. She made an effort to speak brightly. 'I tell you what, we'll try and get your Mam and Dad to come here and see you both.'

Connie shook her head. 'Me Dad can't come, he's ill, he's been ill a long time, ever such a long time.' The woebegone note in her voice brought a lump to Lyndsey's throat. Bette came out into the garden and asked softly what was wrong. When Lyndsey explained Bette, for once, seemed non-plussed.

Janie had her face buried against Lyndsey's neck and Connie said, with an old-fashioned air, 'Janie frets, you see, she loves me Dad and she misses him. Uncle Andrew was like a dad to her and now she misses him.'

This time Bette and Lyndsey exchanged helpless glances. Fortunately the situation was saved by Mrs Petrie calling with a golden Labrador pup.

'There now,' Bette said, 'look who's come to see you. This is Penny, isn't she lovely?' Lyndsey put Janie down and both children brightened. The dog came up and fussed around them, licking their hands, trying to get up to lick their faces. It raced about and the children raced after it squealing with delight when it almost bowled them over.

Bette said to her neighbour with feeling, 'Mrs Petrie, you could not have come at a better time,' and explained their problem.

'I know exactly how you feel,' Mrs Petrie said. 'I had four evacuees a year ago, two brothers and two sisters, and they all cried themselves to sleep at night. It was heartbreaking. But do you know, within a few weeks they settled down beautifully.' She gave a wry smile. 'I'd certainly rather have children than my two aunts and their husbands. You can control children, but grown people're forever quarrelling among themselves. I was glad to get out for a while. I thought I would call and see if you wanted me to baby-sit while your nephew was here.'

Bette told her he had gone then added, 'But perhaps one

evening this week we can take advantage of your kindness and Lyndsey and I can go to the pictures.'

Mrs Petrie beamed at her. 'That will be lovely, I'll enjoy it. Are you all going to church?'

'Church?' Bette eyed the children. 'Mmm, I suppose now I have a family I should take them. Lyndsey, would you come?'

Lyndsey hesitated. She had not been to church since her parents and grandparents had been killed, vowing there was no God. Now she looked at the children and said, 'Yes, I'll come with you.' Bette went upstairs.

When she came down she was wearing a black coat, a black pudding basin hat and was without make-up. They all stood staring at her. 'Have I overdone it?' Bette asked.

'I'll say you have!' Lyndsey exclaimed. 'It's just not you. Why change your appearance? If people don't like the way you are they can lump it!' She turned to the children. 'We like the other Auntie Bette, don't we?' They nodded vigorously and Bette laughed and went upstairs again.

This time when she came down she was wearing a short musquash fur coat and brown felt hat with a turned-up brim, and was not quite so heavily made up as usual. Lyndsey and the children approved.

As they set out down the road Bette asked the children if they went to church at home and Connie said only when her Auntie Flo had been married, but added that she and Janie always went to Sunday School. She then said, 'And we like it, don't we, Janie?'

Janie took her thumb from her mouth and said, 'Yes.' It was the only time she had spoken that morning.

There were no church bells to summon them to prayer, it having been decreed that they were only to be rung in case of invasion. Invasion? Lyndsey gave a little shiver. She looked up at the sky. There were no clouds. Was Andrew up there at this moment? There were dog-fights going on most of the time, over the Channel and along the coast.

As they neared the small stone-built church they joined the people converging on it from all directions. Lyndsey recognized some of the evacuees, some of the mothers recognized her and stopped to speak. There were good and bad reports. There will be billets where the people were mean, where the food was poor and the beds hard, there were those where their landladies were kind, they were well-fed and had lovely feather beds . . .

Two boys began running around the churchyard and had their ears boxed by their irate mother who informed them they were bloody well going to church and that was that!

Bette grinned. 'Religion to order. I wonder what the Lord will have to say about that?'

Lyndsey replied under her breath, 'I should think He'll be pleased that the mother is trying.'

Trying? Was this what *she* was doing? Giving the Lord a second chance? The church was cold and had the musty smell of their church at home. Memories came flooding back of her childhood, the long service, but of her enjoying the hymns. Bette led the way to a back pew, remarking in a whisper that she did not want to incur the wrath of any of the villagers by sitting in *their* pews. Janie was looking bewildered and Lyndsey lifted her on to her lap and held her to her, feeling an affection for this small child with the skinny limbs and dear little face with its snub nose.

The organ had been playing softly but then, as the notes died away, there was the usual shuffling and coughing and blowing of noses before the organist struck up the chords of the processional hymn. The congregation rose to their feet as the choir came singing from the back of the church and walked down the aisle to the choir stalls.

Lyndsey smiled to herself as she remembered falling in love with a choir boy when she was a child. He was about nine and she seven and she had been thrilled when, at a party, he called out her number in the game of Postman's Knock. He had given her a peck on her cheek and she thought she would die with joy. Soon afterwards he left the district and she was bereft.

The vicar came into the pulpit and the congregation sat down.

'Dearly beloved brethren, we are gathered here today in the sight of God . . .' and so the proceedings began.

He took as his sermon the Good Samaritan, and talked about the evacuees and the people in the village who had opened their homes to them and the conflicts that often arose, and how rewarding it was to close one's eyes to faults when one thought of the conflict that was going on in the world, where husbands and sons and relatives were involved, when civilians were bombed out of their homes and maimed and killed.

The people were still, there was not even one cough. Most of them had relatives in the forces – army, air force and navy. Bette had pointed out one family, parents with five daughters, who had recently lost their only son, killed in a submarine.

The congregation had sung 'Fight the Good Fight' with great fervour, but when they sang 'Eternal Father Strong to Save,' a few voices wavered. Even as a child Lyndsey had found the hymn emotional and now as they came to the line, 'Oh, hear us Lord, we cry to thee, for those in peril on the sea,' she was unable to sing it for the lump in her throat.

It was a relief when eventually they came out in to the thin sunshine of the September morning. Bette and Lyndsey were approached by a number of villagers. How nice it was to see them at church with the children. Perhaps they would care to join in the social life. One of the women said to Bette she had heard she had been on the stage and asked if she would be willing to help with the drama group, whose producer had recently joined the Army. Bette said she would be delighted and yes, she would love to join in the social life of the village.

When they left the women Bette laughed softly. 'That

sermon must certainly have hit home to them. I've been here several months and no one has approached me about joining anything. By the way, Lyndsey, did you get that information from your uncle's wife about caring for the battle-weary servicemen?'

'Oh, Bette, I'm sorry, I forgot. I should have a hard rap over the knuckles. I'll write to Marian today. I *promise*.'

Bette's eyes were shining. 'I'll be in the swim again at last. It'll be great to be busy. How about you joining the drama group?'

Lyndsey protested, as she had done previously, that she had never done any acting but Bette was not listening. There were a number of trunks in the attic full of costumes, she said, some of which had belonged to her parents for their double act and others containing costumes and small gadgets she and Rupert had used in their magician's act. They would open them up and see what was in them.

Then, as Bette became aware that Connie was speaking, she said, 'And you, my two darlings, can help. You can spread newspapers on the attic floor ready for our adventure after lunch!'

Adventure was the key word, for Bette made it seem so with her fund of stories as they emptied the trunks. The floor was a sea of colour, the bright red skirts of gypsy and Spanish dancers vying with an emerald ball gown, the brightly embroidered waistcoats of Regency gentlemen, the purple, yellow, green satins and silks of their ladies and the blue and gold uniform of a Hussar.

The task proved to be the panacea for what ailed each of them. Even little Janie chatted happily. Bette pulled out a tambourine, rattled it and gave it to Janie. To Connie she gave castanets. 'And what is this?' she exclaimed as she brought out a small ukulele. She twanged a string and handed it to Lyndsey saying, 'See what you can do with that.'

Lyndsey tuned it up, grinned, and gave a rendering, in a Lancashire accent, of George Formby's song, 'When I'm

Cleaning Windows.' When she had finished Bette sat back on her heels and stared at her.

'I don't believe it! You let me think you couldn't do anything in the way of entertainment.' Lyndsey laughed and said she was terrible, she croaked. But to this Bette exclaimed, 'Croaked? You have a marvellous throaty voice, and with the *right* song – *sexy*. You'll knock the servicemen for six!'

'What servicemen?'

'First of all those who are wounded, but tomorrow I'm going to start enquiring around to get up a show for the forces.' She gave a firm nod. 'Yes, I am. The children won't be neglected, I promise. I'll work in the evenings, *some* evenings, and when I'm out Mrs Petrie will baby-sit. Now then, we are going to have a sing-song.'

She picked up two red and white spotted scarves, tied one each round the heads of the children, placed a wide-brimmed straw hat on Lyndsey's head and put a clown's hat on her own head. 'Now then, Connie, you and Janie shake your instruments, Lyndsey will play the ukulele and I have here a tin whistle. What shall we sing? Something lively, how about "Daisy, Daisy, Give Me Your Answer Do"? If you don't know it, hum it.'

When they had given a rendering of the song they all collapsed in laughter.

Afterwards Lyndsey knew it was something she would always remember, the dusty attic, sun motes floating, the beauty, the joy on the faces of the children, Bette's effervescence, her red hair tinged with gold . . . and their laughter. She must tell Andrew all about it when she wrote.

That night when the children were in bed Bette began making plans for the following week. She had something arranged for each day and evening and when Lyndsey realized she was included in every evening's plan she said, 'Look, Bette, I couldn't travel back and forth every morning and evening, but I could stay overnight in the middle of the week, then come for the weekends – if that's all right with you?'

Bette eyed her in dismay. 'Oh, Lyndsey, I was counting on you; I want you for my spearhead.' She gave a sudden wry grin. 'You were to be my star attraction when I approach . . . some official at one of the camps and ask if they would be willing for me to put on a show for the troops.'

'I'm no star attraction, Bette, and it's just that – well, I feel I want to help when there's a raid.'

'But there are people to deal with raids – wardens, the fire brigade, people like that.'

Lyndsey was silent for a moment then she said, 'Last week I was caught up in some bombing. I saw a couple running out of a house, their clothes alight. I was too far away to be of any help but later I heard a man say that if only more members of the public would help to put out the incendiary bombs less property would be damaged and fewer people would be burned.'

Bette said quietly, 'It's brave people like you who – '

Lyndsey's head came up. 'I'm not brave, Bette, I'm terrified. It's just that something urges me to do these things.' After a pause she added, 'If, when you get organized, you need someone to fill in with ukulele strumming, I'll do it – ' She laughed. 'But heaven help them.'

'That's a promise and I won't let you forget it. I have all sorts of ideas for you, but that's my secret for the moment. And don't look so alarmed, I'm not going to ask you to come on the stage nude and pose.'

'I should hope not! You'd have Uncle Richard and Marian take to their beds with shock.'

'Lyndsey – where will you be staying in London? At your uncle's house?'

'Yes, why not? I feel as Mrs Grey does that if you're destined to be killed by a bomb you'll get it wherever you are.'

48

Bette sighed. 'I suppose you're right.' She got up. 'I'll make some cocoa.'

Although Lyndsey was not afraid of sleeping in the Mayfair house on her own she had to admit to feeling a sense of desolation when she stepped into the chill of the hall the following morning. Fires were ready laid in the kitchen, the drawing room, the dining room and two of the bedrooms. She lit the one in the kitchen then put on the kettle to make a cup of coffee. She drank it black and pulled a face. If she was going to stay here she would need to get organized with food.

After some debating Lyndsey decided she would shop on her way to the Centre that afternoon and had just washed up the cup and saucer when she tensed, sure she heard movement in the hall. Footsteps coming towards the kitchen. They were too heavy for Marian. An intruder?

The door opened and a khaki-clad figure appeared. Lyndsey's shoulders went slack. 'Uncle Richard – what a fright you gave me. Did you know that Marian is away?'

'I did.' He came forward, a tall, attractive, fair-haired man, with a grave expression. He kissed her then stood back and demanded, 'What are *you* doing here? I understood you were staying in Kent.'

Lyndsey stood stiffly to attention and saluted.

'Only for the weekend, Colonel, sir – I have work to do in London.'

He smiled then and gave her a hug. 'It's nice to see you, but I would prefer for you to be away from harm.'

She repeated what she had told Bette and he replied a little wryly, 'I think that fate needs a little help sometimes. It's no use looking for danger.' He nodded towards the hall. 'I called at Fortnum and Mason's and got them to fix me up with a lunch basket. There'll be enough for both of us. Shall we eat in here? It will be more – homely.'

Lyndsey glanced at him. There had been something wistful in his tone. She saw then how tired he looked. When she mentioned it he said, 'I've been travelling for days,

49

with very little sleep. I think I shall sleep tonight, even if there are ten raids.' He got up and brought in the lunch basket.

As Lyndsey laid the table she thought it was not much of a homecoming for a man to find only a niece to greet him. But then, he was lucky to get home occasionally; there were thousands of servicemen who would be glad to change places with him.

During the meal Richard asked Lyndsey how she was coping with the evacuees and with the raids but he never once mentioned Marian.

During a lull in the conversation she said, 'Don't you miss Marian not being here when you come home?'

'Of course I do. I miss her dreadfully, but there's a war on. One must accept these separations.' He had spoken sharply and immediately apologized for it. 'Blame my tiredness, Lyndsey. I feel boorish but I'll be all right after a good night's sleep. What are your hours of duty? Could you manage to fit in a theatre matinée this week?'

Lyndsey said she was sure she could and would look forward to it.

Richard was now only picking at his food and his eyes were closing. Lyndsey suggested gently that he go upstairs and lie down. He drew his fingertips across his eyes, said he thought he would, then added, 'Just promise me if there's any heavy bombing you'll go into the shelter.'

Lyndsey made no promise. She urged him to his feet. Richard touched her on the shoulder and gave her a grave smile. 'When all this is over, Lyndsey, we'll make it up to you, you're missing so much.'

'I don't have such a busy social life,' she replied quietly, 'but I have gained an awful lot of experience of life, of people.'

'I think this war has helped a lot of people to grow up, Lyndsey, older people too . . . like me.' With this enigmatic remark Richard left, leaving Lyndsey puzzled.

It was not until some time later that she recalled once,

when she was small, asking her mother why her Uncle Richard was away so much and her mother replying quietly, 'I think he wants to run away from life.'

Had something dramatic happened in his life to make him want to run away? The sudden wailing of the air-raid sirens interrupted Lyndsey's train of thought. She stood listening. Although there was the sound of distant ack-ack fire there was no droning of planes overhead. Perhaps it was just a stray raider. There were clouds. The all clear sounded twenty minutes later and Lyndsey went out shopping.

When she came back she made preparations for dinner but Richard was still asleep at seven o'clock and she found he had undressed and got into bed so she did no cooking. At half past seven the sirens went again and this time there was the sound of explosions, but they were not close. She went up to the attic window. Once more the East End seemed to be the target for the raid, for there were fires in that direction. How many more people would be made homeless?

Lyndsey was coming back downstairs when the phone rang. It was Bette, she sounded excited. She had had *such* a busy day. There was an army camp not far away, not large, about a hundred soldiers, and she had spoken on the phone to a captain about putting on a show for the men and he was very interested. He had arranged for her to see him the following day. 'And that's not all,' Bette enthused. 'I think I've rounded up quite a lot of talent in the village. When I do get organized, will you do your act for me, *please*?'

Lyndsey laughed, finding it impossible to resist Bette's enthusiasm. She said she would be willing to strum the ukulele but the men would have to do the singing. Bette told her she had something else in mind for Lyndsey to do, but for the moment that was her secret.

'Do *what*?' Lyndsey demanded.

Bette chuckled. 'Don't get so worried, it's something

51

exciting. I shall tell you when you come. The children are missing you, but I do feel at last that Janie has stopped fretting to go home. I hope so. I had a quick call from Andrew this afternoon. You do know, darling, that he's already head over heels in love with you? He's going to write to you. How did *you* get on when you got back home?'

Lyndsey told her about Richard turning up and Bette declared it was some inner sense that had told her she must return home. She asked how long Richard would be staying and when Lyndsey told her it could be a few days or two weeks Bette suggested if he was still there at the weekend to bring him to Kent. That is, if his wife would not be at home.

Lyndsey said she would ask him, and wondered how her uncle would respond to Bette's flamboyancy, her effervescence – and decided it might be interesting to find out. They chatted a few minutes more and ended their conversation by Bette promising to phone the following evening to let her know the results of her interview at the army camp.

Lyndsey looked in on Richard several times, but he still slept. At nine o'clock she listened to the news on the wireless.

At half past nine she went to bed – and slept soundly.

The next morning she took Richard's breakfast up. He opened one eye and asked if the raid had been a heavy one. Lyndsey told him no and set down the tray. By then he was fast asleep again. She left a note for him saying she was going to the Centre and would not be home until early evening. No doubt he would lunch at his club.

Although the raid had been much lighter than on previous evenings there were still a number of homeless to be dealt with, to be clothed and fed, and more important still, to be comforted. This was the most difficult. What could one say to these grey-faced people, who were not only devastated with grief at the loss of family, relatives or friends, but who had lost everything they owned.

Ann came breezing in. 'Hello there! A better night last night, wasn't it? Freddie and I went dancing.' She paused. 'What's up, Lyndsey?'

'Nothing more than usual.' Lyndsey nodded to the people sitting around waiting for attention, to those sleeping on mattresses on the floor. 'It's impossible to think about pleasure when you come here.'

'You have to, Lyndsey, or you won't be able to do it.' Ann spoke quietly. 'You must have a life outside the Centre. I'll ask Freddie to bring a friend tonight. We'll make up a foursome and go dancing.'

Lyndsey shook her head and explained about her uncle being home. And because she did not want Ann feeling sorry for her she added, 'I think he will be taking me out to dinner this evening.'

Ann grinned. 'Lucky you. He's the wealthy one, isn't he? Perhaps *he* has a friend and will ask *me* to make up a foursome. See you.' She turned away and a few minutes later she was soothing a fractious child. That was Ann.

Lyndsey found herself watching the older volunteers dealing with the homeless, and, becoming aware of their helpful manner, with an underlying cheerfulness, realized that Ann was right. You had to force down your own feeling of depression. But even with this maxim in mind Lyndsey felt drained when she left to go home.

To her surprise, when she opened the front door a delicious smell of cooking drifted to her. Could Marian be at home? But then Marian was no cook. Hearing Richard calling to her from the dining room Lyndsey crossed the hall and went in. Then she stood staring. The table was beautifully laid with lace mats, crystal and silver. From a four-branched candlelabrum the flickering flames of candles cast moving shadows on the walls. She noticed then that the table was laid for three. Lyndsey looked at Richard who was smiling gravely. 'Is Marian due home? Who did the cooking?'

'Marian will not be home and I did the cooking. I've

invited a guest, a colleague of mine. I met him unexpectedly when I lunched at the club. I haven't seen Elliott for some time.'

Lyndsey's spirits sank. A colleague of Richard's would be a liability. The talk during dinner would be all of war – as usual. She was trying to think up some excuse to get out of meeting this man, one that would sound valid, when Richard said, 'Elliott Warrender is a loner, a rather stern-looking man, but although you may not take to him at first I think you'll get to like him. He's a major, an interesting man. You go upstairs and get changed, Lyndsey, I'll see to the meal. It will be ready in about fifteen minutes.'

As she went upstairs she wondered how many more sides there were to this uncle of hers. Where had he learned to cook? She had never heard it mentioned.

Although Lyndsey had been determined not to dress up for their guest she found herself carefully selecting what she would wear, and chose eventually, a pale beige pure silk two-piece, the skirt finely pleated and with a dolman-sleeved top. With it she wore emerald green shoes, an emerald necklace and matching earrings.

When she went downstairs Richard held her at arm's length and declared she had done him proud. 'You have a wonderful poise for one so young, Lyndsey, but then you truly are a beautiful girl.'

Lyndsey wished at that moment she was dressed up to meet Andrew, and wondered when she would hear from him. Perhaps in the morning.

Five minutes later she was being introduced to Elliott Warrender and was taken aback at the impression he made on her. He was not tall, but he had a presence and was a strong-looking, dynamic man with a stern face and a quiet yet compelling voice.

'Miss MacLaren, it's a pleasure to meet you, your uncle has told me so much about you.'

The greeting was formal, one any man might make, but although Elliott Warrender delivered it as though she was

someone important he wanted to meet, there was not the
studied air of a man who was a womanizer, no charming
smile. There was no smile. His hair was dark, thick and
she suspected would curl if not brilliantined and brushed
flat. She thought his eyes were grey, but could not be sure.
Aware that she was studying him closely she said quickly,
'I'm so glad you could come, Major Warrender. My uncle
will be glad too of your company, he's missing Aunt
Marian. And I am not here all the time.'

He said, 'Unhappily war separates families. It's hard,
but necessary.'

Lyndsey wondered why Elliott Warrender should make
her feel flustered. There was nothing superior about his
manner. On the contrary he was listening in a courteous
fashion, almost, one could say, in a sympathetic way.

Richard said, 'I've poured drinks. Shall we sit down?'

They sat by the fire and Lyndsey sipped her cocktail,
finding it difficult not to stare at Elliott Warrender. He
was younger than she had expected, possibly in his early
thirties. His eyes she noticed now were a blue-grey, eyes
she imagined that could hold an iciness if he were angry.
He had a well-shaped mouth, but it did nothing to soften
the sternness of his features. As he picked up his drink he
noticed that his hands were square, with blunt fingertips.
Strong hands. She imagined them touching her and felt a
tremor go through her.

Heavens – where were her thoughts leading her? She
took a quick drink and choked on it. Immediately the
efficient major whipped out a snow-white handkerchief and
handed it to her. She took it and dabbed at her lips. Then
she handed it back. 'Thanks. I drank my drink too quickly,
like eating too quickly and getting a crumb in one's throat.'

What was she jabbering about? Settle down, she told
herself, he's just a man.

No, not just any man, not the type who would pass
unnoticed in a crowd. He had a commanding presence, he

would be a leader, one who would instil confidence in his men in a difficult situation.

Lyndsey smiled to herself, wondering what Elliott Warrender would think of her thoughts. No doubt he would condemn her as being a silly romantic girl. And he could be right – about her being romantic anyway. She had always had a leaning towards strong men. Her father and her grandfather had been strong and she had adored both.

Realizing that Richard and Elliott were discussing the Far East Lyndsey tried to appear interested. Richard said, addressing her, 'Elliott was born in China. His father was an army man.'

'And my grandfather and *his* father before him,' Elliott said with a wry smile.

'So that is where you get your forbidding expression from,' she said. 'One look from you would put the fear of the Lord into any raw recruit.'

Before Lyndsey had finished speaking she realized how gauche she had been, how rude, and was not surprised when Richard said, 'Lyndsey – ' in a gently rebuking tone.

She apologized and Elliott said, 'There's no need to, Miss MacLaren. You are obviously a young lady who speaks her mind, as I speak mine.'

Lyndsey, anxious now to make amends for Richard's sake, said, 'Uncle Richard used to talk to me about China when I was a child. I loved hearing about it. And I can remember his telling me about Bangkok, describing the beautiful temples and the floating market. I used to think it would be most exciting to go shopping from all the little boats.'

Richard laughed. 'It was noisy, brash, and colourful, so many tongues.'

Elliott said to Lyndsey, 'I think what the ladies used to appreciate was being able to choose beautiful fabrics and have sewing women make up clothes to their own design – in a matter of hours and for very little cost.'

'Yes, I've heard about it. The poor who slave for a pittance to keep the wealthy in luxury.'

'Hasn't it been the same from time immemorial?'

'But it shouldn't be so.'

Elliott leaned back and steepled his fingers. 'Tell me, Miss MacLaren, has there ever been a time in your life when you knew people poorer than yourself?'

'Y—yes, when I was younger and lived at Echo Cove. But they were not downtrodden people. I played happily with all their children.'

'Were not the poorer classes affected by the depression in the thirties?'

Lyndsey said yes again and Elliott asked, 'So did you share your food with them?'

Colour rose to her cheeks. 'I didn't because it didn't occur to me. I was young. I'm sure my parents helped – they were always trying to help people – but then their trade too suffered in the depression. What upsets me now is the way the poorer homeless are treated. I'm not complaining about the volunteers at centres, they are marvellous, it's the people in offices, the bureaucrats who treat the poor like dirt.'

Richard laughed and got up. 'I'm going to see to the meal. Don't fall out, the pair of you, while I'm gone.'

'You are like a lot more people, Uncle Richard,' she called, 'you run away from problems.'

'I live with problems!' He turned and went out, leaving Lyndsey feeling she was putting herself in a worse and worse light with Elliott Warrender.

To mitigate it she said earnestly, 'I might have made a lot of mistakes in my life, and I'm sure I shall make a lot more, but I really do think that someone should do something about the homeless. There are families, elderly people, frail people, who are put in bug-infested and rat-ridden houses and when they complain they are told they can take them or leave them.'

Elliott pointed out that with the heavy bombing the

amount of property available would be limited, which remark had Lyndsey edging forward on her chair, really angry now.

'Major Warrender, let me point out to you that whole streets of houses, vacated by people who've sought safety in country areas, are available but because they are better-class houses they are not available to people who come from tenements because they might destroy them! The people who have lived in them don't *own* them, they're rented. Their furniture is in store!'

Richard came in carrying a tureen of soup. 'Come along, folks, sit down and have this soup before it gets cold!' He set the tureen on the table then asked how their discussion was progressing.

Elliott got up leisurely. 'Your niece spoke at great length about the dilemma of the homeless, the poverty-stricken ones.'

Lyndsey gave him a sharp glance. Was there a note of amusement in his voice? She got up too. If he had said no more at that moment all might have been well, but as he went to the table to draw out a chair for her he went on, addressing himself to Richard once more, 'It really was a *most* impressive, stirring speech,' and this time Lyndsey was positive there was a derisive tilt to his mouth. She flared.

'The plight of the poverty-stricken homeless might be an amusing subject to you, Major Warrender, but it is certainly not to me, nor to anyone else I should imagine! And now, if you will please excuse me!'

In the split second before she turned to leave she was aware of the two men exchanging astonished glances, but she hurried out, tears blinding her.

FOUR

Lyndsey sat on her bed in her room trying desperately to control her tears. What a fool she had made of herself. Would she never learn to stop flying into a temper whenever someone disagreed with her.

There was a gentle tap on the door followed by Richard saying softly, 'Lyndsey, may I come in?' She got up, unlocked the door and went back to the bed. Richard came and sat down beside her. He put an arm around her.

'What's wrong, love? What upset you? We're both bewildered. Elliott is upset, feeling that he was responsible yet swears he did not mean anything.'

'The fault was mine,' Lyndsey said in a low voice. 'I flare up. I thought he was amused at the way I talked about the homeless. I know I get carried away –'

'On the contrary he was most impressed by your earnestness, your dedication to your job. He said it was a pity there were not a lot more people like you. Will you come down? My lovely meal is spoiling.' Richard had spoken this last sentence in a light-hearted way. And Lyndsey attempted a reply in the same vein.

'All that slaving over a hot stove –'

He squeezed her shoulder. 'That's my girl. There's no need to feel embarrassed at what happened, Elliott will understand. I'll leave you to powder your nose, then come down.'

Lyndsey was on her way downstairs when the phone

rang. She ran the last few steps and grabbed the receiver. It could be Bette. It was.

'Hello there, darling. Just had to tell you what a fantastic day I've had. I saw the officer in charge at the camp about doing a show for the troops and he agreed. Isn't that splendid! And do you know what? I've a number of people lined up to take part, tap-dancing twins, a boy and a girl – they're very good – a trick cyclist who plays a mouth organ while he rides around, some dancing girls – they're attractive but need some tuition to get some sparkle into the act. Then there's a comedian, his jokes are corny but he's got the sort of face that makes you laugh. Do you know what I mean?'

Lyndsey said she did and Bette rushed on, 'I'm going to try and arrange a rehearsal for this weekend,. Isn't it exciting?'

'Better miss me out, I really don't think I would fit in. For one thing I would be terrified in front of an audience.'

'Not with servicemen, you wouldn't, they're most appreciative and you really would be doing them a good turn. You *must* say yes.'

She gave in reluctantly and was about to ask after the children when Richard came out of the dining room. He pointed to his mouth, made chewing movements, then looked at his watch. Lyndsey said to Bette, 'Uncle Richard's making signs at me. He's cooked the dinner and I think he's afraid it's going to spoil.'

'Cooked the dinner? What a clever man. I hope you've talked him into coming for the weekend.' She chuckled. 'I could do with a handsome chef. But you go now, my love. We'll be in touch. Lots of love from all of us.'

The phone call had relaxed Lyndsey, and she was no longer worrying about facing Elliott Warrender. He stood up as she went into the dining room and said with concern, 'Miss MacLaren, I'm truly sorry if I said something to upset you. I assure you it was unintentional.'

'The fault was mine, Major Warrender. I think I'm over-sensitive to people's reactions and I ought to have known you would not be be mocking me over such a serious issue.'

'Definitely not. I admire your views. Shall we call a truce?' His smile, this time, softened his stern features.

Lyndsey said, 'Yes, of course, Major Warrender,' and Richard suggested they dispense with the formality of surnames. They both agreed and at last they settled down to the meal.

After the soup Richard produced a curry, which he said he knew was a favourite of Lyndsey and of Elliott. It made their eyes water but they both declared it excellent. For afters he brought in cheese and biscuits, apologizing for not producing something more exotic, but was told it was just right. Lyndsey was about to ask him where he learned to cook when the sirens went. Richard went to the attic to see what was happening. Minutes later he came back and suggested they wait and see what happened since at the moment there was little activity.

Elliott dabbed at his mouth with his table napkin. 'I think the public are getting blasé about the raids. No, that is the wrong word. Perhaps I should have said becoming reconciled to them. It never fails to surprise me how people all over surface from shelters and go to their jobs, some of them who won't have slept a wink all night.'

Lyndsey looked up. 'Why are you surprised, Major Warr – Elliott? We're all in this war together. Servicemen can't have a lie-in or stay in bed all day because they've been up all night fighting.'

'How right you are.' He gave her a brief smile. 'I seem to have been making fatuous remarks all evening.'

Lyndsey, feeling he was annoyed with himself for saying what he had, answered brightly, 'Don't we all at times?' then she mentally cringed, realizing she was agreeing with him that his remarks *had* been fatuous.

Oh, dear, it was going to be difficult making conversation with this man if she had to examine her words carefully every time before speaking. But then she might not see him again after this evening.

Richard began talking about the shows in London and told Elliott he was thinking of taking Lyndsey to one of the matinées. He then asked him if he would care to accompany them.

Lyndsey held her breath. With his sombre manner Elliott Warrender could be a death's head at a musical show, which was what she was hoping to see. He inclined his head and said, 'I would enjoy that very much, Richard, thank you.' Lyndsey released her breath, accepting that she must put up with this major – for Richard's sake. After all, it would be for just an afternoon.

The all clear sounded and afterwards they listened to the news.

After that both men talked about various countries they had visited and Lyndsey was surprised at just how many her uncle *had* visited. At eleven o'clock Elliott got up to take his leave. He thanked them both for their hospitality and said how very much he had enjoyed himself. His clasp was warm and firm.

Lyndsey was standing by the drawing-room fire when Richard returned after seeing Elliott into a taxi. 'A nice chap, Elliott,' he said. 'He's not actually a social animal but I know his pleasure was genuine this evening. I think he's a lonely man.'

'Is he married?'

'No. And in fact his only living relative is a sister and she took her children to America to stay for the duration of the war. I think this upset him. He could understand her sending the children to safety but having come from an army background I think he felt his sister should have stayed and done "her bit", as they say.'

Was Elliott Warrender lonely? This had not occurred to Lyndsey.

'He had some leave,' Richard went on, 'and decided to

spend it in London. I did think of asking him to stay with us but thought it might not be wise.'

'Why not?'

'I don't know whether Marian would have approved.' Richard smiled and touched Lyndsey's cheek. 'I have a few people to see and I couldn't leave you in the house alone with a strange man.'

'Oh, Uncle Richard, do you honestly think that Elliott Warrender would have taken "advantage" of me?'

'No, I'm sure he wouldn't, but Marian is a stickler for conventionalities.' For a moment a bleakness came into Richard's eyes, then it was gone. 'So what show shall I try and book for tomorrow?'

Lyndsey asked him then if he would be interested in spending the weekend at Bette's house, saying the invitation had been issued by Bette. He showed some interest but would not commit himself.

Lyndsey felt disturbed, sure that her uncle's marriage was not as happy as Marian had made it out to be. She asked where Elliott was stationed and Richard said at the moment he was working on the admin side, going from camp to camp, and added that he was recovering from wounds received while he had been abroad.

'Oh, poor man. I wish I had known.'

'So what would you have done?' Richard teased. 'Mothered him?'

'I would have been nicer.'

Richard looked alarmed. 'Oh, for heaven's sake! Don't fall in love with the guy, he's much too old for you.'

'Don't be silly, of course I'm not falling in love with him. But may I remind you that Grandfather was years and years older than Gran and look how wonderfully happy they were. A true love story.'

Richard tapped her on the arm. 'Come along, Romantic Rosalind, there's work to be done.' They had cleared the table after the meal, and Elliott had insisted on helping, but Richard had also insisted that the washing up should be left until later.

Romantic Rosalind was a nickname Richard had given her when she was younger and had come home from the cinema drooling over some handsome film star. Now she smiled at him and told him she would do him a favour, he could dry, she would wash up.

A domestic Richard was something she had never seen and she was astonished how he whipped the dishes away after he dried them. When she asked where he had learned to cook and attack domestic duties he said, 'I've lived rough many times during my life, and when you spend three months alone on a small boat you learn to put everything in its place after use otherwise it would be chaotic.'

Lyndsey lifted a dish out of the soapy water and put it on the draining board, then she looked up at him. '*You* are a strange person, Uncle Richard, do you know that? Every time you came home from your trips I used to feel I had learned a little more about you, but in spite of it I felt I never *really* knew you. But don't get me wrong, it hasn't stopped me from loving you.'

Richard dried the dish slowly and Lyndsey saw the bleak look come into his eyes again. But as before, it was gone very quickly. He put the dish on the kitchen dresser then turned to face her, his expression now tender.

'You've always been someone very special to me, Lyndsey. You always gave me such a loving welcome. Not that I didn't get a warm welcome from the family, but you were my lost youth. I regret in one way all my wanderings, and yet I learned so much about people, about human frailties. Sometimes I wish I could have been born with the common sense that I've acquired over the years. Then I would not have hurt those I loved.'

Lyndsey waited for him to continue, her hands resting on the edge of the sink, but instead he said, teasing, 'Come on, you're slacking.'

She said with gentle reproof, 'And you are infuriating,

Uncle Richard. I was interested in knowing what mistakes you had made, so I could avoid them, then you abruptly close the subject.'

'I think we can only learn by our own mistakes, Lyndsey.' He spoke quietly. 'Situations are different, my problems will never be yours, thank the Lord. I was deeply hurt by something that happened in my life, but it's not something I can talk about, not now. Perhaps I shall be able to sometime in the future. And now to domestic business.'

While they worked Lyndsey talked about Bette arranging some acts for her show and Richard, cheerful again, laughed and said he would like to meet her and would go to Kent at the weekend if at all possible.

She was going to tell him about Andrew but changed her mind, not wanting to be questioned about him.

Later, in bed, she settled to think about Andrew and wondered if she would hear from him the next morning, but it was impossible to picture him because Elliott Warrender's image kept intruding. Lyndsey remembered her first impression of him, his strength, the appeal he had made to her. It was only afterwards, when she had behaved stupidly, that she had gone off him. He had talked most interestingly of his travels and had laughed with Richard over little anecdotes. Then he had seemed so different, just as Richard seemed a much more relaxed person without Marian. Had his bleakness when her name was mentioned been because he was missing her? Or had Marian exaggerated the success of their marriage?

The following morning Lyndsey picked up a letter in the hall and felt her heartbeats quicken when she found it was from Andrew. He said he had only time to pen a few lines, but there were two pages both eulogizing about his weekend. How wonderful she and Bette were (he called Lyndsey his lovely darling girl) and how had he ever managed to live without her in his life. He was going to try and manage some leave at the weekend, even if it was just a couple of hours. He *had* to see her. There was more about some of his friends, but Lyndsey read the bits over about herself several times. She hugged the letter to her, praying that he would manage to get some time off. He ended the letter by begging her to write to him, even if it was just a few lines. It would mean *so* much to him. He signed it, Yours adoringly, Andrew.

It was flowery, but to Lyndsey, who had lost out on her family's affection, to be wanted was balm, something she needed.

Richard had left the house early, leaving a note saying he would not be back until late afternoon. She was not to prepare a meal, he would take her out for dinner. She picked up the newspaper.

The Times had been opened at the column giving news of the war. She read about Mr Churchill's words of cheer, British defences better than ever. The RAF keep hitting back. There was news of the bombing of Germany, great fires at Hamburg, and Bremen Docks. Hamburg bombed for four hours . . .

Was the tide turning at last, would the war soon be over? How wonderful it would be if all fighting ceased and everything could get back to normal again. Not that some people's lives would ever be normal again, their relatives and friends killed, possessions gone. Lyndsey laid down the paper and went to make her breakfast. She must try and accept the state of affairs and not let the tragedies tug constantly at her emotions.

She cut a slice of bread, impaled it on the toasting fork and held the bread out to the red glow of the kitchen fire. She found herself thinking of Andrew, who could be up in a plane at that moment, involved in a dog-fight with the enemy. How frail the thread of life easily, cut by a burst of gunfire from an opponent . . . a torpedo from a submarine . . . a bomb falling . . .

The pungent smell of burnt toast filled the kitchen. Oh,

damn! She painstakingly scraped at the blackened parts. Bread must not be wasted, there was a war on.

Stop it! Stop thinking about the war, she chided herself. Think of something more cheerful. Richard was going to take her out to dinner that evening, he was going to book seats at a theatre, she was going to see Bette and the children at the weekend, perhaps Andrew.

In a brighter frame of mind Lyndsey stoically ate the uneatable toast, washed it down with coffee and prepared to go to the Centre.

There was a lighter feeling there too when she arrived, the feeling of the tide having turned. From now on the RAF would give the German cities a 'pasting'. Central London had not suffered at all the night before, and the casualties were light in some of the suburbs. There were a few pessimists of course who declared it was just a lull, wait until later, or until that night to see what happened.

There was little activity that day and she arrived back home to have Richard greet her with the news that he had booked seats for the following afternoon's matinée at the Coliseum. 'It's a musical,' he said, '*The White Horse Inn*. I was lucky, I got cancellations. There were four seats available and I took them.'

When Lyndsey queried in surprise 'Four?' Richard went on to say he had asked Elliott to come too and he had agreed. He smiled, 'And I thought you could perhaps ask your friend Bette to make up a foursome.'

When Lyndsey made no reply Richard said, serious now, 'Did I do wrong?'

'No, no, I'm sure Bette would thoroughly enjoy it but I'm not sure how your major would react to her. She's . . . flamboyant, a colourful character and Elliott is so . . . serious.'

'Shall I tell you something, Lyndsey. When I first met Elliott he was in his mid-twenties. Then he was a bit wild, a great rugger player, popular with everybody, no big party was complete without him. Then he got into trouble, began gambling, ran up big debts, got a rollicking from his father and a bigger one from his regiment. It sobered him. Believe me, there's a vibrant, passionate man under that cool, stern exterior.'

A slow smile spread over Lyndsey's face. 'Bette has a feeling for what she calls rich words. I like your word "vibrant" '. She wrapped her arms around herself. 'Mmm, makes me feel all goose-pimply. I can imagine him carrying off his woman and – '

'Lyndsey, you stop it.' By this time Richard was laughing. 'I told you last night, Elliott Warrender is too old for you.'

She turned round, innocent eyes on him. 'I wasn't thinking of him for myself, but for Bette. She will bring out the fun in him, I know it, and who knows – '

The phone rang. It was for Richard and Lyndsey guessed by his manner that it was Marian. He was quiet, serious. Lyndsey prayed that Marian had not suddenly decided to come home. Then felt guilty. How could she, they were man and wife and for all she knew they might adore one another.

When Richard came in he said, 'That was Marian. Unfortunately it's impossible for her to get home for the weekend. She's terribly disappointed, of course. She says she may be able to manage a couple of days in the middle of next week.' He gave a rueful smile. 'Quite possibly I shall have gone away again by then. But that's war, isn't it? By the way, she's given me an address you asked for, it's to do with caring for war-weary servicemen. I wrote it down.'

Lyndsey explained about Bette having thought she might open her home to them for short stays then said, 'You'll be able to come with me to Kent at the weekend. We can go on Friday evening or Saturday morning.'

Richard told her he would be pleased to come then asked if she was going to ring Bette about the matinée.

Lyndsey phoned her right away and Bette was excited.

How marvellous it would be to see a show, she would go and ask Mrs Petrie at once if she could baby-sit. She would ring Lyndsey back.

In less than five minutes Bette was on the phone, breathless. Mrs Petrie was delighted to take charge of the children, wasn't it lovely of her. Lyndsey then told her about Richard agreeing to come and stay for the weekend and also about the address where she was to write to accommodate the war-weary soldiers, and by this time Bette was ecstatic. Everything was happening at once, wasn't it wonderful!

They talked for about another ten minutes, concluding the conversation with Bette saying she would meet them outside the Coliseum at two o'clock prompt and would be there even if bombs were raining down all around her.

When Lyndsey repeated this last piece to Richard he laughed. 'You're a pair of talkers. You'll be seeing her tomorrow to get all the news.' Lyndsey grinned and nodded, but by tomorrow Bette would have accumulated a mass of things to talk about, she was like that. To which Richard exclaimed, 'Heaven help me, what have I let myself in for?'

Lyndsey could not help wondering what Elliott's reaction would be when he met Bette. Would she be done up like a music hall star, or would she tone down her make-up?

When they did arrive the next day outside the Coliseum Lyndsey didn't recognize Bette at first. She was wearing a pale grey coat with a silver fox collar, a darker grey velvet hat, close fitting, and matching shoes. Her make-up was modified. She looked quite elegant. Lyndsey had not told her about Elliott coming and her surprise was lovely to see. She didn't greet him coyly, but she was unable to suppress her pleasure.

'My goodness,' she said, '*two* handsome escorts. Aren't we honoured!'

Richard seemed at ease with her at once, but Elliott,

although courteous, seemed a little stilted. People were milling all around them as friend greeted friend. There were uniformed men from most of the services with a good proportion of American GIs. Chatter was bright with a mingling of dialects. Although the raid alert was on it was impossible to imagine they were involved in a war. Both Richard and Elliott, having recognized someone they knew, excused themselves for a moment and while they were away one of two GIs said to Lyndsey, 'Ma'am, we're mighty curious to know what service you belong to.' He indicated the emblem on her hat.

Realising they had mistaken the embroidered disc on the front of her cream, corded military-style hat she said, straight-faced, 'I'm a putter-out of incendiary bombs.'

They both looked mystified then the other one said, 'Don't reckon we've heard of that service, ma'am, but it sounds mighty courageous.'

Lyndsey then felt ashamed. 'I'm sorry, I was joking. I have put out incendiaries, but it's not something I do regularly.'

One beamed at her and the other one laughed. Then she was asked if she and her friend were on their own. Lyndsey smiled. 'We're with my uncle and a friend, and here they are now.'

When Richard heard what had happened he was annoyed. It was foolish to have joked with them, it was simply encouraging them. Bette spoke up saying they were very courteous young men and no harm had been done. And as the people were moving to go in and take their seats no more was said.

Lyndsey had a feeling that Richard was manoeuvring to get Bette next to Elliott, but somehow Elliott managed to get himself seated next to Lyndsey, who had Bette on her right, while Richard was on Bette's right.

Elliott then explained his action to Richard by saying with a brief smile, 'One must never separate women at a theatre, they *must* discuss the clothes and the scenery.'

Lyndsey responded to this in a teasing tone, 'You sound, sir, as if you are used to making up foursomes.'

'Of course,' he replied and she thought she saw a twinkle in his eyes.

When the orchestra struck up Bette was almost tearful with pleasure, saying how wonderful it was to be back in the atmosphere of the theatre, there was nothing else quite like it. Lyndsey knew what she meant, remembering from when she was younger that lovely feeling of expectancy of wonderful things about to happen, of entering into the magical world of make-believe.

One of the moments that Lyndsey enjoyed the most was when the orchestra had finished the overture and there was a hush. Then a rousing tune began as the curtains parted and went back with a swish, on this occasion to reveal the exterior of a Tyrolean inn. The magic was about to begin.

The story-line was thin, but the costumes were colourful, the dancing and singing lively, and when, two hours later, they came out to hear the wail of the sirens no one took any notice.

During the interval Elliott had teased Lyndsey and Bette when they were enthusing over the show. He pointed out the faults, the fact that the hotel was short-handed because the men staff had been called to the war, yet there was a chorus of waiters singing.

Both Bette and Lyndsey rounded on him. He was a spoil-sport, one did not take notice of things like that. Why had he not just sat back and enjoyed it.

'I did,' he said, the twinkle evident once more in his eyes as he began to hum one of the tunes. Bette laughed and declared she would rope him in to sing a duet with Lyndsey in one of her camp shows. This, of course, brought questions from Elliott. What camp shows and did Lyndsey sing?

'Like a frog,' she said, laughing, 'but Bette won't accept it.'

71

'She has a lovely voice,' Bette declared, 'throaty, sexy – '

'Oh, indeed, then she must sing on her own. I would ruin the act. Shall we go somewhere for a meal?' He suggested going to his hotel and when it was agreed he hailed a taxi. When they arrived at the Savoy Bette whispered to Lyndsey, 'And the Savoy too!'

The relaxed atmosphere, waiters on silent feet, was the balm after the excitement. The majority of the men there were in uniform, officers, apart from some immaculately dressed elderly men.

Bette, who wore a rapt expression, gave a deep sigh as she looked around her. 'I'm being completely spoilt and thoroughly enjoying it.'

'You deserve to be spoilt,' Richard replied gallantly. 'You are not only caring for evacuee children but trying to get up a show for the troops.'

She grinned. 'I would like to be a martyr and say, yes, it's all terribly hard work, but having the children is a joy and so will arranging a show be, if I can manage it. I think I can.'

'I *know* you can,' Lyndsey said. To Elliott she added, 'Bette and her husband used to do a magic act together. Already she has a number of people lined up and we are going to rehearse this weekend.'

'*You* are rehearsing? A singing act?' His eyebrows were up.

'With a ukulele,' Bette enthused. 'She's good, she'll knock the troops for six.'

'I'm sure she will.' Elliott was smiling at Lyndsey, not with amusement this time, but with the suggestion of admiration. 'I should like to hear you sing and play.'

'Heaven forbid,' Lyndsey declared fervently. 'I'm a fool for having agreed to do it, but Bette can be very persuasive.'

'I should imagine so.' Elliott's gaze was now on Bette but this time Lyndsey could not assess what he was thinking.

Bette sat up. 'Richard and Lyndsey are coming to me for the weekend. Would you care to come too, Major Warrender?'

Lyndsey looked quickly from one to the other, not wanting Elliott to accept. It would be all right for Richard to be there but not Elliott.

'I'm sorry, Mrs Bascony, it's good of you to ask me, but I have already been invited out. Some other time, perhaps, if you would be kind enough to ask me.'

'Of course, Major, any time, you'll be most welcome.'

Lyndsey felt relieved and also mean for not wanting him at Bette's, but it would have spoiled things if Andrew was able to get time off.

They had a pleasant interlude. They discussed the show and others they had seen in the past and Elliott asked, with a seeming genuine interest, about Bette's life on the stage. Bette told them some amsuing incidents then she looked at her watch and said she must go to get her train, she did not want to leave Mrs Petrie too long with the children, it would be imposing on her good nature.

They saw her off at the station; then Elliott said he must leave them, he had a number of letters to write. He thanked Richard for the invitation to the show then asked if they would have dinner with him on the following Monday evening. Richard asked Lyndsey if she would be free and when she told him yes, he said they would be delighted to accept, and hoped he would not be called away before then.

In the taxi home Lyndsey said, 'And so, what is your opinion of Bette?'

'She's a very likeable person, warm and affectionate, I should imagine. I felt that Elliott was quite taken with her, didn't you?'

Lyndsey shook her head. 'I'm not sure. Major Warrender is a little like you, Uncle Richard, giving nothing away. At one time I felt he was fighting shy of her when he decided to sit beside me and you were manoeuvring to get him seated next to Bette.'

'I was not. I was not manoeuvring anything. It just happened that way.'

Lyndsey grinned. 'Oh, yes? There are times when I can see through your moves. Anyway, I shall tactfully try to get to know how Elliott feels about Bette on Monday evening, just in case she asks him again for a weekend. And I must stress that when she asked him it was not because of any designs she might have on him, but out of the goodness of her heart.'

'Oh, I'm sure of it,' Richard said, but he was smiling as he said it and Lyndsey realized that a man might view Bette's motives in a totally different way. It would be interesting to see how they did get on together at the weekend.

FIVE

Although Richard was allowed a petrol ration in connection with his job he said they would go by train since this journey was for pleasure and it was not fair to use petrol that could be needed. Lyndsey saw his point but would have enjoyed the drive.

They left London on the Friday evening about six o'clock, when families were making for the Underground and other shelters to settle for the night, even though there had been no air-raid warning. They came in droves, carrying mattresses, blankets and food to see them through until morning. One man was carrying a concertina and another a violin. It was said that some people enjoyed the music, but others complained it – and the sing-songs – kept them awake. But whether they slept or not they all came up from the shelters the following morning pale-faced and lethargic, and some red-eyed.

Then there would be the exodus of people going to work. Lyndsey felt guilty at going away for a weekend to enjoy herself.

Bette was there on her own to meet them when they arrived. The children were in bed, Mrs Petrie was baby-sitting. Connie and Janie were excited that Lyndsey was coming. Bette was her own flamboyant self again in a bright red cape and a piece of black velvet tied around her forehead. If Richard was surprised he gave no sign.

'Bette, now nice of you to meet us.'

She grinned. 'I always think it's so exciting meeting people off a train, especially those who are to be your guests. How are things in town? Come along, I have a meal ready. I've had one rehearsal with my "turns" for my show and we are going to have another one in the morning. *You* don't have to come if you don't want to, Richard. How is the Major?' Bette gave a throaty chuckle. 'You haven't been here two minutes and I'm talking my head off. It shows how excited I am.' She paused and looked from one to the other. 'I really *am* delighted to see you both.'

'And we are delighted to see you, Bette.' Richard linked arms with them both and stepped out up the road with Lyndsey thinking how different her uncle was in different company and a different setting.

Mrs Petrie greeted them with the news that although the children were in bed they would not go to sleep until they had seen Auntie Lyndsey and the 'gentleman'.

Lyndsey and Richard went upstairs. Connie and Janie were sitting propped up in bed, hair brushed, faces shining with cleanliness. They both held out their arms to Lyndsey and she went over and drew them to her. Then she introduced Richard, saying, 'This is my uncle Richard and he'll play with you tomorrow.'

Richard laughed. He talked to the children, but although he was not as easy with them as Andrew had been he did not talk down to them as some people did. Connie said shyly, 'You're a soldier; have you killed any Germans?'

'Not yet, but who knows, perhaps one day. I've brought you some sweets. Auntie Bette says you can have one each now and you will get the rest tomorrow.'

'And he's brought you some storybooks,' Lyndsey said. 'I'll read one story now and then you must go to sleep, it's way past your bedtime.'

Before she had finished the story their eyelids were drooping. Lyndsey settled them, gave them a kiss, then she and Richard went downstairs.

'Nice kids,' he said.

Bette greeted them with a smile. 'Guess what, Lyndsey. Andrew has just phoned. I didn't call you down, he only had a few seconds. It was to tell you he'll be with us tomorrow afternoon but only for two hours.' Bette explained to Richard about Andrew being her nephew, then added, 'I'm sure that you two will get on fine together.'

Lyndsey fervently hoped so.

They chatted over the meal about the show they'd seen together, discussed the war news, then listened to the news on the radio. The RAF were repulsing the raiders over the Channel. Only a few bombers had got through so raids were light and scattered. 'Thank goodness for that,' Bette said. 'How about going for a drink to our local pub? Do you fancy it?'

Both Richard and Lyndsey agreed and after Mrs Petrie was brought to baby-sit they groped their way through the blackout to the pub. Some singing and a buzz of chatter and laughter greeted them as they opened the door. Cigarette smoke escaped in a misty cloud.

A lot of people were crowded round the bar; another group stood by the piano, but there was no pianist. Bette pointed to a small table in the corner. When Richard asked what they would have Bette decided she would have a small port and Lyndsey, being under age, said she supposed it would have to be lemonade. Bette tried to persuade her to have a shandy but Richard gave a firm no, and when he went to order the drinks Lyndsey pulled a face saying, 'Uncle Richard strongly objects to young people drinking.'

Bette grinned. 'We'll have to educate him. A shandy wouldn't have done you any harm. How is Major Warrender? What a handsome fellow. A bit starchy, but' – her smile spread – 'I reckon we could educate him too, given the chance. He certainly had his eyes on you yesterday afternoon.' When Lyndsey protested Bette gave a quick nod. 'Oh, but he did, I watched him. Greatly taken with you.'

'I think Uncle Richard had him earmarked for you. He said yesterday that although Elliott appears to be a bit stiff he's sure that underneath there is a vibrant, passionate man.'

Bette gave a long drawn out, 'Ooh, what a *lovely* word – "vibrant". I like it, but stop it, it makes me feel all wooshy. And anyway, he's *your* man, he's too young for me.'

'Uncle Richard said he's too old for me. I believe he thought I had fallen for him.'

'And have you?'

'I – like him, but I'm – well, I'm looking forward to seeing Andrew again, if you must know.'

'And what better niece-in-law could a woman have than you,' Bette said softly. Then her eyes clouded. 'But . . . don't get too fond of Andrew, Lyndsey. He's flying and – '

'I try not to think about it,' Lyndsey said.

The landlord suddenly shouted for silence. Then he said they had just had word their pianist was ill and he asked if there was anyone there who could play and who would take his place. Lyndsey heard herself say, to her astonishment, 'Perhaps I can help out.'

'You can play?' exclaimed the landlord, beaming. 'Well, come on then, tickle them ivories. Get going.'

Lyndsey gave a frantic look at Bette and said, 'I must be mad!' She appealed to the landlord, 'I haven't been taught to play the piano, I just sort of – strum.'

To her further astonishment she heard Richard say, as he came from the bar with drinks, 'My niece is good, she's a natural. You can hum any tune you like and she can play it.'

After this she was seized by two stalwart men, almost carried to the piano and placed on the stool, with one of them asking what she wanted to drink.

By then Richard was there and putting the glass of

lemonade on top of the piano. 'She has one for now, thanks.' To Lyndsey he added, smiling, 'Well, go on, you got yourself into it.'

Well, she thought, in for a penny in for a pound as Ivy would have said. She was out to enjoy herself so why not help other people to enjoy themselves. She asked them what they wanted her to play and there were requests from every part of the room. Lyndsey picked one out, 'On Mother Kelly's Doorstep', and began to play.

Within seconds the roof was almost lifting off with the volume of sound as they all joined in. When Lyndsey glanced across at Bette and Richard they were yelling with the rest of them.

She went from one song to the other, from the rousing to the sentimental. She played 'Knees up Mother Brown' and the older women got up and performed. They also did a 'Hands, Knees and Boomps a Daisy'. After that there was a call for 'The White Cliffs of Dover'.

When the landlord called time there were protests. 'Oh, come on, Albert, we're just getting into our stride! Give us another ten minutes.'

But he was adamant, there were other nights, and he didn't want George Beasley on his back again. George Beasley was apparently the local constable. The crowd begged to sing 'Land of Hope and Glory' and he gave in, but that was the lot.

As Lyndsey said afterwards with feeling, 'No choir could have put more feeling into it. I felt a lump come into my throat.' Bette said so had she, and it always did whenever she heard it played or sung.

'I enjoyed it,' Richard said. 'It's a long time since I joined in a sing-song. And you, Lyndsey dear, played very well indeed.'

'Yes,' Bette exclaimed, 'you certainly did and I have a bone to pick with you. Why didn't you tell me you could play the piano? You can get a chorus going in *my* shows.'

They began a No, I won't, and a Yes, you will, session,

with Richard bringing it to an end by saying, 'I think we can leave that discussion until another time. We've had a good evening, let it rest there.'

They talked quietly as they neared the house but in the stillness of the night they could hear revellers singing as they wended their way home.

Lyndsey offered to help Bette make a bedtime drink and some sandwiches but Richard said, 'You sit down, you've done your share this evening, I'll help Bette,' and a few minutes later she heard them both laughing in the kitchen, and trying to control it.

When they came into the sitting room still trying to stifle giggles Lyndsey thought she had never seen Richard so relaxed, so full of gaiety.

'What's the joke?' she asked.

They stood looking at one another for a moment, then Bette began to giggle again. 'I don't know, do you, Richard?'

He shook his head and burst out laughing. He put his hand over his mouth then picked up a cushion and put his face against it. Lyndsey found herself laughing too. It was so good to see him so happy. But she said, 'How much did the pair of you have to drink?'

'We only had one drink each,' Bette said, trying to straighten her face. Then she was away giggling again and in the end, all three were clinging to one another laughing helplessly.

Bette was the first to sober up. 'Come on, stop it, the cocoa will be getting cold. We're like kids, or at least, like I was when I was younger. Once I started laughing I couldn't stop. I was always terrified that something funny would happen when I was on stage with Rupert and I would tell him if it did to give my arm a good pinch. He had to do it about four times and it worked, so if I get hysterical again, just give me a sharp nip.'

Richard said, 'I'll remember.' Then he looked at Bette and added quietly, 'And I'll remember this evening too for a good long time. It was good, thanks to you, Bette – and to you, Lyndsey. You really were on top form this evening. It's ages since I heard you play. Do you remember that Christmas when Jake came to stay and we got him to sing to your playing and we discovered that he had a marvellous voice . . .'

Jake was Richard's friend when he was young but Jake had married and gone to America and they only heard from him at Christmas time.

They reminisced about all sorts of things, some of them funny, but there was none of that crazy spontaneous laughter that had made Richard such a different person. It made Lyndsey wish that Andrew could have been there with them. He would have enjoyed the evening.

The following morning after breakfast, a man came from the village to suggest to Bette that they use the village hall for their rehearsal as some of the older men in the choir would like to join the show. There were five of them and it would make it a bit cramped with the other 'acts' in Bette's house.

'From the choir?' Bette said. 'Well, I'm not sure that the forces would want to be listening to hymns. They need cheering up.'

'These men would do that all right,' the man assured Bette. They sang rousing songs, he said, like 'The Drinking Song' from *The Student Prince*, and 'John Brown's Body' –

'Right,' she said, 'we'll hear them. We'll be at the hall in about half an hour.' When the man had gone Bette raised her shoulders at Richard and Lyndsey. 'I can't afford to miss any plum turns, can I? They might just lift the show. I'll soon know when I hear them. Don't come if you don't want to, Richard, you can always read a book.'

He said he was coming if it was only to look after Bette and Lyndsey. Heaven only knew what could happen with five elderly singers on the loose! They all laughed and started to get ready.

The children were quiet at first, seeming, Lyndsey

81

thought, a little in awe of Richard, but before they reached the village they were asking questions, about what were they going to see. Lyndsey explained.

They were about to turn the corner to go to the hall when someone hailed them. It was Andrew. He came sprinting towards them shouting as he ran. 'I got a few extra hours' leave. Your neighbour told me where you were bound for.' He came up, gave Bette, Lyndsey and the children a hug and a kiss then turned to Richard and held out his hand. 'You must be Lyndsey's uncle Richard. Glad to know you, sir.'

Richard acknowledged him with a curt nod. Bette looked taken aback for a moment then she said with a bright smile, 'This is my very unpredictable nephew Andrew.' When Richard stood wooden Lyndsey was furious. This was an informal occasion, not a parade ground where Richard's seniority would perhaps demand more formality.

They walked on with Andrew saying how delighted he was to get a little extra leave, and wanting to know why they were going to the village hall. Bette explained and he said, 'Oh, that should be interesting.'

When they arrived at the hall they found a group of people outside. To Bette's query if there was some other activity on at the hall that morning a woman spoke up. 'We were waiting for you, Mrs Bascony; we were told you were interviewing people who were willing to take part in a road show for the troops.'

Bette looked at them in dismay. There were people of all ages, some of them youngsters. She told them she had already decided on some 'acts' and they were, in fact, about to start rehearsing. A man then called out, 'But you don't know what talent you're missing among us, Mrs Bascony.' Bette agreed and told them if they could come back in perhaps an hour she would talk to them.

Andrew suggested that he could at least take their names and addresses and find out what they could do. He grinned and added, 'Lyndsey can help me.'

At this Richard offered to help, his manner so stilted it left no doubt in Lyndsey's mind that he was determined she should not be alone with Andrew. She felt like saying something but as Bette accepted the offer of both men she left it at that for the time being.

Andrew's manner, in contrast, was most pleasant. 'Right, sir,' he said, 'we'll need pencils and paper, to take down names and addresses and qualifications.' Bette provided them then she and Lyndsey and the children went into the hall.

There was no heating on and those who had come to rehearse were huddled in chairs, sitting apart, looking most depressed.

'Morning,' Bette called and walking briskly towards them said, 'Now then, when we had a rehearsal in my house, and you were all warm, you were cheerful. Today, because you have no heat, you're miserable. But if you want to entertain the troops there will always be times when you have to change for your act in freezing conditions, so you'll need to look animated, even if you don't feel it. I suggest that if you can't make up your minds to ignore the conditions then you would be wise to drop out of the project – *now*.'

This had everyone sitting up. No one looked exactly merry and bright but they all agreed they were willing to put up with any conditions as long as they could be a part of the show.

Bette smiled. 'Good! That was what I was hoping to hear. There has to be a team spirit. I want these to be lively, entertaining acts. We have a group of people outside waiting to be auditioned. The army and the air force are taking down particulars of the talent! So it's up to you people whether your acts are going to be the right ones. We'll start our rehearsal right away. Joe, would you like to be first?'

Joe was the trick cyclist. He was a wiry little man, with

83

a bald head and a big handlebar moustache. An outsize harmonica jutted from his jacket pocket.

He mounted the one-wheel cycle, rode round in circles two or three times then went into his act, doing intricate twists and turns and doing head stands on the saddle while he played 'Roll out the Barrel' on the harmonica. He was good and Bette declared herself pleased with him. Then she invited four dark-haired girls to do their tap-dancing routine. One of the girls said they usually danced to the tune of 'Tiptoe through the Tulips'. Joe offered to accompany them on the harmonica.

The girls were attractive but solemn, and to Lyndsey, their dancing lacked zest. Bette stopped them. 'Listen girls, you're expected to cheer up the men – so smile! Get some zip into your feet. You should be able to set *their* feet tapping. You did better last night.' One of the girls said they were nervous and Bette told them that every actor and actress was nervous before going on stage, even the professionals, but they overcame it once they were in front of an audience. She told them to try again.

In less than a minute Bette stopped them again. 'Girls, you have lovely teeth but we don't want to see them bared in a grin. We're not advertising toothpaste. Imagine there's a gorgeous man in the audience who's asked you for a date and that you are dancing *especially* for him.' It did the trick.

George, the stand-up comic, was next. He was bean-pole thin but although quite ordinary to look at when he first got up, by pulling a mournful face and sucking in his cheeks he brought a laugh, and it was his comical expressions and stances that brought him laughs for the most ancient of jokes.

The children, who had been sitting close up to Lyndsey, had sat up when George performed. Connie said, chuckling, 'I like that man, he's funny, isn't he? Janie likes him too, don't you?' Janie nodded vigorously, and asked if he was going to pull some more funny faces. Lyndsey, seeing

84

Bette beckoning to her, said, 'Not at the moment, I think Auntie Bette wants me to play the ukulele.'

Bette did and Lyndsey was surprised to find she was not feeling nervous. No doubt playing the piano in the pub had broken her in. She struck a few chords then launched into 'Run, Rabbit, Run,' and before long she was aware that feet had started tapping. When she finished they called for more and at a nod from Bette she played, 'We're gonna hang out the washing on the Siegfried Line'. At the end of this there was some clapping. Joe said, 'You were great, lassie, you'd have my vote any day!' Bette gave her a thumbs-up sign. Lyndsey sat down, well pleased, especially as Connie and Janie gave their smiling approval.

Bette then invited the five men from the choir to do their act. They were all men in their forties. They hummed a few notes then launched into 'Little Brown Jug'. They harmonized beautifully and all of them had excellent voices. A little ripple ran through the audience. They then went into a rendering of 'Yes, We Have no Bananas' and the expressions on their faces as they stressed the word '*Yes*' brought chuckles. When they had finished they got loud applause. Bette's face was wreathed in smiles. 'Excellent, excellent, I'm delighted.'

At this point the door opened and Richard and Andrew looked in, with Andrew saying, 'What treat are we missing? Something good, obviously. We have the complete list of the talent outside so what do you want us to do now?'

Bette said she would come and have a word with them. The three of them went outside. In the hall the atmosphere had miraculously changed, there was a general chatter, with a sixteen-year-old, who was a magician, declaring it would be impossible to follow the last turn.

The 'choir', who said it was the first time they had done harmony singing for fun, were delighted with the response. Lyndsey was praised for her singing and playing, George the comic, saying, 'You certainly have style, miss. A professional, are you?'

Lyndsey laughed. 'No, very much a raw amateur, but I think it could be fun.'

Bette came back with Richard and Andrew. She had apparently arranged for the people outside to come to her in groups during the following week for auditions, adding, 'Richard and Andrew seem to think we have some good talent among them, especially a boy who's an excellent mimic, but we'll see. At the moment we must get on with the other acts.'

Bette told the young magician after he had gone through his routine that he still needed to polish up his act. She would help him. She also told the mother and daughter who sang duets that they must be more lively. She would explain what she wanted them to do and would arrange for all the acts to have another rehearsal.

To Lyndsey's relief Richard was most amiable now towards Andrew. They laughed as they related some of the remarks from the people outside the hall about their 'talents' and chatted to the people who had taken part in the rehearsal. Both of them said they had been impressed by the quality of the harmony group, who they heard from outside through closed windows and door.

Bette was excited about them. 'They really are marvellous. I should like to make them my star turn; they'll go down well, *very* well.'

Andrew grinned, 'So apparently will Lyndsey, judging by what I've heard from your trick cyclist and stand-up comic. They were both raving about her. A beautiful, sexy voice, Joe said, that made your innards tremble.'

Bette laughed. 'She'll make a lot of innards tremble when I explain a certain idea I want her to carry out.'

She would not enlarge on it then, and it was not until they were walking home, with Richard and Andrew and the children in front talking to the mother and daughter act, that Bette outlined the innovation for Lyndsey.

'I thought if you wore a flimsy chiffon dress, not *quite* see-through, you could go across the stage in between two acts, kicking your height, first right leg then left, do a couple of twirls then do some more kicks and off before they had a chance to really take stock of you. Their mystery girl!'

Lyndsey eyed her in alarm. 'Bette! I couldn't possibly do such a thing. Just think what Uncle Richard would say if he knew.'

Bette grinned. 'But he wouldn't know, would he? We would lift up your lovely chestnut hair, fastening it with a chiffon band with flowing ends. Your dress would be flowing too. Lyndsey, it's a marvellous idea, those lovely long legs of yours – '

Lyndsey threw out her hands. 'No, no, no! I couldn't do it.'

'You could, you know,' Bette spoke softly, coaxing. 'Just think what you would do for the men. Give them someone to dream about, this lovely vision – '

Lyndsey kept saying, 'No, no,' but with Bette's persuasive voice the no's became less positive. She began to see the craziness of the whole thing, the fun. It was a long time since she had done anything crazy.

In the end she said, 'I'll think about it, but I'm not promising.' Bette gave a grin of satisfaction when she saw how her eyes were sparkling.

SIX

On the way back to the house the talk was all of 'Bette's acts' and the people who were anxious for an audition. Richard at this stage was at his best, easy, relaxed, amusing as he related bits and pieces of their conversation. He told them about one woman grabbing his arm and saying, 'Hey, general, will you gi' me a chance? I can sing louder than anyone else.' Which had apparently brought a retort from another woman that if they had a few more like her they could do away with the air-raid sirens!

'It was fun,' Richard said, laughing. 'And you really have some talent among them, Bette. One chap is an excellent mimic. He took off a number of well-known people – Churchill, Ramsay MacDonald, Cary Grant – and, believe it or not, Marlene Dietrich! In fact,' he added, with a mock superior air, 'we probably had as good a show outside as you had inside.'

Bette nodded. 'That's possible. Time will tell. I'll have to employ you and Andrew as my stage managers.'

Richard became serious. 'About finance, Bette. Have you thought of the cost? I know you said that all the people taking part were willing to give their services free, but there will be travelling costs. And what about transport? You'll have props as well as people to deal with.'

Bette said she would be able to finance the project, at the beginning anyway. She would hire a van and do shows at nearby camps and if the show 'took off' and they wanted to travel further afield then she would have to try and work out a plan. The important thing at the moment was to get started.

The two children, seeing Mrs Petrie's labrador Penny, went running ahead and while Richard went on talking earnestly to Bette about finance, Andrew drew Lyndsey behind them.

'I've enjoyed this morning but I want some time alone with you. I have to leave about six o'clock.'

She looked at him in dismay. 'So soon? I thought you were here for the evening. Oh, Andrew, it's so short. I hate to think of you flying, it's so dangerous.'

'No more dangerous than being in a submarine where you could have depth charges dropped on it, or torpedoed on a ship, or being blown up in a tank. I worry about *you*, Lyndsey, being in the air-raids in London.'

'I've become philosophical about raids. I think like Uncle Richard's housekeeper, Mrs Grey, that if you are destined to die by bombing nothing will stop it.'

'I think I believe that too . . . and yet – Lyndsey, would you give me a mascot, something small, something you've handled? I would like to take it with me when we go on missions.'

She nodded slowly. 'Yes, I have something with me, Andrew, it's a one-eyed teddy bear called Buffy. It belonged to my mother, she loved him and so do I. I would very much like you to have him. He's a rather tattered little fellow now but I think you'll like him, he has such a lovable, wicked look.'

Andrew stopped and turned her to face him, saying softly, 'I know I will. If he's precious to you, he'll be precious to me, and I promise I shall bring him back safe and sound when this war is over. Yes, I shall, I know it in my bones that we shall be together again.' He put a finger under her chin. 'Will you be my special girl, Lyndsey?'

She was moved by the wistful note in his voice, but

although she was more than a little fond of him she did not want to be too serious. But because she was aware of his homesickness and because she knew how necessary it was for him to have someone special to come back to she said gently, 'Yes, of course, Andrew, and I shall always try and come to Bette's when you manage to get some leave.'

He beamed at her. 'Great, now I can tell the chaps that the teddy bear was given to me by a wonderful girl with gorgeous legs and lovely midnight blue eyes.'

'They're grey,' Lyndsey protested.

'They are when you're in a thoughtful mood, but they're like midnight blue velvet when you are tending lovingly to the children. I want to see them midnight blue when you look at me.'

Andrew made to put his arms around her, but drew away when Janie came squealing down the road, Penny lolloping joyously beside her. Janie held out her arms to Andrew and he swung her up, demanding to know what the trouble was.

Connie came running, 'Penny knocked Janie over.'

'Because you were teasing her I bet. Penny is playing, she won't hurt you. Look.' Penny was sitting on her haunches, looking up at them, tongue lolling. 'She's happy, enjoying herself. Come along, we'll throw her a stick.'

Andrew found a piece of twig and threw it and Penny went racing after it. Janie wriggled to be put down and she and Connie went running after the dog.

Andrew turned then to Lyndsey with a rueful smile. 'Our beautiful love scene ruined. We must try to get out this afternoon on our own.'

But they had no chance to be alone. After lunch there were two phone calls that altered plans. The first was for Bette to ask her if she could board two soldiers, both corporals. They would be there the following day.

Bette had apparently said yes at once, and explained to Lyndsey the call was in reply to her letter offering to board servicemen who needed somewhere quiet to recuperate. She then explained to Richard and Andrew that the men had not been wounded but were suffering from war fatigue, after being in combat for a long time.

Richard looked worried. 'But Bette, how can you possibly manage, where will you find the time? You have the children to care for and you're planning to do shows for the troops.'

Bette seemed to have it all cut and dried. The children were no problem, they were quiet, she would take them shopping, for walks. As for the shows, they would only be on occasions, and then Mrs Petrie, she knew, would baby-sit and see if the men needed anything. Richard was not to worry, everything would work out splendidly.

Andrew said, smiling, 'Knowing you, Bette, I'm quite sure it will.'

Ten minutes after this the phone rang again. Bette took the call then came in to tell Richard it was for him. It was his wife. Richard jumped up. 'Marian?' He hurried out.

When he returned he looked regretful. 'Bette, I'm terribly sorry, but I have to return to London, my wife is at home, she managed to get some leave. I must look up the trains.'

Bette told him there was one due in half an hour and Lyndsey thought she detected a note of disappointment in her voice. Then Bette was smiling. 'We're sorry to lose you, Richard, you hardly seem to have arrived, but how nice to have your wife at home. You must come again sometime.'

Richard promised he would and went up to pack his bag. 'Well,' Andrew said, 'Richard's visit is shorter than mine.'

Bette, who had been standing looking thoughtful, said, 'I think it might be a good idea if I try to arrange a small private sitting room for the two corporals, as well as a bedroom each. Perhaps you could give me a hand to move some furniture around, Andrew, it won't take long. We'll wait until Richard leaves.'

When Richard came down he thanked Bette for her kindness and told Andrew how much he had enjoyed their morning 'interviewing'. He then gave him an invitation to visit them in London if he had the opportunity, and with a glance at his watch said he must go. Lyndsey offered to walk with him to the station but he told her no, she was to stay and enjoy herself. She walked to the door with him where he asked her when she would be home, reminding her of their dinner date with Elliott on the Monday evening.

'I hadn't forgotten,' she said, 'but will Marian want to dine out? After all, if she's home for only a short visit – '

Richard seemed surprised at the question. 'Of course she'll want to dine with Elliott. They know one another, get on well. What time shall we expect you home?'

'I shall travel back on Monday morning, but will go straight to the Centre. I'll be home sometime in the afternoon.'

After Richard had gone Lyndsey was surprised at how much she resented Marian being a part of their dinner date, and although she could not say exactly why she resented her so much, she was sure the evening would not be the same with her there.

She had closed the door and was standing with her back against it when she heard Andrew say, 'And who is this Elliott you'll all be dining with on Monday?' Andrew was standing at the foot of the stairs ready to take up an armchair. It was Bette who answered.

'He's a handsome army captain who made up a foursome when Richard took Lyndsey and me to see *White Horse Inn*. But you needn't be jealous, Richard thinks that Elliott is too old for Lyndsey.'

Andrew sat down in the armchair and crossed one leg over the other. 'But what does Lyndsey think?' Although there was a teasing note in his voice Lyndsey was aware that his expression was serious.

'Elliott Warrender is a very nice person,' she said, 'but I don't want to talk about him. I'm annoyed with Marian. When she was leaving in connection with her war job she was quite content for Richard to sleep in the house and get his meals at his club, but as soon as she knew that he was coming to stay with you, Bette, she hurried back home. She's jealous, that's what.'

Bette shook her head. 'I doubt that. I could be a doddery old lady for all she knew.'

'But she would *know* you weren't a doddery old lady. Richard would have told her all about you and about the four of us going to a show the other day.'

'All right,' Bette grinned, 'so he described me, what has Marian to worry about? I'm not exactly every man's dream of bliss.'

Andrew uncrossed his legs and sat up. 'I've noticed quite a few men cast their eyes in your direction, Bette Bascony. You are a most attractive woman.'

'Oh, come on,' she said, 'who started this conversation? We have furniture to move.'

'Andrew started it by asking about Elliott Warrender,' Lyndsey snapped, 'which proves that he was jealous too and it's just so stupid.'

'Aren't you jealous of me?' Andrew demanded, 'with all those hundreds of Waafs chasing after me.' He was laughing but Lyndsey would not come round.

'Of course I'm not. I wouldn't care if every girl in all the services was after you.'

'Oh, that's bad,' Andrew replied, a mournful note in his voice. 'Much worse than I thought. I leave soon to fight the enemy and she doesn't care, she doesn't love me, doesn't care if I never come back!'

'Don't!' Lyndsey exclaimed. 'Don't say such things, not even when you're joking.' She gave a little shiver and Andrew got up, concerned now.

'Lyndsey, I'm sorry, it was a silly thing to say. I won't do it again, I promise. Come on, let's help Bette to sort out this room then perhaps we'll have time to go for a walk and a chat.'

Bette made a very comfortable little sitting room and the view from the window was restful. But no sooner was the job completed than Mrs Petrie came running in to ask Andrew's help in getting her brother-in-law on to a couch after a fall. Andrew said it might be better to get the doctor's advice before moving him and Bette went to phone.

Once the patient was settled in bed, Mrs Petrie insisted on making a cup of tea for them all, and in the end Andrew and Lyndsey were denied their walk.

'Next time I get leave,' he said, 'I'm going to whisk you away where we can have a lovely weekend on our own.'

Lyndsey told him they would need to do a great deal of talking before anything like that could be arranged, and warned him she had been brought up with strict moral codes. She had tried to keep her tone light, but Andrew took her to be serious and said she would have no need to worry on that score, they could sleep in separate hotels if she wished! She laughed and said it might be wise if they did!

Bette began to talk about Andrew and Richard that night when the children were in bed, saying how pleased she was that the two of them had ended up getting on well together. Then she said, with a thoughtful look at Lyndsey, 'Why were you so upset about Marian coming home? It wasn't only because you presumed that Marian was jealous of me, was it?'

After a moment's silence Lyndsey shook her head. 'Not altogether, although I do think it was the reason for her suddenly rushing home. It's Uncle Richard. He's so different when he's with you, sort of free, free to laugh, have fun. With Marian he's stilted. He's my only living relative and I hadn't realized just how important he's become to me. I've always been fond of him, but now, well, I suppose he's someone to – cling to. Is that the right word? I'm not sure. No, I don't want to cling to anyone. I love him, I want him to be happy.'

'But Marian might be right for him,' Bette said earnestly. 'He's been a loner and now he wants to settle down he's probably quite happy with her. Perhaps he knows she's not likely to run off with someone else. Loneliness is a great leveller. Take Andrew. He's homesick, so he's clinging to you. I think he's genuinely falling in love with you, but – '

'But don't get too serious about him, is that what you were going to say? I don't want to, Bette. I like him, like him very much, and perhaps I am a little in love with him, but there's so much I want to do. I just don't want to be tied down to one man.'

'No, you don't, not yet, there's plenty of time. Oh, heavens, aren't we getting morbid. Let's change the subject. Would you like to go for a drink at the local? They'll be pretty well packed, it being Saturday night, and you might get roped in to play the piano.'

Lyndsey, sensing that Bette was not too keen to go out that evening, said, 'I'm not fussy. Let's sit and talk, go over your "acts". Let me know how you feel about them.'

'Yes, let's, we'll have a sherry.' Bette was effervescent again and Lyndsey enjoyed the rest of the evening.

They didn't go to church the next morning because Bette had a phone call to say that the two soldiers would be arriving at eleven o'clock. Mrs Petrie, who was there at the time, offered to take Connie and Janie, for the morning at least, pointing out the men might not feel like talking to children. Lyndsey suggested that she be out too when they arrived but Bette asked her to stay. 'It's stupid,' she said, 'but I'm nervous. Yes, I, who've been used to playing to audiences.'

By ten to eleven Lyndsey was as nervous as Bette, but when at five past eleven an army car drove up and the two men got out with a sergeant in charge, all Lyndsey's nervousness vanished. So apparently had Bette's, who said with great feeling, 'Oh, the poor souls.'

Both men appeared to be in their mid-thirties; they were hollow-eyed, their cheeks gaunt, and they walked slowly, like sleep-walkers.

The sergeant introduced them but said, 'Just call them by their Christian names. The fair one is Harry, the dark-haired one Frank.'

'Sit down, won't you,' Bette said gently. 'I'll make some tea, the kettle should be boiling.' Lyndsey offered to make it and went into the kitchen. The sergeant followed her.

'I'll let Mrs Bascony have a word with them,' he said, 'try to draw them out a little. They're not mental, just dead weary. You'll see a difference in a few days' time, it's amazing what rest and fresh air will do. It's far better for men in this state not to be in one of the bigger houses. All they want, Miss MacLaren, is peace.'

'They'll get it here, and be well looked after. Mrs Bascony is a very warm-hearted person, most compassionate. She's made a small sitting room for the men if they want to be on their own.' Lyndsey lifted the boiling kettle from the stove, rinsed out the teapot then brewed the tea. 'Tell me, Sergeant Brady, wouldn't the men be better at home with their own families?'

The sergeant shook his head. 'Not as things are, Miss MacLaren. Both their families have been bombed out and are living with relatives. They're overcrowded and the worst thing would be for them to be involved in raids. Shall I carry the tray in for you?'

Although the two men were sitting quiet both were listening with some intentness to Bette describing the country-side and the village.

They drank their tea but refused anything to eat. They looked sleepy and Bette asked if they would like to see their rooms. They nodded. The sergeant went up with Bette and the men and ten minutes later Bette came down alone.

'Harry and Frank want to go to bed and Sergeant Brady's helping to see them settled. He said to let them stay there for the rest of the day, then get them up after breakfast in the morning. He told me to be kind to them, but not to coddle them. Isn't it sad, both bombed out of their homes. I'll have to see that Connie and Janie don't come rushing in squealing with Penny barking at them, and yet it's unfair to try and restrain them.'

'I don't think you should, Bette, it's only occasionally they're playing with Penny, they're quiet children generally. I don't think they'll upset the men in any way.'

'Perhaps you're right.' Bette grinned suddenly. 'I wonder what they're going to think about all the men coming and going. First Andrew, then Richard, and now having to be told there are two soldiers asleep upstairs. And what will the villagers be saying? *I* shall be getting a bad name.'

'No, you won't, not when they know who the men are. It will be just as well if they do know, so they can perhaps show them some kindness when they're able to go out.'

Connie and Janie, when told about the soldiers, accepted them as two more uncles. They seemed quite pleased about it.

The men slept all day and when Bette did take them a light meal in the evening they hardly ate anything. She said to Lyndsey that perhaps they would be more settled by the next day.

The following morning Lyndsey left early and because Bette was preparing breakfast she went to the station on her own, with the promise to try and come one day through the week and stay overnight.

During the journey to London Lyndsey found herself comparing the different lives of people, the two men, their families bombed out and living with relatives, being over-crowded. And yet there was the Mayfair house with only Richard and Marian and herself occupying it. There would be room for two families to live in it. But a home is some-thing precious, not really to be shared. Lyndsey thought of all the times she had stayed with her grandparents as a child, the fun and excitement of the journey, being taken to different places, the show places. How precious those memories were.

When she arrived home Marian was in the drawing room alone. Richard, she said, was in his study sorting through some reports. Then she asked Lyndsey if she had enjoyed her weekend.

'Very much. It was most enjoyable and it was a relief to be away from air-raid sirens wailing and bombs dropping. I heard on the radio that the bombing was light last night.'

'Yes.' Marian paused. 'I was sorry I had to bring Richard back from his weekend; he seemed to be enjoying himself.' She ran a finger along the edge of a small antique table. 'Lyndsey, this Mrs Bascony, what is she like? Richard seemed to find her a most interesting character.'

The casual tone did not deceive Lyndsey. Marian was obviously jealous. She said, 'Bette is a marvellous person, warm-hearted, generous; the two little evacuee children adore her.'

Marian looked up. 'I really was sorry to spoil his weekend, but I did want to see him. There comes a time when missing one's husband becomes an appalling ache. I'm lucky to be able to see him. Other wives are not so lucky and have to accept long separations. This wretched war, I wish it was over.'

There was pain in Marian's voice and then Lyndsey felt sorry for her, sorry that she should suffer from jealousy. It was a soul-destroying thing.

Marian said she would go upstairs, have a bath and get changed and was at the door when she turned. 'I understand that Mrs Bascony is a widow.'

At this Lyndsey felt annoyed. 'Yes, she is, but Bette is not out to snare Uncle Richard. Nor, I feel sure, was he wanting to have an affair with her. He's away a lot; do you always torture yourself wondering if he's with another woman?'

'No, no, of course not.' Marian had spoken with spirit but the next moment it was as though all the life had gone from her. 'Yes, I do,' she said in a low voice. 'I've loved Richard for years and I was overjoyed when he asked me to marry him. But well, I don't think he loves me the way I love him.'

'Men are not so demonstrative as women. My mother once told me that she could only remember a few occasions when my father had told her he loved her. Yet she said she knew he did and they were devoted to one another. I think you'll have to trust Uncle Richard if you want to know any happiness.'

'It seems you have more sense than I,' Marian said with a wry smile.

'It's probably because I've never been madly in love. There could come a time when I'll be thinking about the smug advice I'm giving you. Then *I* shall suffer.'

'I hope not, Lyndsey. You won't say anything about this to Richard?'

'Of course not, you should know me better than that.'

Marian looked hard at her. 'That's just the trouble, I don't. I don't even know myself!' With that she left, leaving Lyndsey puzzling over the complexities of people's characters.

Marian wanted her husband's love yet was dedicated to her job, making it top priority in her life. True there was a war on and loyalty to one's country was important, but surely she could arrange some comforts for Richard when she was to be away, instead of saying he could sleep at home and dine at his club. No, Marian was not deserving of sympathy.

And yet, wasn't it her mother who once said that one must feel sorry for people who were possessive, they lived tortured lives. Lyndsey decided that it was up to Marian to change her ways if she wanted her husband's love. She then went upstairs to get ready for their evening out.

It took her some time to decide what to wear and

eventually she chose a rich jade green silk dress, the fully flared skirt circled by a broad black velvet belt with an intricately designed metal clasp. Her only jewellery was a pair of drop earrings in the same metal as the clasp and studded with jade. She brushed her hair until the chestnut tints gleamed. At first she put it up then decided to wear it loose. It was shoulder length, curling at the ends.

At times Lyndsey had secret longings to be small so that she would be cherished by the man she eventually fell in love with, but this evening she was pleased with the elegance of her reflection, which somehow seemed right for dining with the distinguished-looking Elliott Warrender and her equally distinguished-looking uncle.

When she came downstairs Richard complimented her on her appearance. 'You look beautiful, Lyndsey. You have good dress sense.'

'Yes, she has, hasn't she?' said Marian from the doorway. Lyndsey turned to see her in a black dress, which, without trimmings of any kind, made her look dowdy. What on earth was Marian trying to do? Be a martyr? The phone rang in the hall and Richard went to answer it. As he brushed past Marian he said shortly, 'We *are* dining out, Marian, not going to a funeral.'

Marian's face flushed. She came into the room. 'Why did I decide to wear it? I obviously have a perverse side to my character.' Her lips trembled. 'I suppose I had better go and put something else on.'

'Why not wear that patterned blue chiffon dress you bought when you gave your last dinner party. I liked you in it and so did Richard.'

Marian left to go and change. When Richard came back he said it was Elliott on the phone, he would call for them in about ten minutes. Then he looked around him and asked where Marian was. When Lyndsey told him she had gone to change her dress he said, 'Thank goodness for that! What made her wear such a thing?' His brow creased in a frown. 'She doesn't seem to be herself, I wonder if she's overworking?'

Lyndsey hesitated a moment. 'I think all she wants is a little bit of fuss from you. She's missing you terribly.'

'I miss her, Lyndsey, but she won't believe it.'

'*Make* her believe it.'

A slow smile spread over Richard's face. 'Yes, Grandma MacLaren, I shall take your advice.'

They were laughing together when Marian came in, looking softer and younger in the blue chiffon dress. 'Is that better, Richard?' she asked almost shyly.

'Much better, Marian.' He smiled and touched her cheek. 'Sorry I was rude about the other dress, but black definitely doesn't suit you.'

The front doorbell rang. It was Elliott. Richard ushered him in saying, 'The ladies are ready, but I think we shall have a drink first. Okay?'

Elliott greeted Lyndsey with a brief smile and a hello, then went to Marian hand outstretched, 'Marian, how nice to see you again after such a long time. You look well, hard work must agree with you.'

'It has to be done, it's all in a good cause.' She spoke lightly.

Richard said, 'Sherry for you, Marian? Lyndsey – lemonade or orangeade? I know it's whisky for Elliott.'

Lyndsey refused the drink, feeling annoyed that she had not been offered a sherry or a cocktail, and also childishly piqued because Elliott had not remarked on her appearance.

Which she had to admit was not the most promising start to an evening she had been looking forward to.

SEVEN

Elliott took them to a small restaurant in Soho. It was softly lit with a gypsy orchestra playing in the background. The atmosphere was intimate, romantic. Marian complimented Elliott on his choice of venue, it was so relaxing, not like going to one of the hotels where one was being constantly interrupted by acquaintances stopping to speak.

'Not stopping to speak to me,' she added with a bright smile, 'but to Richard. Such a popular man, with the ladies especially.'

Lyndsey thought, Oh don't, Marian, don't labour the fact that your husband is attractive to women and that you are jealous.

An elderly waiter came up to take their order and after he had gone Elliott remarked how much older all the waiters and waitresses were these days, with the younger ones being caught up in war work. At this Richard looked up.

'Ah, that reminds me of something I've meant to tell you for some time, Elliott. Do you remember when we met in that beer cellar in Vienna and you were greatly taken with a waitress called Rena?'

Elliott nodded slowly. 'Yes, I do. She wanted to be a ballerina. Are you going to tell me that she achieved her ambition?'

'She did, but not as a ballerina. Her real ambition, apparently, was to be an opera singer.'

'An opera singer? Are we speaking of the same girl?'

'We are. She took the job, according to her story, which was well paid, for the sole purpose of having her voice professionally trained. But she was afraid if the proprietor of the cellar knew about this he would want her to sing for his customers and, in that smoky atmosphere, it would be lethal to her voice.'

Marian said, 'Tell me, Richard, where did you meet this girl to get to know all this?' Although she had tried to sound casual there was a sharpness to her tone.

'It was *before* we were married, darling.' Richard looked as if he were thoroughly enjoying himself relating the story. 'It was while I was in Italy and was invited to a weekend party on a yacht. This woman spoke to me. I didn't recognize her at first but she knew my name and she remembered you, Elliott.' Richard laughed softly. 'But you wouldn't have known her, Elliott, she had put on weight, was like a little barrel.'

Lyndsey, intrigued by the story, asked how the girl had got the chance to be an opera singer and Richard said, 'Her music teacher brought some impresario to hear her sing and he was impressed and took her under his wing . . . and into his bed, so I understand.'

'Richard, dear, must you be so crude?' Marian's attempt at a playful, disapproving smile, could not disguise the distaste in her tone.

'It's the truth, Marian, and it's life.' The gentle reproof in Richard's voice took the smile from his wife's face.

Elliott said, his expression rueful, 'I thought myself to be in love with the girl at the time, but realized later it was her tragic appearance that had attracted me. It brought out the protective element. She was so tiny, with an air of frailty about her. It just shows how one can be taken in by appearances.'

'Oh, yes, and don't we know it,' Marian said quickly. 'Richard and I met a most charming elderly man while we were on our honeymoon. Do you remember him, Richard?

He was so kind, so courteous and he turned out to be the head of a gang of bank robbers. Talk about shock!'

Richard added his contribution to this story and while he was talking Lyndsey thought of Elliott's remarks about the ambitious waitress who he had described as bringing out the protective element in him and wondered if he preferred this type of girl. It could explain why he had practically ignored her when he arrived and made a fuss of Marian. Not that she was tragic, or frail looking, but she had a petite figure. Lyndsey had a sudden flat feeling and not even the fact that she had never wanted for boy-friends while she lived at Echo Cove did anything to lift it. She made an effort to concentrate on the conversation.

The waiter arrived with the first course but before he had a chance to start serving it the air-raid sirens began to wail. At this a man came out from the back of the restaurant to explain where the nearest shelters were situated, but he also stated that there was no activity as yet in this area. No one made to leave and the waiter continued serving the meal.

After he had gone Richard and Elliott began to discuss the previous night's raid and how widely scattered it had been, and how efficient the defences had become. Then the man who had made the previous announcement came out once more to say that the 'beautiful Carmelita' was going to sing. There was applause.

Near to where Elliott and the others were sitting was a massed flower arrangement and it was from behind this that the girl appeared. She was wearing gypsy costume and had a sultry, sensuous look. Applause broke out again and the girl blew kisses. The orchestra struck up and the girl began a haunting song about a lost love, moving around the room, appealing to each man in turn to say why had he hurt her so? She sang with pain in her voice, her accent foreign. She stopped beside Richard and held out her hands to him, repeating the phrase. Richard gave a sheepish grin and looked a little embarrassed. The girl then walked behind Elliott and ran her fingertips down his cheek. He sat solemn-faced, showing no emotion whatsoever. She then came round in front of him and held out her arms to him. This time she sang, 'I want you, no matter what the cost.'

Elliott took hold of her hand, kissed the palm and folded her fingers over it. She seemed surprised. Leaning forward she kissed him on the cheek then waved him goodbye and moved away. The notes of the orchestra died away and the girl disappeared behind the screen of flowers, to wild applause and cries of 'More!'

When the girl did not appear a chanting broke out among the customers, 'We want Carmelita, we want Carmelita . . .'

Behind the screen of flowers Lyndsey could hear voices, a man's and a woman's. The man appeared to be trying to coax Carmelita to come out and sing another song. There was a slight lull and Lyndsey heard the girl say, 'I ain't gonna sing again now, Mr Frome, I gotta a bleedin' 'eadache. P'raps later.'

Lyndsey looked at Elliott in utter astonishment. 'She's not foreign.'

'No, she's a Cockney.' Richard and Marian had obviously heard her too. Richard's lips were trembling, Marian sat tight-lipped. Then she looked accusingly at Elliott.

'She's just a tramp, you kissed her hand.'

'Yes, I did, Marian, she's had little romance in her life.'

Richard eyed him curiously. 'You know her?'

'I know the proprietor. He told me her story. She's had a tragic life.'

'Well, whatever it is I don't want to hear it,' Marian said. 'I didn't like her, I didn't like the way she made up to the men.' She took a sip of her wine then put the glass down. 'A woman like that is just trash.'

Lyndsey flared. 'How can you say such a thing when you won't listen to her story? How can you judge her?

Making up to the men is a part of her job, and she probably needs the work, needs the money.'

'She does,' Elliott said quietly. 'But Marian has a right to her opinion.'

At this Marian looked as if she had realized she had gone too far. She gave a faint smile. 'It's just that I have little patience with girls of this type. You say she's had a tragic life, but so do a lot of people. She doesn't have to do this kind of work, there's plenty of other jobs much more rewarding, in factories – dealing with components to help the war.'

'Her mother works in munitions,' Elliott said, 'and looks after Carmelita's baby in the evenings.'

'Oh, an unmarried mother, I see, that explains it.'

The sneer in Marian's voice incensed Lyndsey. She said to Elliott, 'Is she unmarried?'

'No, she has a husband but unfortunately he drinks heavily. She would leave him but apparently when he is sober he's deeply caring about the child.'

'Satisfied, Marian?' This from Richard who could not disguise his annoyance at her behaviour.

The arrival of the waiter with the next course, and the fact that the two men began to talk about amusing little incidents in their work, saved the evening from being a disaster. And all because of Marian's bigoted ideas and snide remarks.

The all clear had gone while they were in the restaurant, but when they left at eleven o'clock there was no sign of there having been a raid, no glow of fires against the skyline, no searchlights.

Marian had just said, 'Let us pray for a peaceful night,' when she and Richard were hailed by two acquaintances.

Elliott and Lyndsey walked on to where they had left the car. She said, 'It's been an enjoyable evening in spite of the upset over Carmelita. Marian has very set ways.'

'It would be a dull world if everyone agreed with one another.'

'It would be a more peaceful world if there were no wars. You would be thinking differently if you had been bombed out of your home.'

'I have been, Lyndsey, but the odd thing is that I never knew any of my neighbours until I was buried under the rubble. They were so marvellous. There was such courage, among the women as well as the men. They risked their lives to remove beams that had me trapped. And this kind of thing is happening all the time during raids, neighbour helping neighbour. So, in an odd sort of way, the war has done some good, brought people together. Not that I applaud wars.'

When they arrived home both Richard and Marian tried to persuade Elliott to come in for a coffee, but he said, regretfully, he would have to refuse. His leave was up the next day and he would have to make an early start.

There were thanks all round, the three of them thanking him for an enjoyable evening and he thanking them for their delightful company. And after saying he hoped to see them all again soon, he left, leaving Lyndsey feeling let down for some reason. After all, what more *could* he have said?

Pleading tiredness she told Richard and Marian she would go straight up to bed. For a while everywhere seemed quiet but when she went along to the bathroom she heard Richard and Marian arguing, their voices heated. It was the first time she had heard them raise their voices. Just before she went into the bathroom she heard Richard say, 'This stupid jealousy must stop, Marian, or else – '

Marian shouted back, 'Or else what?'

Lyndsey closed the door thinking, poor Richard, his evening spoilt because of his wife's possessiveness. Heaven preserve her from ever falling into such a trap.

It was not until she was in bed that she realized she had been guilty of that very thing, in a minor way, when she had felt let down over Elliott. What was that but a possessiveness? She had wanted his attention, wanted him to say,

'*We* must meet again, Lyndsey.' But perhaps possessiveness was inherent in every woman. *My* man! But why should she feel this way over Elliott and not with Andrew? Because Andrew had told her he loved her and Elliott was aloof?

No, no, that was not the sole reason. Not every man she met made a fuss of her, but this did not make her feel let down. It must be a question of personalities; Andrew had an easy-going nature, Elliott was more mature, a stronger character. Masterful. But did she want to be mastered? Bossed around? No, she wanted to be free, free to do as she pleased. She turned over on to her side and lay humped under the bedclothes. To the devil with Elliott Warrender, he was not important in her life. In spite of trying to convince herself of this Lyndsey found herself going over what he had said about the waitress and wondering how many more girls or women he had thought himself to be in love with. Sleep eluded her for a long time.

Marian, who awoke her the next morning with a cup of tea, showed no signs of the upset of the previous night. She chatted pleasantly about their evening then asked Lyndsey what plans she had for that day. When told she would be going to the Centre Marian said, 'In that case Richard and I will have a lazy morning then go to a tea dance in the afternoon.'

Although Lyndsey knew that they both went to social functions, to balls, she had never heard of them going to a tea dance, which somehow suggested an air of gaiety that did not fit in with Marian's image.

It was Richard who came up to tell her later that breakfast was ready. Lyndsey was up and nearly ready to come down. She said, 'I hear that you and Marian are going to let your hair down this afternoon. She told me you are both going to a tea dance.'

Richard raised his shoulders. 'I doubt whether there's much chance of letting one's hair down at the Savoy tea dances, but I must say they have an excellent orchestra. Would you like to come?'

Lyndsey loved the Savoy Orpheans' Orchestra, which was broadcast on the radio, but apart from feeling sure it would be much better for Richard and Marian to spend the afternoon together she was due at the Centre. When she explained this Richard asked her what time she finished, and when she told him two o'clock he said, 'Good, you'll have plenty of time to come home and change.'

'No, no,' she said. 'You and Marian go on your own, you get little enough time together.'

Richard stood hesitant. 'Marian and I had a few words last night. We – sort of made it up, but I think it would help us if you would come, Lyndsey. I think you'll find that Marian will agree.'

To Lyndsey's surprise she did when Richard put it to her. 'Yes, of course, it will be lovely for you, Lyndsey, there are heaps of young men there, most of them in the forces, on leave or stationed in the vicinity.'

And so that afternoon Lyndsey went to her first tea dance wearing a champagne-coloured crêpe de chine dress, with an accordion pleated skirt and a jumper top with a wide neck and sleeves full at the wrist.

As they went into the Savoy the strains of Glenn Miller's signature tune, 'Moonlight-Serenade', was dying away. It put Lyndsey in the mood for the dancing. A number of people came up to greet Richard and Marian, and Lyndsey found herself being introduced to several young officers, who all asked her for dances.

At first she felt excited after having had a waltz, a quickstep and a one-step in turn with the army, the air force and the navy, but after a few more dances she began to feel bored with the similarity in their conversation. Why had they not met her before? Where had she been hiding herself? They must get together. What was she doing that evening, or the next evening? They knew a 'whizzo' place or a 'top hole' one to go to for dinner.

Lyndsey smiled at each one in turn and told them she already had a previous engagement, and added that, in fact, her boyfriend rather objected to her going out with someone else. Then they would groan, they might have known that a beautiful girl like her would be snapped up.

After two more dances with the same type of men, Lyndsey had a feeling of disenchantment, yet deep down she felt the fault must be hers. Other women and girls appeared to be thoroughly enjoying themselves. Marian, who had had one dance with Richard followed with a variety of partners, looked more animated than Lyndsey had ever seen her.

Later when Lyndsey was in the powder room a girl came bursting in, a joyous look on her face. 'Isn't this absolutely great? So many men to choose from! *And* all this elegance. Oh, I *am* enjoying myself.'

She chattered on, explaining that she lived in Surrey in a little village. Her parents had married late in life and were 'fuddy-duddies' but at the moment she was staying with an aunt in London.

She patted her hair, straightened her dress then gave Lyndsey a beaming smile. 'Thanks for listening, I just had to tell someone how happy I am. See you later perhaps.'

After the girl had gone Lyndsey sat staring at her reflection in the mirror. Such exuberance, why couldn't she feel the same way?

Then suddenly she knew why. She didn't want the elegance, the fancy talk, she wanted to be back in Kent with Bette, who in spite of her flamboyance was so down to earth, so warm. And she wanted to be with little Connie and Janie who hugged her when she arrived and begged her to tell them stories. It would be good too, to see Andrew who was fun, but without the fancy talk, and yes, she would like to see Elliott again, who although more serious had proved to be a compassionate man. She got up. Tomorrow afternoon she would go to Kent and stay overnight.

When they were ready to leave the Savoy, Marian, her cheeks flushed, her eyes bright, said, 'I *have* enjoyed my

110

afternoon and I'm sure you did too, Lyndsey. I don't think you sat out a dance.'

'No, I didn't. I love dancing and I did enjoy the orchestra.'

Richard gave her a quick glance. 'But you didn't really enjoy the afternoon.'

Lyndsey, surprised at his astuteness, sought in her mind for excuses. 'It's difficult to explain. I felt there was a falseness. The young men were too talkative, and there were some women who sat with fixed bright smiles as though they were trying to show they did not mind sitting out the dances. For instance, the woman in the black dress and rouged cheeks with the rather crimped-looking hair – I think her name was Horsley – she – '

'Lyndsey, let me say something.' Richard spoke quietly. 'Mrs Horsley has lost two sons in the war. She has a daughter who is rather plain but who was dying to see what she called "a little bit of life". Her mother brought her to the Savoy as a duty, I should imagine, and her smile was probably fixed to stop her from crying when she saw all the young servicemen enjoying themselves.'

Lyndsey, chastened, apologized. 'I'll never learn, will I, that appearances are deceptive.'

Marian laid a hand on her arm. 'Don't be too hard on yourself, Lyndsey. I knew nothing of Mrs Horsley's life either. Richard talks to people more than I do, and I suppose he gets to know these life stories.'

They were all quiet on the way home, but during the evening Marian recovered some of her animation by relating pieces of conversation from some of the men she had danced with. Some of them were funny little incidents that happened in everyday life, where the men were able to laugh at themselves. Marian then related some of their more serious talk and Lyndsey said that they sounded a lot more sensible than the partners she had danced with.

Then it occurred to her that young servicemen who could possibly be facing death when their leave was up were not likely to be serious. She really must start weighing up situations instead of condemning people out of hand.

The following morning there was a letter from Andrew, a short but loving letter in which he said how much he was missing her. He talked about the teddy bear and told her how Buffy's wicked look made all the men laugh. 'He's a good friend already, and I know he will bring me luck. Think of me, darling Lyndsey, and I'll be with you the moment I get some leave.'

Richard and Marian, who were idly discussing going to visit one of Marian's sisters, decided they would go when Lyndsey told them of her plan to visit Bette that afternoon and stay overnight. Lyndsey then phoned Bette, who was delighted to know she would be coming. 'Couldn't be better timing,' she said, 'we're having a rehearsal in the hall tonight. Things are moving, I'll tell you all about it when you arrive . . . I'll meet you at the station.'

When Lyndsey told Ann Matley at the Centre that morning about going to the Savoy tea dance and her reaction to it, Ann said, 'Cor! You are really living it up yet you say you didn't enjoy it. You must come to one of the Palais tea dances. There, I promise, you'll have a whale of a time. How about Friday afternoon, we're both off together then?'

Lyndsey said she would think about it and let her know.

Bette was on her own when she met Lyndsey off the train late on the Wednesday afternoon. She gave her a bear hug. 'Oh, it's good to see you, love.'

'And you, Bette. Where are the "family"?'

'Mrs Petrie came to take the children for a walk and the men went with them. *And* the dog. I love the kids and am pleased to be looking after Harry and Frank but it's lovely just to have a natter on our own.'

When Lyndsey asked how the two corporals were, Bette linked her arm through hers and they set off to walk up the road. 'There's a big improvement in them, Lyndsey. They still look drawn but they've lost that awful hunted look from their eyes. They've started to talk and to eat, not much of either, but it's a start. I think the children have helped. You know how little Janie can stand and look solemnly at people, well she did with Harry and Frank, then she asked them if they had any little girls and they said they both had. Tears came into their eyes and I felt that was the first breakthrough.'

There was a catch in Bette's voice and she said, 'Oh, Lord, I'm going to bawl.' Then she gave a sniff. 'No, I'm not. They're doing well. Come on, tell me, what have you been doing? Oh, how did you get on at the dinner with Richard and Elliott?'

Lyndsey described their evening and when she told her about Elliott and Carmelita a dreamy look came into Bette's eyes. 'Now wasn't that a lovely gesture, kissing her palm? So, our major is not such a stuffed shirt after all. When are you seeing him again?'

'He's gone back, his leave was up. I had a letter from Andrew this morning.' Bette told her that she had had one too and said how pleased she was to know that he was safe. She then began to talk about developments regarding the show.

'We're doing our first performance next Saturday. Oh, Lyndsey, I'm so excited. I've been talking to some of the men. They're confined to camp for some reason so you can imagine how terribly bored they are. We're having a rehearsal this evening then one on Friday evening. You must come in time for it.'

They had reached the house and Bette went to make tea. Lyndsey followed her into the kitchen. 'Bette, have you any idea when Andrew is likely to get his next leave?'

'I haven't a clue, love, and I don't think he has either. The men take it when it's dished out to them, more often than not at short notice, by what I hear. You know our four girl tap-dancers, they've improved enormously, but they still lack that – well, a sort of oomph. Would you be willing to do your little extra act on Saturday with the flimsy draperies?'

Lyndsey said no, and in spite of all Bette's coaxing she was firm about it. 'Give me time,' she begged, 'I haven't even done my ukulele act yet. I shall probably be petrified. Oh, that cake looks good.'

Bette laughed. 'You're a lovely girl, Lyndsey MacLaren, but you can be as stubborn as my Ralph when he made his mind up about something. Come along, let's go and sit down with our cups of tea before the horde arrives. I asked Mrs Petrie to have tea with us and she was delighted to accept to get away from those demanding relatives of hers.'

They had finished their cups of tea and Bette had just brought the conversation back to Elliott again when there was the sound of barking. Bette got up. 'That sounds like Penny.' She went to the window. 'Yes, it is, here they are. Come and look, Lyndsey.'

The small party were coming across the field. Harry had Connie by the hand and Frank had Janie. Every now and again Connie gave a skip and a jump. Penny ran round them in circles and once when the dog trotted beside Frank he reached out and patted her head. Lyndsey did see a change in the men, but when they came in a few minutes later, with Mrs Petrie ordering Penny to sit, they were both shy with her.

She tried to make conversation with them while Bette and Mrs Petrie laid the table but they answered in monosyllables. Connie said, 'Uncle Harry and Uncle Frank have little girls. They have pictures, don't you, Uncle Frank? Show them to Aunt Lyndsey.'

Frank brought a small wallet from his pocket and took out a snapshot, which he handed to her without a word.

Both men were on it, with, presumably, their wives and children. It was in a backyard, with about eight children between them.

'Oh, it's lovely,' Lyndsey said. 'Such a laughing, happy

group. How old are the children, which ones belong to who?'

Harry got up to show her and tell her their ages, but his hand was shaking. Before he sat down again he said, 'I have a snap like it.'

Janie leaned against Frank. 'Your little Beryl's just like me, isn't she, Uncle Frank?' He nodded and stroked her hair. 'Just like you, pet.'

That was about the sum total of their conversation during the meal, but Lyndsey noticed that each appeared to be interested in what was said, especially by Bette when she was talking about her show.

The men went up to their room after the meal but Bette gave a nod of satisfaction. 'I see a further little improvement after their walk. Another week and I think they might start telling us about their lives. I understand that when men are in combat the constant bombardment of guns, bombs exploding, being without sleep, plays havoc with them. The sergeant did tell me that they do recover a hundred per cent after a rest, but sometimes I wonder if they do, or just appear to do so. It must affect their system.'

She paused and picking up a cup rubbed a finger round the rim. 'Doesn't fate play strange tricks. I thought the children might bother the men but it's helped them. There's a sort of empathy between them.' She put the cup down and became brisk. 'Well, we'll get cleared away and washed up, then into the fray. Mrs Petrie will be back to let us go.'

When, later, they arrived at the hall and the people who were taking part in the show greeted her with such friendliness, Lyndsey had that lovely feeling of belonging, a togetherness.

Bette clapped her hands. 'Well, now that we are all here I think we'll start. I did think, Lyndsey, it might be a good idea if you came on first, played a few tunes, get them singing, warmed up.'

Lyndsey wailed, 'Oh, no, not first, I would die.' When

they all started to tell her she was good, she needn't worry, she panicked and looked around her. 'Will there be a piano there? I wouldn't mind giving a tune on the piano, I could sit with my back to them, or sit sideways.'

'And do them out of a treat, seeing a lovely lass like you?' Charlie the comedian teased. 'I heard about you being a great success at the pub last Saturday.'

'Is there a piano at the camp?' Lyndsey persisted.

Bette gave a dramatic sigh. 'Yes, there is. All right, piano it is.' She appealed to the others. 'She'll have her own way. Come on then, Lyndsey, get yourself sat at the piano over there.'

She sat down, struck a few chords, ran her fingers over the keys then asked what she should play. Charlie called, 'Give them "Down at the Old Bull and Bush", that should get them started.'

When she launched into the tune they all joined in with the singing and what thrilled her was hearing once more the magnificent voices of the group of men from the choir. It set the scene and she no longer felt nervous. She only hoped she would feel the same way on the night.

As each act rehearsed Lyndsey realized the big strides they had made since she had last seen and heard them. The young magician gave a polished performance, but then he had had an expert in Bette to coach him. The quintette had no need of any guidance of course, they were superb, especially with their rendering of 'A Nightingale Sang in Berkeley Square'. It was moving, but before anyone had time to feel too sentimental they launched right away into the rollicking 'Alexander's Ragtime Band'.

The tap-dancers had livened up their act and tapped with great zest, but Lyndsey knew what Bette meant by lack of oomph. They were sweetly pretty but their smiles were mechanical. She wondered then if she dare do the extra act that Bette wanted. After all, she would be on and off so quickly they wouldn't have time to realize who it was. She would think about it.

The result of thinking about it was Lyndsey keeping Bette back after the others had all left and saying she agreed. 'You will!' Bette gave a yell and hugged her. 'Great, we'll have a quick rehearsal. You'll have to take your skirt off. No one will see you, the door is locked.'

Bette stood looking thoughtful for a moment and then began to talk, as though to herself. 'We don't want any music. No, that would savour of announcing an act and it has to be a surprise. And yet we have to capture their attention because when an act is finished they all start talking.' She looked up. 'A drum! Yes, that's it, I'll find someone to either give a bang on a drum or a roll. I'll decide that later. Ready? Now this is what I want you to do.' She took her by the hand and led her to the side of the stage.

'The show is taking place in the recreation room. They're rigging up a stage. There'll be screens at either side. Behind the screens are doors. All those taking part in the show will be in a Nissen hut, the men divided from the women by a blanket curtain. It's the best they can do. When Charlie has finished his magician's act he'll come off and you will be waiting behind the screen to come on. I think we'll make it a roll of drums. The moment it ends you appear. You will give a quick twirl, a double kick, another twirl and another double kick and off. The pace is all important. It must be swift. Try it.'

Lyndsey couldn't start for laughing at first. 'I feel daft standing here in my cami-knick.'

'Forget them, you're in floating draperies – a vision. I want you to be a talking point among the men afterwards, something they can laugh about, take their minds off their boredom. And yes, dream about. Off you go.'

Lyndsey, sober-faced now, came from behind an imaginary screen and followed Bette's instructions. Bette said, 'That's good, but faster.'

She kept saying 'Faster, faster,' until Lyndsey collapsed on a chair wailing, 'I'll drop dead with exhaustion.'

'No you won't, because on the night you'll be doing it only once. Once more and then we'll pack up for tonight.'

At the next go Lyndsey won Bette's approval. 'Perfect, absolutely perfect. While you're here you can practise and keep on practising when you're at home.'

They stumbled as they came out into the blackout and Lyndsey said, 'We shall have to dance our way home,' and began doing high kicks. Bette linked arms with her and high kicked with her. Then a voice came out of the darkness saying, 'Now then, what's going on here?'

It was Alf, the air-raid warden, who demanded to know if they had been drinking.

'No, Alf, not the kind of drinking that you mean. If you must know, we're drunk on success. Good night, sweet dreams.'

Bette and Lyndsey went on up the road giggling help-lessly, which had Lyndsey commenting later, 'Let's hope we're in the same joyful mood on the night of the show, but I doubt it.'

'Pessimist! Of course we will be, just as long as we stop worrying about our nerves and think of the fun we're bringing to the men.'

EIGHT

For Lyndsey it was a wonderful weekend, not only because of the fun they had rehearsing the high-kicking act in a big room upstairs, but because when they had a sing-song with the children and Mrs Petrie joining in, the two corporals smiled for the first time. They could not, however, be coaxed to take part in the singing. Frank said, a shakiness in his voice, 'When we're better. Thanks for asking us.'

To Bette and Lyndsey it seemed to be a big step towards healing their mental wounds.

There had been raids over London on Saturday and Sunday but life seemed to go on just the same. Richard and Marian had enjoyed their visit away and had stayed the weekend, but on the Monday Marian's leave was up and before she left Richard had word that he would be leaving that afternoon. When Richard suggested to Lyndsey that she should pack up and stay with Bette she said no, she would take up Ann Matley's offer to stay with her and her mother for a few days.

But, as it turned out, it didn't work out that way. For one thing Ann did not come to the Centre that day and when Lyndsey returned home that afternoon she found Andrew standing on the doorstep. On seeing him her heart began to beat in suffocating thuds. 'Andrew! What a surprise!'

A slow smile spread over his face. 'I can't believe you're here. I felt so disappointed when I couldn't get an answer

119

and I didn't know how to get in touch with you. I rang Bette and she told me you had come back home. Oh, Lyndsey, I want to give you a big hug. Dare I?'

She laughed. 'Not on the doorstep. You had better come in.' Over her shoulder she added as she put the key in the lock, 'But you can't stay here.'

'Of course not, I didn't expect it.'

Once they were in the hall he took her in his arms and Lyndsey could feel the wild thudding of his heart. His kiss became demanding and she drew away, saying, 'Behave yourself. Come into the kitchen and I'll get you something to eat.'

The fire was still on and she raked the coals and added some pieces of wood, taking time over it, not quite knowing how she was going to handle this situation. Andrew, she felt sure, would see it as the perfect opportunity of them being alone, if he knew that Richard and Marian were both away. She decided simply to say they were out.

But even as Lyndsey thought this she knew it would be exciting for them to be alone. The pounding of blood in her veins was telling her so, plus the tremors that ran over her body. She turned. 'Now – what would you like to eat?'

Andrew moved towards her. 'All I want to gobble up is you!' Although he was laughing there was a seriousness in his eyes. He drew her towards him. 'Oh, Lyndsey, sweetheart, how I've longed to see you. You've been with me on every flight. At times the image of you nearly drove me mad, wanting you, wanting to make love to you.'

Lyndsey drew back but this time he did not release her. 'Andrew, this is dangerous. I can't let you make love to me, so you either sit down right there and let me get you something to eat or I'm going out and leaving you here.'

He let her go then, saying as he ran his fingers through his hair, 'I'm sorry, Lyndsey I'll behave myself. We'll go out to eat later but I wouldn't mind a cup of tea, then we can sit down and you can tell me all you've been doing.'

Lyndsey wished that the longing to be in Andrew's arms

would go and she talked in a feverish way all the time she moved about, filling the kettle, putting it on the stove, bringing out cups and saucers. She told him about her weekend with Bette, about the rehearsal and the improvement there was in the two corporals, but not about the high-kicking.

Andrew said, 'Bette has a heart of gold. I felt a bit mean not saying that I would go over and see her but she understood that I was longing to see you.' He caught hold of Lyndsey's hand. 'Tell me, have you had any dates? I torture myself thinking of you in some other chap's arms.'

Lyndsey pulled her hand free and told him about the tea dance at the Savoy but she did not tell him about being bored with her partners because she wanted Andrew to know that she had to be free to do as she pleased. She went to the fireplace and stood with her back to him.

'Andrew, I won't be possessed and if you keep on being jealous, I shall stop seeing you.' She turned to face him. 'Now I mean this. It's not just idle talk.'

'I know.' He spoke quietly. He got up and came over to her. 'Forgive me. All the time I was away from you I kept telling myself I didn't own you because you agreed to be my special girl, but now I'm here and I see you . . . Oh, Lyndsey, you're so lovely, so – desirable.'

'Well, that's nice to know,' she said briskly. 'Now tell me, Andrew, how much leave do you have and have you heard from your family recently?'

Andrew gave a mock groan. 'All right, I get the message. I have to be back tomorrow night. And yes, I have heard from home – this morning. They're all well, the sheep are fine, the weather's good at the moment and the kettle's boiling. Will you make the tea or shall I?'

Lyndsey laughed and went to get the teapot.

Over their cups of tea they talked about general things, Andrew about his air-crew, about their lives, how unreal everything seemed to be at times, and Lyndsey told him little things about Connie and Janie, how the children were unknowingly helping the two soldiers towards recovery.

She picked up her cup and held it in her fingers, circling it, a dreamy look in her eyes. 'Bette was telling me that the men are getting up early and going into the little spinney at the side of the house. She's watched them and they just stand there listening to the birds. Then in the evening about sunset they go to the back door and stand looking out over the fields.' Lyndsey put her cup down carefully, then said softly, 'For me, the loveliest part of the day in the country and by the sea is when the night sky is closing in. If you've been sailing the wind then seems to drop and you tack with only the faint lapping of the water against the bows. In the country there is the last few cheepings of the birds before they settle to roost and the faint rustling of small animals in the undergrowth. There's something so peaceful, so soothing about it.'

There was a silence then Andrew said quietly, 'Thanks, Lyndsey, for making me remember the simple things, the beautiful things in life that still exist in spite of the horrors of war. I remember . . .'

Andrew talked with nostalgia of days of hard riding and of coming home and seeing the lights in the window and the family waiting for him; of walks in the evening with his father and the smell of his pipe tobacco. 'He's a philosophical man, Lyndsey, and it was not until I came to England that I began to realize the wisdom of his words. He would like you, Lyndsey. You are surprisingly wise for your years. Who was your teacher, your father, your mother?'

'Both, I think, in their different ways. Then there was Ivy who ran the café at Echo Cove. My mother worked for Ivy and her husband Tom, who ran a little general shop at Stoke, in the potteries. Ivy was tough, but she was kind. She helped a great deal to discipline me. I needed it,'

Andrew eyed Lyndsey with some curiosity. 'You say your mother worked in a general shop. Bette told me that your parents were comfortably off and that your grand-parents were wealthy, both master glass blowers in their own right.'

'That's true, but my grandmother came from a poor family and was in service when she was young. She met Ivy there. Ivy became a part of the family. She was my anchor when both my parents and grandparents were killed in an accident. And it was a great grief to me when Ivy died not long afterwards from pneumonia.'

'Poor Lyndsey,' Andrew said softly. 'What happened in the accident? Can you talk about it?'

'Yes, I can now.' Lyndsey explained about the mountain slide burying them during a holiday in Italy and he gave a low whistle.

'And I think that I have troubles because I get home-sick.' He laid his hand over hers. 'I promise I won't pester you any more, Lyndsey. *Not* that it will be easy.'

'I'm sorry, Andrew, it's just that – '

'Say no more. By the way, Buffy sends his love. He's a cute fellow. I told you, didn't I, that he makes my pals laugh. It's something we need at times to break the tension when we're on a mission. But there, no more war talk. Where shall we go for something to eat?'

Lyndsey brightened. 'I would like very much to go to Piccadilly Circus and eat in Lyons' Corner House. I've heard it's fun.'

'You do know that it's full of servicemen, GIs as well as our own forces?'

Lyndsey nodded, smiling. 'That's why I want to go, to make eyes at all the men.' Then, as she saw Andrew's eyes cloud, she added, her expression solemn, 'I'm only joking. It's the liveliness I need. How could I want the attention of anyone else when I shall walk in with the handsomest man of the lot.'

'Flatterer! Come on, let's wash the cups and go before I start getting . . . *aggressive* again.'

When Lyndsey said she would just check that all the

blackout curtains were properly drawn Andrew came with her and got intrigued by the books on the shelves in Richard's study. He began leafing through one on the early history of London and said he could spend a very pleasant weekend browsing. Lyndsey was tempted to say he could stay overnight then decided against it. It would certainly be putting temptation in his way and heaven knew what Richard and Marian would have to say if they found out that she had invited him to stay. Lyndsey also had to admit that it would be putting temptation in *her* way too. She took the book from him and put it back on the shelf. 'I'll get Richard and Marian to invite you to stay on one of your leaves then you can study the history of London while I play a game of patience.'

Andrew laughed and gave her a quick hug. 'Come on, off we go.'

They went out into the blackout and bumped into someone before they had gone a few steps. There were apologies on both sides and Andrew drew Lyndsey's arm through his. 'I haven't been eating any carrots lately. I must start again.' It seemed to Lyndsey to be a particularly dark night and she said they should be thankful; it should lessen the chances of a heavy raid.

Lyndsey had not walked along Piccadilly at night, and was surprised that the wide thoroughfare was as difficult to negotiate in the blackout as the narrower streets. It was strange too to find it so deserted after the remembered bustle of before the war on her visits to London. Then it was a joy to mingle with the pedestrians and gaze in the brightly lit shop windows.

But once they reached Piccadilly Circus the scene came to life. There were people all around, chatting, laughing; there was a constant movement of people outside Lyons' Corner House and Lyndsey was aware of a mingling of accents, the nasal twang of the American GIs predominating.

When Andrew and Lyndsey went in they both blinked

against the light. The restaurant was busy. Although there were three floors there was a small queue of people waiting for tables. The atmosphere was different to that which Lyndsey had expected. Outside there had been a gaiety among the groups of people, a little brashness. Here there was a decorum, voices, muted laughter.

Andrew said, 'We'll wait for a table in the Brasserie.' He gave her a teasing smile. 'There's a gypsy orchestra. Very romantic.'

It reminded Lyndsey of the evening she went with Elliott and Richard and Marian to the restaurant in Soho, where the girl Carmelita sang. She found herself wondering what Elliott was doing at that very moment.

There were two couples behind them, two flying officers with two girls in WAAF uniforms. The six of them got talking, the men discovering they had mutual friends and the girls talking to Lyndsey about the Wrens. And when the commissionaire announced there was a table for six in the Brasserie they decided to make up a party and went downstairs.

By the time they had finished the meal they had decided to go dancing together. Andrew said in a low voice when they were leaving, 'I hope I didn't push you into it.' He grinned. 'I thought at least I would have a valid excuse for holding you in my arms.'

Lyndsey smiled and said, 'I enjoy dancing, a favourite pastime.'

The hall was crowded. A number of people were standing around but the majority were on the floor dancing to the dreamy strains of a Strauss waltz. They were in semi-darkness, the only light coming from a mirrored ball suspended from the ceiling which flashed colours as it revolved, and gave a beauty to the haze of cigarette and cigar smoke.

Andrew and Lyndsey had agreed to stay with the other two couples for the rest of the evening and Lyndsey was relieved that Andrew raised no objections when one of the men suggested that they alternate partners. His name was Lofty, the other man was known as Chips, and the two girls as Petal and Angel. Petal was small with a jolly face and Angel was tall with a saucy smile. Lyndsey liked them both.

And so they waltzed, they foxtrotted, one-stepped, did the Lambeth Walk, the Palais Glide; they rumba'ed, did the samba and snaked all over the hall in a conga. In contrast to the tea dance at the Savoy it was a madhouse but Lyndsey loved every minute of it.

Andrew was a good dancer but Lofty was an expert and if he had had his way he would have had every dance with Lyndsey.

'You're a great kid,' he said, 'and we fit together like two birds in a nest. How about us having a night out together?' When Lyndsey pointed out that her boyfriend might have some objection he grinned and told her that what the eye didn't see the heart wouldn't grieve over, but she remained adamant, and he accepted it.

Each of the men bought drinks and after Lyndsey had her third gin and orange she not only felt a little drunk, but very sentimental. She laid her head against Andrew's shoulder and whispered that she wished the dance would go on for ever.

His hold on her tightened. 'So do I, my darling.' He sought her mouth and they clung together. But it was Andrew who drew back this time. 'Stop it, boy,' he chided himself, 'you promised to behave.'

Lyndsey looked up at him. 'Where will you stay tonight?'

'Oh, I shall find somewhere. If not there's always a bench on the Embankment.'

This alarmed her. It was impossible, he would catch his death of cold. She stopped. She must talk to him, she said, on their own. They went to the far corner of the dance hall, and there Lyndsey explained about Richard and Marian being away. 'You can stay at the house, Andrew, but there can't be anything else but you sleeping there.'

He cupped her face between his palms. 'Lyndsey, my sweetheart, I don't think I could trust myself, knowing you were sleeping somewhere near.'

'But you won't be,' she replied, her tone teasing. 'You will be in the basement where there's quite a comfortable bed and an electric fire. I shall be sleeping on the second floor.'

'It's not far enough away. I wish I were more of a cad and that you were not so sensible.'

'Do you, Andrew, do you really?' She searched his face, her expression earnest. 'If I let you make love to me it might occur to you later that as I had given in to you so easily, I might let other men make love to me.'

He denied this vehemently, but Lyndsey persisted. 'It *could* happen, Andrew, it happened to a friend of mine. Her boyfriend happily seduced her then called her a whore a few days later.'

He stared at her, shocked. 'I can't believe you could think such a thing of me.'

'I wouldn't have believed that Janet's boyfriend would have said such a thing. He seemed such a nice person, rather gentle, but where strong emotion is concerned, including jealousy – '

'Say no more!' Andrew held up a hand. 'Let's go and rumba, it's safer.'

After the rumba the men went to have a drink on their own at the bar, the girls not wanting any more and Angel asked Lyndsey why she didn't join one of the women's services. Lyndsey explained she hoped to join the Wrens soon and Petal said, 'Why not the WAAFS? It's fun. We drive lorries all over the place, sometimes through the night. We have dances, parties; you'd enjoy it.'

Angel shook her head. 'I think Lyndsey would fit into the Wrens better, they're a bit more upper crust, and she has a posh voice.'

'What do you mean by posh?' Petal was indignant. 'We had a Lady Penelope somebody or other in our lot and

Princess Elizabeth has joined the ATS, and you can't have anyone more posh than that! Don't you listen to her, Lyndsey, you come in our lot, you'll have a whale of a time.'

Lyndsey told them she had lived by the sea all her life, it would have to be the Wrens, but by the time the girls had talked about servicing their own lorries and sometimes staff cars and being asked to drive officers, plus the chance of perhaps getting to France, her mind began to waver. She had liked tinkering with cars when she was at home, and she had helped boyfriends to take down engines. One of them had declared her to be a born mechanic. It could be interesting. On the other hand, there was the sea . . .

When the men came back Angel announced that Lyndsey had decided to join the WAAFS and although she denied this, saying her mind was not made up, the thought was established for her to mull over.

The dance ended at midnight and the orchestra played 'Good Night Sweetheart' for the last dance. All talk ceased as though everyone realized they might not meet their partners again. Not only servicemen and their girlfriends, but civilians too, for who could tell what all the bombing would bring.

But once the music had ended a burst of talk broke out. There was a rush to the cloakroom for coats and shouts of 'Wait for me, I won't be long!' When Lyndsey managed to push her way out of the cloakroom against the crowd pushing in she found Andrew and the two couples waiting for her. Lofty suggested them all going to a night spot he knew. It was a bit sleazy, he said, but great fun and not too expensive.

Lyndsey shook her head at Andrew and he got out of it by saying that Lyndsey had to be home by half past twelve, her family were strict.

Angel commiserated with her. 'You should get your folks to go to the shelters like my folks and Petal's, they go at six o'clock every evening whether there's a warning or not.

They never know what time we come home – when we *are* at home, of course.' She grinned. 'You've got to get all the enjoyment you can, chick, in these days. Isn't that right, Petal?' Petal nodded.

They talked about all of them meeting up again but with Andrew having to return to base the following day there was no opportunity. They all agreed it had been a great night and perhaps with luck they might meet up again sometime.

Andrew and Lyndsey came out of the hall to find a raid in progress, although no one would ever have guessed it by the laughing chatting groups standing around. They were dim shapes, until one's eyes became accustomed to the blackout. There was the sound of planes overhead but not that awful constant drone as wave after wave had come over on other nights. There were thunderous bursts of anti-aircraft gunfire and the sky was alight with flash and flame and the screaming of shells through the air. But this evening there were no searchlights probing the sky. Andrew cupped a hand under Lyndsey's elbow and hurried her towards the road saying if they were lucky they might pick up a taxi. Taxi drivers were known to give preference to the American GIs who, with more money to spend, were lavish with their tips.

Andrew was lucky, the taxi driver who stopped had a son in the air force. When Lyndsey gave her address he told her that one or two bombs had been dropped around that area, but not much damage had been done. 'Our lads are getting the upper hand of the Luftwaffe, thank the Lord,' he said. 'They stop them over the Channel and at the coast now, but there's a few got through and some poor folks'll suffer.'

He went on talking about relatives he'd lost in raids and what he would do if he laid his hands on any Jerries. Lyndsey pointed out that there would be German people who would be saying the same thing about the British pilots after the big raid on Berlin.

129

The man agreed but added fiercely, 'All the same, they deserved it.'

As they got out of the taxi there was the scream of a bomb. Andrew and Lyndsey ducked and the explosion seemed to rock the pavement. The taxi driver urged them to hurry to a shelter, because, he said, you never knew where the next one would land. The next one was further away but Lyndsey tried to get the key in the lock without using her pencil torch. At last she found it and opened the door. 'Quick, Andrew,' she said, 'nip inside.' She closed the door then picked up a large torch from a ledge. 'We'll go straight down to the basement. I'll go first and put on the light.'

After she had switched on the light and the electric fire Andrew looked about him, remarking how cosy it was, how luxurious in fact, in comparison to some of the shelters he had been in.

'We have a primus stove,' Lyndsey said. 'I'll make a cup of tea. We make a habit of bringing fresh water down each morning in case we're trapped in a heavy raid. Nothing like a cup of tea, is there?' Lyndsey, aware that Andrew was smiling at her, stopped, then added, 'I'm gabbling, aren't I?'

He took her by the shoulders. 'Well, that bomb was close enough to upset anyone.'

Lyndsey said yes, but it was not the reason why she was agitated. She had been as close to falling bombs before. It was the fact of being alone with Andrew in the house, something she knew deep down she had wanted, her body told her so. She lit the primus stove, filled the kettle from a large can of water and set it to boil. She then brought out cups and saucers, sugar, dried milk and a tin of biscuits.

'This is *really* cosy,' Andrew said.

The floor was carpeted, there were armchairs, three single beds, a table, stools and two shelves of books. Andrew examined the books. 'Who reads the crime novels? You, Lyndsey?'

'Yes, I do and Uncle Richard. The books on psychology are Marian's.' When Andrew remarked that they didn't look as if they had been much handled Lyndsey stood thoughtfully for a moment. 'I haven't seen her reading any of those, but she is interested in psychology, although, to be honest, I don't think it does her much good.'

'Why do you say that?'

'Well, because' – Lyndsey raised her shoulders – 'I don't think she understands people. I'm sure she doesn't understand Uncle Richard. On the other hand –' she paused and looking up searched Andrew's face, 'do we understand ourselves? I don't think I understand myself.'

'Does it matter?' he said softly and kissed her. Lyndsey's senses, her blood, leapt in response but she drew away.

'Perhaps not.'

'Lyndsey, when we were dancing tonight you wanted me as much as I wanted you, I could sense it.'

'I had had too much to drink.' She picked up the biscuit tin and removed the lid. 'Have a biscuit, I'll make the tea.'

He took a biscuit and sat down. 'All right, you win . . . for *now*.' The words 'for now' and his wicked smile sent her nerve ends tingling. She conjured up all sorts of situations she knew were wrong, but she also knew they would lead up to them eventually.

Andrew nibbled on the biscuit then said, 'So what do we talk about? Tell me about your life at Echo Cove, if you can bear to talk about it. You have this great love of the sea. Did any of your family go to sea?'

'No, none of them had been brought up beside it. I loved the life, loved the little cove, and the echoing cliffs. I remember my mother telling me once that before she and my father were married how he shouted out for everyone to hear, "I love Julie van Neilson!" She got such a shock because Dad was a quiet man, a very strong character.'

Lyndsey made the tea then stood with the pot in her hand. 'My mother wasn't in love with him at the time but I often wondered if it was this declaration that swayed

131

her.' She set the teapot down then looked at Andrew. 'Is love something that grows? Can you be fond of someone then find out later that you're in love with that person? I've always felt that love was something that hit you suddenly.'

'It hit me that way when I met you,' Andrew said quietly. 'I knew there would never be anyone else for me but you. But you didn't feel the same, did you, Lyndsey?'

'I liked you on sight,' she said, smiling. 'I thought you were *very* handsome.' Then she became serious. 'I'm fond of you, Andrew, and I think perhaps I am a little in love with you, but I'm not sure.' She poured the tea and was aware that her hand was shaking. She began to talk about Petal trying to persuade her to join the ATS, and Andrew said why not the Waafs, then they might both be established at the same base. They began to give fors and againsts, making a game of it, with Lyndsey feeling sure that Andrew was talking for talking's sake as she was, to take their minds off their need for each other.

She had put the tin of biscuits back in the cupboard when Andrew came up behind her and put his arms around her waist. 'Lyndsey, I want you,' he whispered. She tensed and he turned her to face him. 'Is it so wrong, darling? We're young, life is surging in us, it's nature; how much time do we have left to give ourselves to each other?'

Lyndsey, knowing that Andrew was not meaning how much time had they together that evening, gave a wail of despair. 'Oh, Andrew, I want you too, I only wish I hadn't been brought up to be . . . sensible. My body urges me to say yes, but my brain is telling me it's wrong.'

'But is it, Lyndsey, is it?' There was a feverish note in Andrew's voice now. Reaching behind her he began to pull down the zip of her dress, slowly, sending shivers of excitement up and down her spine. She wanted to say 'Don't' but felt powerless to speak. Then he slipped the dress from her shoulders and it slid to the floor. And there she stood, clad only in a scanty pair of white satin cami-knicks. As Andrew gave a quick indrawn breath pulses began to beat all over her body.

Suddenly she felt ashamed, not because of Andrew seeing her so scantily clad but because she was enjoying his scrutiny for the wrong reasons. There had been no warm rush of love for him, just a sensual excitement, and yet she made no protest when he slipped the straps of the cami-knicks from her shoulders, baring her breasts. She wanted to experience what other girls had talked about. But she had not been prepared for such a surge of emotion. When Andrew buried his face between her breasts she closed her eyes and gave a little moan, which excited Andrew more. His lips moved over her skin to her throat and then to her mouth. They clung together and little shivers of ecstasy had Lyndsey trembling.

Picking her up he carried her to the nearest bed and laid her down. Quickly, he divested himself of tunic and trousers and was dragging at his tie when there was the sound of movement from upstairs. Fear ran through Lyndsey. 'Someone's come in,' she whispered.' Uncle Richard? Marian? She shot up on the bed and swung her legs to the floor. She pulled the straps of her cami-knicks on to her shoulders, grabbed her dress and pulled it on. Andrew was just standing there and she said in a fierce undertone, 'Andrew, for God's sake, get dressed!'

He came to life and, like Lyndsey, dressed at speed.

Heavy footsteps crossed the parquet floor of the hall then stopped. Lyndsey held her breath then released it as a voice boomed, 'You down there in the basement, Miss Lyndsey?'

To Andrew she whispered, 'It's Mr Thomson, the air-raid warden.' Unable to pull up her zip she grabbed her coat and put it on. 'Yes, Mr Thomson.' She went up a few of the stairs. 'I've been to a dance and hurried home out of the raid.'

'The best place. Just wanted to check that you're all

right, since the door was open. I promised your uncle I would. Although he did say you might be going away.'

'Tomorrow,' Lyndsey said quickly. 'Tomorrow I'm going to Kent, so you'll know I'm away.'

'Right, I'll leave you then. Good night. Ah, there's the all clear. No more trouble tonight, we *hope*.' The front door slammed.

Lyndsey sank on to a chair. Andrew stood looking at her then they began to laugh. Andrew ran his fingers through his hair. 'Oh, Lord, that was a narrow squeak, we'll never be so near again.'

Lyndsey, aware that her laughter held a note of hysteria, tried to calm down. 'No, we never will. It would have been terrible. Just suppose Mr Thomson had come straight downstairs. I would never have lived it down. I would have felt – '

'Stop it, Lyndsey,' Andrew spoke sharply. 'It didn't happen, so you must forget it.' He added, his voice suddenly wistful, 'I'm not sure whether I'm sorry or glad that we were interrupted.'

Lyndsey got up. 'I'm glad, Andrew. We let ourselves be carried away. I think we would both have regretted it afterwards.'

A sudden impish twinkle came into his eyes. 'I don't think I would.' He made to draw her to him. 'And as Mr Thomson is not likely to come back, having checked that you were all right – '

'No, Andrew, let's leave it at that.' Lyndsey drew away.

He sighed and began to fasten his tie. 'Perhaps you're right.' He was silent for a few moments then he looked up. 'I think I've just realized how badly I've behaved, Lyndsey. You invited me into your home to shelter from the bombs and I took it as a licence to let me make love to you.'

'It was circumstances,' Lyndsey said. She gave a wry smile. 'Ivy would have said that the devil put temptation in our way.'

'He didn't have to try very hard.' Andrew's smile too

held a wryness. He stopped to fasten his shoe-laces. 'I'll leave now and look for somewhere to stay.'

Lyndsey protested that it was foolish to try and find accommodation at this hour. 'You sleep down here,' she said, 'and I'll go upstairs.'

Andrew straightened. 'Lyndsey, even if we were ten floors apart and I hadn't even kissed you, what would the neighbours think when I walked out of here in the morning? Your reputation would be in shreds, and Richard and Marian would be blamed for leaving you on your own.'

'I think you're over-reacting. For one thing you could be my brother, or my cousin, and for another we have little contact with neighbours. I suggest you stay and get some sleep and in the morning we'll leave early and go to Bette's. She'll be delighted to see you.'

Andrew rubbed his chin. 'Well . . .'

'Then that's settled. I'll leave you now, Andrew.'

'Just like that?' There was a wistful note in his voice which tugged at Lyndsey's emotions. If they had made love it could have been for the first – *and* the last time.

She went to him, heartbeats quickening, not sure what she wanted. His kiss was gentle and she found she was glad.

But when she was in bed and went over all that had happened Lyndsey was not sure whether she was pleased or sorry that Mr Thomson had interrupted their little interlude.

NINE

Although Lyndsey and Andrew had not made love she felt
closer to him than she had ever done. He was tender with
her and apologized again for his behaviour. She put a
finger to his lips and told him to forget it. 'And we'll try
and forget the war for today,' she added, 'and enjoy the
lovely countryside and have fun with Bette and the chil-
dren. Andrew, will you talk to the two corporals and try
and make them talk to you? They need to be drawn out.'
He promised to try.

Bette was overjoyed to see them and the children made
a great fuss of both Lyndsey and Andrew. Bette made
coffee and the two corporals came to have some too.

Janie stood by Andrew's chair looking at him in her
solemn way. With her elbow on the arm of the chair and
her chin cupped in her palm she said, 'Haven't we got a
lot of uncles now?' She began to count them off on her
fingers, naming some of her uncles at home, about six or
seven, but which added up to about fifty as she counted
them on her fingers. Then there were the 'uncles' at Bette's
and by then the score had reached a hundred.

Connie tut-tutted like an old woman and said, 'When
are you going to learn to count proper, our Janie?'

Janie looked at her wide-eyed and stated that she *had*
counted proper. She did a recount and this time the
number reached a hundred and twenty-six.

When Andrew teased her and asked her how she had

managed to get that number she buried her face in the crook of his arm, giving her infectious little giggle. 'I must have missed some uncles out the first time.'

They all laughed, including the two corporals. Frank said, 'She's just like my little girl. She can't count properly either.'

Andrew asked him how old his little girl was and that set a conversation rolling. Frank asked him in turn about New Zealand and what were the chances of the likes of Harry and himself and their families emigrating when the war was over. And when Andrew said he thought there would be very good prospects, questions came one after the other. Bette, catching Lyndsey's eyes, gave her a quick nod and smile of satisfaction.

Later she said, while they were preparing the meal, 'Isn't it marvellous to hear Harry and Frank talking normally? They still tire easily, but they've lost that awful hopeless look. The sergeant called yesterday and he said he thought they had made marvellous progress. It's so satisfying, isn't it? *And* when we've done our little show – ' Bette was gleeful at mention of the show. 'The rehearsals have gone splendidly, Lyndsey. I want you to try on the costume for your special act this evening, but we'll wait until the children are in bed. What time does Andrew have to leave?'

It was a rewarding day in which the weather helped. There wasn't a cloud in the sky and the air had a lovely nip in it to give it a freshness that they all enjoyed when they went for a walk in the afternoon. The men didn't have much to say on the walk but their pleasure was evident in the way they watched the children running about playing with Penny and listening intently to what the adults had to say.

The time came all too soon for Andrew to leave. Connie and Janie wanted to go to the station with Andrew and Lyndsey but Bette told them 'another time', Uncle Andrew and Aunt Lyndsey had a lot to talk about.

The two of them walked down the road their arms

around one another's waists. Andrew said softly, 'You really are my *very* special girl now. You will keep writing to me?' She promised and Andrew gave his promise to write as often as he could. There were two more servicemen on the platform, each with a wife and children. The women were evacuees who Lyndsey recognized.

'Shakespeare was wrong,' Lyndsey said, 'when he wrote "Parting is such sweet sorrow." I hate partings.'

Andrew lightly tapped the end of her nose. 'I'll be back before you know it. We'll live it up again, go dancing, or perhaps, if I come here we can have a sing-song in the pub again, I enjoyed that.' He went on talking, making further plans and Lyndsey realized why he was talking so brightly when the porter announced the imminent arrival of the train.

They kissed, clinging together, then the train puffed in and Andrew boarded it. Doors slammed and she blew him a kiss. He returned it, calling, 'Now don't forget to write.' She called no, she wouldn't, then the train was on the move. Lyndsey noticed the two wives hurrying away with their children but she waited until the train was out of sight. By then she was tearful and full of regrets. She ought not to have denied Andrew. It had not been fair to him. According to what she had been told men suffered if they got all worked up and were denied. Andrew could be suffering at this very minute, he could go on suffering.

Lyndsey turned away and walked slowly back to Bette's. Although she had her tears under control by the time she arrived the discerning Bette said gently, 'Do you need a shoulder to cry on?'

'Oh, Bette,' there was a catch in Lyndsey's voice, 'can I talk to you? I feel I behaved badly to Andrew last night. Where are the children?'

'With Mrs Petrie. Come along, sit down.'

A few weeks ago Lyndsey would not have been able to speak of intimate things, but somehow Bette not only invited confidences but she had great understanding.

Lyndsey told Bette about going to the dance, their return home and the situation they had been in when the air-raid warden had come into the house.

'I think the man came at the right time,' Bette said gently.

'But don't you see,' Lyndsey spoke earnestly, 'it left Andrew in a state – un – unsatisfied. It was cruel. I was told that men really suffer if they're left in such a state. Andrew will be flying, his mind won't be on the job.'

'It will. Listen Lyndsey, nature has a way of taking care of things like that. Andrew no doubt would dream of you after you had gone, and it would be as if, well, as if the two of you had made love. Do you understand what I mean?'

'I – think so. I just felt so mean this evening. I was so moral last night. "You stay down in the basement here," I said, "and I'll go upstairs." '

'And it was the best thing you could have done, Lyndsey. I'm very fond of Andrew, he's a lovely person, but he's a man and if you had made love he could have left you pregnant. What then?'

Lyndsey defended him fiercely. Andrew would not have done that, she was sure of it.

Bette sighed and said she thought it was time that Lyndsey had some sex education. By the time she had finished talking Lyndsey was a lot wiser and knew of a lot of pitfalls she had not envisaged. Bette concluded, 'So just remember this, Lyndsey, you must avoid getting yourself into such a situation again. Andrew is in love with you, I'm sure of that, but some men make war an excuse for a lot of things. They say they could be dead tomorrow so need to live it up while they have the chance. I can understand how they feel, but how many girls suffer in consequence?'

Bette paused then added with a grim smile, 'I suppose it's easy for me to talk, I was married young. In your position I might have felt the same, but it's not as if you're in love with Andrew. You're not, are you, Lyndsey?'

'No,' she said in a low voice. 'Just very, very fond. I could never imagine myself being married to Andrew, but at the same time I felt I couldn't bear for him to be hurt. And, to be fair to him, he didn't force his attentions on me, and he could have done. We were alone in the house. He was most apologetic afterwards for the way he had behaved, but Bette, I was just as much at fault. I wanted *him*. I feel there's something wanton in me.'

Bette gave her deep-throated laugh. 'Oh, Lyndsey darling, if every girl was classed as a wanton because her feelings were strong for a man the world would be full of nothing else but wantons. Forget it. Just take care, that's all, never allow yourself to get into a position that you feel you can't control.' Bette wagged a finger at her, 'Remember this, you are talking of going into the Wrens and if you get there you'll find that girls are in the minority. You'll have your pick of men. *That* is the real time to worry.'

Lyndsey shook her head. 'No, I can be firm if I make up my mind to be. Thanks, Bette, for letting me talk to you, it's helped tremendously.'

Bette got up. 'Right, now let us get organized. I'll get the children in and start getting them ready for bed. They've done a lot of running about today, they've been excited. Later, when they're in bed I want you to try on your costume for your special act.'

Mrs Petrie came in with the children and after they were in bed she stayed chatting, so it was nearly nine o'clock before Bette brought the dress down for the 'special' act.

The costume of white and honey chiffon had straps at the shoulders and handkerchief points at the hem. Lyndsey held it up. 'Heavens, there's not much of it, is there?'

'If there was any more you could go to a church social. Try it on, the room's lovely and warm now.' Bette had brought down a full-length mirror which she propped against the wall. She talked as Lyndsey started to undress.

'I had an idea this afternoon. I want to add a little piece. After we have the roll of drums I'm going to ask our singing five if they'll sing, "You are my honeysuckle and I am the bee." I think it will be a great lead up to the act.'

When Lyndsey had donned the costume she stood staring at herself in the mirror, aghast.

'Bette, it doesn't cover my bottom!'

'The points do. Oh, I nearly forgot, there's a petalled hat to go with it and a pair of panties, here.'

Lyndsey held up both. 'The hat is a lot of help, isn't it? And look at these panties. They won't cover my navel.'

'Darling, the men won't be looking at your navel, it's your lovely legs they'll be fascinated with. And all they'll get will be a quick glimpse and you'll be off so quickly, they'll be wondering if they've dreamt it all.'

Lyndsey groaned. 'And I was worried about having immoral thoughts! If the censors see this outfit I'll be locked up!'

'Nonsense, you're well covered. Let's clear the decks and you can go through your routine.' They pushed the furniture aside then Bette said she would time Lyndsey. 'Remember, roll of drums, the men singing, then you're on. Kick, kick, twirl, kick, kick, twirl. Kick, kick – you're off.'

Bette set a stop watch. 'Ready – go!' Lyndsey went through the routine and at the end of it Bette announced. 'Ten seconds! That's all it took, that really is splendid. So how much of you are the men going to notice in that time? Your beautiful legs, of course.'

Lyndsey began to feel an odd excitement and for the first time began to understand Bette's dedication to stage life. It might after all be a lot of fun. 'Let me try the routine again,' she said. 'I have a horrible feeling that I might slip up on the spin, or the twirl as you call it.'

'You won't, your precision is perfect; you've never once slipped up on it, not after you'd mastered the changeover.

141

Oh, Lyndsey, we'll have a great night, I know it. I can't wait.'

She went over the details again. 'When you come off you do know that I'll be waiting behind the screen with a fur coat to wrap around you. Then you run across to the Nissen hut . . .'

Lyndsey felt then that *she* could hardly wait for the night.

Unfortunately it was a bitterly cold evening with a driving sleety rain. 'Oh, great,' Lyndsey wailed, 'I'll be like an ice statue and won't be able to move by the time my turn comes to go on.'

The young magician declared that his fingers had gone dead and that he wouldn't be able to pull even a handkerchief out of the hat let alone a rabbit. One of the 'singing five' said he was sure he was losing his voice and began to spray his throat. Bette took it from him. 'That's enough, you're all persuading yourselves that these things are going to happen. Think of all the pleasure you're going to bring to the soldiers. Smile, look happy, *think* happiness! Ha, ha, ha!'

Bette's big grin, her false laughter, her cheerfulness, gave them all confidence. Before long they were all chatting and getting their things together for when the van arrived to take them to the camp.

When it did come they packed into it, with Bette methodically checking equipment. 'Right, off we go, and the best of British luck!'

Bette and Lyndsey had spent hours trying to find a suitable name for their show. Bette had wanted to use the name Bascony and had wanted to have a B to begin the second part. They had chosen a final three – Bascony Buccaneers, Bascony Trail Blazers and eventually Bascony Boomerangs. They settled for the Boomerangs.

'It has movement,' Bette said, 'and it has a sort of punch. Boomerangs keep coming back and that's what we want to do.'

They had a ten-mile ride with a rather erratic driver and

the at times bumpy roads, and they were all relieved when they at last arrived at the camp. They got VIP treatment, with several officers and a number of sergeants waiting to welcome them. A Captain Marshall made the introductions and said coffee would be served to them. After the show a meal would be laid on for them if they wished. Sergeant Willis would show them to the Nissen hut where they were to change. He added that the men were already assembled in the recreation hut for the show, but they were content to wait.

The rise and fall of voices and bursts of laughter left no doubt as to where the men were assembled. A Waaf came to join Sergeant Willis to take them to the hut the party would use. It was divided by a large plywood screen, to separate the men from the women. By this time Lyndsey was aware of the underlying excitement among the party, they were here, it was *the* night. Weather was now no longer of any importance.

While they all sat sipping at their steaming mugs of coffee Bette gave them a final pep talk. 'Think of yourselves as professionals and act accordingly. Remember that there could be a talent scout in the audience to whisk you away to stardom.' At their murmurs of laughter she said, 'Oh, yes, it could happen, it's happening all the time. And you, or you, or you, could be the one. To combat that first-night feeling take deep breaths, it helps. Don't ever let it come into your mind that these people are just soldiers who want a little bit of entertainment. They want the best! And we are going to give it to them. Right?'

'Right!' they chorused. Bette then turned to Lyndsey and told her as she would be playing the introduction songs she had better start getting changed as soon as she had finished her coffee. It was then that Lyndsey's stomach began playing her up, churning over and over. Determinedly she began taking some deep breaths.

The Waaf, who had sat quietly with them, now said to Lyndsey, 'Do you want to go to the john? It's not far away.

I'll take you.' Lyndsey decided she had better go. They ran all the way, Lyndsey with a scarf over her head. She shivered all the way back. Huts were just vague outlines, the recreation hut looking larger than she had expected. There was a laugh when she returned because she had set them all off and there was a queue waiting to go.

Then at last the moment came and to Lyndsey's surprise she was utterly calm. She had changed into a beige trouser suit and matching jumper, wanting to try and be inconspicuous, and she wore a dark snood over the back of her hair. Bette, who would be with her behind the screen, linked her arm through hers. 'Now, off we go.' They ran the space between the huts.

The screens at either side of the platform were quite large. From them three broad steps led up to the stage. There was a backcloth of a country scene. A fug of smoke hovered near the high-vaulted roof. There was some shuffling, some coughing, then a silence as the captain in charge of entertainment began to speak. He kept his speech short, more or less introducing the show, saying how lucky they were to be entertained by such a professional group as Bascony's Boomerangs. He knew the men were in for a treat and would they show their appreciation in the usual way. There was a burst of applause, a few cheers.

He then said, after glancing at his paper, that Miss Lyndsey MacLaren would start the proceedings by playing them into a sing-song. He gave her the signal and Lyndsey braced herself and walked out to the piano. There was more applause and a few louder cheers. She sat down at the piano and went straight into 'Little Brown Jug'. Any worry she might have had about them not joining in at once was immediately dispelled. There was supposed to be only about a hundred men but judging by the sound there could have been a thousand. They 'ha-ha-ed' and 'he-he-ed' as if their life depended on it, and Lyndsey responded to it with a feeling of glee. Before the notes of 'Little Brown Jug' had died away she went on to play 'I'm Only a Bird in a Gilded Cage'. This was no less well received and to Lyndsey was heart-warming. She got up after this, prepared to leave, but they yelled for more and to the captain's nod she sat down again. She played two more then the captain held up his hand as he glanced at his watch. He said if there was time he was sure that Miss MacLaren would oblige again later but he must now introduce George Fellows, a well-known local comedian.

George had them right away and the room was filled with laughter. They went from one act to the other and everyone got the applause that a star turn might merit. For her ukulele act Lyndsey had changed into something more glamorous, a midnight blue satin dress with a boat-shaped neck that emphasized her fair skin and chestnut hair. Even before she had sat down she was getting wolf whistles and shouts of what they wanted her to play. She went through a repertoire and they went mad, kept on demanding more and more. Again they had to be brought to silence.

The singing five were next and they were rewarded by complete silence, which Lyndsey thought must have been most gratifying to them. Not a sound could be heard when they sang 'Danny Boy', the words and the harmonizing were so moving.

While they were singing Lyndsey had gone to change into the honey-coloured and white outfit and was then so nervous and so chilled she was actually trembling. She tried to persuade Bette to let her cut it out of the programme but Bette was adamant. It was what the boys needed.

The singers had great applause and when at last they left the stage a buzz of conversation burst out. The man who was to play the drum roll was ready, and Bette told Lyndsey to get prepared to go on. Lyndsey panicked. 'I can't do it, Bette, I can't, I feel daft, petrified.'

'You look beautiful. Get ready.' She gave the signal for the drum roll. It captured the men's attention. There was silence. Bette then signalled for Joe to play the line of the

song, 'You are my honeysuckle, I am the bee'. As it ended
Bette gave Lyndsey a push. 'Now!' Lyndsey took a quick
breath and ran up the steps. She went through the routine
and ran down the steps to where Bette, who had run behind
the stage, was waiting to wrap her in the fur coat. It was
over so quickly there was a hush. Then a man yelled,
'More! We want Honey!' The other men took up the chant,
there was wild applause, a stamping of feet and more
chanting, 'We want Honey! We want Honey!'

Captain Marshall said, 'You really must go on again,
Miss MacLaren, I'm sure that some of the men hardly
realized what was happening.' Bette said no, that was part
of the act, the mystery. The captain smiled but Lyndsey
thought he looked disappointed. He went on to the stage
and held up his hand for silence.

'Sorry, men, you can't have Honey again tonight, but
there'll be another time, I'm *sure*. And now, I want to
introduce you to – '

Fortunately the girls of the tap-dancing act were pretty
enough to capture the attention of the men, but even when
the show was over and the captain was about to make a
speech one man got up and yelled, 'We're not leaving until
we see Honey again.' And the cry was taken up.

The captain then asked Bette to come up and he intro-
duced her. Bette talked to the men, said how much they
had all enjoyed doing the show, and how marvellous the
men had been with their response. Then she smiled and
added, 'As for Honey, as you call her, she's terribly shy.
It was a fun thing that I decided to introduce as a little –
tease?' This brought a burst of laughter. Someone shouted,
'Tease is right! None of us'll sleep a wink tonight.' Bette,
laughing with them, said they would definitely come back
if invited, and yes, Honey would be with them.

All the players were invited into the officers' mess for
drinks and although all the girls came in for some attention,
Lyndsey was the biggest draw. She was surrounded. The
men were intrigued by her. Was she a dancer by profession?

She said no and asked them how they had recognized her as she was so quickly on and off the stage. This brought such a gale of laughter that the others turned to see the reason.

One blue-eyed lieutenant said, 'Miss MacLaren, you carry your trade mark with you. I would recognize those beautiful legs anywhere.' The man next to him grinned. 'I'd recognize them in the blackout!'

Bette came to her rescue. 'Sorry, gentlemen, I must take Miss MacLaren away, Captain Marshall wishes to speak to her.' At the howls of protest she added, '*Purely* for business reasons!'

Bette explained to Lyndsey as she led her to a table in the corner that the captain was trying to persuade her to join ENSA and she didn't want to. 'I need your support, Lyndsey. The others, of course, will have to be consulted later.'

The captain very patiently explained that it was solely in their interests that he had suggested them being members of ENSA. 'I know that all your performers have been generous enough to offer their services free, Mrs Bascony, but they are all *most* professional and could be in demand in a few months' time.'

'Lovely thought,' Bette said, beaming.

The captain spread his hands. 'But what then? You are financing them now as far as expenses are concerned, but supposing you were asked to go somewhere where you would need to stay overnight?'

Bette became serious. 'Let me put it this way, Captain Marshall. I know ENSA are having troubles. Some shows are arriving hours late, some have been directed to the wrong town. There's incompetence, which they are trying to sort out. We need experience and we'll get that by doing as many shows locally as possible. By the time ENSA has got themselves sorted out we might be ready then to go further afield.'

The captain smiled. 'And your performers will earn ten pounds a week, as well as expenses.'

'Splendid. And now we'll have those drinks you offered.'

It was late when they left but although they were all tired there was still the excitement of the success of the show. 'When's the next one?' Joe asked. 'Soon, I hope, I enjoyed tonight. But here, what was all this talk about Lyndsey doing a dance? *We* never saw a thing.' Lyndsey told them she would give them a private showing and the men asked her to promise. 'I do,' she said, feeling a warm glow from the drinks she had had and enjoying Bette's pleasure that the show had been so successful. She must write and tell Andrew all about it.

Even when they arrived back to Bette's they still didn't go straight to bed. It was her big night and she wanted to talk about it. She said if only she could get someone to sponsor the show, she would deal with the business side of it. They might even get as far as entertaining the troops in France. 'Wouldn't that be really marvellous, to play to battle-weary troops? Then they would all feel they were really doing their bit.' A slow smile spread over her face.

'And you, Lyndsey, were wonderful. How the men all loved you. I was talking to a little corporal. He said he was right at the back. He couldn't see your face but he just knew you would be beautiful. He asked me so wistfully if you would give him a photograph of yourself if you ever came to the camp again to do a show. It's things like this that make it all so worthwhile.'

They sat in silence for a while then Bette gasped and sat up. 'Just look at the time! Half past three. Come along, bed, this very minute. It's a good job you don't have to catch a train in the morning. We'll have a lovely lazy weekend.'

But they didn't get their lazy weekend. The members of the show came to visit, wanting to talk about the show. Some came on the Saturday and some on the Sunday. The Singing Five came after church and the most rewarding part of this was them singing at dusk, for the two corporals. Lyndsey felt there could never come a time when she would be more moved. They sang in the garden and it was as though every bird and every animal had stopped to listen.

They sang gentle songs, 'Roaming in the Gloaming', 'If I Should Plant a Tiny Seed of Love', 'After the Ball', 'Clementine' . . . Then, at the request of Tom, whose wife was named Maud, they sang, 'Come into the Garden, Maud', and their harmony was so exquisite that Lyndsey was not the only one who wept.

But to conclude, the men sang 'The Galloping Major' and afterwards one of them told jokes, which had them all so helpless with laughter that Bette declared he should be on her show as a stand-up comic as well as with the singing group.

Lyndsey left on the Monday morning, saying she would be back that evening about six.

But again things did not turn out as planned. When she arrived at the Centre Ann approached her the moment she went in and asked her if she would come home that afternoon to have tea with her and her mother, and stay overnight. When Lyndsey hesitated Ann said, 'Please say yes, it is important.' There was such a desperate expression on the small freckled face that Lyndsey had to ask why.

'Because – well, my mother thinks that I've been staying overnight with you on one or two nights and instead – '

'You've been staying with your boyfriend.'

Ann nodded. 'I know I shouldn't have done, but I'm really in love with Colin. He's so different. His family go to the underground shelter every night and, well, with Colin and me being on our own, it was so tempting, but I don't suppose you understand.'

Oh, yes, Lyndsey thought, she did understand, she understood only too well the temptation and she did not even pretend to be in love with Andrew.

'My mother is always asking me to ask you to come and stay with us,' Ann went on, 'but of course I was wanting to be with Colin as often as possible. Then – ' she paused dramatically, 'this morning Mother announced she was coming to the Centre to ask you herself! And I thought, oh, Lord, if she should get to you first! If you would agree to come today, Lyndsey, I can phone them at the bread shop and ask them to give Mother a message. I don't *want* her coming to the Centre, this is *my* special domain!'

There was a fierceness then in Ann's voice and Lyndsey was puzzled. Why should the Centre be her special domain? 'Yes, I'll come today,' she said. 'I can phone Bette and let her know.'

Ann had never talked about her family and it was not until they were on the bus that afternoon going to her home that she told Lyndsey about her father having walked out on them two years before. For another woman.

'Mother's never got over it, she's so bitter. She can't understand why my Dad would want anyone else. I could certainly understand it, she never stopped nagging him. We're not hard up, both Mother's parents and two uncles and aunts left her money when they died but she won't spend any of it. She'll moan how hard up she is, but don't take any notice of her, Lyndsey. I'm glad you've agreed to come, I think she's got it in her mind that you're too stuck up to come and stay with the likes of us. I've told her differently, but she had to see you for herself.' Ann smiled. 'Thanks for coming, it'll make life a little easier for me.'

It was one of a row of small terraced houses with a strip of garden in front, with the iron railings and front gate missing, gone to help the war effort. According to Ann there was a front room, a living room and scullery and three bedrooms upstairs, one little more than a box room.

The houses were in quite good repair, windows shining and the lace curtains in every window spotless. Because of this Lyndsey was unprepared for the air of poverty inside the house. The room was sparsely furnished, with lino on the floor and only a strip of carpet in front of the fire. The only chairs were straight-backed and the only adornment

150

in the room was a picture above the mantelpiece of an industrial scene. There was little more than two tiny flames trying to push through a layer of coal dust on the fire.

'Oh, really,' Ann said angrily, 'she could at least have let us come home to a decent fire. I'll see to this.' She called, 'Mother, Lyndsey's here.'

A small, thin, tight-lipped woman came out of the scullery, rubbing her hands on a small fancy apron. 'Well, Lyndsey, so here you are at last,' she greeted her. 'I was beginning to think you were just a myth, invented by my over-imaginative daughter. Sit down, the kettle's on, I'll make a cup of tea.'

'And while you are doing that,' Ann snapped, 'I shall make up the fire. It's freezing in here.'

'There's a war on,' Mrs Matley called after her. 'You seem to forget that.' To Lyndsey she added, 'She doesn't have to provide, I do. Won't even get herself a job where she gets paid. Voluntary work! It's all right for you, you don't need to work, but our Ann does, never contributed a penny to this house.'

Ann came in with some sticks and a bucket of coal saying, 'Lyndsey doesn't want to know all our domestic problems. Lyndsey, sit down, you can keep your coat on until the fire burns up. *I* shall make a job of it!'

Lyndsey was appalled at having to spend an evening in such a dreadful atmosphere. The fire did eventually give out a good heat but the tea consisted of thin slices of bread and margarine, sparingly laid on, three scones, three thin slices of gingerbread and a tiny dish of jam. Mrs Matley apologized for the meagre meal, pointing out how difficult it was to manage on the rations. Did Lyndsey realize that the tea ration was two ounces a week, but probably she would not know these things, the richer people being able to buy on the black market.

'An ounce of cheese a week,' she went on. 'What can anyone do with that, a bare mouthful – and two ounces of bacon. Our Ann doesn't realize either the struggle I have to manage.'

'Just ignore her,' Ann said smiling, giving Lyndsey a wink. 'She never stops talking.'

'How dare you speak to me like that! If I had spoken to my mother the way you speak to me – ' Mrs Matley turned to Lyndsey, 'You seem to be brought up right, you are at least polite, but our Ann . . . Treats me something dreadful. Her latest is she wants to join the women's services. Well, I won't say no, but she gives no thought to me, does she, being on my own. She's all I've got.'

'Mother, why don't you tell the truth?' Ann wagged a piece of bread at her. 'What about your other two daughters, and your grandchildren?' Ann explained to Lyndsey that they lived in the next street.

For the first time Mrs Matley's face softened a little. 'Yes, the grandchildren, they're the only ones who care a jot about me. Lovely children.' But the next minute her lips were tight again. 'As for my other daughters, they come to visit and can't get away fast enough.'

'And can you wonder?' Ann said, laughing, 'with a tongue like yours going non-stop and grumble, grumble all the time.'

Even when Lyndsey was in bed she could still hear Mrs Matley's shrill complaining voice. She shared the twin-bedded room with Ann and although a hot water bottle had been put in the bed there was no eiderdown on, just three thin blankets. Lyndsey, not caring if anyone was upset, got up and spread her coat over the bed, but Ann seemed not to notice.

When she got into bed she spoke in whispers, because, she said, her mother would be sure to complain that they were talking about her.

'How do you put up with it?' Lyndsey asked.

'You get used to it. It's like when you first live on a busy main road and are unable to sleep for the noise, but after a week you never hear a thing. I just close my ears most of the time to Mother's talking. It's the only way to survive. But I will be glad to get into one of the services. I thought of trying for the ATS, but I'll see. I can't apply until January. Lyndsey would you mind if – ' Ann broke off as the air raid siren went. 'Oh, no! We'll have Mother fussing around, wanting me to go to the shelter and I'm just not moving from here.' Before she had finished speaking Mrs Matley was in the bedroom ordering them to get up and get dressed.

Ann turned over in the bed. 'You go, Mother. Lyndsey and I are staying here and taking our chance.'

'Well, don't expect me to come and dig you out if a bomb drops on the house.' She stormed out.

When the front door slammed Ann began to laugh. 'Peace at last!'

She drew herself up in the bed. 'Now we can talk. You mentioned earlier that Bette had done the show. How did you get on?'

Lyndsey described the acts but did not mention her own special one. Ann then talked about her boyfriend Colin and how he had asked her to marry him, but as much as she loved him, she said, she was not yet ready for marriage. At times she had to raise her voice against the barrage of anti-aircraft guns. Lyndsey was on the point of dropping off to sleep when, during a lull, Ann, sounding sleepy said, 'The bombing sounds a good way off. If it gets any nearer you'd better get under the bed. Don't attempt to wake me, I'd sleep through an earthquake!'

'So would I,' Lyndsey said, stifling a yawn. She turned over on to her side. 'Good night, see you in the morning.'

Lyndsey was not sure what time she awoke, or what had awakened her, she only knew there was something strange about the house, a faint rustling like the patter of mice feet running up and down the wallpaper. No, not mice, it was a sort of faint tearing sound. She rolled over on to her back. Plaster from above fell on to her face. She wiped it away then suddenly sat up. Great heavens, the house was moving! She leapt out of bed shouting Ann's name then shaking her.

'Get up! The house is collapsing.' Ann muttered something and Lyndsey, throwing back the bedclothes, grabbed at her and dragged her off the bed.

'What the hell – ' Ann protested, then suddenly realizing what was happening she gasped. 'Under the bed, quick.'

Lyndsey was hardly under the bed before there was the sound of splintering glass, a great rumble, then she was falling into space. For seconds she was conscious that debris was dropping all around and that her throat and nostrils were full of grimy dust, then she blacked out.

When she came to she was aware of a great weight on top of her and of someone moaning. She called Ann, but she was unable to speak because of the awful dryness of her mouth. She found she was able to move her right arm and she groped around – and touched a hand. Ann? She gripped it, then she felt the rings on the fingers and her heart began a mad pounding. Ann wore no rings. Oh, God, who could it be?

TEN

When Lyndsey suddenly realized she was still holding the hand she released it quickly. She had never felt the skin of a dead person before and touching it made her flesh crawl.

More rubble began to fall, raising a cloud of dust that threatened to choke her. She tried to move and found that although she could move her arms she was trapped from the waist down. A terror made her sweat. Were her legs paralysed? She forced herself into some degree of calmness. She must think. Although her legs were trapped there was not the crushing weight of a heavy beam on them, so it was probably debris. She became aware of a strong draught. Had the roof, or part of it, caved in? But if so why could she not see the sky? There was an impenetrable blackness. And everywhere was so quiet. The people in the street might be in the shelters, but where were the street wardens? Had they all been killed? An icy shiver ran down her spine.

For moments her mind seemed a blank then she touched her face. That was all right. She reached up and grazed her hand on – wire? She felt around. Of course! It was the wire of the bed-frame. The rubble had fallen on it and the strong metal legs had saved her from being buried. Buried . . . Ann? Where was Ann? The panic was on her again. For seconds she found it impossible to think how the beds had been placed, then she remembered. Ann had been on her right. She put out a hand but all she felt was rubble. Then she became aware that something was dropping on to her wrist. Her first thought that it was blood sent a terror through her, but then she realized the drops were cold. She put her wrist to her mouth and felt a blessed relief. It was water, nectar!

She held out her wrist again and again until at last the moisture enabled her to speak. She called to Ann and heard a low moan. It was close and Lyndsey told her about the water and asked if she could manage to put out her left arm. There was movement, then after what seemed an eternity came a croaked whisper, 'Lyndsey – '

With pauses to moisten their lips they discussed the situation. Ann too was trapped from the waist down. She said she could move her toes, but felt if she were to try and move her legs she might bring down more rubble. Then she said, 'Why is it so quiet?' And added the next moment, 'Listen – men's voices, can you hear them?'

Lyndsey did hear them but they seemed to be fading.

'They're going in the opposite direction!' Ann exclaimed. 'They must know the house has collapsed.' Then as there was a creaking followed by a further fall of debris she added, panic in her voice, 'Oh, God, are we going to be buried alive?'

Lyndsey, trying not to think of a slow, agonizing death, made an effort to soothe her, pointing out that the raid might have been widespread and the damage heavier elsewhere. 'They'll come eventually, Ann, I *know* they will.'

The silence seemed to last for hours yet was possibly only minutes, then voices were heard again and this time they were coming closer. Footsteps slowed then stopped. Then a man called, 'Anyone in here?'

They both shouted yes together. Ann told them they were buried under beds but neither of their voices had any strength and Lyndsey, having touched a piece of wood earlier, felt for it and banged on the floor with it. It brought a response. 'Right, we're coming for you.'

The front door was jammed and each heave seemed to

156

bring down a shower of plaster. 'Let's go to the back,' one of the men shouted. There seemed to be a number of them and Lyndsey knew eventually they were in the house by the crunch of glass underfoot. The beam of a torch played round the floor then a voice said, 'Here they are.'

To Lyndsey and Ann the man added, 'Whatever you do *don't* attempt to move. We're getting help.'

They talked about heavy rescue equipment and Lyndsey's only fear was that they would all be buried before this help came. The foundations at times seemed to be shifting.

There was suddenly a great deal of activity, bells ringing, fire bells, ambulance and police. While they were waiting for the rescue equipment Ann said, right out of the blue, 'I think there's someone else buried under the rubble. It could possibly be my mother.' Her voice had gained some strength.

Lyndsey felt a dreadful coldness creeping over her. Mrs Matley? The hand? But how did Ann know that her mother might have come back into the house?

It *was* Mrs Matley. She was dead. Ann had insisted on knowing. Mrs Matley's body was taken out and by then the rescue equipment and an ambulance arrived.

It was not until they were in the ambulance that they were told what had happened. There had been a big explosion a distance away that had caused a row of houses to collapse including the Matley house. Mrs Matley must have come back to the house to try and persuade both girls to come to the shelter. Lyndsey then had the weight of guilt on her shoulders. If they had gone to the shelter in the first place, as Mrs Matley had wanted, the woman might still be alive.

When they arrived at the hospital they were taken to an emergency room where women volunteers were washing other people caught in the bombing and changing them into cotton nightdresses. Afterwards they were given cups of tea and wheeled away. When Lyndsey's turn came she thought she would remember it as one of the greatest treats of her life, to feel her face being sponged with warm water, to have the dust brushed out of her hair and to feel warm tea going down her utterly parched throat.

The hospital was so overcrowded that beds filled every corridor. Lyndsey and Ann were put side by side in one near a door where staff were constantly coming and going. Some patients were moaning, some crying out for relatives lost in the raid and others shouting out with pain.

In spite of the overcrowding it was not long before a doctor was examining the two girls. He announced there were no bones broken and that with luck they should be back home the next day. Ann said drily, 'What home?' and the doctor replied, 'Like that, is it? I'm sorry. Someone will come and talk to you about it, but it will probably be in the morning. You need rest now.'

The doctor gave them both an injection and Lyndsey remembered no more until the next morning when she was awakened by one of the voluntary helpers with a bowl of water for her to wash. Ann, who was stifling a yawn, said, 'How did you sleep? I slept like a log. I expect my sister Maggie will be here later, she lives nearest and must have heard the news by now. Then there'll be weeping and wailing, but I don't know why, it was the best thing that could have happened to Mother.'

Ann's detached manner had Lyndsey staring at her for a moment then she decided that the girl must be suffering from shock. 'It really *is* the best thing that could have happened,' Ann went on. 'Mother has never been happy, never, not even when Dad was living with us. It doesn't even worry me that I no longer have a home to go to. I'll get myself a flat. Lovely!'

Ann's eldest sister Maggie arrived later, distressed. She had just heard the news, and ten minutes after this Bette, to Lyndsey's astonishment, came up to the bed.

'Hello, my love, how are you?'

'Bette – how did you know, who – told you?'

'They phoned from the hospital because you had given my name as your next of kin. I'm glad you did, glad I know, but I'm afraid Richard might be upset, my love, at you giving my name as family.'

Lyndsey was mystified. She said she must have given Bette's name after she had had the injection. 'Bette, I'm sorry you've come all this way. What about the children – and Frank and Harry?'

'Mrs Petrie is looking after them, they're all right. You couldn't leave the hospital unless you had someone to look after you. Thank goodness I *can* do that. I don't know whether you'll be strong enough to travel. It seems they need beds for urgent cases.'

After both Ann and Lyndsey had been examined by the doctor they were given permission to leave, on condition they promised to rest at home. Bette said *she* could promise that in Lyndsey's case.

While Ann was getting ready her sister came over to have a word with Lyndsey. Lyndsey told her she was sure Ann was suffering from shock and Maggie gave a wry smile and said, 'Don't worry about her, she's a survivor.'

When they were ready to leave Ann gave Lyndsey a cheery wave and said she would keep in touch. Then she and her sister had gone.

Bette suggested Lyndsey going to the Mayfair house and she would stay with her until she felt well enough to travel. Before Lyndsey was out of bed she would have urged for them to go straight to Kent, but once she was on her feet she realized her weakness. She agreed to go home.

And it was there that Lyndsey told Bette the whole story. Bette said fervently, 'Well, thank God you came out of it all right. It's no use saying you must take more care, because it could happen to any one of us at any time. And you must stop blaming yourself over Ann's mother, it was fate, it had to be.'

Lyndsey slept nearly the rest of that day and while she slept Bette had written to Richard and Marian giving them

159

the news and telling them she was taking Lyndsey to stay with her.

After another good night's sleep Lyndsey said she felt well enough to travel, adding, 'And your lovely fresh air will do the rest.'

Lyndsey wanted, for some reason when she arrived, to spend some time on her own. Bette said she understood, and so would Frank and Harry. *They* had wanted to walk on their own, not speaking to anyone. But she did advise Lyndsey not to go too far away from the house. She could tire easily.

Lyndsey set out across the fields, enjoying the crisp autumnal air, stepping out with a wonderful feeling of well-being. How good it was to be alive.

A few minutes later she stopped and looked up at the sky. Although she had known that dog fights took place nearly every day behind the clouds and had heard the planes, this was the first time she had witnessed a fight taking place. The machines were like little silver insects against the sun, the silver vapour trails developing into delicate silver loops. It was a scene of beauty . . . disguising the hidden brutality. The awfulness of war. Lyndsey shuddered and walked on slowly. Andrew could be up there among them. Neither she nor Bette had heard from him.

The majority of swifts had migrated but a few stragglers soared, screaming their last song. Family groups of starlings drifted over the fields, alighting silently to feed among the grazing sheep. Some of them fought for morsels, in spite of there being plenty for all. Greed, greed . . . it was the reason for wars.

Further on she came upon a dead badger near the grass verge of the narrow country road, killed no doubt by a passing vehicle. More slaughter. Suddenly needing sanctuary from the violence Lyndsey went into a nearby wood. Here it was dim and the only sound the soft rustling of leaves underfoot. At first as she saw the changing colour of the trees she thought of death again, but as she came

160

out into a clearing, a shaft of sunlight shining through the branches of the trees gave a glory to the profusion of golds and reds and russets. She felt a sudden uplift. The migrating birds would return in the spring, there would be a new growth. How foolish to allow herself to get into such a state.

When she came out of the woods she heard the rise and fall of voices and bursts of laughter, and following the sounds came to where people were hop-picking. Before the war there had always been an influx of workers from London. Now the workers were the evacuees. Children were working as well as adults, working hard. Bette had insisted on her taking some boiled ham sandwiches, a piece of cake and a flask of tea. And now Lyndsey was glad of this snack. She sat under a tree near a small farm where hens clucked around her and came pecking at the small pieces of crusts she threw to them.

Later when she came to a village she phoned Bette to say she was all right and enjoying her day. She would be back about four o'clock.

Lyndsey tramped all afternoon, but although she had been able to walk many miles when she was at Echo Cove, she found herself still weak after the awful experience of the raid. Gradually her footsteps slowed and during the last half mile she wondered how she was going to make it.

When she arrived Bette exclaimed, 'Good heavens, Lyndsey, you look like a ghost!' She insisted on her going straight up to bed and Lyndsey needed no urging. Bette had promised to bring up some food, but the moment Lyndsey laid her head on the pillow she was asleep.

She awoke some time during the night to the deep country darkness and felt a swift panic as she remembered the feeling of entombment when the Matley house collapsed; gradually her heartbeats slowed. If she switched on the torch it would take away that awful blackness. The battery was getting low but it might last long enough to

161

help her to get to sleep. She settled herself under the bed-covers, and soon slept.

When she next awoke it was from a nightmare where she had been buried in a deep pit and was fighting for breath. The fighting for breath was real. She shouted and although she felt she had not made enough sound to bring help two people came into the room. The battery of the torch had all but run out but she made out the figure of a man. He spoke sharply.

'Stop it, Lyndsey, you've been dreaming.'

She felt incensed. 'I was in a black pit,' she retorted, but her voice still lacked strength.

Then Bette was speaking. 'I'll go downstairs and warm some milk. Perhaps it would be better if you could bring her downstairs, Elliott.'

Elliott? Lyndsey tried to get him into focus but everything was blurred. It couldn't be Elliott Warrender, he was miles away, and anyway he would not have spoken to her so sharply.

She was scooped up in his arms and she thought whoever it was he was certainly strong. He carried her effortlessly down the stairs and into the living room. Two lamps were lit and with the blurring gone Lyndsey saw that he was indeed Elliott Warrender. He sat in an armchair with her on his lap and Bette came and put a rug around Lyndsey's shoulders.

'Feeling better?' Elliott enquired, as he tucked the rug around her.

'You shouted at me,' she accused.

'I had to, it was necessary to snap you out of your nightmare.' Lyndsey waited, expecting him to apologize for speaking so sharply, but he said no more and she felt an animosity towards him. Andrew would have been gentle, understanding. She looked up. 'When did *you* arrive and why did you come?' Her tone was now belligerent.

'I came to see if you were all right, Lyndsey. I had a phone call from Richard. He was worried after having had

Bette's letter, and as he knew I was coming to London for a meeting he asked me to call and see how you were.'

He had spoken more gently this time and Lyndsey saw an expression in his eyes she was unable to fathom. A caring? She made to try and sit up and his arms tightened around her. He drew her head to his chest and pushed her hair back gently. Then she felt she wanted to cry. It was such a long time ago since anyone had cuddled her. She gave a small sigh and closed her eyes.

It was daylight when Lyndsey next awoke and she lay looking around the bedroom as though trying to get her bearings. Had she dreamt that Elliott had been here, in this house, had carried her downstairs? The bedroom door opened and Bette looked in.

'Oh, you're awake, love. I didn't want to disturb you.'

Lyndsey drew herself up in the bed. 'Bette – was I dreaming last night or was Elliott Warrender here?'

'He was here, still is, he's having his breakfast. You had a nightmare, Lyndsey.'

Yes, of course, the nightmare, how could she have forgotten it. But then it did not seem so bad in daylight. She threw back the bedclothes and Bette said, sounding worried, 'I do think I should get the doctor to come and take a look at you.'

'No, Bette, I'm fine. I behaved stupidly yesterday. You warned me not to go too far but I wouldn't listen, would I? I *will* take it easy today, I promise.'

When she did come down, Elliott, who was sitting having his breakfast, got up and apologized for not being fully dressed. He was wearing grey slacks and a white open-necked shirt with the sleeves rolled up. Lyndsey was surprised to feel a small sensual tremor go through her at seeing this attractive, strong-muscled man, who had held her so closely during the night.

She said brightly, 'It must feel good to be out of uniform for a change.' Then she called to Bette who was in the kitchen, 'I'm down, Bette. I just want a slice of toast, I'll come and do it.'

'No, you won't,' Bette called back. 'You'll have a proper breakfast: porridge and bacon and eggs. I was given some lovely home-cured bacon yesterday by one of the farmers.'

'And I can recommend it,' Elliott said, smiling. 'It's delicious.' He drew out a chair for Lyndsey and she sat down. Then she looked out of the window. 'Connie and Janie are in the garden, but where are the two corporals?'

'They left early this morning,' said Bette coming in with a bowl of porridge, 'they were due to leave. I didn't tell you because they didn't want to say goodbye. They felt it would be too upsetting. They send you their warmest regards and promised they'll be back to see us. I hope so. I'll miss them.' There was a catch in her voice and after putting the plate on the table she hurried out.

'Bette has such a big heart,' Elliott said quietly. 'How are you feeling this morning, Lyndsey?'

'On top of the world,' she declared, and started on the porridge. There was silence and when she glanced up she found Elliott watching her with a sort of concerned scrutiny – and something else. Lyndsey thought it was a look of love, then quickly dismissed it. Of course not, she was allowing her judgment to be clouded because of that warm feeling she had when he held her.

He began to talk of Richard, how worried he had been. Elliott added that Marian had been worried too when she knew what had happened and was talking of trying to get compassionate leave to come home.

Lyndsey was quick to reply that it was quite unnecessary; she had not suffered any injury, and she then repeated what she had told Bette earlier, that it was her own stupidity that had made her ready to drop into bed the evening before.

'It seems I'll never learn,' she said wryly. 'My mother told me often enough that I must think before I started making plans, that a foolish action could affect other people. By walking much too far yesterday I caused Bette unnecessary worry. I must try and become a more responsible person.'

Elliott broke a piece from his bread roll. 'My grandmother used to say that it was impossible to put an old head on young shoulders and I realized later how right she was. I was a little wild when I was younger and must have caused my parents, my mother in particular, a great deal of worry. I refused to listen to advice that was offered. I think that adolescence is the worst part of anyone's life.'

'I'm not sure that I agree with you,' Lyndsey said.

'I do,' this from Bette who came in with a jug of coffee and bacon and egg for Lyndsey. She poured them each a cup then sat down with her own cup between her fingers. 'Mind you, I didn't think so at the time. I was married when I was sixteen and thought I must be the happiest girl alive to have a husband like Rupert.'

'So what changed your mind?' Lyndsey asked.

Bette looked thoughtful. 'Time . . . retrospect. I realized what I had missed was adventure.'

'Adventure!' Lyndsey exclaimed. 'How can you say such a thing. How much more adventure could you have than being on the stage? You were on the move all the time, meeting people; there was the glamour of the footlights, the – '

'It was repetition, Lyndsey. It was work. Oh, I'm not going to say that I didn't enjoy the life. I did and I wouldn't have wanted any other. It's only now I realize all the things I missed as a young girl by being married so young. Do you realize I never knew what it was to have a date with a boy, never knew all the excitement of dressing up? I never went to a party where there were all young people. All the parties I went to were behind stage, with the actors and actresses. And those parties were few and far between.'

Bette, a wistful expression on her face, smiled at Lyndsey. 'I remember you telling me about the fun that you used to have by the sea, the excitement of sailing, having a sing-song around a bonfire on the beach at night, the dances in barns, the sneaking out with a boy, walking in the moonlight . . .' Bette's voice had dropped. 'Those were the things I realize now I missed.'

'But you had a happy marriage,' Elliott said quietly. 'Isn't that worth something?'

'Yes, it is. I know I was lucky, but there was something else I realize now I missed, a sense of achievement. Rupert was the magician, I his assistant. He was the boss of the show. It wasn't until I put on the show for the troops that I had that sense of achievement. It was me – not my husband or any other man – who was responsible for giving pleasure to an audience. And I think what gave me the most pleasure was the applause that those taking part received. It was great.'

Bette sat a moment, a faraway look in her eyes, then she said, 'Oh, I didn't tell you about Lyndsey, did I? What a wow she was!' Lyndsey gave her a frantic warning look and Bette smiled and nodded. 'She not only plays the piano and the ukulele but she sings; and what a voice, husky, sexy, she nearly brought the house down.'

'I can imagine it,' Elliott said to Lyndsey, looking amused. 'I hope I shall have the pleasure of seeing the show sometime.'

The children came running in. 'Auntie Lyndsey, Auntie Lyndsey,' cried Connie, 'you're up! Are you better?' Janie leaned against Lyndsey's knee and said in a woebegone voice, 'Uncle Frank and Uncle Harry have gone. Will you stay, Auntie Lyndsey?'

Lyndsey gathered them both to her. 'I shall be here for a whole week, then after that I shall travel back every night from London and stay over all the weekends. How's that?'

Connie beamed and Janie gave her slow sweet endearing smile. Lyndsey thought how lucky she was to be with such loving people. Elliott then got up and said he must start getting ready, his train left in twenty minutes.

Lyndsey was taken aback. 'Oh – are you leaving so soon?'

'I don't want to go, but duty calls.' His voice held a teasing. 'But I hope I shall be invited sometime in the future.'

'You're welcome any time,' Bette said, 'you don't even need to phone.'

He thanked her and when he glanced at the children, Lyndsey thought she saw a look of longing in his eyes. Was he a lonely man? Did he long for children? Lyndsey was not going to suggest going to the station with him, thinking he might prefer to go on his own, but when he came down ready to leave he said lightly, 'So who is going to see me off?' and in the end they all went.

'Just like a proper soldier,' he said, 'having his family to give him a big send-off.' Then little Janie slipped a hand into his and looked up at him in her solemn way, as though she understood, which touched Lyndsey.

Elliott told her he would be in touch with Richard as soon as he arrived in London and would stress that she was perfectly all right, there was no need for worry. She thanked him.

When the train was sighted Elliott kissed Bette and Lyndsey then picking up each child in turn he gave them a hug and a kiss, and he seemed then very much a family man. They waved to him until the train was out of sight. On the way home, while the children ran on ahead, Bette and Lyndsey discussed Elliott, both sharing the opinion that he was a very lonely man in need of a lot of love.

ELEVEN

Bette and Lyndsey were on their way upstairs to bed that evening when the shrill ringing of the phone had them looking at one another, Bette's worried expression echoing Lyndsey's thoughts that anyone who rang at this time of night must be the bearer of bad news. Bette ran downstairs to answer it.

The next moment she was saying, 'Who?' and then, 'Andrew? Well hello . . . is something wrong?' There was some talk then Bette said, 'Measles, at your age. Good heavens! . . . Yes, Lyndsey is here. . . . Yes, I'll explain everything. You take care, do you hear? Get back to bed. What? . . . Yes, I promise, cross my heart. What? . . . Oh, 'bye.'

Bette stood looking at the receiver, then she replaced it and came back to Lyndsey. 'It was Andrew. I expect you heard. Measles, of all things. It's a mild attack apparently, but he's in the sick bay. He got up to phone us because – well, he had heard rumours that his squadron are going to be moved. He doesn't know where.'

'Oh,' Lyndsey said. 'What else did he say?'

'He told me to tell you he loved you. He ought not to have been out of bed, silly boy, he could have got his death of cold.'

Lyndsey gave a little shiver. Catching one's death of cold was a common enough expresssion, but it not only made her think of Andrew risking his life every time he was flying, but it brought Ann's mother to her mind. She said, 'I wonder when Mrs Matley is to be buried? I don't particularly want to go to the funeral, but I suppose I must.'

'You are not going to any funeral,' Bette said firmly. 'You are here to recuperate, to forget what happened. And don't get it into your mind that Andrew is seriously ill, the attack is mild. Come on, bed.'

Lyndsey had the last word. If she was not going to the funeral then she must send flowers. They would have to find out in the morning where Ann's sister lived. The evacuation people would know.

As it turned out there was no need to start enquiring. There was a letter from Ann the next morning.

'Dear Lyndsey,' she wrote, 'Sorry not to have been in touch with you. I think I was suffering from shock when we parted. Mother is being buried the day after tomorrow. I don't suppose you'll want to come to the funeral. And quite frankly, I would rather you didn't. All our awful relatives will be there and there'll be weeping and wailing and gnashing of teeth. But knowing you, I feel sure you would want to send flowers. The family will be pleased if you do since they hold great store by having masses of flowers and lots of people attending the funeral, but as you are not a close friend or related in any way, it's best you don't come. They're all hypocrites and the only one not to hate Mother is Maggie. She seemed to understand her. I certainly never did. Let me know how you are going on after our awful experience.' It was signed, 'Yours, Ann.'

Lyndsey read it over again then handed it to Bette. 'What do you make of it? I feel that Ann must still be suffering some shock. It's dreadful the way she talks about people.'

After Bette had read it she looked up. 'I don't know what to say. She's certainly sick. All that hatred in her. A real nastiness. What is she like normally?'

Lyndsey was a while in answering. 'Deep down I don't

think I like her. And yet she loves children, is really caring with them, so she can't be all bad.'

Bette nodded. 'We'll see about getting some money sent off for flowers then you'll feel better.'

Lyndsey wrote several letters: to Ann, enclosing money for flowers; to Richard and to Andrew and to Elliott. She asked Richard to forward Elliott's letter, which also contained a note from Bette and contributions from the children.

It was not until Lyndsey had written the letter to Andrew that she realized how unconcerned she must have seemed to Bette the night before. But then the tragedy of Mrs Matley had dominated her thoughts. Now it occurred to her that if Andrew's posting was a long distance away there would be no more lovely surprises of finding him standing on her doorstep on a twenty-four-hour pass.

She had gone over that evening many times, especially remembering that awful moment when the air-raid warden had arrived, interrupting what could have turned out to be a disaster. Neither of them had had control over their emotions. She could at this moment have been pregnant; then there would be no joining the Wrens, no more fun at a camp show. And it had been fun. Although she had told herself she did not want to be recognized in the flimsy costume doing the high-kicks and twirls, she had to admit now that she had enjoyed the ovation she had received, and the flattery.

Lyndsey came to realize during the next few days that the time she had been given to recuperate after the raid was the best medicine she could have had, and here in the country was the best place to spend it. The pace was slower, there was the country quiet, the peace. In London, there was the crush of rush-hour travel, the sirens, the noise of ack-ack guns, the explosions of bombs. It all seemed a necessary part of life until one was away from it. Here, although there were days of high winds, of showers, they walked over the fields, through narrow lanes, and Lyndsey felt completely relaxed. In the evenings they read, listened to the wireless or had Mrs Petrie in for a game of cards or a chat.

On the Friday morning there were four letters for Lyndsey. She opened the one from Ann first. It was short. She thanked her for the money for the flowers and the only mention she made of the funeral was to say she was glad it was all over. She added that she was returning to the Centre on the Monday and hoped to see Lyndsey there.

Lyndsey put it aside and read Richard's letter next. He said he was pleased to hear from Elliott that she had come to no harm. If she ever needed him she was to send a telegram at once. He said that he and Marian would most likely be home sometime the following week. He would let her know.

Andrew's letter was full of his attack of measles, and was amusing at first as he described how he discovered the first spots. Then he said how bored he was, and how he longed to see her. 'Oh, how I've longed for you, my darling,' he wrote. 'I felt I wanted to abscond and pinch a car and drive to see you. I've thought many times of that lovely evening we spent together, the dancing, the being together in the basement shelter, and that wretched air-raid warden spoiling everything. But perhaps it was all for the best. I don't know. In these times one is apt to cast caution to the winds. Fine for me, of course, but not for you, but I wouldn't hurt you in any way, my darling. I would always take the utmost care of you, you're too precious to me to hurt. Do you think of me? You said you did in your very welcome letter, but I think of all the other chaps who find you so desirable and then I have to fight down my jealousy because I know you hate me to be jealous. Bette will have told you I think our squadron may be posted elsewhere. Have no idea where yet. In the meantime, my beautiful, precious girl, I send you all my love and many, many kisses, Yours forever, Andrew.' There was a P.S. 'Even the pretty nurses I have meant nothing to me. It's you and only you I want to see.'

Lyndsey felt a sudden wave of love for him sweep over her. Poor Andrew, bored in sick bay yet risking his life when he was better and flying again. If only she could have visited him. If only he would phone and speak to her. Why didn't he? Was he still ordered to stay in bed?

She sat for quite a while thinking about him and fingered Elliott's letter for some time before opening it.

'Dear Lyndsey, How kind of you to write to me, and also Bette. I welcomed too the dear little note from Connie telling me she "loved me", and the many rows of kisses from Janie. What delightful children they are. Their parents must be missing them terribly. What sacrifices families have to make during wartime. It was good to know that you are recovering from your appalling ordeal. I understood how you felt, having suffered once being buried by rubble myself. It's at least good to know that our airmen are holding their own with the Luftwaffe and in many cases beating them off. Will you thank Bette and the children for their messages. I shall write to each in a few days' time. I'm on the move again today. Do take care of yourself, Lyndsey. Yours sincerely, Elliott.'

Lyndsey felt that there was a warmth in the letter, a sincerity and only wished she could know more about his life. She would write again sometime, not too quickly, perhaps in a couple of weeks' time, just to keep in touch and let him have a post; Andrew kept saying how important it was.

By the time Sunday evening came and Lyndsey was making preparations to return to London the following morning her ordeal in the collapsing house seemed like a dream. 'I feel really well,' she told Bette, 'and it's thanks to you and all your fussing and caring. And now that we know we are doing a show next Saturday for the troops I can tell you now that I shall be with you.'

'You will? Oh, that's marvellous, love. I wouldn't have

pressed you to come if you hadn't felt like it, but it'll be great to have you. Now you look after yourself when you get back to town, do you hear?' Lyndsey smiled and promised.

It felt strange to her the next morning to be back among the rush-hour travellers, many of them having the pallid look from having stayed in shelters overnight. One woman said to her as they clambered over rubble and glass, 'I don't know whether our office will still be there. The building my sister worked in was completely demolished the night before last.'

They passed an overturned bus and a taxi, shops with their windows blown out, but no one seemed to spare a glance; such things being so commonplace.

Ann was already at the Centre when she arrived. She said, 'Hello, Lyndsey, so you are back too,' then she walked away. Lyndsey was standing looking at her retreating back when one of the women came up and asked her if she was fully recovered. Lyndsey said yes, she was, and the woman then looked in Ann's direction.

'But Ann is acting strange, isn't she? Do you think she's still suffering from shock?'

'I think so, and I think it might be best if we don't say too much to her today. What is there to do first?'

There were some people who had been made homeless but not so many as on previous occasions. Although Lyndsey had always been sympathetic towards the homeless she now had a greater understanding of their awful feeling of loss. She kept busy all the time, yet in spite of it the day dragged. She was uncomfortable and knew it was because Ann seemed purposely to have avoided her. At last she sought her out and said, 'Ann, do you blame me for your mother's death? If so, tell me, instead of avoiding me.'

Ann stared at her in wide-eyed surprise. 'I haven't been avoiding you, I've been busy, and no, I don't blame you for what happened. I told you, it was fate, and I'm glad to be free. Would you like to go dancing tonight?'

Lyndsey, taken aback by the sudden change of attitude, stood for a moment torn by a feeling of loyalty towards Ann, wanting to help her over her trouble, yet not feeling at all in the mood for dancing. At last she said, 'I don't particularly want to go socializing this evening. Perhaps tomorrow?'

'I have a date tomorrow.' Ann walked away, leaving Lyndsey feeling terrible. She could have gone but she had been thinking only of herself, of getting back to Kent to Bette and the children. She went after Ann and saw her talking to one of the younger ambulance drivers. Ann was all effervescent as she was saying to him, 'Oh, that's fine, I'll be ready at seven o'clock. Where shall I meet you?'

A meeting place was arranged and as Ann turned away smiling and saw Lyndsey she said, looking her up and down, 'I'm glad you didn't want to come with me, I shall have a much better time with Johnnie.' Then she added with a sneer, 'A fine friend you turned out to be.'

Ten minutes later when Lyndsey left the Centre she came face to face with Ann's sister Maggie. Before she could tell her that Ann had left Maggie said quietly, 'It's you I came to see, Lyndsey. Is there somewhere we can talk, have a cup of tea perhaps? Have you time?'

Lyndsey told her yes and indicated a small café further along the street. Although she wondered why Maggie should want to see her so specially, her curiosity was not satisfied until they were sat down in the café with their cups of tea. Then Maggie, after stirring her tea slowly, looked up, her expression worried.

'I felt I had to come to see you Lyndsey, to talk to you about Ann. She's been nasty to everyone since Mother was killed and was calling you blue yesterday. She doesn't mean you any harm – in fact I feel sure she's quite fond of you – but my sisters and I thought you ought to know the way she's been behaving – and why.'

Maggie, who had gone on stirring her tea, now laid the spoon in the saucer. 'What Ann is suffering from, we feel, is

174

a guilt complex. As a child she wanted Mother's approval, wanted to be her favourite, which she never was. Mother, for some reason, always seemed to have a knife in her. Ann did well at school but when she tried to show her reports, or prizes she had won, my mother would thrust her aside and tell her she was no better than anyone else.'

'How awful,' Lyndsey said, 'how – tragic.'

Maggie nodded. 'Yes, it was, but something more tragic was to occur. Ann, after a scolding one day, told Mother that Dad was seeing another woman, that he was in love with her and they were together. It was a lie, but although Dad swore on the Bible that it wasn't true, Mother refused to believe him. After that there were so many awful rows that Dad walked out. He started drinking, he lost his job and two months later he took his own life.'

Lyndsey just sat staring at her, shocked. Then Maggie went on, 'When Mother accepted that Dad had been telling the truth she thrashed Ann until she was black and blue, and all the time Ann was shouting that she had done it because she wanted Mother to love her. It was dreadful, Lyndsey. Ann ruined all our lives and it's this guilt she's suffering from now. She's to be pitied really. I feel very sorry for her, and I did hope you would bear with her for a while until she's got over the shock of Mother's death.'

'Yes, I will, Maggie, I'll help her all I can.'

'I thought you would, love, thanks a lot. Give Ann time, she's not always easy to deal with at the best of times, but she can be loving. She's marvellous with all our children.' Maggie gave a brief smile. 'I always say that if a person loves kids there's got to be some good in them.' She got up. 'I must go. Thanks for listening, Lyndsey, and offering to help, I'm grateful.'

It was late evening before Lyndsey had a chance to tell Bette about her talk with Maggie. Bette said, 'How do you really feel about Ann? I've often had the impression that you're not too keen on her as a friend.'

'No, I'm not, but without knowing why. I've always

175

admired Ann for her dedication to her work and for the way she cares for the children. She's marvellous with them. Poor Ann. It must have been awful loving her mother so much yet never having that love returned.' Lyndsey was silent for a moment, then she went on:

'It's made me realize what a sheltered life I led when we lived at Echo Cove. Nothing like the relationship between Ann and her mother has ever touched me. What unhappy people they both must have been. I never heard anyone rant on the way Mrs Matley did.'

Bette said gently, 'Although you may not realize it now, Lyndsey, I think this experience might help you in the future, make you more conscious of the various types there are in the world, the mean ones, who can't bear to hear of anyone getting promotion, the catty, the gossip-mongers, the liars, the cheats. I've met them all in my stage career, but I learned to accept them because there were always the other types to make up the balance, the loyal ones, the ones men are always willing to help, those who make you laugh, who have no malice in them. Wherever you go, there are always the good and the bad. Be tolerant towards the ones who seem to be the worst because they are the ones who need your help, but never, and I repeat *never*, let anyone sit on you!' Bette studied Lyndsey, her head inclined, 'Somehow I don't think you will. In spite of your soft heart you can speak your mind.'

Lyndsey smiled. 'I do come from a plain-speaking family, but I was often told I had too much to say, that I was *too* plain speaking.'

'I don't think so. Anyway, we'll change the subject. Did I tell you that we'll be playing to an audience of about five hundred on Saturday? If we can please that number then we can be satisfied we're progressing.'

Before they were due at the camp on the Saturday Bette asked Joe if he would play the tune 'Daisy Bell' on his harmonica instead of 'You Are My Honeysuckle' as a prelude to Lyndsey's special act. When he asked why she said, 'Because if they shout "We want Honey" after her act, instead of "Daisy", then I shall know that the news of the act has gone ahead on the grapevine, and that will delight me. Fame, Joe, fame!'

The men did yell for 'Honey' and Bette's face was alight with pleasure. 'Splendid. Now we shall really be in demand.' And they were. The next week they had ten enquiries for dates. The Boomerangs celebrated. They were on their way.

Lyndsey tried twice to tell Bette that she would need to employ someone else for the special act when she went into the Wrens, but Bette, as usual, dismissed it as being something that belonged to the future. Live for the moment was her motto, she declared.

This next show took place in a hangar. A proper stage had been erected with draw curtains and as each member had a peep through and saw the sea of faces, a panic set in. They would never be able to do it they declared. Bette told them firmly, yes, of course they would, they were *troupers* and they were not to forget it, not for a moment!

Lyndsey had been rehearsing to the tune of 'Daisy Bell' to get the kicks and twirls in unison but she said her legs felt like jelly. Again it was Bette who gave her confidence by saying, '*Don't* think of the numbers out there, think of the *pleasure* you're going to give to the men.'

There was tumultuous applause for each act and in between there was a din of chatter and bursts of laughter. But when there came the roll of drums preceding Lyndsey's special act, the noise began to die down. And there was complete silence when Joe began to play 'Daisy Bell'.

When Bette said, 'Now!' Lyndsey went into her routine and was off the stage and the fur coat wrapped around her as usual in seconds. But then she realized that strong hands were gripping her arms, and while the men were yelling 'We want Honey' she was turned and found herself staring into the stern face of Elliott Warrender.

Her mouth went dry. 'You!' she whispered.

'And *you*,' he answered grimly, 'are the Honey with the beautiful legs I've been hearing so much about.'

The roof of the hangar was just about lifting off with the clamour, the clapping, the shouting and stamping of feet. Lyndsey looked around her. 'Where's Bette?'

'Never mind Bette, *you* are coming with me, I have something to say to you,' and with that Elliott pushed her in front of him. 'Out.'

Oh, Lord, Lyndsey thought with despair. This could mean the end of the shows for her if her Uncle Richard got to hear about it.

TWELVE

Elliott took her to a hut a short distance away and Lyndsey, having by now regained some confidence, asked cheekily, 'Well, am I to be court-martialled?'

'You ought to be flogged! So should Bette. Sit down'.

Lyndsey walked to the stove in the corner and held out her hands to its warmth. 'I would rather stand, thank you'.

'Sit down, Lyndsey'. Although Elliott had not raised his voice she found herself obeying him. He then asked her if her Uncle Richard knew what she was doing.

'No, and I don't want him to know. I'm not doing any harm, it's fun, we enjoy doing the show and the men enjoy it'.

'I'll say they do'. Elliott's lips trembled but any smile that might have developed was immediately controlled. 'Your act is a byword in the camps. The high-kicking one, I mean.'

'So what's wrong with that? I repeat, I'm not doing any harm. Now am I? Be honest.'

Elliott seemed suddenly to relax. 'None, I suppose, and you might think it's none of my business what you do, but Richard did ask me to keep an eye on you if I was anywhere around.'

'Oh, he did, did he? Well, let me tell you I don't need anyone to keep an eye on me; I'm not a ten-year-old.'

'And it was not Richard's intention to have you treated like one,' Elliott said quietly. 'For instance, when you wrote about having been involved in a raid, I was able to relieve his worry by coming to see you.'

'Oh, I see,' Lyndsey said. 'I suppose it must have been a surprise seeing me on stage.'

'I didn't believe it at first when I saw you sit down at the piano, then later when you played and sang to the ukulele. I went round to the back of the hangar to see if I could find you and there I met Bette. She told me about your *special* act and you can imagine my shock when I discovered that *you* were the Honey with the beautiful legs I've been hearing so much about. I offered to take the fur coat to put around you and Bette handed it over. I think she thought it a great joke, my taking her place.'

'She would', Lyndsey said earnestly, 'and please don't spoil her pleasure. She's been marvellous, getting us all organized, taking us through routines, badgering us, wanting our acts to be as good as we could make them.'

A slow smile spread over Elliott's face, then he was laughing. 'Oh, really, Lyndsey MacLaren, you are the end! No, I won't spoil it. You better go and find Bette and you'll want to get changed. I understand you are all going to have drinks and eats at the officers' mess.'

'Yes, that's right. And Elliott – thanks! You're a sport.' On an impulse Lyndsey went to him and kissed him lightly on the cheek. 'See you later.'

She was at the door when he called her name. She turned and he said, a twinkle in his eyes:

'You *do* have beautiful legs.'

She bobbed a curtsy. 'Thank you, sir, glad you approve.'

When Lyndsey walked to the hut where they were to change after the show she had a feeling of walking on air. Perhaps she was being a little foolish but Elliott having admired her legs meant more to her for some reason than all the other compliments put together. It was probably because she felt that with Elliott, compliments would not be lightly given.

The hum of conversation when she opened the door of

180

the hut stopped as she went in. Bette said, 'What happened? I thought Elliott was taking it all as a joke when he first saw you, but afterwards, after he had taken the coat, he looked thunderous.'

Lyndsey dismissed it. 'He was all right, just a little worried as to what Uncle Richard would think. It was all settled amicably.'

'Good.' A sergeant came then to escort them to the officers' mess and there was no more time for any further discussion.

The men tended to gather around Lyndsey, but she, not wanting to cause any jealousy among the other members, excused herself and went to where Elliott was talking to Bette and George. Elliott laid an arm across her shoulder and said, his tone teasing, 'It's a good job the men are not due to go into battle, otherwise they would be thinking about legs instead of the enemy.'

'I would say it was a good thing to think about,' George said with a grin. 'If you're going to get a bullet in you, far better to be wounded with a lovely image in front of you than the ugly mug of the enemy.'

Elliott nodded. 'True, true. Now, how about drinks?'

There was no opportunity for any further talk with Elliott. Officers kept coming up to congratulate Bette on her show, and to tell Lyndsey how much they had enjoyed her act and to congratulate George.

After that they became part of a much larger group and it was nearly one o'clock when they broke up. Before they did leave Elliott had accepted an invitation from Bette to come to lunch the following day. At first he had told her he would come after lunch but Bette insisted he come for the meal, explaining she had been among the first twenty lucky ones in the butcher's queue that morning and had got a chicken. 'And I also got some sausages,' she said, 'so although we won't exactly have a feast I think we'll have enough to make us feel thankful.'

'To make us feel thankful,' Elliott repeated softly. 'I like that Bette. How good-hearted you are. I can understand why everyone loves you.'

'Oh, stop it,' she scolded, 'you're making me blush and that is something I haven't done for years.'

When they got back from the camp they found Mrs Petrie sitting knitting over the dying fire. Usually, when she was baby-sitting she stayed overnight at Bette's and was in bed when they arrived. She said she had waited up to tell them that Andrew had phoned and so had Lyndsey's Uncle Richard. The news from Richard was that neither he nor his wife would be home for another week or so. He would be writing. Andrew's news was that the squadron were moving, he had no idea where but would let them know later. He was over the measles. He sent his love to all of them.

'Well at least we didn't come home to bad news,' Bette said.

Mrs Petrie asked how the show had gone and after they had talked for a while she went up to bed.

Lyndsey, whose mind had been full of dreams about Elliott on the way home, began now to think of Andrew and to wonder what exactly her feelings were in regard to each man. There were times when she felt really loving towards Andrew and wanted to be with him, but this evening she had felt she could be in love with Elliott. He was so masterful, his very strength gave her a thrill. But then, did she want to be mastered? Was she perhaps fickle-minded without realizing it? She sat eyeing Bette for a moment, then she sat up.

'Bette, did you ever feel you were in love with two men at the same time?

Bette, who had kicked off her shoes and was stretching luxuriously, stifled a yawn. 'Darling, I've been in love with five men at the same time. I met so many in the profession, attractive men who could charm the birds off the trees. When I was only fifteen I had such a mad crush on a six-foot baritone who could almost melt your bones with the way he sang that I felt I would have died for him. It didn't even make my pain any the less when I found out he was married with six kids.'

'But then you were only fifteen!'

Bette threw out her hands. 'Fifteen, eighteen, *thirty* – women are always falling in and out of love. Yes, even though I adored Rupert. Not, mind you, that I ever had an affair. It's just a sort of dreaming, Lyndsey. I suppose men dream too. I listened sometimes to Rupert flattering a girl he'd been really attracted to, but I knew it would never go further than that.'

Bette added softly, 'Who are these two men you feel you're in love with? Andrew and Elliott?'

Lyndsey nodded. 'They're so different.' She gave a wan smile. 'But I don't feel ready to die for either one.'

'And a good job too! Having a crush on someone can be hell.' Bette waved a warning finger. 'You wait until you get into the Wrens when you'll have dozens of men to pick from. The ratio of men to women must be about fifty to one.' Bette grinned. 'Lucky Wrens.'

'Bette – do you think you would ever marry again?'

'I don't know, Lyndsey. At the moment no, but I do miss having a man in my life, miss loving and being loved. It's nature, isn't it? But no matter how much I fell for someone I could never go into an affair.' Bette grinned. 'To be truthful I wouldn't dare. I would imagine Rupert there scolding me and saying, "Bette, how *could* you".'

Lyndsey laughed. 'Oh, Bette, you are funny.' Then soberly she said, 'You told me that Rupert was a kind and understanding person. Surely he wouldn't want you to remain unmarried for the rest of your life. You're still young.'

A faraway look came into Bette's eyes. 'When Rupert knew he was dying he begged me to marry again. Perhaps I will at some time in the future, if the right man comes along.' She smiled suddenly. 'And that would be all right with Rupert. Oh, yes, marriage, but no playing around.'

The subject was still on Lyndsey's mind when they were ready to go to bed, and it must have been on Bette's too because she said suddenly, 'My mother used to say it was harder to be good than bad, but much more rewarding.' Bette chuckled softly; 'But do you know, Lyndsey, she was wrong. It was hell at times to be good!' The grandfather clock struck two and she added, 'And on that note we'll get to bed and dream of princes on white chargers coming to kidnap us and carry us off to fairy-tale castles on top of mountains.'

They were both giggling as they went upstairs.

But Lyndsey's dreams that night were not of princes or fairy-tale castles. Her most vivid dream was of picking her way over a path of flinty stones, barefoot, to where her lover was waiting outside a broken-down cottage. And when she did arrive a faceless man told her to go and do the journey again, she was not yet ready for love.

The next morning when she related the dream to Bette she wailed, 'And that will be my lot! Travelling stony paths before I can get married.'

'But how rewarding,' Bette teased her, 'to know that you'll find true love in the end.' Lyndsey picked up the tea cosy and threw it at her, accusing her of being a Job's comforter, and had Connie asking 'What's a Job's comforter, Auntie Lyndsey?'

Lyndsey, to save long explanations said, 'Guess what, Uncle Elliott is coming today for lunch.' And that was enough to take any thought of Job out of Connie's mind.

Elliott was to travel by car, and to save the children hanging around in the road waiting for him to arrive and asking the time every few minutes, Lyndsey agreed to take them to church while Bette prepared lunch.

When they returned the delicious aroma of roast chicken and thyme and parsley greeted them. 'Ummm,' Lyndsey said, 'it makes me feel ravenous.' Bette said the meal was nearly ready and she hoped that their guest would not be late. He had told them he would arrive about half past twelve, and he was there as the clock was striking the half hour.

The children, in spite of their excitement, were shy with him at first, but after he had given them a bar of chocolate each, Connie at least talked him to death. Janie's one contribution to the conversation was to say that Bessie, one of the pigs at the farm, had had a lot of babies. 'Seventeen!' she added in an awed voice.

'Seventeen!' Elliott repeated. 'My goodness, that's a lot of babies isn't it? I think we must go and take a look at them this afternoon, don't you'? Janie nodded vigorously and leaned against him in a gesture of affection.

Lyndsey thought Elliott's offer a lovely start to the visit and hoped he would remember to keep his promise. He did and suggested after lunch that they should all walk to the farm. The air was crisp and invigorating. Connie kept skipping about but when Elliott started to tell Janie about when he was young and kept rabbits she walked by his side and listened.

'I started with only two,' he said, 'but before long I seemed to have about sixty.'

'Sixty?' Connie screeched. 'Where did they all come from?'

Bette said to Elliott under her breath, '*You* have started something, *Major* Warrender.'

But Elliott took it all in his stride. He explained there was a mummy and a daddy rabbit and they had children, just as their parents had Connie and Janie. And before Connie could ask any more questions he began to tell them about a family of rabbits who lived in a forest and he made their adventures sound so exciting that no more genealogical problems arose.

'Very clever, sir,' Bette remarked.

The farmer's wife greeted them when they arrived and when she knew why they had come she waved a hand in the direction of the pig sties. 'Go and take a look. They're greedy little things. I believe they'd feed all day if Bessie would let them.'

Bette stayed to talk to the farmer's wife while the others went to see the piglets. Their mother was on her side, lying passive as the little squirming bodies clambered over her seeking a place to feed. When all but one were sucking avidly, tails waving ecstatically Connie began to giggle. But Janie was very concerned by the fact the smallest one of the litter was being constantly pushed aside. 'The poor little thing will die,' she said, distressed.

'Just you wait,' Elliott said, 'This piglet is small but it seems to me he's a very pushy little thing and there is a place for him. Look! He's found it. Oh, I could tell you a lot about farming.'

Lyndsey, remembering that Elliott's family had lived out in India, asked where he had learned about farming.

'From an uncle, who liked to be thought of as a 'gentleman farmer'. My parents sent me to boarding school in England when I was young and I went to stay with my uncle and aunt during the vacations. They were some of the happiest times of my life. I loved the farming life.'

'Better than being an army man?'

'I would have liked to have taken up farming if soldiering had not been a tradition in the family.' Elliott then drew the children's attention to the ducks on their way to the pond. They laughed at the way they waddled towards the pond in single file but soon turned back to watch the piglets and, fascinated by their antics, stayed a long time.

What fascinated Lyndsey that afternoon was Elliott's absorption with the children, his concern to keep them near and the way he gently soothed Connie when she fell and hurt her knee.

Later they stood smiling, listening to Connie scolding Janie for getting dirty.

'Just look at your hands, our Janie, they're filthy. What would our Mum have to say if she saw them?'

Janie held out her hands and studied them in her solemn way. Then she looked up. 'They're not *very* filfy, are they?'

'Yes, they are.' Connie drew a handkerchief from her knicker leg, spat on it, and rubbed vigorously on Janie's palms. 'There, that's better. Now, don't you get them dirty again, do you hear?' After replacing the handkerchief she laid an arm companionably across Janie's shoulder and said she would ask Auntie Lyndsey if they could go and see the chickens.

Elliott said softly, 'Bless them, they almost bring a lump to one's throat, the way Connie bosses little Janie, but shows that she loves her. And Janie happily accepts her sister's seniority. Do the parents visit?'

'Mrs Howard has only been once, but apart from the fact that she does have a job she also has an invalid husband to look after. She told Bette in a letter that although she longed to see the children, she was afraid if she came again they might want to come home with her, and that would defeat the whole project.'

They discussed evacuation and how it worked for one family and not for another, then Lyndsey told Elliott about Andrew, his measles, and how his squadron had moved. To this, Elliott said quietly, 'You'll miss him; he's quite a lively person, I understand.'

'Yes, he is. By the way, Elliott, are you stationed at the camp where we did the show, or was it just one of your admin visits?'

'I shall be there a week.' Elliott smiled at her. 'I may be able to get over and see you all, if that would be all right with Bette.'

'Bette would be delighted, I know.'

'And you, Lyndsey? Would you be pleased to see me?' His tone was light.

'Why – yes, yes, of course.' Lyndsey, feeling her colour rising, was glad when Bette hailed them to say that the farmer's wife had made them some tea.

Lyndsey came to learn that day there were many sides

to Elliott Warrender. When the farmer and his wife were talking of the difficulties of farming under wartime conditions without sufficient men on the land, he was the perfect listener, nodding from time to time, but afterwards he became the politician, putting his own views, although seeming at the same time to agree with everything the couple had said. The farmer said to Bette before they left, 'Yon's a clever fellow, likeable, down to earth, and he knows a fair bit about farming. You'll have to bring him again another time.' Bette promised she would.

On their way back home they met Mrs Petrie who was taking Penny for a walk. It was obvious she had been crying and Bette said, 'What's wrong, love, those relatives of yours again? Come and have a meal with us, it'll help you to get over it.'

Mrs Petrie often complained of her relatives but never at any length. But this time, while Bette and Lyndsey were preparing the meal she told Elliott all her troubles over the years, how she was never free of her relatives. Even before the war, they would come for a few days and then would stay weeks.

Bette whispered to Lyndsey, 'Oh, dear, I didn't think she would go on so. Poor Elliott. You had better go and rescue him. See if you can steer the conversation into another channel.'

But by then Elliott was doing the talking, pointing out to Mrs Petrie that it might be better to have troublesome relatives than none at all. Didn't she agree?

She thought about it a moment then she nodded slowly. 'You could be right.' A slow smile spread over her face. 'If they were all goody-goodies I wouldn't have anything to talk about, would I? I'm glad I've met you, Major Warrender. I had heard a good deal about you from Bette and Lyndsey. *And* nothing but good, I must say.'

Mrs Petrie was once more her cheery self. She got up and called to Bette that she wouldn't stay for a meal. And when Bette came in to try and persuade her to stay she said, 'No, I'll go and spread largesse to my *dear* ones.' She laughed. 'And give them the shock of their lives!'

When she had gone Bette said to Elliott, 'Well, you've done enough good deeds to last for several days. It was nice of you to cheer Mrs Petrie up. She's a marvellous neighbour and we're all very fond of her.'

Lyndsey, feeling in a mellow mood, was thinking what a lovely day it had been when Joe, the trick cyclist in the show, called to see Bette about something. When he was introduced to Elliott he said, 'Have you seen her do her act in the show? She's great.' Then he added, 'Very versatile, our Lyndsey. A couple of weeks ago she played the old Joanna like a veteran in the local pub when the usual bloke was ill and had everyone singing.'

'I wish I had heard her', Elliott said, his voice conveying nothing. Lyndsey groaned inwardly thinking that Elliott would probably be picturing her as a high-kicking chorus girl and a piano player in a pub! What an image.

A few minutes after Joe had gone Elliott got up to leave. Bette asked him if he would care to come again the following weekend and to Lyndsey's relief, he accepted at once.

When Elliott had gone Lyndsey turned to Bette. 'Wouldn't Joe just turn up at that moment! Heaven knows how Elliott sees me.'

Bette grinned. 'Don't worry, dukes have been known to marry chorus girls.'

'Oh, Bette, don't joke about it. *Playing the old Joanna – in a pub*. It sounded awful.'

'I've told you, there's nothing to worry about, Elliott is greatly taken with you. He thinks you are a very beautiful, talented girl.'

'Not his words, I'm sure,' Lyndsey protested.

'That was exactly what he did say, cross my heart. And would he have accepted an invitation to come again next Sunday so readily if he had thought you a – '

'A slut? Oh, I do wish I had remembered to tell him

189

that Uncle Richard had raised no objection when I played in the pub. He actually encouraged me. He – '

'Lyndsey!' Bette spoke firmly. 'Stop this. Right now. Stop putting words into Elliott's mouth.' More gently she added, 'You must be very fond of him indeed to need his good opinion so much.'

'I'm not, I – oh, I don't know how I feel. I seem to be all at sixes and sevens lately. Let's forget it.'

Later Lyndsey found herself trying to analyse Elliott's reactions to all that had been said while he was with them and instinctively knew she was interpreting things he had said in ways he probably had not meant at all. When Joe had mentioned about her playing in the pub Elliott had shown no reaction. She had taken it that it was because he disapproved of what she had done. Yet actually, when he had disapproved of her doing her special act he had been angry. So how could she possibly judge him? As Bette had said, she must stop putting words into Elliott's mouth.

Once she realized this she felt more relaxed.

On the Monday morning, before Lyndsey left for London she said, 'Bette, I'm going to stay in town overnight this evening. I really must go and take a look at the house. I know I would have heard if it had been bombed because I left your address with the warden, but still, I feel I ought to open some windows, give it an airing. I'll be back on Tuesday. Thanks for everything.'

Lyndsey had mentioned going to the house on impulse. She had felt restless. Was this an omen? Had some damage been done? She prayed not.

When she arrived at the Centre, Ann came hurrying up to her, all excitement. 'Guess what, Lyndsey? I have a little flat. The woman who keeps the small general shop-cum-greengrocers, is letting me have it rent free. It's above the shop and although there's a lingering smell of oranges and oh, all sorts of things, I don't mind. It will be my very own little home.'

'Oh, I'm so pleased for you,' Lyndsey enthused. 'Is it furnished?'

'Partly, and the family are going to give me all sorts of bits and pieces. The woman in the shop was friendly with my mother. No, not really friendly, they chatted, Mother wasn't friendly with anyone. Lyndsey, would you come and take a look at the flat when we finish here today?' Ann was more like herself and because she was so eager for Lyndsey to come she agreed.

Every time the two of them met during their work that morning Ann went on about her luck in getting the flat. Once she said, 'Although there's been some bombing in the area there hasn't been so much as at other places. I feel it's going to be a lucky flat. I can't wait to get moved in. Just think, no more nagging from Mother or from my other sisters. Maggie's all right, she's understanding, but I think even she is pleased I've managed to get a place on my own. Roll on two o'clock.'

Lyndsey was surprised at how easily Ann could talk about her mother. Even now Lyndsey found it difficult at times to think about her parents and her grandparents without feeling emotional. But then they had been very different people to Mrs Matley.

When they left the Centre at two o'clock to go to the flat the air-raid sirens began to wail, but Ann and Lyndsey, like the majority of people, ignored them and went on their way. Even the people who were regular users of shelters at night ignored them during the day, not finding the bombs so frightening in daylight.

The district where Ann had her flat was in a poorer-class area but although paint was peeling from windows and doors there was an air of cleanliness in scrubbed steps, shining window panes. The shop was double-fronted, with one side boarded up, but as they passed the unboarded one Lyndsey could see that many of the shelves were bare. The door to the flat was to the left of the shop and as Ann put the key in the lock she said, 'Mrs Turner told me she can't give me any extra rations, but has promised to let me know when she's expecting any unrationed goods, like tins of salmon or sardines.' The stairs were narrow and steep, but the small landing opened on to two decent-sized rooms, a living room with a small scullery beyond and a bedroom with two windows. 'Not exactly luxury,' Ann declared, 'but I just know I shall be happy here.'

The rooms were sparsely furnished and when Lyndsey asked who had lived in the flat previously she said, 'A middle-aged couple. They went to visit a daughter and were killed by a bomb on the way. You never know what's going to happen from day to day, do you?' She spoke in a quite unconcerned way, then went on talking about the various items she would buy to brighten up the flat. Lyndsey was not quite sure whether Ann was trying to forget the tragedy of the couple or whether it had not really affected her.

They had a cup of tea then Ann looked at her watch. 'How about going to see a film? I just feel like going to the pictures tonight.'

Although Lyndsey was not keen, she agreed for Ann's sake. She enjoyed the film and when they came out Ann suggested they went to Lyons' Corner House for a snack. She agreed and experienced a similar excitement, the sense of adventure, as on her previous visit with Andrew. They pushed through the crowds milling around outside the restaurant and went inside, blinking against the lights after the blackout. It was several seconds before she noticed that there was a much longer queue of people waiting than on her previous visit.

Ann noticed that many of the servicemen in the queue were without girlfriends. 'Take your pick,' she whispered, 'but go for the Yanks, they have the money.'

Lyndsey, determined not to give in to Ann's avaricious whims, stared straight ahead and found she was gazing at the back of a GI uniform. Then, as though aware of her gaze, the soldier turned round and half-smiled from Ann to Lyndsey.

Then he said, 'Excuse me, ma'am, but aren't you the young lady who is a "putter out" of incendiary bombs?' His smile was wide.

The other American with the one who had spoken smiled too, but his was a slow shy smile. Suddenly remembrance came and Lyndsey laughed. 'You were the two Americans that my friend and I met in the foyer of the theatre – *White Horse Inn.*'

'That's right, ma'am, my name is Brad and this is my friend Ed. Would you and your friend care to join us for supper?'

Before Lyndsey had a chance to answer Ann said, 'Yes, lovely thanks. I am Ann Matley and my friend's name is Lyndsey MacLaren.' Within seconds Ann was chatting brightly to Brad while Lyndsey found herself talking to the quieter man, Ed.

Actually, they turned out to be courteous and pleasant; what Lyndsey didn't like was Ann telling them about both of them being buried in all the rubble after the raid. Ann seemed to thrive on the drama of it. Ann was certainly at her most vivacious when men were involved. Lyndsey's first impression of her when they had first met was of a rather small, plain girl with freckles. Now she could see how male company brought out the best in her, made her seem attractive.

Ann, obviously looking to the future, asked where they were stationed and if they were on leave. It was Brad who answered the second part. Unfortunately, their leave was ending; they were due to return to base the following morning.

'Oh, what a shame,' Ann said. 'We could have shown you around London.' Lyndsey felt embarrassed at her forthright manner.

Brad smiled and touched Ann's hand. 'Another time,

perhaps.' Then he looked at his watch. 'But the night's young. How about us all going dancing?'

Ann said, 'Great.' Lyndsey excused herself, said she didn't really feel like dancing and Ed said that he didn't dance anyway.

'Right! That suits us fine.' Ann got up. 'Brad and I will go and enjoy ourselves while you two stick-in-the-muds can stay and bore each other to death.'

Lyndsey bridled, but Brad laughed. 'Nothing boring about these two. I bet they'll enjoy themselves just as much as we will. See you . . .' He gave them a wave then he and Ann were gone.

Ed watched them go, his smile indulgent. Then he turned to Lyndsey. 'I'm afraid I am a bit of a stick-in-the-mud at times.'

'And so am I,' Lyndsey declared happily. 'And what is wrong with that? I go to stay with a friend in Kent and I think how lovely it is, how satisfying to go and stand at a field gate and watch the sheep cropping the grass, or to sit by a river and watch it wending its way lazily among the water meadows.'

Ed had rather gentle brown eyes but at that moment they twinkled with pleasure. 'I just knew that you and I had things in common, ma'am.'

Lyndsey told him it was strange to be called ma'am and he promised to use her name.

Later they found they had a lot more in common than watching grass growing. Ed asked her where her home was and she told him about living in London, but explained about having been born and brought up by the sea. Ed coaxed her to talk about it and she did, but made no mention of the loss of her family. Ed was delighted to hear about Echo Cove and said they were practically soul-mates. She had the sea in her blood and so had he.

'My home is in Chicago,' he said, 'but when I was younger we lived in Hawaii. My father worked as an

194

engineer there. It's just so beautiful, Lyn, all the islands are.'

He talked about the joy, the adventure of surfing, about the foliage, the tulip trees with their orange flowers, the pink shower trees, the white flowers of the mangoes with their pink-fringed edges, the beautiful cream of the frangipane . . . He described a waterfall that looked as if the water was running upwards, and how the spray held rainbows in the sunshine. 'They called it the Upside Down Waterfall,' he said, and added, 'as if you didn't guess.'

'How beautiful it all sounds, Ed.'

They talked about swimming, about boats, collecting shells, and Ed wanted to know more about the fishing fleet and the echoing cliff and the time flew.

When Lyndsey eventually looked at her watch she said, 'Oh, Ed, I'm afraid I must go, it's late. I've loved hearing about Hawaii.'

'Plenty more to tell,' he said with his slow smile. 'That is, if you're interested. I'd be glad to oblige.' 'And I would love to hear about it,' she said softly. 'Thank you for a lovely evening.'

He insisted on taking her home in a taxi, and he made no attempt to kiss her, for which Lyndsey was glad. It would have spoilt the evening.

THIRTEEN

Lyndsey had a short note from Andrew the next morning, simply saying that he was feeling much better, that he was missing her terribly and hoping to get some leave soon. 'I love you, love you, love you,' he said, '*please* write soon. I'll phone you when I can.'

'It's so unsatisfactory', Lyndsey said to Bette when she arrived on the Friday evening. 'A short note, and a scrappy conversation when he does phone.'

Bette sympathized with her and said he would be sure to get some sick leave once he was properly over the measles. Then she told her that Elliott was coming again on the Sunday to spend the day with them. And Lyndsey felt a little guilty at realizing how pleased she was to hear it.

He arrived half an hour earlier than he had done the time before and Bette said, 'Lovely, we can have a coffee and a chat before we have lunch.' She went into the kitchen and Elliott smiled at Lyndsey.

'So, here I am again. It's good to see you, Lyndsey..

'It's good to see you.' She laughed. 'And now that we've dispensed with the pleasantries we can discuss the weather.'

'No, we won't, tell me what you have been doing. Are Richard and Marian back home?'

'Yes, but I don't know for how long.' There was some shouting from outside and Lyndsey got up and went over

196

to the window. Elliott had brought a small bat and a rubber ball for Connie and Janie and a neighbour's three young children had joined in their game.

Lyndsey remarked that poor little Janie seemed to be doing all the running to fetch the ball and added, 'It's always the good-natured one who gets put on.'

Bette came in with the coffee. 'How true that is. By the way, I'm going to take you all this afternoon to see a wonderful garden that I saw the other day. It's full of chrysanthemums of all shades. Really beautiful.'

But they never did get to see the chrysanthemums. The children who were wrapped up in their game of rounders could hardly finish their meal, wanting to get back to the field again to play. Bette told them they would get indigestion running around on full stomachs but indigestion meant nothing to them, not when their friends arrived wanting to know if they were ready to come and play.

Bette said, 'Off you go then, but don't leave Janie to go running after the ball all the time, she's only small.'

They promised and away they went with gleeful shouts.

The three adults had sat back to enjoy a cup of tea and a chat when Elliott suddenly sat up. 'I can hear a plane.'

Bette dismissed it as a dog-fight going on somewhere but Elliott said, 'No, it's a single plane and – ' He got up and went to the window and Lyndsey and Bette followed. Lyndsey could now hear the drone.

Suddenly there was the sound of an explosion and the drone became louder. Elliott shouted, 'Get down!' Lyndsey yelled, 'The children!' but he had Bette and Lyndsey pinned to the floor. When the plane's engine faded into the distance Elliott let them up. They ran outside. Lyndsey's heart was beating so wildly it threatened to suffocate her. Then as she saw the children looking up into the sky she went weak with relief. Thank God they were all right.

Seconds later she realized that Elliott and Bette were standing motionless, both looking beyond the group of children to where a small bundle lay. Lyndsey's stomach contracted.

'Stay here', Elliott said quietly, and started to move away. Lyndsey, her tongue feeling twice its size, ran past him. He caught her up saying, 'Lyndsey, no, let me!' but she thrust him aside and raced on.

Janie lay on her back, two fingers against her cheek as though contemplating some problem. For a few moments Lyndsey thought she might have just been knocked unconscious, then she noticed that both shoes were missing from her feet and an icy finger ran over her spine. Bomb blast . . . Oh, no!

Elliott knelt down and felt Janie's pulse; and Lyndsey knew by the sorrowful way he looked at them that the child was dead. She dropped to her knees.

'Oh, God, why? Why little Janie?'

Bette came up and drew Lyndsey to her feet and they stood, deeply shocked, grief stricken, holding one another, not quite knowing what to do.

Then Elliott took off his tunic and covered Janie with it, tucking it around the tiny little body almost tenderly. He was about to pick her up when there was the sound of people talking excitedly in the road at the front of the house. Someone shouted, 'The Willoughbys' farm has caught it . . .'

The garden gate was suddenly flung open and Mr and Mrs Hall, the children's parents, came hurrying in. The mother, seeing them, gave a glad cry. 'They're safe, thank the Lord.' Her husband touched her on the arm and nodded in the direction of the small khaki-clad figure. Her hand went to her mouth momentarily then she was saying quietly, 'We'll take Connie with us, Bette.'

'Thanks, Mrs Hall, it's good of you.' Bette spoke in a mechanical way. The children, who had all been standing like statues, began to move and when Connie came towards where Janie was lying Bette hurried forward and spoke to her.

198

Elliott said to Lyndsey, 'I must do some phoning.' He turned once more to pick Janie up then paused, adding, 'I had better wait until the children are gone.'

Lyndsey touched his arm. 'You go and phone, I'll see to Janie; I want to, *please*.' He hesitated a moment then left. Bette had taken Connie's hand and walked with her outside the gate where she left her with the Halls.

Lyndsey stooped and picked up Janie. It was not until she moved the coat so that she could wrap the child in it the better to carry her that she became aware that Janie's back and buttocks were bare, her clothes having been torn off by the freakish blast. Bile rose in her throat. It seemed such a violation of tender innocence that she wanted to scream.

Then Bette was there and tears were streaming down both their cheeks as they went inside and Lyndsey laid Janie down gently on the divan in the living room. Seconds later Mrs Petrie came in and went to make some tea.

By the time she was handing round the tea Bette and Lyndsey were calmer.

Elliott told them the results of his phone calls. The police would inform Mrs Howard, and the doctor and ambulance were on the way. They were all silent, everyone realizing it was one time when no words were necessary.

The doctor came in the ambulance. 'A sad time,' he said. 'I'm so sorry, Mrs Bascony, where is – ?'

'This way,' Elliott said.

Bette looked at Lyndsey, her lips trembling. 'I can't let her go without saying goodbye. Will you come with me?'

'Yes, of course.'

With their goodbyes said and the doctor telling Bette he would call later, the ambulance left.

When they went back to the kitchen Mrs Petrie had gone. Bette said to Elliott in a strangled voice, 'What am I going to say to Mrs Howard? She and her husband are going to regret letting the children come to stay with me. I feel so responsible.'

'You mustn't blame yourself, Bette, and I'm quite sure the parents won't. It's – ' The phone rang and Elliott went to answer it. It was the first of a number of calls from people shocked by Janie's death. Then the doorbell rang and Elliott attended to this too. He came into the room with a police constable.

The constable removed his helmet and said, looking uncomfortable, 'I'm sorry about your trouble, Mrs Bascony. It's a terrible thing, a stray Jerry drops his bombs before making for the Channel and he wipes out five of the Willoughby family and this little lassie.' He paused, cleared his throat then went on:

'We've had word from London. They've contacted Mrs Howard and told her what happened and she says she'll come when she can, but it won't be tonight'.

Lyndsey, incensed, exclaimed, 'Not tonight! Her child's been killed. Is it too much trouble?'

'No, no, it's not like that, miss. It's, well, you see – ' The man pulled out a handkerchief and mopped his brow. 'Well, it's like this. Mrs Howard has other troubles . . . Her husband died this morning'.

The silence that followed was so complete that the droning of a bee outside the window seemed magnified a hundredfold.

'I know how you feel,' the constable said. 'A dreadful thing.' He picked up his helmet. 'I'm sorry, terribly sorry.' Elliott went with him to the door.

'Connie will have to be told,' Bette said, 'and I don't think I can face it. Would you, Lyndsey?'

'Yes, of course.'

Mrs Hill brought Connie back at six o'clock. 'I would have kept her overnight,' she said, 'but she wanted to come home. She hasn't cried but she's been very quiet.'

When Mrs Hill had gone Connie said, 'Auntie Lyndsey, I want to go to bed. I'm tired.'

To Lyndsey it was more heartbreaking than if she had asked about Janie. It was the request of a bewildered child.

'Come along, pet,' she said gently, 'and I'll get you ready.'

When Connie was in her nightdress and clutching her doll she said, 'Has Janie gone to heaven, Auntie Lyndsey?'

The woebegone look on the child's face made Lyndsey lift her on to her lap and hold her close.

'Yes, she has, Connie. And – so has your daddy.'

Lyndsey was not sure whether she was doing the right thing but felt it would be terrible if after having been told about Janie the child would have to learn about her father.

'Dad?' Connie drew back, puzzled. 'Why has he gone?'

'Because he's been ill such a long time and been in a lot of pain. Now he'll no longer have any pain.'

'He won't? I'm glad. He cried once he was hurting so much, but he didn't let Mam see him, only me. He held my hand tight.' Connie was silent, fingering a button on her nightdress, then she looked up. 'Auntie Lyndsey, I'll miss Janie. Would you stay with me until I go to sleep?' Connie's voice was tearful then and Lyndsey had difficulty in controlling her own tears.

'Yes, I will, pet, I'll lay beside you.'

She held Connie close. Poor little soul. The two children had probably slept together since Janie was old enough to sleep in a bed. What childish secrets had they shared?

When Connie was asleep Lyndsey crept downstairs. Bette looked at her, worried. 'How did she take it?' Lyndsey repeated what had been said and they both shed a few tears.

Elliott, who had been talking to someone on the phone, came in. 'It was Andrew,' he said. 'He was shocked, he'll phone again tomorrow.' Elliott looked at his watch. 'I must leave soon, Bette. Is there anything else I can do? I'll come again in the morning.'

She said there was nothing else he could do and thanked him. What would they have done without him.

It was seven o'clock when he left leaving a dreadful void. Mrs Petrie called and it was a welcome diversion, then the vicar and his wife arrived and after that there were a number of phone calls. At nine o'clock Bette and Lyndsey decided to go to bed, both dreading Mrs Howard's coming the next morning.

She arrived at eight o'clock just after Bette and Lyndsey had finished their fourth cup of tea. Without a word being said they went into one another's arms and wept together. When they drew apart Mrs Howard said, 'You are not to blame yourself, Mrs Bascony. It was the Lord's will.' Lyndsey thought she had never seen anyone's face so drained of colour.

Bette drew out a chair. 'Sit down, Mrs Howard. I'll make you some breakfast.'

'Thanks, but I couldn't eat anything, Mrs Bascony. How is Connie?'

'Lyndsey told her about her father – she thought it would help – and Connie seems to have accepted that Janie was taken so she would be company for her Dad.'

'How good of you.' Mrs Howard flashed a grateful look at Lyndsey, then thanked Bette for all she had done. 'You've no idea how much it meant to me and my husband to know that the children were so well looked after. We –' She paused and shook her head, unable to control her emotion. The next moment she straightened.

'I'm sorry, it's all been such a shock. I have to be grateful that Connie wasn't taken too. God has been kind in that way.'

'Kind?' Bette queried sadly.

'Yes, Mrs Bascony. God moves in mysterious ways. I don't pretend to understand His motives, but I do know there have been many times when a pattern has emerged.' She paused and wiped the corners of her eyes. 'If one loses faith, one has nothing. When I first heard about Janie I wondered if I was being punished for making her my favourite child, which is a terrible thing for a mother to do, but then I realized that God would never punish me for a thing like that. He's a just God. He allowed my

202

husband to go peacefully at the end. It's a great comfort to me to know that if Janie *had* to die, she'll be with my husband. They were very close. He loved both children, but it grieved him that Janie had to leave home at such a tender age.'

The kitchen door opened and Connie appeared. She had dressed herself and stood a moment clutching at the skirt of her dress, then she said 'Mam' in a choked voice and came running.

'Oh, Connie.' Mrs Howard smoothed back the dark hair. 'It's been awful for you, but we do know that your Dad and Janie will be happy together, don't we?'

Connie nodded then she looked up.

'Mam, I will be going back with you, won't I? You'll need me now you haven't got Dad. I'll look after you.' Mrs Howard looked distressed for a moment then recovered and said they would have to talk about it later.

Mrs Howard was faced with the harrowing task of having to identify Janie. When she got up to go to the hospital and Bette offered to go with her she accepted gratefully.

After they had gone Connie came over to Lyndsey and said earnestly, 'Mam does want me, doesn't she, Auntie Lyndsey?'

Lyndsey found herself comparing Connie with Ann. Both needing love. Connie must have been aware of her mother's greater love for Janie, but she had never showed any jealousy. She had mothered Janie because she wanted to, had loved her.

She said gently, 'I know she'll want you, Connie, but we must wait and see what she says.'

Not long after this Connie decided she had better go and say goodbye to Mrs Petrie and Penny just in case her Mam wanted to leave for home when she got back. Lyndsey made no attempt to stop her.

She busied herself washing up and tidying things away but all the while Janie's dear little face kept intruding.

Would she ever be able to forget the moment when she saw the still form on the grass? Without warning she burst into tears, and it was in this state that Elliott found her.

He folded her in his arms. 'Oh, Lyndsey, my dear. I know how you feel. Come and sit down.'

Lyndsey made an effort to pull herself together. This was only the beginning, there were the next few days to be got over, possibly without Connie, the funeral . . . and afterwards. She realized just how much she would miss the children, and how Bette would miss them more. She had been with them all the time.

'I don't know what Bette will do,' she said. 'We'll have to make some plans.'

Elliott was gentle with her. 'This is the wrong time to make decisions of any kind, Lyndsey. You are both under stress. Don't attempt to make any plans now. Things will work out, you'll see.'

'I wish I had your faith and that of Mrs Howard.'

She repeated what Mrs Howard had said and Elliott shook his head. 'I don't have that kind of faith. Mrs Howard has nursed a dying husband and loses him and her child in one day, yet she feels comforted because she is sure they will be together in another world. I think perhaps that courage comes into it too. Mrs Howard belongs to a certain breed of people.'

'Yes,' Lyndsey said, and hoped that she might learn something in the future from Mrs Howard's faith and courage.

FOURTEEN

Lyndsey came to think of the time of Janie's death and the days following as some of the most emotional she had ever experienced. Connie had gone home with her mother. It was not that Mrs Howard had wanted it, having reasoned that on balance the child was safer staying with Bette than anywhere else, but Connie's pleading and finally her tearful, heartbreaking question, 'Don't you want me at all, Mam?' settled it. Mrs Howard had broken down and taken her in her arms.

After the funeral Bette decided to go and visit a friend at Coventry. 'We worked together in the theatre,' she said. 'I've been promising for ages to go and see her. I'll be back in a few days' time, Lyndsey. It's just, well, I want to get away from the house. I'm sure you'll understand.'

Lyndsey did. The funeral had upset *her* more than she had imagined, and at home that evening she wished there was something more she could do for the war effort to avenge Janie's death.

As it turned out an opportunity came in an unexpected way. She was roused from sleep by the steady drone of planes. The alert was on but she had not bothered to go to the basement shelter. Lyndsey lay listening. There seemed to be an awful lot of activity outside, people shouting. She got up and peeped behind the blackout curtain; then gave a gasp. The street was lit up with the fiendishly beautiful silvery phosphorous sparkle of incendiary bombs. They were everywhere. She pulled on a siren suit, pushed her feet into her shoes and with a fast-beating heart, ran downstairs.

When she opened the front door she came face to face with Fred, one of the wardens. He yelled, 'There's incendiaries on your roof! Tell your uncle.' Brushing past her he made for the stairs. Lyndsey followed, explaining that her uncle and his wife were away.

The incendiaries were cylindrical tubes no more than twelve inches in length, but dropped from the height they were, they easily broke through tiles and wedged themselves in the timbers. Within seconds a fire would start up. One had come through the attic skylight and the floorboards were burning. Lyndsey grabbed the stirrup pump and put out the blaze. Fred, who was already out on the roof, threw sand on one that had lodged in the gutter.

Planes were going over in a steady drone and incendiaries were raining down. Some just clattered into the street but Lyndsey saw one go through the window of a house opposite and something in the room catch fire. Fred had seen it too. He climbed back into the attic then started to run. Lyndsey followed. He shouted to her to go into the shelter but she ignored him. The more incendiaries that could be put out the less blazing targets there would be for the bombers who would follow.

There were more volunteer helpers in the street than Lyndsey had seen anywhere. The ack-ack guns, exploding bombs, the clanging of fire engines' bells, ambulances, men yelling instructions made a deafening noise.

Lyndsey heaved sandbags on incendiaries, threw buckets of water over fires that had started and worked stirrup pumps until she felt her arms would drop off. When she sat on a step for a moment to regain her breath she suddenly thought of Mrs Grey. She ran back to the house and up the stairs shouting 'Mrs Grey, Mrs Grey, get up, at once.'

The woman, who was already out of bed, was pulling a

thick woollen cardigan over her dress. 'What's going on?' she demanded. 'There's enough noise to rouse the dead.'

'And you could be dead if you don't get out of here, now!' She went back down the stairs, with Mrs Grey following, wanting to know if the house was burning down. Lyndsey called, 'Not now, but it could be.'

Mrs Grey worked side by side with Lyndsey and Lyndsey realized just how strong the housekeeper was.

Perhaps because so many fires had been extinguished very few bombs were dropped in the vicinity. It was half past three when the all clear went and Mrs Grey said, 'Come on, let's get inside, I want a cup of tea.'

As she filled the kettle she said in a grudging way to Lyndsey, 'You did very well.'

'So did you, Mrs Grey. I always think if more incendiaries were put out many more lives would be saved.'

Mrs Grey retorted, 'If all the folks who go to shelters stayed at home and their houses were bombed the death rate would shoot up, wouldn't it? The trouble is that these houses are too big; they should be let to folks for flats and at rents they could afford!'

It was Mrs Grey's pet subject and Lyndsey let her rant on, her own satisfaction being that she might have helped to save some buildings that evening, if not lives.

Although Lyndsey dropped into bed exhausted she found it impossible to sleep. Her mind was too full of impressions of movement, of people, voices. When she did sleep her dreams were full of faceless people, but the next morning when she left to go to the Centre she was able to put faces to the voices of the night before. The street was usually quiet when she left but this morning there were groups of people standing around. A man, immaculately dressed, raised his bowler hat and greeted her. 'Good morning, Miss MacLaren. I've just learned your name. How splendid you were last night, you worked like a Trojan. Didn't she, Miss Mancy?'

'Indeed she did.' Miss Mancy was tiny, frail-looking,

with the sweetest of smiles. 'Lovely to meet you, Miss MacLaren. I did enjoy myself last night. I met so many people.'

A big woman, with a booming voice, said 'I thought they were all a snooty lot here, but I changed my mind last night. Enjoyed our little party. Looking forward to our get-together next Wednesday.' She poked Lyndsey on the shoulder. 'You should come. Miss Mancy is holding it.'

'Oh, do,' said Miss Mancy, beaming at her. 'It'll be fun. Seven o'clock. I'm in number twelve.'

Lyndsey thanked her and said she would love to come, then asked to be excused, she had a bus to catch. They all gave her a wave.

As she walked away she marvelled at the change a war could make with relationships. For months she had passed people in the street and although she had half-smiled a greeting they had walked past her. People said they had found a great friendliness in shelters, neighbour helping neighbour. They had sing-songs, concert parties, celebrated birthdays. 'We're just like one big happy family,' declared one woman. 'Wouldn't have missed this experience for the world!'

Richard had phoned while Lyndsey was out to say that he and Marian would be staying a couple of days longer. Mrs Grey said, 'I didn't tell him about the raid, no use worrying folks unnecessarily,' which Lyndsey thought was a definite change of attitude on Mrs Grey's part. Perhaps she was beginning to feel more neighbourly.

On the Thursday evening Bette phoned. She sounded excited. 'I'm back home, Lyndsey, and guess what? I've heard from Andrew that he's coming on leave. Tomorrow. Can you come, he's particularly asked to see you?'

A joyousness flooded through Lyndsey. 'I'll be there.'

She was with Bette on the station platform the following afternoon when Andrew arrived; he dropped his kitbag and came running.

He swept Bette off her feet first, then Lyndsey, but before

he set Lyndsey down he held her to him, saying softly, 'My sweet, darling girl, I can't believe I'm here,' and his voice was not quite steady.

The elderly porter-cum-station master shouted, 'I'll see you get your kitbag, Mr Bascony. Off you go and enjoy yourself.'

'Thanks, Mr Edwards. I have some tobacco for you. See you later.'

The three of them went up the road arm in arm and people came out of houses and shouted greetings and Andrew told each one, 'I'm home for a week, I'll see you,' and they waved and called 'Good luck.'

When they were inside the house a silence came over. Bette said, 'We'll talk about little Janie later. We can at least talk about her now without bursting into tears. We want to hear *your* news, Andrew.'

He talked and talked in a feverish way, then suddenly without warning he was fast asleep in the armchair. Bette put a rug over him saying gently, 'Poor Andrew, he must have been going through hell.'

He roused at ten o'clock and was furious for having slept so long, wasting his precious leave. When Bette went into the kitchen he said to Lyndsey in a low voice, 'Darling, we must spend some time alone together. I want to hold you, love you. Where can we go tomorrow?'

Lyndsey explained that she must go to the Centre the following morning because they were short-handed, but added that she would try and get away a little earlier and he could meet her off the train.

'And what then?' he asked.

Bette came in with a tray saying, 'You two will have to entertain yourselves tomorrow afternoon, I have a bandage-wrapping session. I won't be late back.'

Andrew gave Lyndsey a wicked grin, as though to say what an opportunity. Lyndsey's pulses had leapt when Andrew told her he wanted to love her, knowing that what he meant was to *make* love to her. She longed for love and asked herself why should she deny him. He could go back from leave and be – killed. But her upbringing niggled at her. It was not her mother's voice telling her to behave herself with boys but Ivy's. And Ivy did not mince her words.

'It's the easiest thing to give in to a lad when you're both on heat,' she had said, 'but just you think of the consequences. He could go off and you could find yourself left with a bastard.'

Then she saw Andrew's lovely blue eyes full of pleading and she decided to let things take their course.

He was there waving to her the next afternoon when she got off the train. He hugged her wordlessly for a moment, then led her out of the station. But instead of going in the direction of Bette's he went the opposite way. She looked up at him. 'Where are we going?'

They had taken a right turn and were walking towards a gate that led to a field. He pointed towards some derelict buildings and cottages. 'We're going there. It looks like rain and *we* are going to take shelter, my darling.' He was smiling. 'Bette didn't go out, the bandage-wrapping ladies came to her.'

Lyndsey said, 'Are you sure there aren't people living in the cottages, or that there aren't any animals in the barns?'

'No, I've been to look.'

'You schemer!'

'Of course I am, I'm a man who wants to be alone with his woman.'

Lyndsey felt tremors running through her body at the thought of what could happen and she knew a longing she would never have imagined, an unbearable ache.

Before they reached the first barn it began to rain, big drops, and within seconds it was deluging down. Andrew took her hand and ran with her, laughing joyously. She felt caught up in his mood.

They had reached the barn. Andrew put his shoulder to the stuck door and they fell in and collapsed on a pile of straw. They lay there laughing, then Andrew, his expression serious, pulled off her peaked cap and lay looking at her.

'Oh, Lyndsey, darling, you're so beautiful. The times I've dreamed of a moment like this.' He pulled out a handkerchief and wiped the raindrops gently from her face, then wiped his own. He laid his own cap beside hers, then he began to unbutton her coat. She laid a hand on his, staying him.

'What if someone comes?'

'There's no one near.'

'It's wrong, Andrew.'

'Is it?' He put her hand to the buttons of his tunic and after a moment she began to unbutton them. The raindrops pattering on the roof seemed to keep rhythm with the wild beating of her heart.

When at last he slipped the straps of her cami-knicks from her shoulders and cupped her breast she drew in a quick breath. He pulled off his jacket, tossed it aside, undid his tie and took off his shirt. By this time Lyndsey's blood was on fire.

He buried his face against her neck groaning, 'Oh, my love, I want you – *now*.'

Although a little afraid of the strength of her own feelings Lyndsey wrapped her arms around him and pressed her fingers into his back. She felt a quickening of her pulse as he responded to her touch. Her actual knowledge of the act was limited to what she had been told by other girls when she was at Echo Cove. A fisherman's daughter had once said with a knowing nod, 'I can tell you this, Lyndsey MacLaren, you'll get a surprise the first time you do it with a feller.'

She had omitted to say what the surprise was, but Lyndsey realized now she had been surprised to know that the satiny feel of Andrew's skin could bring a sensual arousal in *her*. He nipped her ear lobes gently between his teeth and she cried out as pulses came to life in every part of her body. Andrew responded by moving his lips over her breasts, her throat, his breath quickening.

Then she became aware of a rustling in the straw, of something moving beneath her, and when she heard a squeaking sound she yelled, 'There's a mouse under me,' and pushed Andrew away. He rolled from her and began to laugh.

'I've heard of some passion dampers,' he declared, 'but never of a mouse!'

'It's not funny.' Lyndsey scrambled up and began to get dressed. 'There are not many things I'm afraid of but I go ice cold when a mouse comes anywhere near me.' She gave a sudden shiver.

Andrew got up and, picking up a bundle of straw, let it shower to the ground. 'There, not a mouse in sight, I should think you scared the hell out of that one!' He took her by the hand and tried to pull her down but Lyndsey resisted, saying, 'Oughtn't you to be getting dressed?' She began putting on her blouse.

'All right, I'll get dressed but don't let us rush away. It's cosy in here, just listen to that rain.'

Andrew, who had all but completed buttoning his shirt, took her by the hand. 'Lyndsey, sweetheart, you know I love you. It's because I love you so much and because you are seldom out of my thoughts when I'm away that I wanted to make proper love to you.' He kissed her gently and she found herself relaxing.

Then suddenly she tensed and stood, head cocked.

'Lyndsey, what is it?'

'There's someone outside. Listen!'

The sound she had heard came again and Andrew gave a shout of laughter. 'It's a cow – coughing! I don't think it's likely to come barging in.'

'But it might not have been a cow,' she protested. 'It could have been a man, a farmer, and what then?'

'I would have died!' Andrew exclaimed. 'Simply died on this *very* spot with fright.' He began to laugh, then Lyndsey

212

was laughing with him. He pulled her down on to the straw where they lay giggling helplessly.

'A coughing cow,' Andrew kept repeating. 'Oh, just wait until I tell the boys.'

Lyndsey sat up, alarmed. 'Oh, Andrew, you won't?'

'I wouldn't say who it was. Oh, darling,' he pulled her back against his shoulder and now he was tender with her, 'I would never make a fool of you. It's just that when we first set off on a mission we're tensed up, we talk a lot, say silly things, think up jokes to tell. Later we settle down. Do you know what I mean?'

She leaned up on her elbow and smoothed a hand over his thick fair hair. 'I'm sorry for making a fuss. Such a trivial thing when there are so many important issues at stake. Sometimes when I think about you setting off on a raid, I feel all curled up inside.'

Andrew said, 'In our quiet moments I often think of Echo Cove. I've never been there, as you know, but I feel I know it through you, the cobbled streets, the harbour, the fishing fleet going out. When this war is over I'm going for a visit.' He knuckled her under the chin. 'You can come with me if you like.'

She felt a sudden pang. Would that opportunity ever come? She said brightly, 'Oh, thank you very much. Perhaps *you* can show *me* the town. I'm sure you know more about it than I do.'

'I know where the church is and the bread shop and the shop where the man used to sell rolls of wallpaper for twopence a roll. And I shall stand in the harbour and shout, "I love Lyndsey MacLaren" and the cliffs will echo my words and everyone in the place will know how I feel about you.'

Lyndsey felt like saying, oh, don't, but she kept silent. Her father had declared his love for her mother in the harbour . . . and now they were both dead.

Andrew nuzzled his cheek against hers. 'I'll have a lot of memories to take back home, but this will always be

213

very special. A stormy afternoon, with a beautiful girl in my arms *and* I'm content not to be making wild and passionate love. And do you know why? Because I've realized that quiet times can be so full of love. And that is what marriage should be. Don't you agree?'

'Yes,' Lyndsey whispered, wanting to cry.

FIFTEEN

It was not until Lyndsey was in bed that evening that she had a chance to think about their time in the barn. She and Andrew had not made love and she had thought then it was perhaps just as well, but now she wondered if it would have been wrong had they done so. Wasn't the physical act of love as true to nature as the elements?

When the rain had died down they had walked home, arms about one another's waists and Andrew had said lovingly, 'We still have nearly a whole week, my darling, and when we do make love it will not be in a barn where mice abound!'

But it seemed they were destined to fail. During the next two days there was no opportunity, and on the following morning when Lyndsey came down for breakfast Andrew received a telegram recalling him to his unit.

'Goddam!' he exclaimed, 'I've hardly arrived on leave.' He folded the telegram and put it in his pocket, adding, 'There's only one reason, there must be something big on.'

Lyndsey felt sick. 'Something big' usually meant heavy casualties.

She never did find out what the action was, but she was only too thankful to learn a few days later that Andrew was all right. He was not his usual self but he did seem to make an effort to be bright. He teased her about the mouse, said it would be something to tell their grandchildren. It worried Lyndsey that all through Andrew seemed to take

215

it for granted that they would marry. She felt she loved him but at the same time was sure there had to be something else to make her long for marriage. Then she thought if she did not want to get married then it was time she stopped letting her emotions carry her away.

Ann had been away from the Centre for a few days and when she returned and Lyndsey told her about the fiasco of Andrew's leave it was lost in Ann's news that Brad and Ed would be in London soon, and were to stay for a while since they had been transferred.

She went on to say she had had a lovely letter from Brad. 'He seems quite taken with me, Lyndsey, and he said that Ed has never stopped talking about you.'

Although Lyndsey knew she would be pleased to see Ed again her mind was too much on Andrew at the moment to concentrate on the two GIs.

The next two times that Andrew phoned Lyndsey was aware of a change in him. She said to Bette, 'I don't think it has anything to do with his flying, he's being cagey, as though there was someone else.'

Bette dismissed it as being imagination and added, 'You must realize the strain he's under – all of them are.' Lyndsey accepted it, but still felt it was not the answer.

Two days after this she met Elliott in Piccadilly. He had hailed a taxi and kept it waiting while he spoke to her. 'I was on my way to see you, Lyndsey. Can I take you home? I have something to tell you.' He seemed unusually happy and she accepted.

On the way he said, 'I feel I've been boorish lately, but there was a reason. When I was wounded some time ago I had a fall and I was knocked unconscious. It affected my eyes. I thought I was going blind.'

'Oh, Elliott, how awful.'

'But half an hour ago I learned that my eyes are all right, and I feel like doing a Highland fling.' He seemed years younger and although she could not imagine Elliott doing a Highland dance she could certainly understand his relief.

'How about celebrating?' he said. 'Would you have dinner with me this evening and perhaps go dancing?'

Lyndsey accepted the invitation, thinking that it might be a most interesting evening, judging by the saucy look in his eyes.

When they arrived home and Lyndsey invited him in he said, 'No, tell Richard and Marian I'll see them some other time.' He paused. 'I want this to be *our* special night, Lyndsey.' The saucy look had been replaced by a seriousness that made her want to catch her breath. He left after saying he would call for her at seven o'clock.

Lyndsey had to catch her breath many times that evening.

When Elliott had talked about dancing she had imagined them waltzing and foxtrotting, perhaps a little sedately, to the Savoy Orpheans' Orchestra, instead of which he took her to a restaurant where, in the cosmopolitan atmosphere, they quickstepped, tangoed, did the conga and jitterbugged, and she loved every minute of it. Lofty had been good at jitterbugging, but Elliott surpassed him and, like many strongly built men, he was amazingly light on his feet.

From the moment they were on the floor their steps synchronized as though they had been dancing partners for months. With right hands held he flung her from him and she whirled back, her skirt flying out. They twisted and spun, kicking out, tapping; he danced around her and she danced around him; he lifted her over his right shoulder, then his left, he slid her between his legs and swung her over one hip and then the other, and she laughed her delight.

After a while people stopped to watch them. One girl said, 'Gosh, what style that man has, what rhythm.'

'What a doll,' exclaimed an American voice, 'what legs!'

When the dance ended and they came off the floor

Lyndsey said, 'Talk about an unknown quantity! *You*, Elliott Warrender, are a perfect example.'

He laughed and dabbed at his brow. 'Would you believe it if I tell you that I came first in a dance championship some years ago? My family wouldn't believe me. Recently I took lessons in jitterbugging. Thought it might come in useful sometime and, well' – he spread his hands – 'here we are.'

'But how did you know that *I* could jitterbug?'

'I just knew it. You were marvellous. I should like to do it again sometime if you – '

'I'd love to.'

The revolving coloured lights flashing across his face softened the strong features. The band had struck up a tango but they made no move, just sat gazing into one another's eyes with Lyndsey wondering how this stern-looking man could convey such tenderness in a look.

Then he stood up and held out a hand and she put hers in his and they went on to the floor. And to the tune of 'Lola' and the sensuous rhythm of the tango she was aware of a fire in him, a passion, and she felt a pleasurable shiver of expectancy run through her as she thought of later, when he would bring her home. After all this love play of eyes and body he could not leave her standing on the doorstep without some show of emotion . . .

But Lyndsey's pleasurable anticipation of a tender love scene between Elliott and herself when he brought her home, ended in chagrin when he kissed her lightly on the cheek and said, 'Thank you again for a lovely evening, Lyndsey. Will you tell Richard I'll give him a call to arrange about an evening out.' He did wait until she had found her key and opened the door but then he left. And did not even turn round to give her a wave.

She stood on the doorstep fuming. 'Of all the infuriating, the insufferable – ' She went inside and slammed the door, switched on the light and threw her coat over the chair by the telephone table.

Elliott Warrender had used her. All he had wanted was someone to share his good news, any other girl would have done. But would she? There was the tender way he had looked at her before they tangoed, and there was the emotion while they danced . . . a sensuality. Had he been afraid to trust himself when he brought her home? She had invited him in, but he had known that Richard and Marian were away.

Well, it was no use speculating. At that moment she didn't care whether she ever saw him again.

When she told Bette about her evening out with Elliott, Bette laughed. 'I always thought there was a bit of a devil in him, but jitterbugging! It just shows you can never really tell with people. Mind you, I admire him for the way he behaved when he brought you home.'

Lyndsey was indignant. 'But, Bette, what a let-down after all the build-up.'

Bette said she ought to be grateful that he had shown her such respect, then added, 'It proves what will-power he has. You were excited and so was he after his good news and the dancing. It's the easiest thing in the world to let your emotions run away with you, but hell at times to control them. And don't you forget it, darling.'

Lyndsey, remembering the incident in the barn with Andrew, felt a flush of guilt steal over her face and was glad when Bette changed the subject by talking about their next show in a fortnight's time. Lyndsey had dropped out of the last two, but she agreed, at Bette's coaxing, to do this particular one.

During the following week Ann asked Lyndsey to come and meet Brad and Ed. She had asked her twice but Lyndsey had made excuses. Now she accepted. And was glad she had, if only to see Ed's heart-warming smile. 'It's great to see you, Lyn, I've been thinking a lot about you.'

Later, when Brad and Ann left to go dancing, as they had done previously, Lyndsey said, 'Now, Ed, tell me more about Hawaii. You've had me dreaming of tulip trees, frangipane and upside-down waterfalls!

'I could tell you some legends,' he said eagerly. 'There's one I particularly like that my mother told us when we were young. It concerns a young couple and a white flower called naupaka.' When Lyndsey said she would love to hear it Ed began:

'This girl and boy were deeply in love, but unfortunately their parents were enemies and they were forbidden to meet. They defied the·order and the boy was then told he was to be sent thousands of miles away across the ocean. They were heartbroken but the boy swore he would come back to the girl. He plucked two white flowers and handed one to her saying, "Wear this next to your heart and have faith that we shall be together again."'

'And did they get together?'

'Yes, but unfortunately only in death. The girl was dying a slow death pining for him and in the end she cast the flower into the ocean. It travelled to the boy and he, guessing what had happened, killed himself so they could be together.'

'Oh, but Ed, that's terribly sad,' Lyndsey protested.

'I think it's beautiful,' he replied softly. 'They were reunited. And I think the really beautiful part of it is that when the flowers bloomed again, it looked as if two of them had been joined together. And they still have that appearance.'

'Now I feel like weeping,' she said.

'Then I shall tell you something more cheerful . . .'

Although Lyndsey enjoyed the evening it worried her a little that Ed at times looked at her with an expression almost of devotion in his eyes. But he still made no attempt to kiss her when he brought her home.

In the middle of the following week Elliott phoned and asked Lyndsey out to dinner for the next evening. She guessed it was to apologize for his abrupt behaviour and although she would have liked to refuse, still feeling piqued about his treatment, she agreed.

There was no dancing that evening. Elliott told her over dinner that he was being posted abroad, then after a short pause said, 'I wanted you to know that I'm in love with you, Lyndsey. I did hesitate about telling you, then I remembered my father once saying to me, "Never stumble over obstacles, my boy, tackle them head on or you'll never get anywhere." '

'And I suppose I am the "obstacle" in this case?'

'Yes, Lyndsey, you are, because I don't know how you feel about me.'

'I – I don't know. There have been times when I felt I was in love with you, but you've never given me a chance to get to know you. We haven't had any real conversation, – not a meaningful one.'

When he looked at her puzzled she told him about Ed, about the talks they had had. She told him the legend of the flower and added, 'He's a shy person but he has this feeling for beauty in him. I know you can dance, Elliott, know you can be fun, but that's all.'

Elliott was silent for a moment then he looked at her, his expression sad. 'I think you've answered my question, Lyndsey, you don't love me.'

She stared at him, bewildered. 'I'm not in love with Ed, if that's what you're thinking.'

'No, it's because you said you didn't know me. When I first met you I knew at once that you were the only girl for me. But I didn't know a thing about you.'

'So! Elliott Warrender decides that Lyndsey MacLaren does not love him and that's it! End of scenario. You'd make a rotten director. Films have to end happily.'

'And how would you end it?' he asked quietly.

'Well, there has to be a lot of obstacles before hero and heroine get together . . .'

A smile played around Elliott's lips. 'Such as the man going to war, not knowing if the girl loves him and tortures

221

himself through all the shell blast and bombs dropping, thinking of her in other men's arms, dancing, laughing, having fun. I'm sure that is what the film would show.'

'Ah, yes, but when she got home the mask would fall and we would see her weeping, not knowing whether she should write and tell him that she really does love him. It's pride, up to then, that has prevented her.' Lyndsey was beginning to enjoy herself.

'So, what does she do?' Elliott was openly laughing now. 'She can't write and tell him she loves him because that would end the film too soon.'

'Oh, she would write, but then she would tear the letter up. She's very dedicated to this pride stuff.'

'Poor hero. I could write and tell you about my life. Not all of it, of course, because then you might never fall in love with me.'

'I have a bit of a weakness for villains,' she said softly.

'Then I seem to be your man.' He was serious now. 'If I wrote to you, Lyndsey, would you write in return?'

'Yes, I would, Elliott.'

They were silent for a while and Lyndsey wondered if he was thinking, as she was, about their coming parting.

When he brought her home he kissed her with a lingering gentleness and then with a mounting passion. But before Lyndsey responded he drew away and touched her cheek.

'Take care of yourself, Lyndsey.'

'And you – God bless. I will write, I promise.'

This time he turned to raise a hand in farewell and she felt a lump come into her throat. There were so many partings these days, and for so many people. When would this wretched war end?

The raids continued, some concentrated on London and others over a wider area. Although there were some rural areas that hardly knew there was a war on, they were the exception. Every industrial city suffered attacks, some worse than others, and all the ports were constantly being bombed. The East End docks, which had already taken a battering, were still being pounded. But at least the Luftwaffe were not getting their own way. Now Germany was beginning to suffer for the RAF's day and night attacks.

In the middle of October bad weather brought a welcome lull, then on a full moon night the Luftwaffe came over in waves, causing heavy casualties, and it was the weekend following this when Lyndsey had been run off her feet at the Centre, helping to deal with the homeless, that she learned from Bette that Andrew had another girl.

For a moment she was unable to speak and Bette said gently, 'I know it does happen, and we can blame war. Men need solace, they're lonely, but I somehow didn't imagine it of Andrew. But there, every man has his weakness.'

'And every girl,' Lyndsey said. 'One minute I would feel myself to be in love with Andrew and the next with Elliott. Perhaps this is my punishment for wanting both to love me.'

'No, Lyndsey, don't ever say that. You're young, you could be in love, or think you're in love with a few more men. It's a natural thing. Andrew said he didn't want to talk to you because he couldn't bear to hear the hurt in your voice. He did say he would never forget you. And said he still loved you.'

Lyndsey looked up. 'Could he have got a girl into trouble?'

Bette shook her head. 'It did occur to me, but I felt somehow he would have told me. I don't know what to think. We'll go out this evening, cheer ourselves up.'

Lyndsey agreed but knew there was nothing that would cheer her. At first she was deeply hurt, then angry. She *could* have been pregnant. It was all talk with Andrew about being so much in love with her. Well, she would simply have to put him out of her mind, which she knew even as she thought it, would be impossible.

Then, as though fate had decreed she had not suffered

enough she had to face an upset over Ann's odd behaviour. A letter from Ed asked her if she could meet him on her own at Lyons' Corner House. It was important.

She thought of all possibilities, that Ed was going to be posted abroad; that he was going to propose to her; that he had had bad news from home, but nothing prepared her for Ed telling her that Ann had been saying terrible things about her.

He had the bewildered hurt look of a dog who had been punished for no reason.

'Tell me these things aren't true,' he begged. 'She told me you had called me a stupid oaf, that you thought I was good for a laugh and nothing else, that I helped to pass an evening.'

Lyndsey stared at him, stunned. 'Ann said those things? I can't believe it.'

'It's true, I swear it. I didn't want to believe it, Lyn, but she spoke as if it was the truth. She told me she was warning me not to trust you.'

Lyndsey shook her head. 'How could you believe her, Ed? Did you honestly think I would say such things?'

He looked utterly miserable now. 'I didn't want to, and I probably wouldn't have done had I been . . . well, clever, but – '

'Ed, I think you are one of the nicest people I've ever met,' Lyndsey said gently. 'I've enjoyed our evenings, every one. I don't know what's made Ann behave in such a way. I shall certainly have it out with her.'

'She would deny it, she told me she would if I told you. She kept saying it was to protect me from you.'

'There *has* to be a reason, Ed. Can you think of anything?'

He said no at first, then after some thought he looked up. 'There could be. The other night Brad said to me in a joking way that he must get it across to Ann that he was not in the running for the marriage stakes. Supposing he had told her this and – ' Ed shook his head, 'But that would be no reason for taking it out on you.'

Yes it would, Lyndsey thought, and could see the pattern now. Since knowing Brad Ann had at times lived in a seventh heaven, seeing herself a bride and going out to live in the States with him after the war. Lyndsey had warned her not to get too carried away, that Brad could be moved and she might never see him again. Ann had turned on her, told her she was not the only one who could get boyfriends . . . it was the first time Lyndsey realized that Ann might be jealous of her friendship with Andrew and Elliott.

She told Ed about Ann's love for her mother and the tragedy of her father's death, adding, 'Ann needs to be loved. I must remember that, and make allowances.'

Ed warned her not to make too many allowances because Ann could cause her harm, but although he suggested that the two of them start meeting on their own, Lyndsey thought they ought to go on with the foursome, for the time being at any rate. Her main reason for this was that she did not want to meet Ed on his own in case she became more deeply involved.

They were so busy at the Centre the next few days it was easy to avoid Ann, but one day she caught Lyndsey and said, 'How about meeting Brad and Ed this evening? Brad said they would be at our usual meeting place.' Lyndsey agreed, thinking to herself that if Ann caused any unpleasantness then it would be the last time.

She was all right at first but then Ed made some simple remark and she said with a sneer, 'At what age did you leave school, boy? Ten?'

Lyndsey flared. '*You* might think you're very clever, Ann, but I'm sure you're the only one who does think so!'

The sneer was still on her lips when Brad said, 'Hear, hear, I couldn't agree with you more!'

Ann looked at him startled, then she became distressed.

225

'I was only joking, I didn't mean it. It was just fun, *really* it was.'

'Right!' Brad said, 'but remember this, we don't like those kind of comments. Ed's my best friend and he's a great guy. They don't come any better.'

She looked so contrite he added, 'Okay, okay, no need to bawl.'

Ann was so different then it was impossible to believe she had said such awful things. And Brad, in spite of not wanting to be caught up in the 'marriage stakes', was loving towards her, teasing her.

When the two of them had gone dancing Ed looked at Lyndsey and spread his hands. 'Could that sweet girl be the same one who told me such lies? She must have a double personality.'

'Yes,' Lyndsey said, and made up her mind she was not prepared to make any more excuses for Ann's behaviour. She wanted to be free of her.

Although Lyndsey knew she would not be accepted for the Wrens until she had reached her eighteenth birthday at Christmas she decided she would put in an application. It would be a start.

SIXTEEN

They were so busy at the Centre the next day it was easy to avoid Ann, but the following day Ann told her, 'I heard from Brad this morning that he and Ed are to be posted abroad. They're leaving tomorrow. He asks that we all meet this evening at the usual time, okay?'

Lyndsey wondered with a feeling of sadness how many more people were to go out of her life? . . . First Andrew, then Elliott, and now Ed.

She had tried hard to make excuses for Andrew's behaviour. They had not been engaged, nor had any promises been made, but when she thought of Andrew's words in the barn, when he said he had realized that quiet times could be so full of love, and afterwards mentioned about marriage, she could not make the excuses seem real.

But would she have agreed to marry Andrew if he had asked her outright to marry him? She had to admit she would have said no, she was not yet ready for marriage.

Elliott had kept his promise to write and tell her about his life but although the tone of his letter was light she sensed a lack of parental love in his life and a loneliness. He wrote of being sent to England to a boarding school at a very early age, and although he made no mention of a boy's homesickness at being so far away from home, it became apparent when he spoke with a warmth of spending his vacations with his uncle and aunt on their farm.

'I enjoyed being with the animals, Lyndsey, riding on

the hay cart, so many things, but mostly it was the feeling of freedom.'

He talked about his wilder days as he grew up but although he tried to give the impression of having had a wonderful time there was still that underlying feeling of something missing in his life.

She had written back, telling him as much as was permissible in letters that were censored. She told him about Bette and the members of her concert party who were wanting to join ENSA and added, 'It would get them further afield, perhaps abroad, which I think would be good for Bette.'

Lyndsey did not tell him that Bette was finding it hard to get over little Janie's death, nor did she tell him about Andrew. She mentioned Richard and Marian, how they would be home together for a while and then one or the other would be away again.

For a concluding humorous note, she told him she was working out a 'scenario' for their 'big film' and said there were so many twists and turns in it to get hero and heroine together that she might have to make a serial of it.

Elliott had signed himself 'yours affectionately', so she used 'affectionately' too when she signed her letter.

When Lyndsey and Ann arrived at Lyons' Corner House that evening Brad was smiling, but Ed had a sadness in his eyes. He said to Lyndsey, 'I'm going to miss you terribly, Lyn. You've been great.'

'Hey, cheer up,' Brad said, 'it's not the end of the world. We'll be back sometime – I hope.'

They had a meal together then Ann said to Brad, 'Well, are we going to our favourite ballroom for a final fling?'

Brad said, 'Yeah, yeah,' and got up. He kissed Lyndsey before they left then whispered, 'Ed needs cheering up. Been nice knowing you, Lyn, we'll be back again soon, I'm sure of it.'

Ann just called goodbye to Ed and then they left.

Ed sat for a while looking at Lyndsey then he brought

out a small box and held it out saying it was just a small gesture of the happy times they had spent together.

Lyndsey lifted out an oval silver locket that would pin to a dress. 'Open it,' he said. She had expected to find a photograph of him inside but instead saw a white flower that looked as if it had been cut in half.

When she looked up and said, 'Oh, Ed . . .' she saw tears in his eyes. He laid a hand over hers.

'Please don't think I intended it to be like the legend, Lyn. I just thought if you had one half you might think of me sometimes. I have the other half, but I will never need to be reminded of you.'

Lyndsey felt so choked it was impossible to answer. She was aware of the murmur of voices around them, the different accents. Brad had once said that the restaurant had become like a home to them, and she knew that it would always hold a special place in her heart.

'Thanks, Ed,' she said softly. 'I shall treasure it always.'

He ordered a bottle of wine and tried to instil a feeling of lightness into the evening, but they were both very much aware of their coming parting. When he brought her home he took her in his arms and kissed her gently. And she clung to him and begged him to take care of himself. They repeated their promises to write to one another and then he was gone.

Lyndsey cried herself to sleep that night, cried with the ache of loss and cried for Ed too, who was so unhappy.

The next morning when Ann came into the Centre she looked like a little ghost. Lyndsey, concerned, said, 'Are you ill, Ann?'

'Depends on what you mean by ill,' she retorted. 'Brad, it seems, had no intention of marrying me. Oh, he liked me, he said, he liked me a lot, but – ' Ann started to walk away saying, 'Well, at least it will give you something to gloat over.'

Lyndsey caught her by the arm. 'Stop that, Ann, you know perfectly well I wouldn't gloat.'

'Yes, well, perhaps not,' she admitted in a grudging tone, then added, a sudden defiant look in her eyes, 'But you needn't worry, I won't lose any sleep over him!'

And apparently Ann had not lost any sleep because when she arrived the following morning she was all merry and bright.

'Guess what? I'm leaving here and going north. I have an aunt who runs a boarding house in Newcastle. I phoned her last night and she said she could do with some help. She boards naval officers.' Ann laughed. 'I'll help all right, help myself to a handsome officer. It should be great fun.'

Three days later Ann left without saying goodbye to anyone. At first Lyndsey thought it was a good thing she had gone, but afterwards she was surprised at how much she missed her. Ann had always been at the Centre to chat to; they went to the cinema together and spent odd evenings at Ann's flat, listening to the wireless. And Ann had been responsible for them getting to know Brad and Ed.

The days went by in a meaningless sort of way, there were raids, some lighter than others, then there was a lull at the end of October and it was strange not to hear the ack-ack guns, the bombs exploding, sirens going. But in the second week of November Coventry had a very heavy raid. How heavy was not really known until news began to filter through by word of mouth. Lyndsey heard about it when she went to visit Bette that weekend and found Bette's friend Mary from Coventry staying with her – to get a rest.

Mary described the raid, the fires that could be seen for miles around, the dreadful devastation. A large portion of the city was destroyed, including their lovely cathedral, only the spire remaining. Hundred of people had been killed and many more injured. She said she had gone into Coventry that day to do some shopping and had called on a friend. When the bombing started they went to a shelter – but that was bombed.

'We were running to find another shelter when we had the most terrifying experience. We found ourselves fleeing from what seemed to be a river of burning oil, but learned later was butter from a factory. We just managed to escape by running up some steps of a church, but one man was caught in it. Oh, dear, I'll hear his screams to my dying day.'

Bette and Lyndsey said how dreadful, then Mary went on to say there had been no gas, no electricity, and no water. The bombing had continued night after night, as though Hitler had been determined to raze Coventry to the ground in revenge for the RAF's bombing of Bremen, his favourite city, where the Nazi party had been born and flourished.

Thousands left the city each night, Mary said, seeking a place away from the continual bombardment. Some would pay half a crown a night to sleep on a bus – or on the floor of a cottage or barn, and many had to sleep out in the woods. And many found they had no homes to come back to the next morning.

Bette said quietly, 'And Mary has lost her home too.'

Mary nodded, 'Yes, but although I came here in a sort of desperation I'm going back after the weekend. Yes I am!' There was a fierce note in her voice. 'There'll be something I can do. Hitler won't get *us* down, we'll build again – *and* again if necessary!'

Mary went back to Coventry on the Sunday afternoon and Lyndsey said to Bette after she had gone, 'Such courage, it puts me to shame. I was upset because I felt I was losing so many friends.' She told her about Ed, then after a pause she asked hopefully, 'Any more word from Andrew?'

Bette hesitated for so long before replying Lyndsey knew she had and knew it was not good. 'Tell me,' she said.

'I had a letter from him yesterday. You were right, he had got a girl into trouble. They were married two days ago. I'm sorry, Lyndsey.'

'It's all right. I'm glad I know, so I can stop thinking that some miracle might happen and – Oh, well, it wasn't to be. I have a terrible bleak feeling at the moment, yet I ought not to, because I really didn't want to get married. I didn't, Bette. I felt there was so much to do, I mean it, I really do – '

Lyndsey suddenly burst into tears and Bette held her, soothing her.

When Lyndsey was calm they talked about it. 'The girl is a nurse,' Bette said. 'He had only known her a week. I have a feeling he knows he's made a big mistake, although he hasn't said so in so many words. There must be hundreds of cases like this.'

Lyndsey told her then about the afternoon in the barn. 'I'm telling you, Bette, because I realized how easy it is to make love. Andrew was so lovely, teasing me, gentle, tender. I'm not going to say that we wouldn't have made love some other time, because I feel sure we would have done. It's circumstances, the war, the partings, you feel you must experience everything in case you never have the chance again. And I can't blame Andrew for what has happened. I only wish – No,' Lyndsey shook her head, 'it's no use wishing, I can't change anything.'

'I'm glad you've told me,' Bette said gently. 'I felt bitter towards Andrew because he had said so many times how much he loved you. I'm glad to know that he didn't try and talk you into making love. And now,' she said, 'I think we had better get on to something else.'

They talked about many things that weekend. Bette said she thought she had learned all there was to know about people in her stage career, but since coming to live in Kent she had found another world.

'A domestic world, Lyndsey, a home life, something I had never known, where women talk about recipes, their children, schooling, sewing. I had never ever been aware of a sunrise or a sunset and had never seen the exquisite beauty of a raindrop on a cobweb in a shaft of sunlight. Oh, so many things.'

Lyndsey felt deeply moved because these were things she had taken for granted when she lived at Echo Cove. It had not occurred to her either until then just how hurt Bette had been over Andrew. She had once said he was like the son she had never had. Lyndsey talked about Elliott, his letter, and how she felt he had missed so much in his life. Bette said she had the impression when they were talking the afternoon they went to the theatre that his father had been a strict disciplinarian, and added that Elliott had told her, laughing, that he must have had more beltings than fifty boys put together.

'Poor Elliott,' Lyndsey said.

She went back to London on the Monday morning with many things on her mind.

As the weeks went by the talk was of Christmas. There had been no rationing the year before but this one was very different. In fact, some women had started saving small portions from their meagre rations in the summer so they could make their Christmas cakes and puddings. And when shops had a supply of dried fruit they queued for hours; but in many cases the fruit ran out before everyone could be supplied.

There were not as many toys in the shops as the year before, but even then people who had lost everything in the bombing could not afford to buy them. Centres appealed for secondhand toys and books and games and they came in sackfuls. Some fathers fashioned toys for their children with wood from the demolition, forts, dolls houses, prams and small wheelbarrows (when wheels were available). Women made rag dolls and dressed them from scraps.

Very few holly trees showed berries that Christmas, the result, it was thought, of the previous severe winter. People improvised, making tiny berries from small pieces of red cloth, others painting leaves with Epsom salts dissolved in water, which gave the effect of frost.

Then from America came a shipload of parcels to be distributed to those people most in need. To the Centre where Lyndsey worked were sent turkeys from a big estate and everyone was full of glee that the bombed-out people would be able to enjoy the traditional Christmas dinner.

The volunteers at the Centre wanted to decorate the hall with paper chains but no coloured tissue paper was available. One woman said she would ask God for some, and the next day a batch came from a newsagent who said he had found it when clearing his attic.

When Lyndsey asked the woman, in a joking way, if she would send up a prayer for some oranges and apples the gentle reply came that she could not be too greedy, perhaps someone else should ask. Whether anyone did was not known, but oranges and apples were delivered the next day. Lyndsey said to Bette that weekend, 'And I had lost all faith in God!'

It was Lyndsey's birthday on Christmas Eve and this had caused some difficulty over arrangements for the holiday. She had been invited with Richard and Marian to spend Christmas with Marian's family, but Lyndsey had refused to go.

'I can't,' she said, 'I've promised to help with the parties at the Centre. Bette has volunteered too. I have asked her to stay.'

'But your birthday,' Richard protested, 'we must celebrate it together.'

It had taken a great deal of persuasion on Lyndsey's part to get Richard to agree to celebrate it some other time.

'So that is settled,' she told Bette over the phone. 'Richard and Marian will be leaving the day before Christmas Eve, so come over when you're ready.'

'Lovely! I'm looking forward to it. I'll let you know what time I'll be arriving. Don't work too hard.'

There had been so many people who had volunteered to

help at the Centre with the decorations and the parties that Lyndsey had waited until Richard and Marian had gone before going upstairs to get ready. She was coming down again when the phone rang. She thought it would be Bette to say what time she would be arriving, but it was Mrs Petrie. Lyndsey gave a small shiver of apprehension.

'Hello, Mrs Petrie, is – is Bette all right?'

'No, I'm afraid she isn't, Lyndsey, that's why I'm ringing. She was taken ill late last night and had to be rushed to the hospital. It was appendicitis. She was operated on right away and thank goodness she's all right. She was able to ask me to get in touch with you.'

'Thanks, Mrs Petrie. I'll let the Centre know I won't be coming in then I'll pack some things and catch the first train I can. 'Bye for now.'

Lyndsey stood a moment. Appendicitis? Bette had not complained of any pain. But then, being Bette she wouldn't. What about food? She had better take something with her.

She had packed a bag and was ready to leave when the front doorbell rang. The paper boy for his Christmas box? No, Richard would have dealt with it. She hurried to the door.

When she opened it she stood staring in utter bewilderment.

'Elliott! What on earth – you were abroad – '

'That's right.'

Lyndsey rubbed her brow. 'I don't know what to say, I was just leaving, but come in a moment. I can't gather my wits together. You were the last person I expected to see. I've just had a phone call about Bette.'

She explained what had happened and he asked, concerned, if it would help if he drove her to Kent. She said it would, it would help a lot, and they could talk on the way.

In the car she told him about the phone call. 'I saw Bette last weekend. She looked pale, but then she has been since Janie's death. She showed no signs of having any pain, but then I'm not there all the time. She was coming to stay with me over Christmas. Tell me about you. When did you come back?'

'I was flown back yesterday. I was promoted, Lieutenant Colonel.'

'Well, congratulations.'

'Lyndsey, I do hope you don't feel I'm intruding. I thought I would call and see Richard. No, that's not entirely true. I wanted to see you too. I'm only sorry it's under such unhappy circumstances. But fortunately Bette has been operated on.'

Lyndsey would have liked to know where he had been abroad, but she also knew he would not have told her, everything had to be hush-hush. There were posters all over the place saying, 'Walls have ears', 'Careless talk costs lives', 'Be like Dad, keep mum'. This last one had upset the womenfolk, who felt they were being denigrated. Then there were posters all over showing Hitler, hand cupped behind a large ear listening to two men talking. It was also an offence for a civilian to offer drinks to soldiers in pubs.

Once out of London they encountered a lot of army lorries and Lyndsey realized just how many young ATS girls were driving the heavy vehicles. It set her wondering how long she would have to wait after Christmas before knowing if she would be accepted for the Wrens.

Elliott asked about Richard and Marian and Lyndsey told him about them being away and why she had not gone with them, adding, 'It must have been fate that I didn't go, I would have been grieved not to be with Bette at such a time.'

It occurred to her then to wonder what Elliot had planned for Christmas. When she asked him he said, 'Well, nothing really. I didn't know until the last minute that I would be going home. I do have some very close friends I could go to in Dorset but at the moment I'm only too pleased I'm able to take you to see Bette.' After a pause he said, 'What about her nephew Andrew? Will he be able to visit her, do you think?'

Lyndsey clenched her fists. 'I doubt it, he got married, to a nurse. He's in Scotland.' And as though wanting to torture herself she went on, 'Did I tell you that Ed the American and his friend had been posted abroad? No, of course not, that was recent too.' She nearly followed this by telling him about Ann leaving but stopped herself in time. And because she felt she must go on talking to get rid of her feeling of self-pity she told him about the parties at the Centre on Christmas Day, saying, 'I think we shall end up with as many helpers as guests.'

'Well, far better too many than too few. Let us hope the bombing will cease over Christmas and that there will be a truce like there was in the trenches in the First World War.'

'It's what everyone is praying for,' Lyndsey said, 'but thousands of people are not prepared to risk it, they're holding their festivities in the shelters. When I travelled on the Underground yesterday it was all brightened up with decorations and Christmas trees. I thought it quite sad at first, but then I heard people talking at the Centre about how much they were looking forward to it. One elderly lady told me she had spent the last two Christmases on her own, then said, "And now, just look at the lovely big family I'll be with!" '

After a moment's silence Elliott gave a nod. 'Yes, I don't think we realize how many lonely people there are in the world. I've met them in the services. I remember one man who had lived with his widowed mother since he was a child, and when she died he was lost. We were able to get him involved with leisure activities and he changed. When I last saw him he told me he was getting married. A normally shy man, but who that day was positively beaming.'

Lyndsey told him then about the people she had met during the evening she had been helping to put out incendiaries. 'There were three I had never spoken to before, yet they lived in the same street. They invited me to a little get-together the following week. I couldn't stay long, I was meeting Ann, but I found it very rewarding. They were all lonely people who, because of that particular raid, had found friends.'

Elliott laughed. 'We had better be careful or we'll be carrying banners saying, "Let Us Have More Wars And Make Friends".'

'Heaven forbid,' Lyndsey declared fervently. 'About the wars, I mean.' In the next breath she said, 'I wonder how Bette is?'

They arrived at Mrs Petrie's to find her just coming out. She stared at seeing Elliott. 'Well, Major Warrender, what a surprise. I didn't expect to see you!' To Lyndsey she added, 'I was just going to see to the fire next door, I put it on this morning. Come on in and I'll make you a hot drink, then you can go to the hospital.'

She told them on the way how she had been sitting with Bette the night before, talking, when the pains had suddenly begun.

'Excruciating they were, I could see. She had had some pain before but nothing like this. I phoned the doctor and he was here in minutes. He phoned for an ambulance and Bette was whisked away. They operated on her at once, and a good job they did or else . . .'

Mrs Petrie busied herself getting out the key. 'But there, I mustn't go on about the drama of it, we have plenty in our lives. I was told she was as well as could be expected. Oh, don't look so worried, Lyndsey, it's the standard answer when someone has just had an operation.'

In spite of this Lyndsey *did* worry because she knew Mrs Petrie was upset by the quick way she went on talking. She told them about Bette's cat having died two days before, but asked them not to mention it when they saw her because she had been putting on a bright face. Then she said, 'I've fed the goldfish and the canaries and told

238

the milkman to leave some milk. She had cancelled it, you see, because of thinking she would be staying with you.'

'You've done marvellously well, Mrs Petrie,' Lyndsey said gently. 'very well indeed. You've been a good friend to Bette and I know how she values your friendship.'

'She's been a good friend to me, Lyndsey. I'll go and put the kettle on.'

When she had gone Elliott said in a low voice, 'Bette told me once on the phone what a marvellous person she was.'

Lyndsey looked at him in surprise. 'You and Bette talked – on the phone?'

'Yes, we did, at times.'

'Bette didn't say anything.'

'I didn't think she would.' A faint smile touched his lips. 'It was you we talked about, mostly.'

At any other time Lyndsey might have had more to say, but under the present circumstances she let it go. She was wondering whether she would be allowed to see Bette if she went to the hospital, when Mrs Petrie came in with the tray and answered her unspoken question.

'Normally, no visitors would be allowed in until this evening, Lyndsey, but I feel sure they would let you see her for a moment because she was so distressed when she came out of the anaesthetic, wanting you to be told she would not be coming to London. I went with her to the hospital and left my name and address. When I phoned this morning the nurse asked if I knew you and could get in touch. The rest you know. Oh, no, I didn't tell you she's in Fairley hospital. The buses are fairly erratic but perhaps the Major . . .'

Elliot said yes of course he would take Lyndsey, and added that he would wait outside.

Before they left, Lyndsey told Mrs Petrie about Elliott's promotion and Mrs Petrie, with a flash of the humour she so often showed, got up and did a salaam to him. They all laughed, which eased the tension.

239

When they arrived at reception and Lyndsey mentioned the situation she was told to go up to the ward and explain it to one of the nurses. The nurse said, 'Oh, yes, Miss MacLaren, you can see Mrs Bascony for a few minutes but I don't want her to do any talking. You might find her sleepy, but if she sees you she might settle better.'

Bette's eyes were closed when they came up to the bed. Normally she had the lovely creamy skin that so often goes with red hair but she had an unhealthy pallor this morning and her hair looked dull. As though becoming conscious of someone near she opened her eyes. For a moment they lacked recognition then she whispered, 'Lyndsey,' and made an attempt to draw herself up. The nurse admonished her gently, 'Now just you behave yourself, Mrs Bascony. Here is your friend to see you, but let her do the talking and only for a couple of minutes.'

Bette held out her hand and there were tears in her eyes as she whispered, 'Lyndsey – of all things to happen.'

Lyndsey bent to kiss her. 'I've come to stay and I can visit you this evening. You're not to worry.'

'You'll be alone–'

'No, I have company.' She told her briefly of Elliott's arrival and added, 'I have a feeling he would like to stay. Would that be all right?' Lyndsey smiled. 'I could ask Mrs Petrie to chaperone us.'

Although Bette was so weak her pleasure was apparent. 'Lovely, I'm so glad. I feel tons better for that bit of news.' The nurse came up and Lyndsey said, 'Bette, I must go, time's up, but I'll come this evening and bring Elliott.' She kissed her gently, 'Now you do as you're told.'

Before Lyndsey left Bette had closed her eyes again.

Elliott was waiting in reception when she came down and she noticed that it was not only the receptionist who was casting sidelong glances at him, but one or two nurses who were passing. And Lyndsey herself felt a tremor go through her when he came forward with a questioning smile. He was certainly a man to command attention, not only for his good looks, but his whole bearing, a man among men. She held up crossed fingers.

'I think she's going to be all right, Elliott. She was worried at first about my being alone, but then I told her that you had arrived and I sensed then that all her worry had lifted.' They went out and walked towards the car and after a moment's hesitation Lyndsey said, 'To set Bette's mind at rest I told her that you might like to stay, but of course, if you—'

'I should like to stay very much,' he said quietly. 'As I told you, I had made no arrangements.'

'Oh, good, then that's settled.' Lyndsey tried to speak casually, because now she knew he *would* stay strange things were happening to her body. She added quickly, 'I'm sure Mrs Petrie will come and sleep in.'

Elliott glanced at her, smiling. 'Spoilsport!'

Oh, dear, Lyndsey pressed her palms together tightly to control the wanton thoughts that the single word had provoked. It showed what was in Elliott's mind too.

Lyndsey was silent as they drove away from the hospital. Seeing a derelict barn across the fields had brought Andrew vividly to her mind. Did other girls' bodies betray them as hers was doing? It was not so very long ago that she had been longing for Andrew to make love to her and now it was Elliott she wanted.

She could not blame it on a feeling of loneliness, her life was too busy for that, but she had known an aloneness since she had lost her parents and grandparents. It could be a natural longing to belong to someone.

She decided, however, that whatever it was she would have to stifle such feelings. Look what had happened to the girl Andrew had married . . .

SEVENTEEN

They had driven quite a way in silence when Elliott said suddenly, 'Lyndsey, I do have my ration books with me, but I realize how meagre the rations are. Is there somewhere we can eat out?'

Lyndsey explained she had brought food with her and added that Bette would have the food in the house she had been planning to bring with her when she came to stay. She smiled. 'I don't think we'll starve.'

By the time they arrived back a few snowflakes were drifting about. 'A white Christmas perhaps?' she queried. 'It would be lovely, wouldn't it?'

When they opened the door a delicious smell of cooking greeted them. Mrs Petrie called from the kitchen, and said as they came in, 'I thought you would be hungry. How is Bette?'

'Sleepy, which was natural, but she talked to me and was pleased to know about Elliott. I think we shall see a bigger improvement this evening.' Lyndsey paused then said, 'Mrs Petrie, I wondered if you would, well' – she smiled – 'stay overnight? We can't have the neighbours talking while Bette's away, can we?'

Mrs Petrie beamed from one to the other and all but clapped her hands. 'It's just the excuse I need to get out of the house. I know I grumble about my relatives but this time they've really been the end. They've not helped at all with the housework, nor with the Christmas preparations, so they can get on with it. I'll make up a couple of beds later.' She opened the oven door. 'I'm not cooking anything exciting, but I think you'll find it tasty. I've made a pie from one of those tins of American sausage meat. The fat on top of them makes lovely pastry.'

The meal *was* delicious and Elliott praised it and said he wished there was something he could contribute to the Christmas. Lyndsey asked him if he had such a thing as a cigar and when he said he had she told him if he smoked one after the dinner the next day then it really would seem like Christmas.

It was something she remembered from her childhood. Christmas was the only time she saw her father smoke a cigar and she loved the aroma.

It was not until they were clearing the meal away that Lyndsey wondered about Penny. When she asked where she was Mrs Petrie looked sad. 'She's all right, or at least she will be. *She* had to have a small operation and the vet decided to have her stay with him for a day or two to make sure she was all right. She's *such* a miss, but I can see her tomorrow.'

They had a lazy afternoon with Mrs Petrie talking about her life, Lyndsey talking about Echo Cove and Elliott listening, with interest. At six o'clock they made preparations to leave to go to the hospital. Mrs Petrie, who had been asked to go with them, said, 'Perhaps another evening. Let this be your time with Bette.' She handed her a parcel. 'Will you give this to her, she knows what it is and' – She took another small parcel from the table and held it out – 'happy birthday, Lyndsey dear, this is just a small gift but given with love.'

'Why, Mrs Petrie, how kind.' There were three fine lawn handkerchiefs, the initial L hand-embroidered on the corners. Lyndsey gave her a hug. 'Thank you so much, bless you.'

Elliott said, 'Why didn't you tell me it was your birthday, Lyndsey?'

She turned to him. 'Shall I tell you something, Elliott? Until this moment I had forgotten it. I'll go and get my coat.'

She had to make an excuse to get away for a moment because memories of other Christmases spent with her family had come flooding back, making her emotional. When she came down again she had her tears under control.

Mrs Petrie was saying to Elliott, 'Now mind how you go in the blackout. I'll have a hot drink ready for you both when you come back. Give Bette my love.' To Lyndsey she added, 'Don't forget the flowers!'

It was strange driving in the dark countryside with the headlights masked. Lyndsey said, 'It was a good job we came in daylight so you had some idea of the road.' Elliott said it was and after that they spoke very little.

To the surprise of both of them, Bette, who was sitting up in bed, looked almost like her old self. She gave them a broad smile and held out a hand to each. 'Elliott, what a lovely surprise. Sit down, both of you. Oh, Lyndsey, flowers, thanks.'

'They're from Mrs Petrie's garden, and she sent you this parcel. She said you would know what it was.'

Bette took it then held it out to Lyndsey. 'It's for you, darling. Happy birthday. Let me give you a kiss.' They clung together for a moment and Lyndsey had to swallow hard to get rid of the lump in her throat.

She opened the parcel to find a pair of fur-backed gloves. 'Bette! Your precious coupons . . .'

Bette grinned. 'I made them, my love, I went to a glove-making class. The suede was a remnant someone sold to me and the fur came from an old fur coat I had. Aren't I clever? Bette Bascony, glove maker!'

Lyndsey put them on. 'They fit perfectly! I shall treasure them. And I shall take great care of them, because I'm sure I shall never get another pair like them.'

'You can say that again! You'll get your Christmas

present in the morning, Lyndsey, Mrs Petrie will give it to you. It's from us both. Doesn't it look lovely and Christmasy in here? I understand all the patients who can partake are having a traditional Christmas dinner tomorrow, turkey and all the trimmings.'

Lyndsey could see she was near to tears and she put her hand gently over hers. 'Bette, you're getting excited. Calm down or Elliott and I will be told to go.'

'I know, it's just seeing you both and having to be in here.' She turned to Elliott. 'Tell me why you suddenly arrived home?'

He explained briefly and she congratulated him, then said, 'And now, you tell me all you've been doing, both of you, and I'll listen.' Elliott nodded to Lyndsey and she began telling her about the preparations for Christmas at the Centre.

'All the older people brought tinsel and baubles they had kept year after year to put on the Christmas tree. One old chap brought an angel for the top then told me he wanted a kiss for bringing it.' Lyndsey laughed. 'So I kissed him and he said, "Ar-ah, that's good that is, I'll have another one off you tomorrow, gal." '

'And he won't be able to get it,' Bette said, a sadness in her voice. 'And all because of stupid me having to be in here.'

'She can give it to me instead,' Elliott said lightly. 'A sisterly kiss, of course.'

A small, pert-faced nurse who had come up at that moment said, 'Now what girl would want to give this handsome man a sisterly kiss? I wouldn't.'

'Nor would I,' Lyndsey declared, smiling.

The nurse laughed. 'Am I treading on forbidden territory? Sorry.' She turned to Bette. 'Now I hope you are not talking too much, Mrs Bascony. We can't have you getting too excited, can we?'

Bette grinned. 'My lips are sealed.'

The nurse gave Elliott a saucy sidelong glance before

she left them and he said, 'I don't think that *she* will want for boyfriends.' He was smiling and the look in his eyes as he followed her neat little figure along the ward gave Lyndsey a small pang. Did he prefer girls like that? She realized then that although he had told her about some of his life in his letters, she knew very little of his likes and dislikes, or the way he thought or the books he read. It was something she could perhaps get to know over the holiday.

After this Bette kept nodding off and eventually the staff nurse came and suggested quietly they should leave, explaining that although Bette looked so well, she was still far from being over the operation. 'And there's tomorrow,' she added, 'the Christmas dinner.'

Bette opened her eyes as they were preparing to leave and she made no protest that they were leaving before visiting time was up. They promised they would be there the next day and she smiled and nodded – and was asleep again.

When they came away from the lighted building they stood a few moments to get accustomed to the darkness and Elliott said, 'Poor Bette, we're so used to seeing her full of life. But I'm sure once she's over this she'll be back to herself again.' He put a hand under Lyndsey's elbow and as they walked away asked if she was still doing the shows.

'And more important still,' he went on, a smile in his voice, 'are you still doing your high-kicking act?'

'Not recently, but who knows, any day I could be at it again. Bette did a show a week ago. Did I tell you they had applied to join ENSA? Yes, I did, in my letter to you.'

Lyndsey went on talking about the show because the proximity of Elliott, the firm way he cupped her elbow, had emotion stirring in her again. When they got in the car she said, 'I've just realized something, we haven't had any wailing sirens today. Perhaps there will be a truce after all.'

'Could be, let us hope so. But I don't think we are going to have an all-white Christmas.' The earlier drifting of snowflakes had ceased but although there was no layer of snow on the ground, the hedges and the branches of trees were pretty with hoarfrost. Stars twinkled in a midnight blue sky and the air was crisp and clear.

'A lovely evening,' Elliott said, 'a night for romance.'

He had spoken lightly but Lyndsey was aware of a slight unsteadiness in his voice and it sent her heart racing, and brought stirrings of which Ivy would not have approved. Lyndsey thought it was just as well that Mrs Petrie would be there when they got back.

'And how was Bette this evening?' Mrs Petrie asked, and before they could reply she said, a slow smile spreading over the plump face, 'You've no need to tell me, I can tell by your manner she's much better.'

Lyndsey confirmed this. They talked about Bette for a while then Mrs Petrie told them she was going to see Penny for a while, she would be back about ten. Lyndsey said, 'Give her a hug for me,' and Mrs Petrie promised.

When she had gone the house seemed strangely silent. Logs on the fire crackled and a shower of red sparks shot up the chimney. Lyndsey lifted the guard away and the heat reached out to her. She switched on the pink-shaded table lamps and the room took on a warm, almost a sensuous glow, she thought. Would she be tempting fate by being alone with Elliott?

Lyndsey suddenly realized she was equating the situation with the one in the barn, when Andrew was begging to love her. Elliott was a totally different personality, he was stronger, at least she was sure he was. And anyway, it was her own feelings she was having to fight. He came in.

'Here, give me your coat, Lyndsey, and I'll hang it up.' He helped her off with it and she gave a little shiver. It was like Andrew undressing her.

Elliott said with concern, 'If you feel cold in here then you must have caught a chill.'

'No, I'm all right, thanks. Would you like a drop of whisky? I know Bette has some. I shall have a drink of tea.'

He said a small one and she poured it, then went into the kitchen.

When she returned he was standing by the fire, his hands behind his back. 'Close your eyes,' he said, 'and hold out your hand.'

'What? Oh.' She did as she was bid and a small wrapped parcel was laid on her palm. Elliott commanded her to open her eyes.

'As I didn't know it was your birthday, Lyndsey, this will have to be a combined birthday and Christmas present.'

It was a necklace of jade beads. The sizes were graduated but the tiniest one was as intricately carved as the largest. Lyndsey looked up.

'Oh, Elliott, they're exquisite, the carving − how delicate.'

Elliott came over and holding her shoulders he kissed her gently on the lips. 'A belated happy birthday.' When he drew away she kissed him back, her kiss as gentle as his.

'Thank you, Elliott. I shall have pleasure in wearing them.'

With the giving of the gift and the gentle kiss the atmosphere of the room seemed to have changed. A peace stole over her. She remembered Andrew saying in the barn he had realized that a quiet time could also be full of love, and the memory of Andrew at that moment was without pain. She said: 'Tell me about yourself, Elliott. I only know what you told me in your letters. I don't know what kind of books you read, your taste in music, what games you play.'

He looked across at her and she thought he seemed very relaxed leaning back in the armchair.

248

'I read all kinds of books, on farm management, astronomy, psychology, thrillers, in fact on a wide range of subjects. When I was in hospital I was so bored I read anything I could lay my hands on. Even women's magazines! Not that I'm denigrating them, there were some interesting articles.'

'Such as?'

An impish twinkle came into his eyes. 'Such as how to keep your man.'

'That would be interesting, *very* interesting.'

There was a silence and Lyndsey realized that Elliott's smile had died and he was studying her. Had there been a bitterness in her voice? She said with a forced laugh, 'For those girls who *can't* keep a man of course.'

'But you have no problem.'

'I have no problem because I don't want to get involved. Not at the moment anyway, but that's not to say there won't come a time when I realize that I'm madly in love and discover that the man has found someone else.'

'*I* won't, I promise.' The impish twinkle was back in his eyes.

'Big head! You better tell me what music appeals to you before I throw a cushion at your head.'

He talked music and they discovered they had similar tastes, and were discussing various composers when Mrs Petrie came in.

'Oh, there you are, all nice and cosy. It's a beautiful night. I've been listening to the wireless and there's been no raids. What a blessing it will be if there's none over the Christmas. Oh, listen, there are carol singers in the village. Come to the door and you'll hear them better. Put your coats on.'

They stood in the garden and in the stillness of the night the clear, sweet voices came to them: 'Once in Royal David's City, stood a lonely cattle shed . . .'

A lonely cattle shed, Lyndsey felt a lump come into her throat. How many people would be lonely this Christmas, men separated from wives, from families, people having to celebrate the birth of Christ in shelters because of the fear of bombs.

Elliott laid an arm across her shoulders, as though sensing her emotion.

They waited, listened to 'Silent Night, Holy Night', and then there was silence. Mrs Petrie said, 'They'll have gone into someone's house for their Christmas fare.' They went back to the house and there they reminisced about past Christmases. At least Mrs Petrie and Lyndsey did – Elliott listened. But he laughed with them at the funny little incidents they related about their childhood. Mrs Petrie told them a story about the Christmas her father came in after celebrating too well and fell over the coal scuttle, waking the whole household.

'He was dressed as Father Christmas,' she said, 'and when we children all came tumbling downstairs we were thrilled at first to see him but when I smelled his breath and his beard fell off disillusionment set in. It was terrible, the magic had gone.' She laughed and got up. 'Well, on that discordant note I had better get off to bed. Good night, sweet dreams.'

When she had gone Lyndsey dropped to her knees on the hearthrug and stirred the dying embers of the fire with the poker. 'I know what she meant, don't you? I know there's the disillusionment when one gets to know that it's our parents who fill our stockings, but I wouldn't have wanted to miss that lovely magic of early childhood. There's just nothing to compare with it.'

'I'm afraid I never knew it,' Elliott said quietly. 'My parents were realists. They thought it was stupid to let children think there was a Father Christmas who lived in Lapland.'

Lyndsey sat back on her heels and eyed him in dismay. 'Oh, Elliott, they didn't! What a shame. I hate anyone who tells their children when they're just beginning to understand about Father Christmas that he doesn't exist.

It's utterly selfish, it's self-indulgence really, they want to be different.'

Elliott laughed. 'It's all right. It didn't stop me from accepting any magic that came my way as I grew up.'

'I'm glad,' she said softly.

Elliott got up then and pulled her to her feet. He wrapped his arms around her, and there was a teasing in his voice as he said, 'I promise faithfully not to disillusion *our* children about Father Christmas.'

'Now, Elliott,' Lyndsey protested, half laughing. She tried to draw away but she was held firm.

'I want to wish you a happy Christmas, that's all, I wouldn't want to destroy our chaperone's faith in us.' His lips on hers were soft and warm and they moved sensuously. She stood rigid, refusing to respond, having been warned in the past how infuriating Elliott Warrender's behaviour could be. But it was not easy. Tremors were running through her, delicious tremors.

He released her then cupped her face between his palms, and she waited, eyes closed. He kissed her eyelids, moved his hands down to her throat and rubbed his thumbs gently over her skin. Every pulse was beating in her body. She was aware of him moving away from her. She opened her eyes. His were dark with passion, but a faint smile touched his lips.

She was angry, it was a repetition of the evening he had left her abruptly on the doorstep after rousing her. Well, she would give him a taste of his own medicine!

'And now let me wish *you* a happy Christmas, Elliott.'

She clasped her arms around his neck and pressed her body against his. Then she kissed him, following his pattern. He responded immediately. She made to draw away then but he pressed her close to him almost savagely and for seconds there was fire between them. Then he released her and stood looking at her, his expression solemn, regretful.

'I think it's sensible, Lyndsey.'

She knew he was right but felt humiliated because her little ruse had gone wrong on her. She said, her head up, 'I did it deliberately, but that's the end to the kissing games.'

'It was not a game with me, Lyndsey. You know I love you.'

She felt suddenly deflated. 'Yes, I do, Elliott, I'm sorry I acted the way I did. I wanted revenge for the time you left me high and dry on the doorstep.'

'It was enjoyable revenge.' He was smiling now. 'It could be heaven if you–' He rubbed a finger gently across her chin. 'I better not say any more.' They stood a moment, then Elliott became brisk.

'Right, what is there to do? About locking up for the night, I mean. Do you want the ashes raked out? See how domesticated I am.'

Lyndsey found herself laughing. 'You really are the end, Elliott Warrender, as Mrs Petrie says about her relatives. We had better lock up in case a German parachutist decides to land and seeks somewhere to hide. Horrible thought. The fire is too low to spark, I think, but I'll put the guard in front, Bette always does. I wonder how she is. It would have been lovely if she could have been here for Christmas.'

'Yes, it would, she's a lovable, lively person.'

Elliott shot the bolts on the back door then they went upstairs, pausing only seconds on the landing to whisper their good nights.

Lyndsey lay a long time awake thinking about Elliott, his restraint. It was tantalizing, but necessary. If only she was not so quick to respond. But then it was something she had felt with only Andrew and Elliott. She had felt emotional with boyfriends in the past but had never allowed any of them to take any liberties whatsoever.

When she did fall asleep she dreamt of Andrew. He was flying to reach her where she was marooned on a small rock with the rising tide threatening to engulf her. But although the plane was heading in her direction it was receding every second and she was in despair. When she roused from the dream she felt terribly unhappy. But by morning the dream had almost faded.

When Lyndsey was ready to go downstairs she picked up the presents she had brought for Mrs Petrie, a box of candies and some nylon stockings which Ed had given to her. Lyndsey had brought the same for Bette, but with additional presents, a silk headscarf for Mrs Petrie and three chiffon ones for Bette in different patterns and colours. She regretted not having a present to give to Elliott.

But when she went downstairs Mrs Petrie solved it for her. She showed her a beautiful fine cream cashmere scarf she said she had won in a raffle at the church bazaar. 'I thought you could give it to Elliott, then he won't feel out of it. And I want it to be from *you* alone, he would appreciate it all the more.'

Put like that Lyndsey accepted it. She laid the parcels on the breakfast table and noticed there was one beside her plate. A few minutes later Elliott came breezing in. 'Happy Christmas to you both, what a lovely fire.'

A special smile for Lyndsey had her heart giving a lurch. 'Porridge is ready,' Mrs Petrie said, 'but first let us open our presents.'

Elliott looked astonished when he sat down and saw his parcel on his plate. He read the little gift card then he looked up, a slow smile spreading over his face. 'Lyndsey, how did you know it was just what I wanted?'

She thought he probably would be able to buy any scarf he wanted in his position but it made her feel good.

Mrs Petrie exclaimed her delight with the headscarf but Lyndsey, who had opened her present, was sitting gazing at a small framed painting, which had to be Echo Cove. It was a joint present from Mrs Petrie and Bette. She looked up. 'Where did you– Who did it? I–' She could hardly speak.

'Bette knew a wounded soldier who did paintings,' Mrs Petrie said gently. 'She described Echo Cove to him as you had described it to her. We prayed it would be right.'

'It's absolutely right, the harbour, the fishing fleet, the echoing cliffs – oh, even to the old fishermen sitting on the seats at opposite sides of the harbour. Did I tell you that it was so small they could talk to one another across it?' Her voice broke. 'Forgive me if I shed a few tears.' She dabbed at her eyes. 'But there, I mustn't cry on Christmas Day, must I?'

She got up and gave Mrs Petrie a hug. 'It's beautiful, I'll thank Bette too when I see her.'

It was a day that Lyndsey thought she would always remember. She had never expected to enjoy a Christmas Day afternoon in a hospital, but she did. Not only was Bette so very much better but there was a marvellous atmosphere. They had all enjoyed their Christmas dinner and were still wearing paper hats from crackers.

There were no very ill patients on the ward but there were some in pain and these were as happy as the others. A Father Christmas came and everyone got a small present.

One elderly lady said, 'Do you know something, when we kids were young we got an apple and an orange in our stockings, and if we were lucky, *very* lucky, we got a new penny.'

Another woman on the opposite side called out, 'We were lucky if we got a few sweets in ours and I never knew what a Christmas dinner was until some poacher gi' me dad a rabbit. It had to be divided among ten of us so you can imagine how much each of us kids got, but I can still taste that dinner, the gravy and the sage and onion stuffing. My, it were lovely!'

Her son, who was visiting, laughed. 'You've won the prize, no one can better that one!'

Bette said, 'What marvellous people. Those who can get up have been to have a chat with me. And now you two are here.' Lyndsey had thanked her for the painting and

254

Bette had been thrilled with her scarves. 'Just in time,' she declared, 'all my other ones are getting tatty.'

Later 'Father Christmas' led them all in singing carols. They sang softly and it was so moving some of them were in tears, but immediately they were over there was laughter again. 'And there haven't been any raids, I understand,' Bette said. 'Isn't that splendid. Let's hope we can have tomorrow free as well. I couldn't have had more care than I've had here, but I do wish I was home. Elliott, when are you due back? Not that I want you to rush away.'

He said he would have to be back in London on the 28th and Lyndsey said she was due back at the Centre on the 27th, but assured Bette she would return every night so she could come and visit.

To this Bette said in a low voice, 'Darling, I think I might be home by then. According to rumour there's a lot of war wounded coming from abroad and they need beds. I shall be very pleased to let them have mine.'

And it was more or less on that note that they parted. On the way back Elliott asked Lyndsey if she could ride a bicycle. She looked at him in surprise and said, 'Yes, why?'

'Because I was talking to a chap in the ward who told me the best way to see the countryside was on a bike, and he offered to lend us two, his and his wife's. They apparently don't live far from Bette.'

'Great!' Lyndsey declared. 'I haven't been on a bike since I came to London. I'm an expert,' she laughed, 'could ride without hands since the age of five, and many a clout I had from Ivy when she saw me. Swore I would kill myself.'

Elliott teased her. 'And what else can you do apart from being an expert cyclist and a jitterbugger?'

Lyndsey rubbed the backs of her nails down her coat. 'Well – I can swim, sail a boat, ride a motor bike, repair them, drive a car and I've taken down an engine. *Not* that my parents knew I rode motor bikes, or drove a car. They belonged to boyfriends and I always waited until I was away from the Cove before riding or driving.'

Elliott glanced at her, laughing. 'I think you must have been a bit of a problem.'

'I suppose so, but then, on the other hand, I don't suppose I was worse than any other young person. I'm a restless individual always needing to be doing something. I can't wait to hear from the Wrens to know if I've been accepted.'

'I shouldn't think they would be likely to turn you down, not with your sailing background and your knowledge of motor bikes and cars. If you can't get into the boats' crew section I'm sure you could get into despatch or motor transport.'

Lyndsey looked at him and was thoughtful. 'Mm, I never thought about that. I would quite like to be a despatch rider. Oh, well, we'll see what happens.'

Although Mrs Petrie had been determined to stay away from her relatives she said before they left for the hospital, 'I suppose I had better see how they're doing. After all, it *is* Christmas. I'll look in while you're gone, but I'll be here when you get back.'

She was there and so were two more people, Joe and George from the Boomerangs, who had called to see how Bette was.

Lyndsey introduced Elliott to them and right from the start they were 'buddies'. Lyndsey was surprised, then she realized that although Joe and George were easy to get on with Elliott was just as relaxed with them. Mrs Petrie came in and they ended up having a convivial evening. They chatted, George cracked jokes, they had a little sing-song and then played cards.

It was midnight when the two men left. They said they had had a wonderful evening. Joe whispered to Lyndsey, 'You've got a great bloke there, girl. You stick to him, they don't come like that very often.'

Mrs Petrie's eyes were shining. 'Now wasn't that a lovely

256

surprise. I don't know when I've enjoyed an evening so much. Oh, my goodness, look at the time, I'll never be able to get up in the morning.'

'Is it important?' Elliott teased. 'Are you going somewhere special?' She said well, no, she wasn't and went upstairs laughing.

When she had gone Elliott put his hands under Lyndsey's elbows and smiled into her eyes. 'I hear that you are a very popular girl in the show, not only with the troupers, but the forces. I'm jealous.'

'You needn't be,' she said quietly. 'I enjoy their flattery, of course, what girl wouldn't, but I – well, there have been only two special men in my life, you and –'

Oh, Lord, how tactless could she get? She forced a smile and concludeed, 'The other one got married.'

Elliott did not smile, his expression was solemn. 'Andrew?'

Lyndsey took a quick breath, 'Y – yes, but I don't want to talk about it.'

'No, of course not. I'm sorry.'

Lyndsey was beginning to think she had spoilt what had been a wonderful day when Elliott said, 'All right, let's forget it. Where are we going bicycling tomorrow? We must make the most of our time together.'

They discussed plans and ended up by deciding they would go where the roads took them. He gave her a gentle good night kiss, then said softly, 'I'm glad I'm still in the running.'

EIGHTEEN

Lyndsey's and Elliott's cycling expedition the following day was a great success. It was bitterly cold, with the wind stinging their cheeks as they cycled along all the lanes and byways, but there was a joyousness about Elliott as there had been the night they had jitterbugged together. It was as though he was unleashing all his inhibitions.

'Race you!' he would shout, when they were on a straight stretch of road and away they would go, and although more often than not he would let her win, Lyndsey knew he could have beaten her. She would end up breathless, while Elliott showed no signs of having to catch his breath.

When they stopped to have a picnic lunch he said, looking about him, his eyes alight with pleasure, 'This is marvellous, something to remember on the bad days.'

'The bad days?' she queried, worried.

'I mean the mornings when I get out of the wrong side of the bed.' His voice held a teasing but Lyndsey guessed that the 'bad days' had something to do with warfare.

And it was on that afternoon she learned most about his life. Sometimes he joked about certain incidents, such as the time he started at boarding school. 'Would you believe that I was a shy, tongue-tied youngster who wouldn't say boo to a goose?'

Lyndsey told him she could not imagine it and he said, 'It's true! The bigger boys used to play all sorts of pranks on me, reducing me to a jelly. Lord what fun they had.'

Elliott laughed as he said it but Lyndsey thought she detected a remembered pain in his eyes.

'So what changed you?'

'It was advice one of the older boys gave to me. He told me if I didn't start and fight them, or make a show of it, I would be a "punching bag" for the rest of my life.'

'Did it work?'

'It did. From somewhere I found hidden courage. I attacked everyone who played tricks on me. I lashed out and I must say the fact that my father had taught me to box helped. Even then, I had my nose bloodied, my eyes blacked, but oh, the pleasure of being able to get my own back. More important still I won respect.'

'And that is what has made you such a good army man,' Lyndsey said quietly. She poured coffee from the flask and handed it to him. He sipped it then gave her a broad grin.

'I would much rather prove to you that I would make a good husband.'

'Now stop it,' she warned.

'All right, all right, but can I just ask how the serial is getting on? Is the heroine any nearer to solving her problems about our hero who is at the front? She should be getting something clear in her mind by now.'

Lyndsey dismissed it with an airy wave of her hand. 'Oh, there are a lot more episodes to go yet. Have a sandwich.'

Later he talked about his mother and how he had found out when he was older that she had never wanted children. 'I think perhaps she loved us all in her own way, but was unable to show it, possibly because my father was such an undemonstrative man who deplored any outward show of affection. On looking back, I think my mother was afraid of him. The two families arranged the marriage.'

'How sad. I would hate to marry someone I didn't love.'

Elliott smiled. '*You* wouldn't, you're too strong-willed. I should imagine you would have run away and joined the gypsies.'

'Mmm, it might have been fun.'

'Don't you believe it. You would have ended up being a slave to one of the men. They stand no messing. They're rough and tough; they have to be in the life they lead.'

Lyndsey poured out the rest of the coffee then screwed the top firmly on the flask. 'Let's change the subject, shall we? Do you see that farmhouse over there? Shall we cycle to it? It will be a good landmark to make for.' Elliott agreed and a few minutes later they set off.

At four o'clock they arrived back, windblown and ravenous, with some freshly laid eggs, some slices of gammon and a chicken.

'Well!' Mrs Petrie exclaimed. 'How did you manage that?'

Elliott said, 'It was through one of those strange coincidences that happen in life. Their youngest son happened to be in my regiment.'

Lyndsey thought no, it was not coincidence alone, it was Elliott's way of handling the mother, who was worried because they had not heard from their son recently. He had been so lovely with her, gentle, explaining that the boy had been in good spirits when he had left a few days ago and assuring her he would look into it and see that he wrote home.

The day ended with the good news when they went to the hospital that Bette would be coming home by ambulance the following morning. Mrs Petrie had come with them and Elliott waited in the car so they could discuss arrangements. The district nurse would come in, Mrs Petrie would be there and Lyndsey would return from the Centre each evening and stay overnight. Bette was jubilant.

'They've been marvellous in here,' she said, 'but there's just nothing like one's own home.'

A bed was made up for Bette on the divan in the living room so she would not feel isolated upstairs and Lyndsey and Elliott spent most of that day with her. It was a good day, peaceful.

The next morning Elliott and Lyndsey travelled to

London together, but parted when they reached London. There had been a tearful parting from Bette and Lyndsey had difficulty now in controlling her tears. She had found a closeness with Elliott these past few days that she had not experienced before. He held her to him and kissed her and she was aware of his strength and his own controlled emotion. He pressed his cheek to hers and said, with a forced lightness, 'Be good,' and she replied in equally light vein, 'And you.' Then they went their separate ways with Lyndsey seeing the moving crowd of people through a blur of tears.

Bette had tried to persuade Lyndsey not to come back on the Friday afternoon as it would be too much rushing about for her, but Lyndsey did go back. On the Saturday morning she went to do some shopping and was stopped many times by people wanting to know how Bette was and offering help. Lyndsey tried to remember all the names to tell Bette and had them all in her mind when she got back. She went into the living room saying, 'Bette Bascony, you must be the most popular person in – ' and then stopped, and stood frozen as she saw the blue-clad figure sitting by the divan. Andrew . . .

He got up and said quietly, 'Hello, Lyndsey.'

She felt a sudden surge of anger. How could he, how dare he turn up here after what he had done? Then she realized he had every right to be here, he was Bette's nephew.

'Excuse me,' she said, 'I'll put the shopping away.' She went into the kitchen, opened a cupboard then closed it again knowing she had nothing to put into it. She was tipping the potatoes into the vegetable rack when Andrew came in.

'Lyndsey, I came because I heard that Bette was ill, but I did very much want to see you to explain – '

'There's nothing to explain, Andrew.' She put the loaf of bread in the bin. 'It wouldn't change anything.'

'*Please*, Lyndsey, just let me tell you the circumstances.'

'No!' She turned to face him, and was shocked at the dreadful bleakness in his eyes. 'No,' she added more quietly. 'Whatever there was between us has gone. I'll be polite to you while you're here, but don't expect anything more. Please go and talk to Bette.'

He went out and Lyndsey leaned against the table and closed her eyes, feeling the remembered emotion stirring in her. Oh, God, why did he have to come back? He was crucifying her. She didn't deserve it. She waited until she had her emotions under control then she went back into the living room. Bette was alone. She patted the bedcover. 'Sit down, love, I wanted to have a word with you. I've sent Andrew to see Mrs Petrie. Will you give him a chance to explain what happened? The two of you could go for a walk.'

'Bette, I can't. I don't want to talk about it, it would serve no purpose.'

'I think it would. Andrew can only stay until tomorrow evening and I don't want to have an awful atmosphere, which there would be if you didn't make your peace with him. That's all I ask.'

Lyndsey, suddenly realizing Bette's distress, which was the worst possible thing for any invalid, said, 'Yes, I will, Bette, and I'll do my best to be tolerant.'

'Thanks, love. I know there can't be anything between you but I love you both and want you to remain friends.'

Lyndsey tried to remember this when she set out with Andrew later to walk across the fields, because she was still feeling full of resentment towards him.

After walking a short distance in silence he said, 'I'm really sorry for not explaining what had happened, when it did happen. I kept making excuses to myself, that I didn't want to hurt you, but actually it was cowardice. I had done such a big build-up job of telling you how much I loved you. I still do, nothing can change that.'

'Don't, Andrew, please. *Don't* add insult to injury.'

'It's the truth I'm telling you and nothing can change

that. Freda knows it, just as I know she still loves her boyfriend who was shot down over Germany. We met when she was in a low state and in need of comfort and so was I. I was back flying before I was really over the measles and, well, I think I was on the verge of a breakdown. We went out once or twice and – the rest you can guess.'

Andrew was silent for a long time then continued. 'When I knew about the baby I was shocked, so was she. I had taken . . . precautions, but it went wrong. We talked it over for hours. She wouldn't try and get rid of it, not that I wanted her to, and she didn't want to give it away for adoption. But, on the other hand, she knew she could not go home. Her parents were deeply religious people and would consider what we had done a crime, worse than murder, she said. I asked her to marry me and in the end she agreed. And so, Lyndsey, that is the whole sorry story.'

'I'm sorry,' she said, and meant it, for both their sakes, knowing how easy it was to want to make love.

Andrew stopped and turned her to face him and there was pain in his eyes. 'All I ask, Lyndsey, is that you'll forgive me for the way I behaved towards you. You must hate me and I don't blame you.'

'I think I did hate you when I first knew you were married, but afterwards it was resentment I felt and yet I hadn't wanted to get married. Andrew, I must be honest about that. I didn't feel I was ready for it. There's nothing to forgive.'

'Thanks, Lyndsey, for being so decent about it. Freda and I are determined to make a go of our marriage, for the baby's sake. She's in the Waafs at the moment but will be leaving soon. She's a nice person, rather gentle. Under different circumstances I think you would have liked her.'

They walked on again and were silent. Then Andrew asked Lyndsey what she had been doing recently and she talked, but at times felt she was losing the thread of what she was saying. Once when she paused, Andrew prompted,

'You were saying that Ann left abruptly. Have you heard from her?'

'No, not even a postcard. It's perhaps just as well, she was a strange girl. I've sent in an application to join the Wrens and I had an acknowledgement. I should be hearing from them soon to go for an interview.' Lyndsey wondered why her voice should sound so flat when it was something she was longing to hear.

'Lyndsey – I'll be going back to Scotland. I have tomorrow free and I did want to do my little tour around London, the city somehow I've never had the chance to really see. Would you – would you come with me?'

The pleading in his voice pulled at her heart strings. She wanted to go, but knew it would not be wise. She was glad of having the excuse of looking after Bette.

'Yes,' he said, 'yes, of course,' and the sadness of the remark made her say quickly, 'I would have gone with you Andrew, if it had been possible.'

'Thanks for that, anyway. It's good to know you don't feel any animosity towards me. We had better go back.' Andrew smiled then. 'Bette will be anxious to know how we got on.'

When they went in she held out a hand to each of them. 'I can see that you are friends again and that is all I wanted. Now let us have a nice cosy little chat.'

The cosy little chat was denied them. Bette's friend Mary from Coventry arrived unexpectedly. She said to Bette, 'When Mrs Petrie told me over the phone that you were being sent home from hospital I thought to myself that this was the time you needed help. I can only stay until tomorrow evening, but I'll clean the house from top to bottom if you want.'

Bette laughed. 'Just you sit yourself down and talk to me. All the work is done.'

There was no doubt about Mary being good-hearted because she took over the cooking of the meal, insisted on

264

washing up alone and afterwards came in with cups of tea for all of them.

'There now,' she said, 'we can have a little chat and catch up on all the news.'

Lyndsey glanced at Andrew and he gave her a wink then turned to Bette. 'Bette, I was trying to persuade Lyndsey to come to London with me tomorrow and wander around all the old streets and lanes of the city. She told me she couldn't come because she had to look after you, but with your friend being here I thought – '

'You go,' Mary declared. 'Bette will be all right with me, won't you, love? Oh, dear, I've forgotten the teaspoons.' She jumped up to go and get them and Bette said, laughing softly, when she had gone, 'You'd better go the pair of you; Mary won't rest until she has me on my own. Even poor Mrs Petrie has had her nose pushed out.'

It was not until later that Lyndsey managed to get Andrew alone then she said, 'You arranged that *very* nicely, didn't you?'

'*I* thought I had.' For a moment there was the familiar twinkle in his blue eyes then he added quietly, 'For friendship's sake, Lyndsey? We may never meet again, you will be going into the Wrens, and I – well, please say you'll come.'

She told him yes and he said, 'Thanks.'

It was strange she thought afterwards how the whole atmosphere in the house had seemed to change. There was an air of expectancy. Or was it something inside herself . . . inside of Andrew too? Not that there would be anything between them, nothing intimate. This was out of the question and she felt sure that Andrew knew this. He had stressed for friendship's sake. It was probably a tying of threads that had been left undone. She felt no jealousy of Freda, in fact she felt sorrow. She was a gentle girl he had said.

Andrew was talking of going to the station to see the times of the trains, which were poor on a Sunday, when a neighbour who had called offered them a lift. He and his wife were going to visit relatives.

And rewarding it was. Mr Bentley brought to life for them the city as it was in olden times. He described the criss-cross of streets and small courtyards that could bring you to a dead end, but which were, nevertheless, worth exploring. He told them about the streets whose names dated back to the middle ages. Cheapside, taking its name from the Anglo-Saxon word *ceap* meaning market. There was still a market at Cheapside. Beekeepers had their shops in Honey Lane; Bread Lane was self-explanatory. The panyers, or basket weavers, lived in Panyer Alley. Friday Street was named after the fishmongers who sold their fish there on Fridays. He went from one street and alley to the next.

He told them that seeing St Paul's cathedral was a must and described it. He said there were forty-seven churches within the square mile, and added that unhappily some of them had been badly damaged by bombs, but mentioned only one, St Mary le Bow, famous for its Bow Bells because, he said, there were so many still intact.

By the time they arrived in London, Lyndsey's head was so full of all the places she wanted to see she declared it would take a week to see them all! Andrew said he felt the same, but whatever sight-seeing they did he must first go to Buckingham Palace to – he paused and smiled – to pay his mother's respects to the royal family.

The palace had been bombed three times, but the damage was not serious, nor had anyone been killed. And although the Queen's apartment had been damaged she had not been in residence at the time.

Lyndsey and Andrew tramped for two hours and they talked about everything under the sun, with an ease as though the rift had never been between them. When Andrew suggested having a meal Lyndsey agreed and over the meal he said he ached inside for all the beautiful buildings that had been damaged and destroyed. Then he smiled and added, 'Let's have a bit of romance for a change shall we?'

She looked at him, alarmed, and he laid his hand gently over hers. 'Don't panic. It was just that I like Vera Lynn's song, "A Nightingale Sang in Berkeley Square", and I thought I would like to see the Square and' – he smiled – 'perhaps hear nightingales.'

Lyndsey relaxed. 'Nightingales only sing at night, I think, and alas you'll find no romance in the Square; it's dominated by a great big anti-aircraft gun.'

'Oh! Well in that case we'll go and see where bees made honey and the basket weavers weaved – '

They lost themselves in the maze of alleyways and laughed when they came to dead-end courtyards. Once when Andrew's wife crossed Lyndsey's mind she felt guilt for a moment then she thought, no, she was taking nothing away from Freda. Andrew would have come on his own and how much better it was to have a companion to share the experience of what they had seen. By this evening it would be over and from then on Freda would have Andrew to herself.

The afternoon was cold, the sky grey, the clouds heavy. In a way it was a blessing because there was less chance in cloudy weather of a raid. There were few people about and the few there were appeared to be sightseeing themselves. Once when Lyndsey and Andrew were standing looking about them at the ancient buildings an air-raid warden appeared and asked them if he could help.

Andrew explained they were interested in the area and the warden began to talk about the streets and alleyways, which he called a veritable 'death trap'. 'All the buildings are built of stone or brick,' he said, 'but inside they're a mass of timber, wooden staircases, roofing, beams. Get a few incendiaries on this lot and the whole lot'll go up! Where are the fire spotters? In bed, that's what, having their Sunday afternoon's snooze.'

He went on about firms not leaving men in charge and

also locking buildings up without leaving keys with fire brigades. 'Now take Paternoster Square,' he said, 'nearly every building there is chock-a-block with books of every description, millions of 'em. One spark and whoof! the whole lot would go.'

Andrew tried to console him with the fact that the cloudy weather would at least keep the bombers away but the warden was not having that. 'That blasted Hitler would try anything, clouds or not.'

An elderly couple coming up to ask the warden directions allowed Lyndsey and Andrew to escape. 'Talk about pessimists,' Lyndsey exclaimed. 'He would have the whole city burned down if he had his way. Let's go to St Paul's.'

There were many more people about when they reached the cathedral and the majority were looking up at the massive lead-sheathed dome, which was one of the most famous landmarks in the world. 'An impressive sight,' one woman remarked. Men, obviously fire watchers, walked around the balconies, stopping every now and then to look over the city. Lyndsey was about to point the men out to Andrew when two exuberant voices hailed them. 'Andrew – Lyndsey!'

It was Lofty and his girlfriend Petal that they had met in Lyons' Corner House.

'Well, what do you know, fancy meeting you here!' This from Lofty. Petal laughed joyously. 'We've wondered about the two of you. Isn't this lovely, we can make up a foursome.'

Although Lyndsey liked them both she wished they had not met. Andrew told them they were sightseeing and Lofty said, 'Great, we'll come with you!' Lyndsey then had a feeling of resignation, but not so Andrew. He told them he would have to leave about eight o'clock to return to his unit, then added, 'So we can stick together until about six o'clock, then Lyndsey and I want some time together. Okay?' His smile softened the rejection.

Oh, yes, that was fine, Lofty said, they understood.

Petal said as they moved away, 'Wasn't that a lovely night we had at Lyons' Corner House and when we went dancing.'

Memories of it came flooding back to Lyndsey. Andrew had belonged to her then. So much had happened since. She had met and lost Brad and Ed, and Elliott had gone.

Andrew asked about the other couple who had been with them and Lofty said, 'They got married, didn't you know? No, of course you wouldn't. They had what you could call a two-hour honeymoon before he was shipped abroad and Angel hasn't seen him since.'

'And Angel is pregnant,' Petal said in a voice of doom. 'Silly things. I thought they would have had more sense.'

Lyndsey could feel Andrew tense beside her. Seeking frantically for something to say that would change the subject she said, 'Did you know that the Duke of Wellington and Lord Nelson are buried in the cathedral? And so is Christopher Wren.'

'Who's he?' Petal asked, with a wide-eyed innocence that brought a shout of laughter from Lofty.

'Oh, Petal, duckie, you really are the limit. Christopher Wren was the bloke responsible for the cathedral being built. I really will have to educate you.' The smile he gave her was loving. Lyndsey felt her heart contract.

Making up a foursome was not as bad as she had expected. Both Lofty and Petal were so amiable they were soon all laughing together as they wandered about. Andrew suggested later they had a meal and although Lofty was all for going to Lyons' Corner House Lyndsey suggested quickly that they find somewhere nearer.

They sat over the meal so long it was dark before they realized it. And Andrew had just said they really must go when the sirens went.

'A raid in this cloudy weather,' Lofty exclaimed, 'I don't believe it. They'll never hit their targets.'

They paid their bill and left and by then the steady drone of planes was coming nearer. Andrew had just said,

'Come along, you girls, we must get you to a shelter,' when incendiaries came hurtling down, not in small numbers but in the batches known as Molotov Baskets. And they kept coming. Within seconds the whole street was lighted up with the silvery exploding sparkles which someone had once described as beautiful glittering furies. At that moment Lyndsey thought of them as lethal furies.

'Good God!' Andrew said and grabbed Lyndsey by the arm. She shook herself free. 'Get some sand over them,' she yelled.

Petal had already doused several with sandbags. Some people came running to help. The planes were still coming over dropping their loads, but there were no sounds of bombs exploding. One man explained this by shaking his fist at the sky and yelling, 'You bastards! It's Coventry all over again, isn't it! Get the fires going for the bombers to follow! Well, we'll beat you, we'll beat you.'

But beating these loads was something that Lyndsey felt was an impossibility. There were not enough people to extinguish them. All the people there were working full out. The anti-aircraft guns had started with an ear-splitting boom; searchlights were probing from all directions, but this seemed hopeless too, it would be impossible for them to penetrate the thick layers of clouds.

Andrew gave a shout and pointed to a building where a fire had started in the second storey. He and Lofty ran and tried to break down the door, but it resisted. Then a man came running with some axes and at last they had entry. 'Oh, be careful,' Lyndsey prayed.

There would be a lull and they would all heave a sigh of relief but the next moment down would come another batch and they would explode, splintering the darkness with a sort of madness. Lyndsey saw Andrew and Lofty with two men come out of one building where they had put out the fire, but immediately afterwards they had to break down the door of the next building where several fires were burning.

Into the chaos came the clanging sound of fire engine bells, but they were making in a different direction. Lyndsey's back was aching like mad but she didn't stop for a minute. Nor did Petal, who shouted to her, 'This ain't no normal raid, gal!' And Lyndsey agreed with her. Never had she seen fire bombs rain down in such quantities.

Flames were now shooting out of roofs and when a wind sprang up the flames spread until whole buildings were alight. The heat was intense and a warden came running and cleared them all away. 'You should all be taking shelter,' he shouted, 'but they need all the help they can get or the city'll be wiped out.'

It was the pessimistic warden they had met earlier.

Lyndsey realized when they left that street and went to help in another that his pessimistic view could be reality. Fires were blazing everywhere. It was terrifying and awe-inspiring.

'An excellent target for the bombers to follow,' Andrew said. 'They'll see the haze of red through the clouds.'

But this did not stop any of them working. With the help of all the people in the next street they were able to save some buildings, at least for the time being. If the wind changed direction it could bring red-hot fragments to set more fires going.

Southwark across the river was ablaze; they were told that people were fighting fires in St Paul's but that up to now the Guildhall was safe. Then word came that Paternoster Square and Row was a furnace – which was proved when clouds of fragments of charred paper came drifting over. Lyndsey felt at times she had tiny splinters of burnt wood under her eyelids. She was sure her hair had been singed and her throat was so dry she could hardly swallow.

A bomb dropping at the end of the street demolished two houses and sent all the people running. At the end of the street they were met by three women with mugs of tea

271

on trays. 'You deserve a drink,' they said. 'You've all been wonderful.'

The women were told that *they* were wonderful and that the tea was like nectar. Lyndsey had not seen Andrew and Lofty or Petal for some time, but now all three came up. And as they did so the anti-aircraft guns suddenly stopped. Lyndsey looked at Andrew. 'What – why?'

It was Lofty who answered. 'They're obviously sending some fighters up and they don't want to risk hitting them, but if they sent up fifty squadrons it wouldn't do any good. Not with these clouds.'

It was strange, in the sudden silence, to hear the roar of fires. Some sounded to Lyndsey like the low growl of an animal, and others had a rushing, exultant sound as though joyous of their power. A man who came up said, 'St Bride's has gone, the printers' church in Fleet Street. The whole place has collapsed, all but the spire. Waterloo Station's been bombed *and* St Pancras.'

Lyndsey looked at Andrew with dismay. 'Your train?'

'Oh, Lord, I had forgotten.' He looked at his watch. 'I think I'll make it, I have an hour. I want to see you safely home first.'

Lyndsey was protesting that he was not to worry about her when the stranger said, 'No use trying to hurry anywhere, son, streets are closed, taxis have stopped running and so have buses and trams. A tram was blown up on the Embankment, everyone killed.'

Lyndsey was thinking, another Job's comforter, when Andrew took her by the arm. 'We'll get through somehow.' He turned to Lofty and Petal. 'It's been great seeing you both; sorry it had to end like this. Take care of yourselves. Hope we can meet some other time.'

Lyndsey was shouting her goodbyes to Lofty and Petal as Andrew was hurrying her away. Afterwards she said, 'Andrew, I don't think you'll make the station in time, and will there be trains? Can't you phone your unit and explain about the fire?'

'Actually, I have two hours. I took an hour off the time of the train for Lofty and Petal because I wanted some time alone with you, I also want to see you safely home.'

Lyndsey told him he was not to worry about her, she could manage to get home, but he insisted he would either find a taxi or make sure she was safe on her doorstep before he left her. Then he stopped as they turned a corner. The street facing them was piled high with rubble. They took the next turning and got lost.

'Not to worry,' Andrew said, 'we'll find our way out of this maze sometime.'

NINETEEN

Two hours later they were no nearer to getting to St Pancras than when they had set out. Apart from being prevented from cutting through various streets because of collapsing blazing buildings, they had stopped to help in streets where only two or three people were trying to deal with what seemed to be hundreds of the dazzling incendiaries. With these and the fires around it was as light as day. At the end of the street three warehouses were ablaze and as the wind had arisen and was now reaching gale force it would not be long before the flames spread.

There was an office block in the middle of the street and when flames showed in the ground floor a man with an axe broke down the door, went in with a bucket of water and a stirrup pump and soon the flames had died.

It was then a girl, who looked to be no more than fourteen or fifteen, pointed up to a third-storey window and shouted, 'Look, there's a woman up there! She should come down.' The woman, who had a baby in her arms, seemed frozen with fear. 'I'll go and get her.'

The girl ran across the street with Lyndsey following. After them came Andrew yelling for them to come back, he would go, but they raced on, their footsteps clattering on the uncarpeted wooden stairs. They followed the baby's plaintive wailing and burst into a room on the third floor. The woman turned and gazed at them, petrified, eyes wide with terror.

'I'm not coming, you can't make me. I can't come, me and the baby'll be burned alive!'

The woman turned back to the window and pointed with a shaking finger.

'All of London's burning, look at it, we can't escape.'

It was Lyndsey's first view of the scene from a height and she was appalled at what she saw. All around was a massive conflagration that reminded her of a painting she had once seen of Dante's Inferno. There must have been over a thousand separate fires. Flames in every shade of red were interspersed with blast furnace-hot white ones and dense clouds of thick black smoke. Windowless skeletons of buildings glowed crimson.

Then as the wind changed direction the flames became tinted with a beautiful blue and a yellow green, and some became orange and gold – all moving hither and thither in the strong gusts of wind. It was terrifying yet awe-inspiring and Lyndsey could have wept for the beauty of destruction.

Suddenly realizing that the others were all hypnotized by the scene she said, 'Come on, let's go.' She took hold of the woman's arm but she resisted. Then Lyndsey shouted, 'Goddam it woman, you have a child to protect. Move.' The woman came meekly.

They were met by a woman warden who said, 'Oh, Lord, I thought Mrs Ridley had gone visiting with her husband. I was told so. I'll take charge of her, thanks. You better all move, this lot could go up at any time.'

It was astonishing how quickly the flames were engulfing the other buildings. A man called to the warden, 'Where are all the bloody fire engines?' She replied over her shoulder that they were all in use, then she and the woman and child were gone.

Not long after this Andrew and Lyndsey and the other helpers left too, the street was doomed . . . but there was always another one they could perhaps save.

At times it was possible to see flames leap from one

tinder-dry building to the next. Other people who came to help passed on information. Moorgate station had been completely destroyed . . . The Guildhall was past saving . . . St Paul's was still standing . . . The city's main water pipes had been destroyed . . . Electricity had been cut off but was on again . . . The river was at its lowest ebb and firemen were dragging their pipes over mud to get what water they could.

Everywhere they went it was the same, the flames had taken over. The roar of noise never slackened and it took an effort to distinguish its elements, over the hundreds of panes of glass cracking, the thud of buildings collapsing, the roaring flames, the crump of bombs, followed by explosions. The air was stifling. When they met a party of people led by an air-raid warden who was moving them to another shelter a man shouted, 'Don't go down that one yonder, it's as hot as Hades!'

Lyndsey and Andrew trudged wearily away and had stopped, wondering where on earth to go to next when a miracle happened. A taxi pulled up and the driver asked if he could take them anywhere.

'You certainly can,' Andrew said fervently.

Lyndsey declared he was an angel from heaven and the man laughed. 'I might be one later. Jump in, I can at least get you out of this lot.'

He not only knew every street, alleyway and road in the district but seemed to know everything that was happening. He told Andrew there was no hope of getting out of London that night. Every main railway line had been bombed, there was a land mine hanging in the wires above Charing Cross station; Underground stations were operating, but they were few. He told them a lot of firemen had been killed and injured and declared that he wouldn't have their jobs for a king's ransom.

He went on to say that many churches had been destroyed and that although St Paul's was still standing it was sure to go up in the next onslaught.

'Next onslaught?' Lyndsey queried.

Why yes, it had to come, the fires were just a lead for the bombers to follow. Then the whole of the City of London would be wiped out. He hazarded a guess that this raid was just a lead up to the invasion.

He had related this in a surprisingly cheerful voice and when Andrew remarked that it didn't seem to worry him he laughed. What good did worry do, it didn't change anything.

Lyndsey said to Andrew, 'Well, seeing that you won't be able to travel this evening you had better come and stay overnight at Uncle Richard's. He and Marian are away but Mrs Grey said she would be back to light some fires and get the house warmed up.' When he hesitated she said, 'It's the sensible thing to do, Andrew, it would be foolish to hang around the station.'

He nodded. 'You're right, and thanks. I'll phone the base and let them know I can't get back until tomorrow.'

'That is if you can get through,' exclaimed their cheerful driver. 'Most of the telephone exchanges in the City have been bombed. Still, it might be better elsewhere.'

When they arrived Lyndsey asked him if he would care to come in for a cup of tea and he accepted at once saying he was as 'dry as a bone'. Although the fire was burning brightly in the kitchen, with the guard in front of it, there was no sign of Mrs Grey. Lyndsey said, 'She must have gone visiting.'

While they drank their tea the driver told them that although over a hundred fire engines and pumping equipment had been sent out to help, some of them couldn't get to where they were needed because of the piles of rubble. And others, he said, had broken down on the way. 'Do you know what I saw? A Rolls-Royce towing a tender. Never thought the day would come when I would see such a sight. But there, needs must when the devil drives!'

He was still talking non-stop when the all clear went about half past seven. Lyndsey heaved a sigh of relief but their driver and Andrew were staring at one another in astonishment. To Lyndsey's puzzled query as to what was wrong the driver said, 'The all clear has gone, that's what, and it shouldn't oughta.'

Andrew explained that according to the strategy the enemy had been using they expected another wave of planes.

'Bombers,' said their guest firmly. 'They have to come, the fires were the point of the whole raid. Incendiaries first and bombs later.'

They waited and when nothing happened he got up. 'I reckon I'll be off now and find out what's going on. Thanks for the tea, miss, I enjoyed it. And the chat.'

Andrew and Lyndsey went to the door with him and when Andrew opened the door he said, 'Rain – and mist. There's your reason for the no follow-up bombing. It must be worse over there.'

'Thank the Lord for that,' said the driver. 'Ta-ra now and thanks again.' He went to his cab whistling 'Lili Marlene'.

Lyndsey closed the door, switched on the light and turned to face Andrew. 'I thought he would never go.' Then, thinking that Andrew might take it that she was dying to be alone with him she added, 'I never knew a man talk so much, I was beginning to get a headache.'

'I'm glad he went too,' Andrew said, 'because I wanted to have a talk with you before Mrs Grey arrived. I feel there are a lot of things to be discussed.' Andrew spoke softly.

Lyndsey stood tense for a moment then moved away. 'I don't think there's anything to discuss, Andrew. You are married and your wife is expecting a baby. I asked you to stay overnight for the sole reason that you would be unable to get out of London.'

Andrew grabbed her arm. 'Lyndsey, for God's sake! Don't make me out to be worse than I am already. It didn't occur to me to take advantage of the situation.'

Lyndsey's body went slack. 'No, no, of course not. I don't know what made me say such a thing. Put it down to circumstances, meeting you unexpectedly at Bette's, coming to London together, and then the raid.' She began to cry and Andrew put his arms around her.

'Please don't cry, Lyndsey, I can't bear it. We're both tensed up, I shouldn't have come here. I'll go, I'll wait at St Pancras.'

She drew away and dabbed at her eyes. 'No, that would be foolish, you could wait there for hours.'

'Then I shall just sit in the armchair here and cat-nap, I do want to be away early in the morning.'

She gave in but insisted she would put on her alarm and make him some breakfast before he left, but Andrew would have none of it. She was to stay in bed, try and get some sleep. Lyndsey said then, 'Well I shall make some sandwiches now and some tea, then we can have the talk you wanted.'

The talk, as it turned out, was no more than Andrew describing Freda. She was small, fair, with big dark eyes. She was good-natured and quiet. When Andrew started to tell Lyndsey where he and Freda had first met she said, pain in her voice, 'Please, Andrew, not that,' and he flung out his hands with a gesture of despair.

'It's not what I wanted to talk about at all. But then what I want to say I can't and you know why. I can only say that I hope if we meet again, in company perhaps, that we can meet without embarrassment. I hope we can always remain – friends.'

Lyndsey knew then that it was not friendship she wanted with Andrew. She wanted him to hold her, not to make love to her, just to give her a feeling of warmth, of being needed, but as this was impossible she said, 'Andrew, I've just remembered. You must phone your unit.'

He got up. 'Oh, yes, thanks, I will.'

He was away a long time and when he came back he

said he had been told there was a three-hour delay, he would have to explain what had happened when he arrived.

Lyndsey went upstairs to bring a blanket and when she came down again Andrew was fast asleep. She covered him with the blanket, leaned forward to kiss him on the brow then drew back. She could rouse him and he needed sleep as much as she did. She was beginning now to feel utterly exhausted from the events of the day, and being with Andrew was tearing at her emotions.

When she was undressed and ready to drop into bed she drew back the blackout curtains and stood staring at the dull red glow above the rooftops. It could be days before all the fires could be put out. Would the Luftwaffe return the following evening? Heaven help them if they did. She shivered. One could only pray that the weather would remain poor.

Lyndsey slept heavily and when she came down the next morning Andrew had gone. The blanket was neatly folded and the fire had been banked up with slack coal. A few minutes later Mrs Grey arrived. She said, 'A right night it was last night and no mistake.' And that was the sum total of her conversation.

It was a day of gloom all round. Owing to delays in the traffic she was late getting to the Centre and then the talk was all of the raid, with the pessimists declaring that the bombers were sure to be back that night to finish the job. The rain was easing.

Lyndsey returned home in the late afternoon feeling jaded and depressed to find a letter from the Wrens. After reading it she was immediately on top of the world. Hearing Mrs Grey banging pots around in the kitchen she ran in waving the letter.

'What do you think! I have an interview for the Wrens. Isn't it great? I have to report in two weeks' time. I can hardly wait. I wish that Uncle Richard and Marian were here. Have you heard from them?'

'Yes, I have, and I would have told you if you had given

me a chance. They'll be home this evening about six or seven.' She banged a pan down on the shelf. 'And just you calm down, I have a headache.'

Lyndsey went to phone Bette with her news.

As it happened Bette had news of her own to impart. The Boomerangs had been accepted for ENSA. They both talked excitedly about their projects with Bette saying it was the best tonic she could have had and she had been feeling tons better since she had heard. They laughed a lot and before they rang off Lyndsey had given her promise to go to Bette's that weekend. She would have liked to have gone right away and would have done so had not Richard and Marian been due home.

They arrived at eight o'clock that evening and although their greeting to Lyndsey was effusive enough, she became aware later of a coolness between them. When Lyndsey found Richard on his own for a few minutes she asked him if something was wrong.

He raised his shoulders. 'We've had a big row, over her parents. They've never liked me and they were inclined to think that because I travelled the world I'm a bit of a wastrel. I'll accept that, it's their opinion, but it annoys me that Marian appears to side with them.'

It was the first time that Lyndsey had heard Richard say anything against Marian and she guessed that the atmosphere must have been pretty bad for him to have made the complaint.

Mrs Grey had prepared a meal and over it Lyndsey did most of the talking, telling them about the Wrens. Marian warned her not to get too excited, that she may not be able to get into Boats' Crew as it was one of the more favoured sections.

Richard was more cheerful with Lyndsey and told her that he thought it would be a cinch with her sea back-ground and her expertise with boats. At this Marian became tight-lipped and told him it was foolish to raise her hopes. Richard's expression changed, became surly, and to cover the awful atmosphere Lyndsey told them about her involvement in the big fire.

They both eyed her in astonishment and Richard exclaimed, 'But I thought you were at Bette's.'

'I was but – ' Lyndsey told them how it had all come about and was surprised herself at what a long story she had to tell. By the time she had concluded it some of the coolness between Richard and Marian had dissolved in their concern for Lyndsey.

'We ought never to have gone away and left you,' Richard declared. 'You could have been killed.'

Marian replied, speaking quietly, 'She could have been killed anywhere, even walking along the street.' Then she added, 'We must have an evening out together, belatedly to celebrate your birthday, Lyndsey. I felt mean that we couldn't do it at the time.'

Lyndsey tried to stress that there was no need to celebrate it but Marian insisted and fixed a date.

Things seemed to have settled down during the next two days between Richard and Marian, not that they were at all loving with one another but there was none of the resentment present at their homecoming. But then on the Thursday afternoon, when Lyndsey came home from the Centre, she heard angry voices coming from the sitting room, and as she closed the front door quietly she heard Marian shout:

'I'll need more explanation than that, Richard, and you know it! Of course I'm jealous, but only because you've been so secretive about it. Give me one good reason why you should go and visit Bette Bascony, only one!'

Lyndsey, who had crossed the hall to go upstairs, paused and stood tense. Richard – visiting Bette?

Richard came storming out of the room and left without bothering to put on his overcoat, and Lyndsey, not wanting to meet Marian at this stage, went on upstairs, wondering why on earth Richard had visited Bette *and* been so secretive about it. Well, she would be going to Kent the next day so perhaps she would get to know the reason.

When Lyndsey came downstairs Marian was so composed it was difficult to imagine she had been in such a tearing temper minutes before. And when, later in the day, Lyndsey mentioned about going to Kent for the weekend Marian said, 'It will be a nice change for you. I know how you and Bette enjoy a chat and the weather seems settled.'

Bette was up when Lyndsey arrived and they greeted one another joyously. But although Bette was her own effervescent self she was pale and walked slowly. Lyndsey made her sit down then went into the kitchen to put the kettle on to make some tea. At first she talked from the kitchen about the Wrens then left the kettle on the gas and came back into the sitting room.

'Mind you, I would like to be part of Boats' Crew, but if I can get by the sea I'll settle for that. I do miss the sea terribly at times. There are moments when I imagine I can smell seaweed! Crazy, isn't it?'

'Oh, I don't think so, the wind could carry it across.' Bette laughed. 'What I think I can smell at times is more crazy. I feel I can smell the theatre, the greasepaint – ' Her voice dropped and her eyes took on a faraway look. 'It has an atmosphere, a smell all of its own, people, scents, a mustiness, paint, dust . . . and I loved it all. Sorry, I'm letting myself get carried away.'

The kettle began a shrill whistling as it boiled and Lyndsey went to make the tea. When she came back with the tray she said, 'What are the Boomerangs doing at the moment?'

Bette said that they were doing well, doing shows all over the place, but mentioned that they kept saying they missed her guidance. 'I'll be running around soon, Lyndsey. I want to be well enough if we do get the chance to go abroad with ENSA.'

They talked and talked and it was not until the evening

that Lyndsey brought up the subject of the row between Richard and Marian.

'It's not really my business, Bette, but I hate to see Uncle Richard unhappy.'

Bette, who did not look in any way guilty, sighed.

'Richard phoned me last night, told me about the row and asked me not to say anything to you about it, but now that you know what I think it might be wise to tell you the truth. It was before Christmas when he turned up quite unexpectedly, said he was in the vicinity in connection with his work and felt he couldn't leave without giving me a call.'

'But why did he call, was he upset in any way?'

'Yes, he was. Apparently he didn't want to go to his in-laws and said that he and Marian had had an awful row.'

'Didn't you wonder why he should come to you with his troubles?'

'Yes, I did, Lyndsey, and I took it there was no one else he could talk to. He was really distraught. I felt sorry for him, yet I had to be careful what I said because I didn't want to be involved in any marriage troubles. It's for the couple to sort out their problems.'

They were silent for a while and the room seemed to be listening, then a log shifted in the grate and ashes dropped with a soft plop into the pan below. There was a faint cheep from one of the canaries as though one of them had been dreaming. Bette got up and pulled the cover of one of the cages further down. Then, when Bette was seated again, Lyndsey said:

'I think I can guess why Uncle Richard came to see you, Bette. You have a warmth and an understanding that's lacking in Marian. But I simply can't understand why he should tell her that he had been to see you. He really was asking for trouble, wasn't he?'

'He didn't tell her, someone else did. A friend, or should I say a so-called friend, had apparently seen us at the station. I went to see him off. Richard kissed me on the cheek, just a peck, but the sort of thing that would rock empires in Roman times when Emperors had their wives watched and the wives had their husbands watched. And an incident such as ours would be exaggerated a hundred times.'

Lyndsey sighed. 'The more I see and hear of the complexities of human nature, of the little affairs that people have, the less I want to get married.'

'Oh, Lyndsey,' Bette gave her deep-throated chuckle, 'you're talking like an old woman, darling. You're young, far too young to worry about the complexities of anything.'

'But not too young to suffer disillusionment over Andrew,' Lyndsey said quietly. Bette immediately sobered.

'I'm sorry, I had forgotten it for the moment. It shows how wrapped up we are in our own lives. But at the same time I think you must accept this as a part of life, a growing-up process. Few people escape it.'

Bette paused then went on, 'You are an essentially honest person, Lyndsey, and I shall be honest with you. I could find it easy to fall in love with Richard, but I would never let him know this, not even if he were to tell me that he loved *me*, which I'm sure he wouldn't. As I said before, I'm not out to destroy a marriage.'

'I know,' Lyndsey said earnestly. 'But I also know how easy it is for a marriage to go on the rocks. And I have a feeling that Richard and Marian will be heading this way if they're not careful. I blame them both, Marian with her jealousy and Richard for being stupid enough to come and see you when he knows of Marian's jealousy. No, not for coming to see you, but for making a secret of it.'

'I agree,' Bette said. 'But how many times in life do we do the right thing?' She smiled. 'You are at least getting a good grounding in ways to make a marriage work. With, of course, the important ingredient of both of you being in love.'

Lyndsey was silent a moment, staring into the fire, then she looked up.

'Bette, how do you know when you are really in love? I still feel at times that I'm in love with Andrew and at other times with Elliott. Is there a different kind of love which I haven't yet experienced that tells you at once it's the right one?'

'There is something that tells you, at least it did with me, but I should imagine every person, every couple, is different. I fell in love with Rupert at once, but although I was attracted to other men even after I was married I knew that the love I had for Rupert was all enduring, and that I would never love any other man in the same way. It's something one can't explain.'

Lyndsey sat thoughtful for a moment then she said, 'Ivy once told me about a woman who lived in Echo Cove. Her husband had numerous affairs and eventually she left him. Ten years later the husband died and she married again, but she told Ivy that although she loved her second husband the love she had for the first was something that would go beyond the grave. Strange, isn't it?'

Bette gave a wry smile. 'They say that women are attracted to the villains.'

Lyndsey laughed. 'Then I had better look for a villain. In the meantime I'll stop worrying, seeing that I'm not desperate to get married.'

Richard and Marian were not mentioned again until the Monday morning when Lyndsey was ready to leave. Then Bette said, 'Lyndsey, if you get the chance to put things right between Richard and his wife, will you do so?' Lyndsey promised but doubted whether it would ever be mentioned.

In that, however, she was wrong. On the Monday afternoon Marian broached it while Richard was out. She told Lyndsey about the row and said she had been so hurt at Richard's secrecy and asked if Bette had mentioned his visit.

Lyndsey said, 'I told her because I heard part of your quarrel and couldn't understand why Uncle Richard should go to see Bette with his troubles. Bette didn't know either, but I think I know the reason. Bette has a warmth, Marian, which perhaps you lack, or at least you don't show. There's nothing between Bette and Uncle Richard, I can assure you of that, and the person who told you of Richard's visit lied if she put any more into it than just a visit.'

'But if only he had not made such a secret of it!' It was a wail of despair from Marian. Then she gave a sigh. 'I should know why, it's because I'm so jealous, but I can't help it, I really can't.'

Lyndsey was beginning to feel annoyed with Marian. After all she was not a youngster. She said, 'If you don't *try* you'll just go on making your own kind of hell. Bette told me I was too young to worry about the complexities of life, but I think if I don't try and understand all the complexities I'll never be able to avoid the pitfalls.'

'I don't think you will be able to avoid them,' Marian said quietly. 'If we could when we're young there would be no problems later. We make fools of ourselves without realizing it. I've been a fool. Richard didn't want to go to my parents for Christmas because they've always resented him, not because he was a man of the world, but because they wanted to have an unmarried daughter at home. I knew it, but wouldn't say anything, instead I kept defending them.'

'And what about next Christmas? What do you say then? Will you still insist on his going home with you without saying anything?'

'No, I shall have a talk with my parents, long before then. Perhaps I am learning, Lyndsey. Anyway, thanks for listening.' She got up.

Lyndsey wished she could feel closer to Marian but was aware of a barrier still between them, and wondered for the first time if perhaps she was responsible for it.

She stood up saying, 'I hope everything works out all right for you and Uncle Richard, Marian,' and took a step towards her, intending to put her arms around her and give her a hug, but Marian, as though anticipating it, stepped aside.

Lyndsey might have felt a rebuff had she not known that many loving people could not bear an outward show of affection.

As Ivy had been wont to say, 'It takes all sorts of people to make a world.'

TWENTY

Richard and Marian made up their quarrel and although they were not exactly loving towards one another there was no longer that awful tension between them.

Lyndsey's interview was to be held in a school and because she was not familiar with the district she left early. She had been directed through a maze of streets and was still not sure of the place, so she went into a café to ask the way. The girl behind the counter nodded towards two girls sitting together at one of the tables. 'They're going to the same place, they'll show you.'

Lyndsey turned and a solidly built girl with a round, weatherbeaten face called cheerily, 'Hello, come and take a pew.' She introduced herself as Fay Ashton and the girl beside her as Stephanie Leadbitter then said, 'We've just met, but as we are all to be interrogated we may as well share our knowledge.'

Stephanie, a small, sweetly pretty girl with golden hair, laughed. 'I came in here all screwed up with nerves and Fay's made me feel I'm embarking on a great adventure.'

'Of course it's an adventure,' Fay declared. 'None of us knows where we'll be sent. What section do you want to be in, Lyndsey?'

'Boats' Crew,' she replied promptly. 'I was born and brought up by the sea and was interested in boats almost as soon as I could walk.'

Fay frowned. 'Trouble is, most girls want to be on the water. I do and – '

'I don't,' Stephanie interrupted. 'I was brought up in a mining village, left it two years ago and came to London to get away from coal, coal, coal, lived with my married sister and her husband who started, believe it or not, a coal delivery service! I think I would rather like to be a cook.'

'We'll all probably have to take what jobs are offered,' Fay said. 'According to what I hear we'll be placed where we're most needed. I think it might be wise to have a second line to talk about. I wouldn't mind being in Motor Transport, I can drive a car.'

Lyndsey thought about it then said, 'I wouldn't mind doing the same. I can drive a car and take down an engine, and I can also ride a motor bike and repair it.' She laughed. 'Not that my parents knew I did either. When I met my boyfriends it was always well away from the house.'

Fay gave a quick approving nod. 'A sensible girl, a girl after my own heart.'

They still had plenty of time to spare before their interviews and they went on talking. Lyndsey and Stephanie learned that Fay was used to helping her father sail his yacht, but warned them not to get the picture wrong. 'I'm not the daughter of a wealthy man! My family are always on the verge of bankruptcy, have been as far back as I can remember.' She spoke so cheerfully about it that Lyndsey and Stephanie laughed.

Stephanie said, 'They wouldn't be on the verge of bankruptcy if they met my mother, her maxim being "Cut your coat according to your cloth"! And do you know something? I was getting a bit that way myself until I came to London. Then I spent nearly all my savings on going all over the place, theatres and what have you. It was grand! I don't regret a minute of it.'

Fay grinned from one to the other. 'Do you know what,

290

I think the three of us will get on well together, I hope we'll be lucky enough to share a cabin.'

Lyndsey looked up quickly. 'If we got into Boats' Crew would we be on a ship?'

This was when Fay initiated them into naval jargon. The building where they would do their training would have the name of a ship; beds were bunks, bedrooms cabins, windows portholes and floors decks. 'And it's possible,' she added, 'we shall have to scrub and polish these decks *and* clean portholes.'

Fay, it seemed, had a friend who was in the Wrens, and this was why she was so well informed. When the time came for them to leave the café to go for their interviews Stephanie declared she was now ready to face ten admirals, and the whole fleet if necessary, and Lyndsey, who had been a little nervous herself when she set out, felt the same way. She hoped very much the three of them *would* share a 'cabin'.

There were several other girls in the room they were shown into. They all glanced at the three and some gave a self-conscious smile, but then stared at the wall facing them. Fay was the only one who did any talking and even she conducted the conversation in whispers, after having been told by a woman sitting at a desk to lower her voice as an interview was being held in the next room.

They had agreed before they arrived at the school that whoever was interviewed first would wait for the others. Stephanie was called first, Fay followed her some ten minutes later, but as they did not come back into the room Lyndsey presumed they had left by another exit. It was then she began to feel a little apprehensive. She had put down on her application form about wanting to be part of Boats' Crew but now she wondered if she *should* mention she could drive a car or take a chance. She did so much want to be on the sea.

When her name was eventually called she got up, took

a deep breath and decided she would just let things take their course.

The officer Wren who interviewed her, in spite of a rather stern appearance, had quite a pleasant manner and Lyndsey found herself feeling at ease and talked at great length. Afterwards, she felt she had talked too much and when she left and met Fay and Stephanie she said, 'I'm sure I gabbled and talked much more about driving a car than I did about handling a boat. I bet I'll be sent to Motor Transport!'

Fay consoled her with the thought that it was in the lap of the gods and they would not have any say where they wanted to be.

Stephanie sighed. 'And now it's just a question of waiting. I hope it won't be too long before we hear.'

Ten days later Lyndsey had word to say she was to report to the drafting depot at Mill Hill where girls were expected to do two weeks provisional training to prove their suitability for service life, after which they would be drafted to naval bases all over the country.

Lyndsey was jubilant and found it impossible to settle down. She wrote to both Fay and Stephanie and letters came back from both of them said they too would be reporting on the same day. She phoned Bette who made her promise to come for a weekend before she left.

Richard and Marian took her out for a celebration dinner and presented her with a soft leather travelling bag that must have cost the earth.

The weekend before Lyndsey was due to leave she went to Bette's and found that the Boomerangs had arranged a party. It was to be a double celebration because *they* had been accepted for ENSA.

Bette said afterwards, 'I only hope that when you get leave, Lyndsey, I shall be here to welcome you.' They both wept when they parted, but as Bette remarked, they were both starting yet another new life, another adventure as it were, and they would have so much to tell one another they would be filling pages in their letters.

Although Lyndsey was looking forward so much to her new life she could not imagine at that moment her life without Bette being a part of it.

Richard said the evening before she was due to leave, 'If there is anything you need, Lyndsey, any money, or if you need advice of any kind, you only have to ask.'

'I know,' she said, 'and thank you both for taking such good care of me.' She was near to tears and Marian said:

'It's what you want, Lyndsey, and I know you'll enjoy doing whatever it is that's allotted to you. Do keep in touch, we'll be anxious to know how you're getting on.' Lyndsey promised.

Richard drove her to Mill Hill and repeated what he had said previously, that he and Marian would be there if she needed them. He held her closely for a moment then was in the car and drove quickly away.

At first Lyndsey had the feeling of her first arrival at boarding school, the milling around of people and not knowing anyone, but then she saw Fay and Stephanie and there was a joyful reunion, as though they had been friends for years.

While they waited their turn to report Fay told Stephanie that according to a friend of the family cooks were in demand for the Wrens. 'So,' she said, 'you might get your wish.'

'If they're so desperate for cooks,' Lyndsey said gloomily, '*we* two might also be put in that section.'

'Heaven forbid!' Fay exclaimed. 'The one occasion when I made pastry I had to use a hammer and chisel to cut it – same with the cake I made.' They all laughed and a girl in front turned to them and said she wished she could laugh, she was scared stiff. She had been a ballet dancer and had wanted to do her bit for her country. Another girl said, 'You would have been better going into ENSA and entertaining the troops.'

293

The queue began to move and the conversation ended.

After they reported they were sent for a medical, at which, during the examination, they were searched for head and body lice. They were then given bedding and Lyndsey to her joy was to share a 'cabin' with Fay and Stephanie and five other girls. And again it was Fay who initiated them all into the art of folding in the corners of sheets as they did in hospitals, and also saw that the bed-cover was placed to suit the standards of the person who would examine the bunks.

During this they learned that two of the five girls had had office jobs, one had been a shop assistant, the fourth a hairdresser and the fifth a tightrope walker in a circus! Which proved conclusively to Lyndsey that it was not necessarily girls who had connections with the sea, or had a member of the family who was sea-faring that were accepted into the Service. Before this she had thought that Stephanie was an exception.

It was a shock to some of them when they knew they would have to be up at half past five every morning. Lyndsey was a natural early riser, so was Fay, but the girl who had been in hairdressing wailed that she had been used to going for a bus to work at eight o'clock every morning with her eyes closed. Half past five was an ungodly hour.

They soon learned what was meant by a full day's work. There were bunks to be made up, 'decks' not only to be swept and scrubbed but later polished. Latrine blocks were scrubbed. They were drilled, and had several hours of lectures each day. These covered navy etiquette, traditions, terms and customs; ranks, ratings and badges, the division of commands and sub-commands, nautical nicknames and who to salute and when . . . The variety was endless.

A lecture on 'Security' was followed by a film on naval intelligence. There was also an interesting talk by a woman doctor on sex and hygiene.

By the end of three days Lyndsey felt her head was

packed with facts and that she was already part of the navy, especially when drilling, even though they were not as yet kitted out.

The following day the interviewing started. Two days later Lyndsey was summoned to the office and told she was to be sent to Portsmouth for training for their stores there.

'Stores?' Lyndsey echoed, staring in disbelief.

'Clothing. You will issue clothing, all this will be explained to you.'

Lyndsey left feeling dazed. And found Fay and Stephanie laughing their heads off. 'I'm going to be a cook!' Stephanie exclaimed. 'Isn't it great?'

Lyndsey looked at Fay and Fay wiped her eyes and said, 'And I'm going to dish out clothes. Isn't *that* a laugh?'

'A laugh? I've been put in Stores too, I'm furious. What about Boats' Crew and Motor Transport?'

'Not to worry,' Fay said, 'we can always transfer to Boats' Crew when there are vacancies. Who knows, you mightn't even want to transfer, you might become so fascinated dishing out shirts and trousers, and – '

'Oh, don't,' Lyndsey pleaded. 'I can't bear the disappointment.'

Fay then said quietly, 'Lyndsey, lovey, you should have joined to help the war effort, *not* to satisfy your love of boats.'

Lyndsey then felt ashamed. 'You're right of course. Thanks for reminding me. There is one consolation. If we're going to Portsmouth we will at least be by the sea.' Stephanie was to be sent to Plymouth and they were all sorry they were to be parted.

Before they left they were kitted out with uniforms and Lyndsey who was used to wearing pure silk cami-knicks, was tickled to death with the issue of three pairs of thick woollen navy blue knickers, which were apparently known as 'passion killers'. Although she swore she would not wear them until she was forced to she also knew she would have a great feeling of pride wearing the uniform.

Her first impression of Portsmouth was the bomb dereliction. She said to Fay, 'I knew they had had some heavy raids, but I had no idea it was as bad as this. Terrible, isn't it?'

Fay replied, 'I expected to see plenty of naval personnel, but I certainly never expected to see as many as this. They're everywhere.'

They went to the dockyard where they were to report and Lyndsey became excited at seeing so many ships. There were destroyers, merchant ships, minesweepers, MTBs and corvettes.

'Just look at them, Fay, isn't it a magnificent sight?'

'You're certainly dotty about the sea and ships aren't you?' Fay grinned. 'Much worse than I am.'

After they had reported they were taken to a large house at Southsea, which had been commandeered by the Wrens, and there they found they were to share a 'cabin' with four other girls, who all turned out to be friendly.

The next morning they travelled by bus to the dockyard and were taken to Supplies, a massive shed, where shelves were stocked with clothing of every description. A chief petty officer explained their duties. Ratings, men and women, would come on different days to shop and there would be special days for officers. They would all produce clothing chits but would pay for their purchases. The officer then went on to explain that there would be a great deal of paperwork involved and she would now pass them over to someone else to explain this.

Lyndsey decided it would be about the most boring job there was, but within a few days she had to change her mind. They dealt with men who, having been torpedoed, had to be kitted out, and these men were so cheerful Lyndsey didn't know whether to laugh or cry.

One said, 'Cor, it were worth being in an open boat for three days wivout food or water just to have a glimpse of yer lovely smile. 'Ow's about 'aving a twirl round the ballroom tonight?'

The man with him said, 'Watch it, gal, 'e's got two left feet has Sam. Now me, I'm world's champeen.'

'Sorry, fellers,' Lyndsey said, 'I'm on duty tonight.'

'Ow about tomorrer, eh?'

The officer Wren arriving at the window had them all smartening to attention, but before they left they were all fighting cheerfully as to who was eventually to be Lyndsey's escort.

There were also the shy ones who would come to buy handkercheifs, or a tie, or a pair of socks, who would have little to say but who would linger and Lyndsey, sensing they just wanted to talk, would ask them about their family. Then photographs would come out and they would talk about their homes, their Mums and Dads and sisters and brothers and their girlfriends.

'They're the lonely ones,' Fay said, 'the shy ones who have to live on dreams.'

One day when an able seaman came in to buy a collar for his tunic, he asked Lyndsey if he could have one that had belonged to a dead man. She felt an icy shiver go up and down her spine. The man then explained that when a collar was new the blue stripes around the edge ran into the white, but if it had been washed a number of times it was all right. Although Lyndsey had heard the shed described as the dead men's stores, it was not until she had the request for the collar that she felt she was involved with death; and wanted to be out of it.

When she told Fay she was going to apply for a transfer to Boats' Crew Fay said, her tone impatient, 'For heaven's sake, Lyndsey, you are in the navy. Men *do* get drowned. I don't think the powers-that-be would take kindly to you asking for a transfer, not if you're as squeamish as all that. They could kick you out.'

'Yes, of course, it was stupid. Forget it.'

Although Fay always said she looked forward to officers'

day she was just as cagey as Lyndsey about accepting all the dates they were offered, and these men were just as varied. There were the madly attractive ones who were confident of a girl accepting them at once and were taken aback when told they had more dates than they could cope with. There were others who would ask quietly for a date and not try and push when refused.

Fay did accept a date with a chief petty officer and said she had enjoyed the evening so much she had arranged to have dinner with him the following week. 'He's married,' she said, 'and all he wanted was a pair of ears, but he was jolly good company. A nice chap who's madly in love with his wife. Suits me. I don't want any romantic involvements, not yet anyway.'

Lyndsey, not wanting any involvements either, had refused all offers of dining out until the day a lieutenant came in who reminded her of Andrew. And yet, apart from his height he was not a bit like Andrew. His hair was brown, not fair, and his eyes were hazel instead of blue. She must have been staring at him because he teased her:

'How flattering to have a girl look at me with such awe. I know I'm madly attractive, of course, but – '

Lyndsey smiled then. 'Now I know why you reminded me of a friend.'

'And is he fun to be with, like me?'

'I haven't had a chance to prove it,' she said, pert for once.

'Then come out with me this evening. We can walk, talk, dance, have a drink, have dinner, just say the word. Oh, by the way the name is Bill Denning, and I know your name. So, Lyndsey, what about it?'

She found herself agreeing and he arranged to pick her up at her quarters at seven o'clock. He was moving away when she reminded him he had not bought anything.

He gave her a broad smile. 'I didn't want to buy anything. I came in to see you, to see if what the chaps were saying about you was true. An Irishman described you as a gem in a box of fakes. How's that for a description? Another chap said you were a real beaut, with the friendliest of smiles, but up to now no one had been able to persuade you to accept a date.'

Lyndsey flared. 'So you made a bet with them saying that *you* would persuade me to go out with you. Well let me tell you – '

'I didn't make a bet, Lyndsey, honest, I didn't.' He spoke quietly. 'I just wanted to see you and when I had I knew that nothing would give me greater pleasure than to share an evening with you. Please don't let me down.'

She gave in, but was not sure that she was doing the right thing. Well, she would make this a 'one off', then there would be no more dates, not for the time being at any rate. She had hardly had a chance to get settled in.

Lyndsey waited for him that evening outside her quarters. The moon was on the wane, giving sufficient light to recognize him when he turned the corner. He walked briskly, stopped on seeing her and she came down the steps.

'You *are* prompt, Lieutenant!'

'So are you, unusual for a female. I'm *so* glad you didn't stand me up.'

'How many girls have?'

'Well, like George Washington, I cannot tell a lie. None, actually. But then, how could they, it's not often they get the chance of a date with such an attractive bloke.' His smile was infectious and Lyndsey tried hard not to laugh.

'How can you bear to live with such an inflated ego?'

'I must admit it's not easy.' He tucked her arm through his. 'And now, after all that tomfoolery shall we go and have something to eat?'

The air-raid alert was on but so far there had been no activity and the town was crowded with personnel from all the services, the navy predominating.

The restaurant they went to was also crowded, reminding Lyndsey of the brasserie at Lyons' Corner

House, only there was no orchestra playing. And with this Ed came into her mind and she wondered where he was, she had heard nothing from him.

They had to wait for a table and when an elderly waiter came to tell them he had found them one for two Bill said, 'Lucky us.' Unfortunately they were near the kitchen so they had to compete to make themselves heard over the voices shouting orders, the clinking of crockery and the rattling of cutlery.

'Just the spot for a romantic interlude!' Bill declared, laughing.

'People who make wars are no respecters of lovers,' Lyndsey replied, and realized as soon as she had spoken she might be giving Bill the wrong idea. And apparently she was right because he said in a light, but confidential way, 'Don't worry, I know of such places.'

He then asked where her home was, and how long she had been in the services. She just touched on the death of her parents, said she was a raw recruit and asked about his family. He told her, a look of unhappiness in his eyes, that he had recently been jilted.

'Not exactly on the eve of the wedding, but it was only weeks beforehand. We had actually rented a house and furnished it. Then she met this army captain. She told me she couldn't help herself, she felt something for him that she had never felt for me, although she had been so sure she was in love with me.' He spread his hands with a gesture of despair. 'So what can I do about it? Nothing. My family tell me I'm lucky, far better to find out now than after we had been married, but it doesn't help, I still love Carol and it still hurts.'

Lyndsey knew now why he had asked her out, why he had behaved in such a light-hearted way. He wanted company, and had not wanted to show his hurt. She told him she understood how he felt and he began to question her, had she suffered the same fate, and when she told him briefly about Andrew he asked her how she had coped.

'Well,' she said, 'it was different in my case. For one thing we weren't engaged and for another I was not altogether sure that I wanted to get married.' She sat looking at him. 'I don't know how one recognizes the real thing, Bill.'

He nodded slowly. 'Oh, you'll know when it happens. I'm certain of one thing, that I'll never love anyone like I love Carol. She was my world – and I seemed to be hers. She was warm, loving, like a little kitten, all soft and cuddly.'

He gave a self-conscious laugh. 'Oh, Lord, you must think me an utter oaf, taking out a lovely girl and drooling on about my lost love. Forgive me, Lyndsey. Tell me about Echo Cove, I don't know that part of the country at all.'

There was a companionship developing between them that Lyndsey appreciated. She had a feeling that although Bill might want to kiss her there would be nothing further than that. He more or less hinted at it and she was glad.

He asked her if she would like to go dancing after the meal and she told him she would rather walk and talk and he said he preferred it too. And Bill did know the quiet places away from the crowds, where the waning moon touched the waves with silver and ships were just outlines. Lyndsey talked of her love of the sea and Bill said, 'So you would perhaps be prepared to marry a sailor? I think it was the long separations that worried Carol, but then there are always the homecomings, aren't there?' There was almost a pleading in his voice and he suddenly laid an arm across her shoulders and gave her a squeeze. 'There I go again, harping on about Carol, I must stop thinking about her. Seen any good films lately?'

Lyndsey smiled. 'Some good, some bad and some indifferent. I've seen "Gone with the Wind" three times.'

'You have? And I bet you fell for that Rhett Butler, all the girls do, and he was such a swine.'

'But a masterful lover!'

Bill said, laughing. 'This is the part where I should snatch you into my arms and say, "Like this?" but I won't.'

301

They walked in silence for a while then Lyndsey drew in breaths of the cold salty air. 'Good, isn't it?'

Bill stopped and they stood looking out to sea. The moon had gone behind a cloud and the darkness was so complete that for a few moments even the outlines of ships had disappeared. Then Bill suddenly began to whistle, and it was like listening to the sweet clear notes of a nightingale. They tugged at Lyndsey's emotions as she remembered Andrew wanting to go to Berkeley Square, having liked Vera Lynn's rendering of 'A Nightingale Sang in Berkeley Square'.

When the notes died away she said softly, 'That was beautiful, Bill. Where did you learn to whistle like that?'

'I come from a whistling family on my father's side. He could mimic any birdsong and call. People tell him he missed his vocation, but he is first and foremost a man of the sea.'

'And you, can you imitate any other kind of bird?'

'I can. A thrush, a canary and a blackbird. Want to hear?'

He went into his repertoire and Lyndsey felt more emotional then ever, not only because of thinking of Andrew but knowing that for the first time since leaving London she was experiencing her first bout of homesickness.

When the last notes died away Bill said, 'That's it! Show over, that will cost you sixpence.' His voice held laughter.

Lyndsey's voice held a tremor as she said, trying to speak in a teasing way, 'And what happens if I can't pay?'

'Then I shall demand kisses in payment. A penny for each one.'

'Threepence each. I shall pay for one now and the other later.'

'Done!' He drew her into his arms and warm lips covered hers. There was passion in his kiss and she responded, needing love, and knowing that Bill needed it too.

'Oh, Lyndsey,' he murmured in a broken voice, 'will you

let me love you properly?' Aware suddenly of the dangers she drew quickly away and he said, 'Sorry I scared you. I won't do it again.' He gave a shaky laugh. 'Consider the debt paid.'

They moved away and walked in silence. Lyndsey longed to get back to their former light-hearted mood but could not think of anything to say. She had not asked for a late night pass and knowing she had to be in her quarters by ten o'clock she suggested they start making their way back.

On the way Bill said hesitantly, 'I have to return to base the day after tomorrow. Dare I ask you to go out with me tomorrow evening? I promise to behave myself.'

She agreed and once more he laid an arm companionably across her shoulders. 'You really are a great girl, Lyndsey, you've no idea just how good you've been to me. I can't think of any other girl who would have put up with all my drooling over Carol. But then,' he said softly, 'you're not just any other girl, you're someone very special.'

'You better stop that,' she warned, 'or I shall be getting big-headed.'

'Not you.' They had reached her quarters and he drew a finger lightly over her cheek. 'Not you, Lyndsey. See you tomorrow. Sleep well.' He saluted her then was swallowed up into the night.

Lyndsey would have liked to have gone straight to bed, but she met Fay in the hall who said, 'Come on into the mess, tell me how you got on, we've got twenty minutes.'

'It will only take one. He's a really nice fellow who was jilted. But I enjoyed the evening. How did you get on?'

'Great, he's a nice guy too, who as I said, simply needs a pair of ears. Fancy a hot drink?'

In bed later Lyndsey wondered whether she would see Bill again after the following night, or whether they would be 'ships that pass in the night'.

Elliott came into her mind before she slept and she thought it strange that he now seemed so remote, just as Andrew did . . . and Ed. She had not heard from Ed or

303

Elliott recently, nor Andrew, but then unless he wrote to Bette she would not hear anything. He was now someone who really belonged to the past. Or did he? This evening had proved otherwise. He still had the power to cause her pain.

TWENTY-ONE

The following morning there was a note for Lyndsey from Bill to say he had been called back to base earlier than expected. 'I'm upset about it, Lyndsey,' he wrote. 'I was so looking forward to seeing you again. For me it was a memorable evening, to be with such a warm and understanding person. You'll often be in my thoughts in the quiet hours. I pray we can have another such evening. In the meantime, I send you my good wishes. You are a darling girl, Lyndsey. Think of me now and again, will you? Bill.'

Lyndsey felt saddened. Would Bill turn out to be someone who had flitted into her life and out again? She had liked him, had enjoyed his company. She decided not to accept any more dates for a while.

As it happened there would have been little chance of going very far, the raids were heavy again, and, when they did ease, she went with Fay or one of the other girls to see a film either outside or inside the unit and to ENSA shows in the NAAFI. She also started knitting, making gloves and scarves for servicemen.

Fay's married friend had gone back to sea and she said she missed him, he was mature and intelligent. But she did have letters from him. Lyndsey had no word at all from Bill. She did hear from Bette, who told her they were doing more shows than ever and enjoying every one, they were so rewarding. 'And,' she wrote, 'we are quite well

305

known now. I think it's mainly because of our "choir boys", they really are superb. They've had offers of better things, but they're loyal and say they'll stick with us.' There was general news, Mrs Petrie sent her love, Bette said she loved having Lyndsey's letters and asked her to keep sending them.

There were letters too from Richard and Marian but neither had very much to say. A letter from Elliott had been forwarded but his was not even as chatty as they had been in the past. She was pleased to hear from him but felt dissatisfied afterwards that he didn't even this time ask teasingly how their 'serial' was progressing.

When a second letter came quickly from Bette after the last Lyndsey wondered if she had heard they were to be posted abroad, but the first line had her sitting tense. It was to tell her that Andrew's wife Freda had been killed in a raid.

'He's grieving so, Lyndsey, and blames himself, which is of course, all wrong. The poor girl could have been killed anywhere. He speaks with such sorrow of the baby, says the little tiny thing had had its life extinguished before it had hardly begun . . .'

There was more but Lyndsey could not read on for the tears blinding her as she wept for the loss of a girl she had never known, for an embryo and for Andrew who she felt sure had already loved his unborn child. Life was so cruel.

The rest of Bette's letter asked Lyndsey to write to him. 'He wanted you to know,' she said. 'Just a few lines, Lyndsey, he's so far away from home and I feel it will help if he knows someone else cares.'

Lyndsey thought it would be a difficult letter to write but once she started she seemed to find the right words to commiserate with him in his loss without becoming maudlin, which she felt she might have done.

Two days later she was belatedly reading *The Times* when she noticed Bill's name in the obituary column: 'Lieutenant William S. Denning, son of Captain and Mrs Denning . . .

killed in action . . .' She sat numbed, unable to believe it. Bill, so full of life fighting hard to forget his hurt . . . It was in this numbed state that Fay found her ten minutes later.

'Lyndsey – what's wrong?' Lyndsey looked at her in a blank way and Fay took the paper from her, read the piece and took Lyndsey by the arm. 'Come on, we're going for a walk.' Lyndsey was like a zombie and after Fay had dragged a duffle coat on to her and wrapped a scarf around her throat she led her outside and gave her a shake.

'You have to snap out of it, you must. This is war and there's damn all that you or I or anybody else can do to stop the slaughter. Lyndsey, do you hear?' She gave her another vigorous shake and life came back to Lyndsey's limbs.

'Yes, I hear, let's walk.' There was a north-east gale blowing and as they battled along the front an icy drizzle stung Lyndsey's cheeks which, as she said afterwards, restored her to some sense of sanity. They found a small café to shelter from the gusts of wind that almost took their breath away and it was in there that Fay lectured her.

'Your trouble is, Lyndsey, that you suffer everyone's pain. You'll have to stop it, or it'll destroy you.'

Lyndsey unwound the scarf from around her throat. 'Tell me, how *do* you stop it? You either feel it or you don't.'

'You harden yourself. A friend once accused me of being soulless because I didn't weep when my youngest brother was killed. I couldn't weep, dare not, because once I'd given way I wouldn't have been able to stop, and then my mother's grief would have been worse than ever. She needed me, I was her support. I loved Dickie more than I've ever loved anyone else. He was a gentle boy who couldn't bear for a person or an animal to be hurt. But he joined up because it was expected of him.'

'I'm sorry, Fay. I think I understand how he felt. My trouble is that I had never experienced personal grief until my parents and grandparents were killed together. Since then I seem to attach myself to people. I need to love and be loved.'

'Don't we all. That's why I go out with this one and that one, yet never finding what I'm seeking.'

There was a bleak look in Fay's eyes then and Lyndsey realized how vulnerable Fay was in spite of her 'strong' talk.

Two days later when Lyndsey was still upset after the news of Bill, she heard from Brad telling her of Ed's death. He enclosed the other half of the white flower saying:

'Ed asked me if anything happened to him to send you this, he said you would understand . . .'

There was more in the letter but Lyndsey was unable to read it.

Dear, gentle Ed, who had had so much beauty in his soul. He had loved her and she was unable to return it. If only she had lied. but no, one had to be honest with Ed.

Lyndsey began to cry then, slow painful tears at first, then in a flood she was unable to stop. They took her to sick bay, but when the nurse was about to give her a sedative she thought of Fay who could not allow herself the luxury of tears when her brother had been killed. Lyndsey's tears stemmed. There were other people who had lost whole families. 'I'm all right,' she said. 'I'm over it now.'

Lyndsey, thinking to toughen herself, began using the language of the men, but apart from some of the older ones who told her they didn't like to hear it from her, she was approached by the chief petty officer who said, 'Swearing doesn't become you, MacLaren, stop it before it becomes a habit.'

Lyndsey stared straight ahead. 'Yes, Ma'am.'

And she soon realized that trying to be tough was not the answer. An unbearable ache was still with her. Then unexpectedly she was given a four-day pass and she went to spend it with Bette. For Lyndsey it was a coming home, and just having Bette hold her close and say in her warm voice, 'welcome, my love' was a start of the healing process.

They talked and talked that first day, not only discussing Andrew, Bill and Ed, but discussing little Janie's death. Bette called it an emptying of grief and Lyndsey realized she was right as the pain became less.

They walked, sometimes just Bette and Lyndsey together and at other times accompanied by Mrs Petrie and an exuberant Penny, who would race back and forth in an ecstasy of having Lyndsey back again.

Andrew was on the phone one evening to Bette, but to Lyndsey's relief Bette did not mention that she was there. It was too early to talk to him.

'He's over that first awful shock,' Bette said later, 'and he has youth on his side. And by what I can guess he has plenty of flying to keep him fully occupied. I hope that the two of you will get together again, and I'm not thinking in terms of matchmaking. Please don't think that, Lyndsey.'

Several of the Boomerangs came to see them and all talked excitedly of the theatres of war they could be sent to. Some favoured India, some the Far East, others the Middle East. Bette said after they had gone, 'Wherever we're sent won't be a picnic, but I know they all feel as I do, if we can give pleasure to men who are in outlandish places we'll be willing to put up with any hardships.'

At the end of four days Lyndsey felt completely recovered but she and Bette shed a few tears on parting, knowing that if the concert party went abroad they might not meet for a long time.

Fay welcomed Lyndsey back like a long-lost relative and said they must celebrate that evening. There were two sub-lieutenants who would be willing to make a foursome. When Lyndsey began to protest at this Fay said in an exaggerated accent, 'They're *awfully* decent chaps, don't you know.' Then she added in a normal tone, 'They really are a couple of nice fellers, Lyndsey, eager to have a drink and a good sing-song somewhere. They'll call for us in a taxi. There'll be no complications, I promise.'

The subbies, as Fay called them, *were* nice, courteous, and eager to give Fay and Lyndsey a good time. There was an air-raid alert on when they left, but although the searchlights were probing the sky there was no gunfire and no sign of any bombers. They went to a small inland pub that was so crowded they thought they would never get in. But the two men managed to make a way in and then they all stood shoulder to shoulder while a big woman, balancing a tray of drinks on one hand, yelled, 'Mind your backs, please!' and miraculously made her way through the crowd without spilling a drop. Then someone started to strum on the piano and the crowd started singing 'Roll out the Barrel', followed by, 'There'll Be Bluebirds over the White Cliffs of Dover'. Lyndsey and Fay, and the two subbies, yelled as loud as the rest, while the solid mass swayed to the music.

When a drunken soldier leered into Lyndsey's face and said, 'How's about a kiss, duckie,' Alan, the younger of the two lieutenants said, in an authoritative voice, 'Scram, mate, the lady is with me,' and the man raised a hand and turned away to leer at someone else.

Lyndsey said, 'Thanks,' and Alan smiled and replied, 'You're welcome.'

They only managed to get one drink before the beer ran out, but it didn't matter, it was just the atmosphere they had wanted. When they left, the searchlights had been switched off. Fay gave a sniff, 'I can smell fish and chips cooking somewhere. How about it?'

They all agreed and after they had queued at a shop for ages they came out with a packet of fish and chips each, soaked in vinegar, which they ate with their fingers. 'Mmm, lovely,' Fay exclaimed. 'Nothing like eating fish and chips out of newspaper.' The two men laughed and said they agreed and Gordon, the elder subbie, added, 'One of the best nights I've had in a long time.' Alan echoed this.

The night was pitch black, and they kept bumping into things, but it was all part of the enjoyment. Lyndsey was glad she had come.

Afterwards Fay called it a fun night and that was what it had been. No kisses had been exchanged but Gordon and Alan did say before they left they hoped they would all be able to meet up again when they were back in port.

The following day Lyndsey had just come off duty when she was told there was a Lieutenant Colonel Warrender waiting for her. 'Isn't he really something?' the girl said. 'You'd better hurry before he's gobbled up.'

Elliott? Impossible, there must be some mistake. Lyndsey went hurrying away. But it *was* Elliott, standing straight, his expression rather stern, but a twinkle not far from his eyes as he watched two Wrens giving him sidelong glances.

'I don't believe it,' she greeted him. 'This is the second time you've come back from abroad. Are you one of the favoured?' She was surprised at how weak she felt at the sight of him.

'Lyndsey, hello, how are you? I didn't go abroad. I've been here, there and everywhere. At the moment I'm stationed in London. I had an appointment here in Portsmouth this afternoon and wondered if we could have dinner together.'

'Why, yes, that would be lovely.'

He arranged to call for her at 7.30 and Lyndsey raced away to tell Fay. 'Elliott, of all people to turn up, I can hardly take it in.'

'I'm drooling with envy,' Fay said, 'but mind what you're doing.'

'Nothing like that with Elliott Warrender. He's the soul of honour.'

'Don't you believe it, such a man hasn't been born. I want to hear all about it when you get back, all of it mind, the truth, the whole truth and nothing but the truth.'

311

Lyndsey laughed. 'Of course, but you'll be disappointed.'

It wasn't until she went to get washed and to change into her number one uniform that she realized what a mess she looked, her hair windblown and wearing her bell-bottom trousers and thick navy jersey.

It was not Elliott who came for her but his batman, in a staff car. 'The Colonel's apologies, Miss MacLaren, he's been delayed, he'll be ready when you arrive.'

It was not to a restuarant the man took her but to a hotel, and he led the way upstairs. He knocked on the door and when Elliott appeared he left.

'Ah, there you are, Lyndsey. Come in. Sorry I couldn't call for you, I was kept much later than I expected at my second appointment.' He held out a hand. 'Let me take your coat. I've asked for dinner to be sent up here.'

'Oh, yes,' she said, looking pointedly at the double bed in the alcove.

Elliott chuckled. 'There's nothing like that in my mind. It was just that my colleague and I were interrupted in our business talk at lunchtime by a retired major, who, I'm sorry to say, has become the most awful bore. And as he is staying in the hotel – '

Lyndsey said, 'I don't know what your batman would think, bringing me up to your room.'

'Dawson knows me, and knows I would have nothing else on my mind but food.'

'Oh, thank you very much, very flattering. Aren't you trying to play God when you think you can read men's minds?'

'Lyndsey – ' Elliott drew a hand across his hair with a weary gesture. 'I've had a hell of a day and if you want to go back I'll get Dawson to take you.'

'Don't be daft, I'm as famished as you.'

He laughed then. 'I can always depend on you to come out with some down-to-earth remark.' There was a knock on the door and to Elliott's 'enter' an elderly waiter pushed

312

in a food trolley, followed by two boys carrying a table already set. The waiter hovered, asking if he could pour the wine, but Elliott told him he would manage. Man and boys left as quietly as they had come in.

'Well, Lyndsey . . .' Elliott pulled out a chair for her and when she was seated he poured the wine. 'So, tell me what you've been doing lately.'

She covered several things then he mentioned the big fire of London, adding, 'Bette told me you were involved in it.'

'Yes, I was,' she said, 'Andrew was with me – Bette's nephew.'

'I understand he lost his wife in a raid.' Lyndsey, feeling she heard a note of censure in his voice, went on:

'He came to see Bette after you had left. He had heard about her being in hospital. He had to return to London and as I was due back at work the following day we – we travelled together. Andrew wanted to explore the old streets of the city and I agreed to go with him and then, well, incendiaries began to fall and we helped to put them out.'

Lyndscy knew she had overdone the excuses for being with Andrew, but when Elliott sat silent, looking, she thought, disapproving, she bridled.

'I'm not answerable to you for my actions, Elliott!'

His eyebrows went up in surprise. 'Have I suggested you were?'

'Not exactly, but – '

'Lyndsey.' He reached out and covered her hand with his. 'Darling Lyndsey, shall we forget Andrew and talk about the ending of our serial? It really is time it came to an end and it *must* have a happy ending, the audience demand wedding bells.' There was a teasing in his voice then. 'You can't keep them waiting too long.'

Lyndsey thought of all the times they had been together when she was sure she was in love with him. There had been the serious moments, the fun times, cycling together, dancing with him, Elliott surprising her with the expertise and exuberance of his jitterbugging. She had been so wonderfully happy with him.

He got up and coming round to her drew her to her feet, saying softly, 'I love you so much, Lyndsey, need you.' He kissed her and the warm sensuousness of his mouth over hers had her emotions running wild. But although she had a desperate need to love and be loved she prevaricated.

Drawing away she looked up at him. 'Don't rush me, Elliott.'

He eyed her, his expression bland. 'Two weeks, *that* is the limit. Now, shall we see if we can do justice to the meal?'

Lyndsey said, 'But for the fact that I am still famished that vegetable dish would have gone over your head.'

Elliott smiled then. 'Do you know, my darling Lyndsey, I think that marriage with you would never be dull. Now *sit* down and I shall start serving.'

She sat down.

TWENTY-TWO

When Lyndsey told Fay about her evening Fay said, 'You must be mad keeping him dangling on a string. What happened when he brought you back?'

'He told me he would keep in touch, then he gave me a *sisterly* kiss and left. He's so tantalizing, so unpredictable.'

'Just the man for me,' Fay declared. 'You can pass him over any time. I don't want a namby-pamby man, all lovey-dovey and moonshine. He's masterful, yet caring, he's told you he wouldn't want you to resign from the Wrens – what more do you want? You don't know how lucky you are.'

'But what's the good of getting married to be apart all the time?'

Fay gave her a wicked grin. 'But think of the times you'd be together, the services are sympathetic towards married couples arranging their leaves. And think of all the second honeymoons you'd have.'

Lyndsey smiled. 'Stop it, or you'll have me sending a telegram to say, "Arrange Wedding".'

'And why not?'

Deep down Lyndsey knew why not. It was because Andrew was always there in the background. And yet, were her feelings stronger for Andrew than for Elliott? She thought not.

During the following week Lyndsey's emotions were torn this way and that. One day she would decide she would say yes to Elliott and get excited, and the next it would be no, she must wait and be sure.

Then came a morning when everything else was blotted from Lyndsey's mind by the fact that she and Fay had been accepted for Boats' Crew. It was Fay who came running to tell her that their names were on the drafting board. They jumped about together in jubilation then Lyndsey said she must see the proof. Other girls said enviously they wished *their* names were on the board.

Lyndsey remained excited and went about, as Fay said, with a smile that would not wash off. The ratings who came into the stores teased her about it.

'Wot you looking so 'appy about, Legs?' one man asked. 'Is your boyfriend on leave?' ('Legs' had become Lyndsey's nickname with some of them.)

When she told him about being transferred to Boats' Crew *his* face was one broad smile. 'That's orlright then, 'cos I'll see you on our liberty trips. If I get a skinful and fall in the drink will you fish me out and put me to bed?'

'Of course!'

One of the other assistants, an older woman, said sourly, 'And don't think you won't *have* to fish some of them out when they're all boozed up. And I'll tell you this, you'll have more to contend with than using a boathook. They're a lustful lot in drink.'

Fay, who had overheard the remark, grinned. 'Lustful? I wonder where she dug that one up? Straight out of the eighteenth century that.'

There were others who warned Lyndsey about rough weather, icy conditions, getting drenched, suffering from chilblains on hands and feet but nothing anyone could say could destroy her excitement and pleasure at the thought of working on boats.

On the Wednesday morning she and Fay crossed Portsmouth Harbour on the ferry to Gosport and reported at the Regulating Office. There a petty officer examined their papers. Lyndsey was then drafted as deckhand and Fay as stoker.

'Stoker!' Lyndsey exclaimed. 'Marvellous. You'll be able to teach me all about engines.' They did a jig.

Then Lyndsey was handed over to an established coxswain who was to take her for a trial run. The sea was choppy and the boats they had to clamber over to get to the outermost one were moving in all directions. Happily, clambering from one gunwale to the next was nothing new to Lyndsey, who nimbly followed the coxswain without mishap. She thought the woman gave her an approving look before starting the engine. She had given her name as Moreton, and Moreton ran across the thwarts, releasing first the bow-line, then the stern-line, after which she thrust off from the other boats with a boathook. She was so expert it was all done in a matter of seconds.

They circled the middle of Portsmouth Harbour several times, with Moreton pointing out various landmarks, the submarine base, the famous gunnery school at Whale Island. Lyndsey memorized these landmarks and noted the position of buoys, knowing there would come a time when she would be doing this in pitch blackness.

The following morning Fay and Lyndsey and twelve other girls travelled by bus from Southsea to Portsmouth to start their training, Fay with six prospective stokers to go to the Mechanical Training Establishment in Portsmouth Dockyard and Lyndsey with six hopeful deckhands to the Bosun's Hut on the quayside.

The moment Lyndsey stepped inside the hut she was full of nostalgia, back at home in the fisherman's hut in the harbour, with the same mingled smells of hemp, lamp oil, tar, paint, and the pungent smell of driftwood burning in the pot-bellied stove. She looked around her at the rope ladders, rope fenders, sacks, oilskins, sou'westers, sea boots, tins of paint, cleats, Aldis lamps . . .

'You better call me Herbert,' said the man who was to be their tutor. His weatherbeaten face was a network of lines, his eyes the far-seeing eyes of men who have been at sea all their lives. Some naval men had no time for the Wrens, thinking them empty-headed, but Herbert treated them with respect, speaking in a quiet voice. To Lyndsey he was her father and grandfather and all the fishermen she had known as a child rolled into one.

They had their first lesson in semaphore on the quayside and afterwards Herbert talked to them, with the girls sitting on coils of rope or hemp. He showed them how to make knots, bends and hitches and Lyndsey was fascinated. He told them all the things they would have to learn, Morse code; being able to read the position of lights and the colours of them on ships; the management of boats under oars; how to use a boathook correctly, especially to fish a man out of the sea. At this the girls exchanged glances.

Herbert paused, looked round at them all and said, his tone serious, 'I'm not trying to bamboozle you, I simply want you to know just how much you have to learn and how important it is to be proficient. One mistake and it could mean the loss of a life or lives. Never underestimate the power of the sea, ladies, and always allow for the carelessness of other people.' Herbert slapped his knees and got up. 'Now we shall have a break.'

They were served steaming mugs of tea flavoured with the unadulterated rum allowed to naval ratings each day.

When Fay and Lyndsey met late that afternoon they talked non-stop exchanging experiences. Fay was full of talk of Kelvin and Thorneycroft engines, crankshafts, pistons and cylinders and Lyndsey enthused about making fancy knots and splices with names like a Single Matthew Walker and a Double Matthew Walker, a Turk's Head Standing and a Turk's Head Running, a Monkey's Fist . . . and then going on to tell her about that afternoon when they were shown around the base.

Each day that followed was a joy to Lyndsey. They were taken out in the various boats used by the Wrens, pinnaces, cutters, launches; the launches being used mainly as liberty boats. Each boat was spotlessly clean and they were told it would be their job after crewing them to scrub out and polish them.

But the thing that stood out in Lyndsey's mind that week was the church service on the Sunday morning, held on Nelson's ship the *Victory*.

About a hundred Wrens and double that number of naval men marched to the band of the Royal Marines to the dockyard where the *Victory* lay. The first time Lyndsey had seen the black and white painted ship she had been most impressed by the majestic upsweep of the prow and the lovely three-tiered bowed windows at the stern, which reminded her of an elegant Georgian house.

Lyndsey wished she could peep into Nelson's cabin and see the beautiful polished table, whose patina had once been described by a friend as 'resembling water'. They all assembled on the quarter deck and Lyndsey had a feeling of time slipping away, this was where the crew of those bygone days must have assembled for the morning service.

The vicar began the service by repeating the prayer Nelson read to his men on the morning of 21 October 1805, when the combined fleets of France and Spain were in sight.

When Lyndsey had first seen a framed version of the prayer in a seaman's house at home she had felt a lump come into her throat and she felt emotional now on hearing it.

May the Great God, whom I worship, grant to my country and for the benefit of Europe in general, a great and glorious Victory: and may no misconduct in any one tarnish it; and may humanity after victory be the predominant feature in the British Fleet.

For myself individually, I commit my life to Him who made me and may His blessing light upon my endeavours for serving my country faithfully. To Him I resign myself and the just cause which is entrusted to me to defend.

It was not only the prayer that moved Lyndsey so deeply that morning but the knowledge that the men who sang the hymns with such feeling would know they might not return from their next voyage.

Several times that day she felt a rise of tears.

Then the following morning she had a note from Elliott that simply said, 'Serial due to come to an end. Let me know result.' It was unsigned.

She replied, 'Impossible to complete script. Have no time. Been transferred to Boats' Crew.' And she smiled as she put it in an envelope, wondering what reply it would bring.

It brought no reply and although she dismissed it as being unimportant it worried her as the days went by. Surely he was not being petty about it because he had not had his own way. Was he hurt that she was treating his proposal so lightly? Her attitude would deflate his ego. She went over all sorts of possibilities. He could have gone abroad, could be anywhere – her letter might not have reached him yet. He would be a man of decision, he would need to be in his job. Supposing he had thought, well that is the end, he would not pursue it any further?

Lyndsey felt a pang at this, knowing she would be upset if Elliott were to go right out of her life, he represented stability.

Stability? Heavens, what a tag to put on a prospective husband. And yet, stability was important. Then she thought that perhaps dependable would be a better word. Oh, forget it, she admonished herself. There was nothing she could do to change anything. As her father would say, what can't be cured must be endured.

But endurance was not easy to accept.

Two days later when Lyndsey was getting off the bus after duty her attention was caught by a blue-clad figure waiting on the corner near her quarters. Then, as she recognized Andrew, her heart began a slow pounding. She walked across to him and he came forward.

'Lyndsey, I'm sorry for turning up so unexpectedly, but I just *had* to talk to you.' They were words she had heard from him once before and she answered him now as she had answered him then, that it would serve no purpose.

'Just ten minutes, Lyndsey.' The plea, the unhappiness in his voice, had her hesitating.

'Well, all right. Just give me time to wash, I won't bother to change. Five minutes.'

While she washed her hands she thought of his loss, the pain he must have suffered and felt mean that she had tried to turn him away. When she came out she suggested they walk, and they set off through the streets.

Andrew said, 'So you managed to get into the Wrens, Lyndsey. How are you getting on? Do you like the work?' When she told him what she was doing, she felt that although he listened to what she had to say he was waiting to tell her about Freda. And he did eventually, speaking in a broken-hearted way, not only about the tragedy of his young wife but the loss of the baby.

'It was a strange thing, Lyndsey, but even when I first knew about the child I felt I loved it. I would have had a son.'

'I was really sorry about it, Andrew, it was so tragic.' She paused then asked him if he was still based in Scotland.

He told her yes but said there were rumours they would be moving soon, but he had no idea where. Then he looked up and said, a wealth of yearning in his voice, 'Oh, Lyndsey, if only we could go back to when we first met. Do you remember the fun we had in the village pub that time and coming back to Bette's in the blackout, and that air-raid warden all but arresting us?'

Andrew laughed then and Lyndsey laughed with him, but her laughter was mingled with the pain of what had been lost.

Andrew gave a sudden sigh. 'If only we could be given the wisdom of the sages when we're young, how differently we would behave.'

Lyndsey said gently, 'I think if we had the wisdom of the sages we would lose a lot of fun.'

'But avoid a lot of mistakes.'

Lyndsey eyed him thoughtfully. 'Don't you think it was because of men learning by their mistakes that they became sages?'

'Oh, wise Lyndsey. I remember once wondering why a girl like you, with so much common sense, could be such fun.' He regarded her, his expression suddenly serious. 'I think those are two things I'm missing at the moment. I've been steeped in self-pity, feeling it wouldn't be right to enjoy myself in any way, yet by talking to you I realize that life has to go on, that Freda would not have wanted me to go on grieving. In fact, she said as much once. Lyndsey, could we – could we keep in touch – write?'

She thought of him leaving, going back to base, flying, needing someone close to him to care, and knew then that he was back in her life. 'Yes, Andrew,' she said, 'I'll write to you.'

He had had to leave soon after that but for the rest of that evening an image kept coming into Lyndsey's mind of Andrew thanking her for letting him talk to her, and seeing the glint of tears in his eyes as he said, 'You'll never know just how much this means to me.'

It was two weeks before Lyndsey heard from Andrew again and the letter came on the morning of the exams. She read it quickly, then put it aside to read again once she was over the ordeal of exams. Nothing must distract her from trying to pass.

Lyndsey was so sure there would be all sorts of questions she would not know the answers to, and heaved a sigh of relief when she saw the papers. It would not exactly be a walk-over, but at least she was conversant – and more important still, interested – in every question.

There were ten girls in the room with the chief petty officer invigilating, and for four hours there was the scrape of pens on paper. Lyndsey, who was so energetic otherwise, had always been a slow, painstaking writer, and when she got cramp in her right hand in the last half hour of writing, she knew with despair there would be some questions that would have to remain unanswered.

Fay, who had already sat her exams and had felt confident enough to say she felt sure she would pass, did, with 90 per cent marks. All the girls who had sat with Lyndsey passed, the highest with 90 per cent, the lowest with 70 per cent. Lyndsey was in the 80 per cent bracket and was over the moon. 'I didn't think I was going to pass. Oh, Fay, we must celebrate!'

They went dancing and Lyndsey told every man she danced with her news, and was congratulated. One of the able seamen she knew said to three of his friends, 'D'ye hear that, mates? Legs has passed her exams. Come on, let's have a drink.'

It was the first time that Lyndsey had ever been drunk and she vowed it would be the last. The next morning not only hammers were banging in her head but there were bells ringing, a tolling that nearly drove her mad. Fay got her some aspirins and by midday she was beginning to feel a little closer to normal.

'Does everyone feel like that?' she asked with a groan. 'If so, why do they drink? It's not worth it.'

Fay grinned. 'But you must admit you enjoyed yourself last night. You were really on high C. Do you remember singing? You have a lovely voice.'

Lyndsey felt a coldness creeping over her. 'Fay, tell me one thing. Did I do any high-kicking?'

'No. Is that what you usually do when you're tight?' Fay asked, laughing.

'I've never been tight before!' She eyed Fay suddenly in alarm. 'Who brought me back? Please say you were there.'

'I never left your side, lovey. But you know, Lyndsey,

323

they were all decent chaps, they really cared about you. You wouldn't have come to any harm with any of them we were with last night.'

It was not until later in the day that Lyndsey read Andrew's letter again. It was full of praise for all she had done for him. 'It really set me up again, Lyndsey. It had been a constant grief to me that I had let you down so badly. You're a wonderful person, one in a million. Knowing that you don't hate me has restored my confidence in myself, which I was gradually losing. And that's the last thing that should happen in *my* job – or in any other job for that matter. Let me know how you get on with your exams. And forgive me for taking so long to write to you. I had to wait and simmer down a little after I saw you, otherwise I might have been saying things to you that I would have regretted. I think you can guess what they would be, and that's something I know you won't wear. Write when you can, Lyndsey, I'll look forward very much to your letters. And thanks again, Andrew.'

Two days after hearing the results of the exam Lyndsey, Fay and six more girls who had been on the course were drafted to HMS *Excellent* at Whale Island.

Lyndsey eyed Fay with dismay. 'HMS *Excellent*? That's the Gunnery School. Oh, why can't we stay here, we've got to know so many people?'

Fay said, with patience, 'We *are* only a stone's throw away and may I add that we are not in this war to make friends. Come along, we must get our things packed, we have to be ready in an hour.'

Although Lyndsey had complained about having to make the move she soon settled in and found herself enjoying each new experience.

The two crews of four, coxswain, stoker and two deck hands, worked twenty-four hours on duty and twenty-four off. Off duty they were billeted in Wrens' quarters ashore, on duty they shared huts at the end of the pier head, which consisted of galley, mess room and a changing room. They slept in two-tier bunks when they were not called out on a job, which was more often than not.

Their work was varied and Lyndsey never ceased to take an interest in it. She enjoyed the mornings when they ran around the harbour in the liberty boat, picking up men who had to report for duty at seven-thirty. She enjoyed the chat, the quips, loved the mornings when a mist hung low over the water and when a weak sun struggling through the clouds would put all the colours of the rainbow in the flying spray and tinge the barrage balloons with pink and gold. They delivered supplies to ships and messages and mail; they towed the divers' barges, which had no power, to wherever they were needed, sometimes out to Spithead where ships had fouled screws, or had other problems.

They transported gunnery officers to Spithead to await liners and other ships which went on trials for gun emplacements.

They did one week on anti-aircraft patrol in the power boat and this was something Lyndsey really enjoyed. It was an all-day job and they had to leave the harbour early morning and steer for the buoy at Eastney anti-aircraft practice range. The Barracudas flew in from Lee-on-Solent with a pilot and navigator and they towed a drogue for firing practice. If it was shot down it had to be picked up again and Lyndsey and the crew would go full speed ahead out to the Channel boom defence, where there was only one way through.

Another task Lyndsey enjoyed was when they had to go around the harbour at two o'clock in the morning to make sure there were no lights showing in any of the ships. In the stillness after all the activities of the day, if the night was clear and the heavens full of stars and enough wind to set the anchor bells gently moving, she would think of mermaids and underwater caverns.

She never even minded the more mundane task of having to scrub the boat out and polish it at the end of their shift, leaving it ready for the next crew to take over.

But it was not all work, they went to dances on their days off, went to ENSA concerts at the NAAFI and to films. They never wanted for partners and Lyndsey especially never sat out one dance. The other girls would accept dates but Fay and Lyndsey refused. Fay because she said there was no one who really took her fancy and Lyndsey because she felt too involved still with Andrew and Elliott, even though she had not heard recently from either.

But then one day she heard from Elliott and although it was just one of his short, cryptic notes she didn't mind. She had contact with him.

This one said, 'Discard present serial. Audience would have been kept too long on tenterhooks. Do two-parter with decisive heroine and masterful hero. They meet in the first part and fall in love; share dangers in the second and know they could never be happy apart. Finale – wedding bells. Fade out to music – "Hearts and Flowers".'

Lyndsey smiled, thought about it and wrote:

'Don't agree with two-parter. Hasty marriages can spell disaster. Far better thoughtful heroine who *really* cares about making marriage a success. Worth waiting, I think, to bring present serial to conclusion.'

To this Lyndsey had the quickest reply from him she had ever had.

'Will consider suggestion, but may have to change script-writer.'

It gave Lyndsey a jolt. Had he met someone else or – had he *intended* to give her a jolt? If it was the latter he had failed to make her change her mind. She had one more go and penned a reply.

'New script-writer could bring a breath of fresh air to original script. Best of luck.'

Lyndsey, who had been enjoying their brief little notes, was very disappointed when, after two weeks, she had no reply.

Then, as though fate had taken a hand to soften the

disappointment, she heard from Andrew that the squadron had moved – much nearer to where she was and would it be possible to meet him for a few minutes before breakfast the following morning, about seven fifteen. It would make his day.

'Before breakfast!' she exclaimed to Fay. 'To meet for a few minutes. It's crazy.'

'He's crazily in love with you, my girl, and you are mad not to be thrilled.'

The next morning Andrew was there on the corner, his coat collar turned up against the biting wind. He looked frozen.

Fay said, 'Look, go and ask Liz in the galley if you can bring him in the back way for a coffee. She can put the two of you in a cupboard for a few minutes.'

Lyndsey had the giggles at the thought of it before she went out to Andrew. And both had the giggles when they were squashed together in a small pantry smelling strongly of fish. When he kissed her his nose was a piece of ice on her cheek.

He took a drink of the coffee. 'Mmm, just what I wanted. Hadn't time to stop and get anything, and I can't stay. I'm playing truant. Just *had* to see you, Lyndsey.'

Andrew was whispering and she whispered back, 'Playing truant? Oh, Andrew, you must be mad. You could get kicked out of the service and so could I for being here with you. Remember this, if we *are* caught, Liz's name must *not* come into it.'

He crossed his heart and grinned. 'They're too short of heroes to kick me out. But in any case it would be worth it if I were. I can carry this lovely few minutes with me. Here, you haven't asked me about old Buffy lately. He's fine. Pining a little for you I think, at times.'

Andrew put his lips close to Lyndsey's and whispered, 'Like me.'

She put both hands against his chest. 'Andrew, now then – '

He drained the coffee, put the mug on a shelf and said, 'I'm going, right now. See you soon. Keep thinking about me.' He opened the pantry door a fraction and peeped out. 'All clear,' he whispered, gave Lyndsey a hasty kiss, this time on the mouth, then left. A moment later she followed, just in time to see him slipping out of the kitchen.

Liz, an Irish girl with a big heart and a wide smile, said, 'There! And isn't that just the most romantic thing that's ever happened here. It's something to tell your grandchildren.'

'Yes,' Lyndsey said softly, 'now isn't it. Thanks Liz, I'll not forget your kindness.'

'Kindness? It's a kindness to meself. I'll be daydreaming for the rest of the week. A lovely feller.'

'Yes,' Lyndsey said, yes, 'he is.'

TWENTY-THREE

A week of stormy weather gave the Boats' Crew a gruelling time. Mail and stores still had to be delivered, men ferried from ship to shore and vice versa. Men who had suffered accidents because of the gale had to be brought ashore, but no matter how serious their injuries one would find them joking. One man who had injured his leg rather badly said cheerfully, 'It couldn't have felt any worse if I had had me leg chewed off by a shark.'

An ambulance was waiting to take him to hospital and he was still joking when he was carried to it.

'Here, mate, will you tell them if they have to take me leg orf to give me a wooden one in its place. Don't fancy one of them new-fangled tin things.'

No sooner was the ambulance away than there was another call from a ship to collect a patient with appendicitis. One of the Wrens said, 'Think of the summer, girls. Blue skies and pretty golden coins sparkling on the water.' They all groaned.

When their shift was finished they emptied water from their sea boots, hung up sou'westers, oilskins and damp jerseys and fell into their bunks.

When Lyndsey dropped into her bunk this time she swore she would sleep the clock round, but she awoke at ten o'clock, felt refreshed and was pleased to find two letters waiting for her. One was from Bette and the other from Andrew. She opened Andrew's first. He said how wonderful it had been to see her, told her he could perhaps get a 24-hour pass to coincide with her 24-hour shifts and suggested coming to Portsmouth to spend the time together. Bette wrote with the news that the Boomerangs were to go to the Far East.

'I don't know whether I'm on my head or my heels, Lyndsey. For some reason I feel it will be Burma. I'm both excited and scared. We won't be leaving for a month, but there'll be so much to do, to arrange. We'll all have to have jabs. Any chance of you getting over to see me? If not I shall have to come and see you. We must meet because heaven knows when we'll be back. Give me a ring, darling, I want to be assured that I've done the right thing, joining ENSA I mean . . .'

Although Lyndsey was pleased for the sake of all of them in the concert party she had a dreadful feeling of being homeless. Bette it seemed had always been there.

Lyndsey phoned Bette later and the warmth in Bette's voice was enough to make her eyes fill with tears, but she swallowed hard and forced herself to say brightly, 'Hello, traveller! Got your bag packed yet?'

'Oh, Lyndsey my love, how good of you to phone me so quickly, and your lovely cheerful voice is just what I needed. Half an hour ago I was in a panic and had more or less decided I couldn't go.'

'Couldn't go? Of course you'll go. This is the big adventure, and just think what you can do for the troops, perhaps stuck out in some jungle area. Bette, you're a trouper through and through. You'll make it and the best of luck to you all. We *must* get together. I do have a 48-hour pass due soon. I'll let you know.'

They talked until Lyndsey ran out of pennies but at least Bette was back to her old cheerful self by then. Lyndsey was still smiling but her smile died when she came out of the phone box.

What a lot of changes there had been in her life since she had lost parents and grandparents.

Fay said, when she knew about Bette, 'Let's go for a long walk, blow the misery away, although it's not all misery, you know, you have a handsome man dying to be with you.'

'Yes, I know,' and Lyndsey's thoughts turned to Andrew.

When they got back from their walk Lyndsey was handed a letter which had been delivered by hand. When she had read the enclosed note she looked at Fay in bewilderment.

'It's from a Captain Haltane, inviting me – *and* a friend – to dinner. I don't know any Captain Haltane.' She turned over the envelope. 'It's certainly addressed to me, he even has my middle initial correct. Who on earth is he?'

'What exactly does he say?'

'He asks us for this evening, if convenient, and adds if not some other evening could perhaps be arranged. His chauffeur would call for us. There's a phone number to ring if we can make it this evening.'

'You're going, of course?'

'Not until I've found out something about him.'

Fay said to hang on, she would make enquiries. When she returned she was smiling. 'The captain is bona fide. He lives in a big house on a hillside that looks like a stronghold, is a widower and well respected. Now you have no more excuses.'

'Mmm,' Lyndsey stood tapping the envelope on her thumbnail, then a slow smile spread over her face. 'It could be more interesting than Dickens's museum. Yes, I'll go, that is if you'll come with me. I'll have to wash my hair.'

Fay grinned. 'Me too.'

As well as washing their hair they had a bath, scrubbed their lanyards, the hallmark of Boats' Crew, polished shoes until they shone, applied lipstick and a dab of powder and were ready when a chauffeur in a well-preserved Daimler came for them.

Fay whispered she had hoped for a Rolls-Royce and Lyndsey whispered back she was lucky it was not a wagon.

The elderly chauffeur touched his cap to them, opened the car door and when they were seated spread a rug over their knees. Lyndsey wondered then if it was some eccentric old man who had invited them.

But there was nothing eccentric about the tall, straight-backed man who greeted them. Although he had rather sharp features and he spoke in a clipped way, his smile was so engaging that Lyndsey warmed to him at once. When she introduced Fay he said how pleased he was to meet her, then seemed to regard her with more than a little interest. Fay also appeared very much interested in the captain.

A middle-aged woman took them to an anteroom where they removed their hats and gloves. There was a Victorian air about the house, but there was nothing gloomy about it. They were shown into an oak-panelled sitting room and offered sherry. Both Lyndsey and Fay accepted. Lyndsey's puzzlement grew. Would the captain tell her why she had been invited or would she have to ask?

He talked about the Wrens, admitted he had been horrified when he learned that women were coming into the service, but said he was now beginning to accept that they were doing an excellent job. He asked them about their work and kept nodding as Fay and Lyndsey described their duties. A servant came in to announce that dinner was ready – and still no mention had been made of the reason for the invitation.

The dining room could have been a captain's quarters on a ship. The ceiling, walls and furniture were all in dark oak, the pictures on the walls were all of naval battles and there was a bust of Nelson in a niche in the wall. The table was beautifully laid, the white starched cloth gleaming, the cutlery heavy silver and the decanter and glasses in cut crystal. A delicious smell of cooking drifted in from the kitchen beyond.

They started with consommé followed by lobster thermidor and then baba au rhum. Lyndsey had been served with similar courses in the past, but none with such flavour. The meal was a gourmet's dream. When both Fay and Lyndsey complimented the captain on his cook they learned he was married to the housekeeper and was a Frenchman who had lost many excellent jobs because of his drinking.

'I employed him when I had my accident and had to retire early from the navy. He was so good to me, he kept me from deep depression. Pierre is volatile, has a fund of stories, and although he still drinks heavily on occasion they are becoming more rare.' The captain gave them his lovely smile. 'I forgive him his lapses for the variety he brings into my life.'

Lyndsey thought of him as a lonely man, like Elliott.

He did not mention whether the accident had been caused by war nor did he mention why Lyndsey had been invited to his home, and when coffee and liqueurs had been served she broached it.

'Captain Haltane, would you please satisfy my curiosity. How did you know my name and why was I invited here, with a friend?'

He looked surprised. 'You didn't know? Didn't Warrender tell you?'

It was Lyndsey's turn to be surprised. 'Elliott?'

'Yes, we met in London last week, dined at his club. He told me about you being stationed here, said he thought you were working very hard and might welcome a break.'

'Oh, he did. As it happens. I have not heard from him for some time.'

An impish gleam came into the clear blue eyes. 'A lovers' tiff. He's a stubborn man, my dear, but a fine one. I have the greatest respect for him. Don't worry, he'll come around, he's very much in love with you. He promised to come on a visit the weekend after next. I do hope you'll be able to come then too, both of you.'

Lyndsey, who felt annoyed with Elliott, refused to give a definite answer. She said a visit would be dependent on their duties and the captain said he understood.

Later, when Lyndsey and Fay went upstairs to wash their hands, Lyndsey said, 'I'm furious with Elliott Warrender. What a cheek he has, wheedling an invitation for *me*. I can just imagine him saying, "Poor girl, she works long hours, she could do with a bit of a change. Why don't you ask her to dinner, give her a good meal." '

Fay put the plug in the wash basin and turned on the tap. 'I'm quite sure he wouldn't say any such thing. And anyway, I'm glad you got the invitation.' She grinned as she soaped her hands. 'It was a bloody good meal.'

'Stop swearing,' Lyndsey said.

'It's not swearing, it's naval language. You've heard a lot worse than that.'

'I know, but that doesn't mean to say – '

'Stop carping! I don't wonder that your colonel has fallen out with you if you go on like that to him.'

'I don't, I don't get the chance. Oh, forget it. I only know at this moment that I will *not* be meeting him when he does come on his visit.'

'You will. Now shut up. Here, the basin is all yours.'

Lyndsey did not mention Elliott Warrender's name again that evening and in fact did not get the chance because of Fay raving over the captain. What a marvellous character he was, just the kind of man she could go overboard for.

When Lyndsey pointed out that he must be in his mid-forties Fay said with a complacent smile, 'Just the type of man I want to settle down with, someone dynamic, intelligent, and, I should imagine, sensible about money. I couldn't imagine him ever getting on the verge of bankruptcy. I could really love that man.'

When Lyndsey mentioned about his accident Fay said, 'Oh, didn't I tell you, he has some shrapnel in his back.

He is going to have an operation to remove it. I don't know the full story. We shall get to know in time.'

Lyndsey asked how she knew all this and Fay told her she had learned it from the Wren who told her who he was and where he lived. Then she added, 'She also told me he had been married, had a child who died when she was seven years old. His wife died three years ago. I think our Captain Haltane needs some love. If he asked me now to marry him I wouldn't hesitate in saying yes.'

'Well!' Lyndsey said. 'That's really something, isn't it? Love at first sight.'

She certainly had plenty to think about the next day, not only did she think of the captain, who had such charm, and marvelled that a girl like Fay was prepared to marry a man of that age, but of course of Elliott. She was no longer angry, only puzzled that he should trouble to mention her to the captain and get him to invite her to dinner, yet had not bothered to let her know.

She had written to Andrew telling him she would be free on the Friday and as it was not encouraged at their quarters to have boyfriends calling for them she arranged to meet him at the station if he gave her a time. If he would not be free then could he give her another day.

There was a short note from him the following day to say he would arrive about nine o'clock, and could hardly wait to see her again.

Although there was quite a strong breeze on the Friday morning putting a few white horses on the water, it was dry and the sun appeared intermittently from behind the clouds. When Lyndsey arrived, early, at the station she found Andrew already there. He saw her and her heart gave a little lurch as he came striding towards her, his whole face alight with pleasure.

'You've made it! I kept praying that nothing would prevent you, such as a switch of duties.' He linked his arm through hers. 'Where are we going?'

'I thought Hayling Island. Fay suggested it.'

335

'That's okay by me. Should we have a coffee first?'

Over their coffee he asked her what she had been doing, where she had been. She told him about having dinner with Captain Haltane, and because she did not want any secrets between them she mentioned how it had come about through Elliott. Andrew asked if she saw Elliott often and to her relief he did not show any of the previous jealousy he had shown when she had mentioned having been out with anyone else.

'No, I haven't seen him for ages. In fact, he didn't even bother to answer my last letter to him. We do correspond from time to time, brief notes, just to keep in touch.' Lyndsey paused then added, 'I will be seeing him the weekend after next when he stays with Captain Haltane, but I suppose it will only be for a meal. Fay is also invited. She's fallen in love with him. What do you think about that? The captain, I mean, not Elliott. He must be about forty-five.'

'Tastes differ,' Andrew replied, smiling. 'Isn't there a song that says, "It's better to be an old man's darling than a young man's fool"?'

'That's a song, not real life. If they have children the captain would seem more like their grandfather than their father.'

'That's their worry, and anyway it might never happen.' Andrew laid his hand over hers and added softly, 'That's your trouble, Lyndsey, you worry far too much about other people. You and my mother would get on like a house on fire. She would take all the worries of the world on her shoulders if she could.'

'Well *someone* has to do it and it's usually the women's shoulders it falls on. You say I'm just like your mother, well my *father* was just like you, he would shrug off worries saying, "It will all work out in the end." '

Andrew sat back, a sudden light of teasing in his eyes. 'Well now, let's see what other troubles we can deal with then. After we've dispensed with them all, we can start to enjoy ourselves.'

Lyndsey laughed. 'I'm sorry. From now on it will be all happy talk. Let's start with the weather. It's a lovely day, we can explore Hayling Island. Once we get to Havant we can travel on a little local railway that runs alongside the sea. And one is allowed to walk on the beach. I've promised to collect some shells for one of the girls sharing our cabin.'

Andrew grinned. 'Goody, goody, collecting sea shells is the one thing I've been dying to do! Come along, let's go.'

He was the Andrew she had first known and Lyndsey felt joy at being able to spend the whole day with him. They caught the train to Havant then boarded the little train that was known affectionately to the locals as the Hayling Billy.

'Isn't this lovely?' Lyndsey exclaimed. 'I feel I'm a kid again going on my first Sunday School outing. Shall we go right to the end of the line, or shall we get out soon and walk?'

They decided to get out and walk. Although there were sounds, the cries of seabirds, the busy puffing of the train as it drew away and the crunch of shingle underfoot, Lyndsey felt she was in some remote world, possibly because there was not another soul in sight.

The tide was out and when Andrew pointed out there was a stretch of damp sand near the water's edge, this was where they walked. They stopped every now and then and would stand in a companionable silence, enjoying the scene. It was just possible to make out the lines of the Isle of Wight through the hazy mist clouding it. A freighter was in sight and also the Isle of Wight ferry, but nothing more at that moment, and it was somehow impossible to believe there was a war going on.

When they did talk it was about people they knew in their jobs and things that had happened. Andrew spoke for the first time of his spell in Scotland, the isolation, the starkness, yet the grandeur of the scenery.

'At times,' he said, 'I knew a terrible, aching loneliness, yet I felt closer to God than I had ever done in my life. It was a strange experience. I should like to go back in peace-time, do a tour, visit the lochs, the mountains.' He paused then added, 'If I live long enough.'

The next moment he was laughing. 'Lordy, I'm getting morbid. How about trying to find a pub and having a drink?'

Lyndsey told him there was the Ferry Boat Inn at the end of the line, and this was where they made for.

The customers were all older men, local fishermen who had gone through the First World War, and, like all fishermen, had tales to tell. They wouldn't allow Andrew to buy drinks, it was their treat they said, it was the least they could do, the forces were doing a good job.

The proprietor magnanimously made them a snack, apologizing that it was just the inevitable spam, but both Lyndsey and Andrew said it tasted good because the fresh air and their walk had given them an appetite.

When they came out the beach was no longer deserted. There were people walking their dogs, mothers with young children, elderly couples out for a stroll. The wind had risen and the sea was choppy. When Andrew asked Lyndsey if she wanted to leave the beach she said no, she was enjoying it. He told her that he was enjoying it too, but later when strong gusts brought them at times to a standstill he led her to the dunes, which he assured her was sheltered. They arrived breathless and dropped into a hollow, but when Andrew made to draw her to him Lyndsey tensed.

He teased her, stressing he was not the villain of the piece out to seduce the heroine. Lyndsey, trying to keep her voice light, replied pertly, 'No, but strange things do happen in dunes.'

'Not in this case.' Andrew spoke firmly. 'I promise. Now relax.'

It worried Lyndsey that familiar tremors had gone through her body at their close proximity and she began to talk, telling him about the weather she had to face sometimes in her job. 'Waves forty feet high, howling gales, this weather is really mild to what we have to put up with at times.'

'Big head,' he said softly and touched her nose with a stem of marram grass.

Lyndsey didn't bother to make a comeback. Although she had had only two drinks she began to feel sleepy. She lay back – remembered saying, 'Don't take this as an invitation' – and remembered no more.

When she roused she found she was cradled in Andrew's arms and he was smiling down at her. When she made to sit up he stayed her.

'No, don't, let me just have this little pleasure of holding you. That's all, I promise.'

She refrained from telling him that it was nice to be held. Later they set off to walk again.

They walked right along the beach and found a tea garden called The Porch. Lyndsey fell in love with it. The house had a porch and at the side were diamond-paned windows. There was a large garden with tables and chairs, and trees all round, and there was a small thatched hut which they peeped in, but it was empty. She said, 'It's a fairy-tale cottage in an enchanted wood,' and Andrew smiled at her indulgently. 'I'm glad we found it together. Shall we inspect the inside? We might find that Goldilocks slept here.'

'I know there'll be a lovely fire inside,' she said, 'I can smell the wood smoke.'

And she was right. The fire blazed and crackled. They were the only customers and the girl who came to serve them gave them a smile. 'On leave, both of you? Must find you something nice.'

They were served a slice of home-cured ham each, butterfly cakes, home-made scones, toasted teacakes and gingerbread. Lyndsey said, 'There just *had* to be gingerbread!'

They sat in the darkening room, with the wind moaning round the eaves and big drops of rain spattering the window panes but it seemed of little importance, they were sharing something they had once shared before; a closeness, a lovingness, without actually having made love.

Before they parted it was with Andrew's promise that they would get together quite soon and his kiss was gentle.

Back in her quarters Lyndsey had to pull herself out of her make-believe world when Fay told her they had a new girl, adding that apparently one of the other girls had said she must go home soon, she was needed on account of illness.

When Lyndsey asked what the new girl was like Fay said, 'Mmm, small, fair, pleasant enough, but I feel she's one of those people who could cause trouble. Do you know what I mean? Nothing tangible but it's there. Anyway, see what you think about her when you meet her.'

When Lyndsey did meet the newcomer she felt a weakness in her limbs. It was her friend Ann, who had left the Centre without saying goodbye to anyone to work in her aunt's boarding house – the boarders being naval officers.

'Hello, Lyndsey, surprised to see me?' Ann asked, smiling.

'Yes, I am. I – I didn't know that you were interested in joining the Wrens.'

'Didn't you? Didn't I tell you that my father went to sea, also three of my uncles. I come from a sea-faring family.'

Lyndsey, having learned from Ann that her father had worked in a factory from the day he left school, knew then that Fay's assessment of Ann had been right. She could spell trouble.

And the lovely happy bubble of Lyndsey's day dissolved.

TWENTY-FOUR

Ann had been assigned as deck hand and within a week of her arrival had not only gained the respect of the coxswain by her dedication to the job, but had found two of the girls to hang on to her every word during off-duty hours, to her tales of her conquests with naval officers. Although Lyndsey had also admired Ann's dedication to her work and knew that men found her attractive, she could not, however, stomach her descriptions of her amorous adventures. Nor could Fay who said:

'If you ask me there's something sadly wrong with any girl who talks incessantly about men the way she does.'

Lyndsey told her then about Ann's life, her need of love and the awful life she had had with her mother before she was killed in a raid. Then she explained too about Ann's involvement with Brad the American, and the result of their affair.

To this Fay said, 'I think perhaps she has good reason to behave as though she were sex-starved, but actually she's love-starved. She's to be pitied.'

But in spite of this Ann and her friends came in for some sharp remarks from Fay at times when they were hogging the places around the stove.

One evening when Fay came off duty frozen she said: 'Move! Let someone else get some warmth.'

Ann immediately pushed back her chair all wide-eyed innocence, apologizing. 'Oh, Fay, I am sorry, I just didn't think. Come on, girls, move back.' The other two pushed their chairs back a fraction, looking sullen. Ann scolded them gently.

'Now come along, be fair, Fay's been on duty.' The girls moved right back then.

Fay said under her breath to Lyndsey, a wry note in her voice, 'Methinks the girl speaks with forked tongue. Beware!'

A few days after this Fay took over the boat Lyndsey and Ann were on. Lyndsey was delighted. She had wanted Fay as their coxswain.

Ann's underlying jealousy showed when she knew about Fay and Lyndsey going to Captain Haltane's house for lunch on the Sunday. She said to Lyndsey, 'I feel really hurt, I am your best friend, you could have asked me to go with you.'

Lyndsey explained that the invitation was for Fay, she had been before, and when Ann went on about it, saying she was sure that Lyndsey could have asked Fay to swop places, Lyndsey became annoyed.

'Look, Ann, you say you are my best friend. You left the Centre without a word, and I haven't even had a postcard from you since you left. I don't call that friendship.'

Ann's eyes filled with tears. 'I couldn't say goodbye, I would have been too upset and the reason I didn't write to you was that I just didn't have time. My aunt was a slave driver, I worked long hours and simply dropped into bed at night, exhausted.'

'Oh, I thought you had all these naval officers dating you.'

'They were all lies,' Ann said in a low voice. 'Only one took me out and he behaved so badly I wouldn't go out with him again.'

Lyndsey was nonplussed for the moment, not knowing with Ann which was the truth and which were lies. But whatever the reason for the confession it did not make her change her mind about taking Ann instead of Fay. Ann accepted it with what could have been a heartbreaking smile, had not Lyndsey had some experience of her actions.

What did bother her during the next few days was not hearing anything from Andrew. She had written to thank him for their lovely day at Hayling Island, and was surprised that he had not replied. Had something happened to him? But then Bette would have let her know, Andrew had put her down as next of kin in England . . . Or could it be that another girl had come into his life, as Freda had done? Well, if this was so it would be the end of their friendship.

As the date for the lunch at the captain's house approached both Lyndsey and Fay became excited. Lyndsey at the thought of seeing Elliott again, even though she still felt some annoyance with him, and Fay because she would be seeing her 'darling captain' again.

The beautifully polished Daimler arrived at half past eleven on the Sunday morning to pick them up. Those girls who were not on duty peeped from windows. Ann, who was in the hall, said to Lyndsey a wistful look on her face, 'Have a good time, you must tell us all about it when you get back.'

There had been a heavy sea-fret earlier but now a fog had crept over the water and the foghorns were emitting their mournful warnings. The chauffeur made the melancholy remark that the fog could get worse and Fay mouthed to Lyndsey, 'Ain't we cheerful?'

The fog had appeared to be only over the sea but as they approached the house a moving mist surrounding it gave the impression of a haunted castle in a film. Lyndsey gave a pleasurable shiver. 'Ghostly, isn't it?' They both stifled laughter.

But they were both straight-faced by the time they were being ushered into the hall. After they had removed hats and gloves they were shown into the sitting room, where a blazing fire and the captain and Elliott awaited them.

'There you are my dears,' exclaimed the captain, 'and

how good it is to see you both again.' When Lyndsey caught sight of Elliott her heart gave a lurch, just as it had done when she had seen Andrew waiting for her at the station. Elliott came forward.

'Lyndsey, how are you?' The captain introduced Fay and Elliott smiled and told her he had heard so much about her. She replied, 'Nothing but good, I hope?' and he said, 'But of course.'

Coffee was brought in and while it was being poured they talked about the weather, the fog, and the captain said he hoped it would continue to keep lone raiders away. Lyndsey, becoming aware of Elliott watching her, turned to him.

'And you, Elliott, are you well? I was surprised to hear from Captain Haltane that you knew one another.'

'We've been friends for some years. It's good to see you again, Lyndsey.'

'It's good to see you,' she said, and thought, Oh, Lord, all these trite remarks! Would there be an opportunity for a down to earth talk later?

Fay asked Captain Haltane if it was true that houses in the dock area had, at one time in history, been built quite low so that guns could be fired over them.

'Yes, it is true,' he said, 'it was in the seventeen hundreds and it was to allow the garrison guns at the Point to fire on the enemy who might approach from the north.'

'The poor people in the houses,' Fay said, 'having to move around, all huddled up like dwarfs, but then no one cared what the workers suffered. Families of seamen starved because their menfolk were not paid what was due to them. Sailors were flogged for the smallest misdemeanour and others hung from the yardarm. The bigwigs, of course, lived off the fat of the land and could do no wrong.'

'Incorrect,' the captain said smartly. 'Byng was executed by a firing squad and he was an admiral. He disobeyed the rules and others officers were also punished for the same reason.'

Fay spoke up then. 'But Admiral Byng did what he thought was right for his men and the country!'

'He was sacrificed,' Lyndsey said. 'Wasn't it Voltaire who said that in this country it was good to kill an admiral from time to time to encourage the others? I think it was terrible.'

The captain thumped his right fist on his left palm. 'My dear girls, if there was no discipline, no rules, everything would be chaotic. Byng broke the line in pursuance of the enemy and – '

'Oh, Captain, don't be such a stuffed shirt,' Fay said. 'Let's get away from naval jargon.'

Lyndsey looked at the captain in alarm, sure he would have been annoyed, but he was smiling. Fay then turned to Elliott and asked him his opinion on the matter.

Elliott drew himself up slowly. 'Captain Haltane is right, of course, there must be discipline and rules in any service, in life, but over the centuries many men in authority during a crisis have had to make a decision contrary to the rules. Byng had to make a decision and, unhappily, it turned out to be the wrong one. Nelson broke the rules and fortunately for him, and for us, it turned out to be the right move. So – '

'A common-sense answer, Colonel Warrender,' Fay declared.

The captain took this in good part, saying with a laugh, 'That is why he is a colonel.'

During lunch many aspects of the services were discussed and the captain complimented Lyndsey and Fay on their knowledge of naval affairs. Fay then mentioned a book she was keen on reading but had been unable to get and the captain told her he had it in his library and that she could borrow it. After lunch Fay went with him into the library and Lyndsey found herself alone with Elliott in the sitting room. She walked to the window and he followed.

'The fog seems to be closing in,' he said. 'If it gets thicker you and Fay may have to stay overnight.'

Lyndsey, not quite sure if he was teasing, stared straight ahead. 'I don't think our officer in charge would take kindly to that.'

'Captain Haltane would put it right. He's well respected in the neighbourhood.'

'I don't think that would cut any ice if our officer found out that there was also a certain Colonel Warrender staying overnight too.'

'Your officer might be pure in heart.'

'Suggesting that I'm not?'

'Such a thought never entered my head. How could you think such a thing of me.' There was no doubting the teasing in his voice then. Lyndsey answered in equally light vein:

'My knowledge of men has increased enormously since entering the service.' Then, because she did not want to enlarge on this subject, she said, 'Oh, by the way, have you found yourself a new script-writer yet?'

His lips twitched. 'Not yet. Shall we sit down, there's a draught from this window and I wouldn't want you to catch a cold.'

He pulled a chair up to the fire for her, brought one forward for himself then sat opposite to her. He crossed one leg over the other, frowned and said, 'What was it we were discussing?'

The frown did not deceive her, there was a twinkle in his eyes. She waited.

'Oh, yes, of course, the film script. Actually, I didn't look for anyone else. I thought it might be just as well to keep the script-writer I have. She's very slow in bringing the serial to a conclusion, but I might engage someone else who might spoil the last episode. And *that* is the most important.'

'Oh, definitely.' Lyndsey sat solemn-faced and suddenly he smiled. 'Well, one can jump from the frying pan into the fire, and let's face it, she has handled the rest of the script rather well.'

He went through the story, not in the melodramatic way they had concocted it at first, but emphasizing various points and the further he got into the story the more his amusement faded. He talked about the girl, their heroine, her uncertainty in not knowing whether she loved the man enough to marry him, and their hero, distraught that he had to go to war and leave her, his torment as he imagined her enjoying herself, living it up, accepting dates. Then his homecoming, on leave, meeting the girl again and finding her with the same uncertainty.

It was at this point that Lyndsey became aware of a change of atmosphere in the room . . . a sensuality. At first she put it down to the warmth of the room, the cosiness in contrast to the greyness of the afternoon, the fog, but then realized it was Elliott's voice, the softness, and the way he had described the couple meeting, like two lovers, touching and withdrawing. She could almost feel Elliott's fingers on her skin, gently caressing her.

'The girl is so beautiful, desirous to men, outwardly an extrovert, but inwardly not yet fully awakened.' Lyndsey, thinking of the afternoon she had spent with Andrew in the barn and what she was experiencing now, wanted to deny it but she felt herself to be caught in a soporific haze.

She became aware of the muted sound of voices, voices that were coming nearer, and as the haze cleared she knew that the sensuality was within herself, the words were her own thoughts. She had been in that halfway stage between sleeping and wakefulness. Then Fay and the captain were in the room and both laughing. Fay said, 'This man has cheated me, there is no book. He makes the excuse that someone had borrowed it but I don't believe him.'

The captain appealed to Elliott. 'Who can blame me? I didn't have any etchings to show her, just books.' He was so full of boyishness then, it was impossible to think of him with a forbidding expression and she found herself wondering if he had fallen in love with Fay, as Fay had fallen in love with him.

Love? Lyndsey got up and went to the window again, feeling shame at her sensuous feelings. She had known emotions like this before, but not just sitting in a room with Elliott. Had he been aware of it? She fervently hoped not.

The fog suddenly seemed menacing. She turned swiftly. 'Fay, the fog is closing in. I think we ought to leave while it's light; if it gets any thicker and darkness comes – we shall be trapped.'

Fay grinned. 'Oh, I'm all for that. Two defenceless girls trapped in the castle with two handsome pirates.'

'I'm serious, Fay. I've been caught in a London fog several times and that can be terrifying enough, but with the blackout as well – '

'Yes, of course, it might be sensible for us to leave now.' She looked at Captain Haltane. 'Please don't think we want to go. I've enjoyed it very much and I know that goes for Lyndsey too.'

Lyndsey glanced at Elliott and said, 'Yes, I really have. It's been – lovely.'

The captain talked of ringing for his chauffeur to bring the car to the front door but Fay said no, there was no need, she and Lyndsey would walk. She added, 'It might perhaps be safer.'

At this Elliott and the captain agreed. They would walk with them, the fresh air would do them good. Lyndsey would rather have said goodbye to them at the house, but knew there was no way of refusing. Both were determined men.

It was strange going out into a grey world where every sound was muffled, the foghorn, bicycle bells, motorcar horns, people's voices. Lyndsey could smell the dampness in her hair, taste salt on her lips. Disembodied figures appeared out of the mist and were swallowed up again. The captain walked ahead with Fay, saying he would lead the way. The two of them talked and laughed. Elliott and Lyndsey walked in silence for a way, then he said, 'I'm so sorry you've had to cut the visit short. I expect you'll be on duty tomorrow.'

'Yes.' There were sudden shouts of 'Oops!' and 'Sorry' as some people collided with the captain and Fay. After they had sorted themselves out, Fay called, 'Consider the boat sunk, the navigator lost his way.'

Then the captain chuckled. 'There's too many distractions on this ship. Attractive girls should be barred.'

Elliott said in a low voice as they walked on, 'They seem to be getting on very well. The captain needed some company, and Fay seems just right for him.'

'Yes – yes she is.' Lyndsey paused then said, 'Elliott, why didn't you answer my last note? It was just a fun thing I know, but I wondered if – well, if something had happened to you. I didn't even know whether you had gone abroad again.'

'I would have told you if it had been on the cards. I didn't write because I heard that you and Andrew were – were friendly again and I had no wish to intrude. Bette told me when I phoned one evening.'

'You and Bette have become very friendly, haven't you?' Lyndsey heard the little niggling note in her voice and knew it was because Elliott had taken it for granted that she and Andrew –

'Andrew and I are just good friends. He needed company after he had lost his wife in a raid.'

'Yes, I was sorry about that, it was tragic. I wasn't suggesting that you and Andrew were any more than just friends, Lyndsey, but I did know that you and he had been close.'

She wanted to deny it, but couldn't because it was true. The early night sky was closing in, giving a feeling of melancholy to Lyndsey. Two men were in love with her, and to neither could she say 'I love you'.

They were on a rough part of the road and when she

stumbled Elliott put out a hand, steadying her. Until then he had kept apart. His touch sent tremors through her once more. She stumbled yet again and his grip tightened. She said, a slight shakiness in her voice, 'I seem to cope better on the sea, never losing my balance, or at least seldom.'

'I'm glad you lost your balance now, it gave me a chance to hold you,' he said in a low voice. 'I've been wanting to take you in my arms from the moment you arrived today.'

Shivers of ecstasy ran up and down Lyndsey's spine. What was happening? This had never happened before, not out walking in the road. And because all this was a mystery to her she taunted him.

'You had plenty of opportunity while Captain Haltane and Fay were in the library. Your urge could not have been all that strong.'

'If only you knew.' There was a grimness in his voice then. 'You can be so tantalizing.'

'No more than you,' she retorted. 'You are still an enigma to me. I wrote little notes, answering yours and enjoying receiving them. Then suddenly you stop and blame it on the fact that I've seen Andrew again. And being so mean as to put a different interpretation on it.'

'If I did, I'm sorry.' His reply was so abrupt Lyndsey decided it would be foolish to follow it up. They walked in silence again and she thought what an end to what until then had been a lovely day.

Before they had gone much further Elliott said, contrition in his voice, 'Forgive me, Lyndsey, I've behaved like a fool. I've hurt you and that's the last thing I want to do. I shall be coming again to see the captain – we have a project we want to discuss. Can we perhaps meet then, just the two of us?' When she hesitated he said, 'Please, and I promise not to make any more stupid remarks.'

She agreed and coming to a stop he turned her to face him. 'Say you forgive me.' She said it and he kissed her on the mouth and his lips were surprisingly warm, but she forced herself not to respond to him. She was afraid to. He took her by the hand then and hurried to where the captain and Fay were just about to be swallowed up by the cloying fog.

'Nearly lost them!' Elliott sounded much happier. 'Although I can't say I would have minded. It might have been fun, just the two of us alone in a strange world of mist.' He put an arm around her waist and when she tensed he said with alarm, 'You haven't forgiven me, Lyndsey!' and all the happiness had gone from his voice.

'I have, Elliott, I have.'

'Then why such a reaction?'

How could she explain to him her feelings? When he had put his arm around her waist it was as though something had flowed from him, binding her to him. And this was something she was not ready to accept. She thought if she could perhaps explain this and about what she had felt earlier when they were alone in the sitting room – but then Fay called, 'Back at base, folks, all safe and sound.'

Their quarters loomed up and Lyndsey said to Elliott, 'Perhaps we can talk the next time we meet.'

Elliott smiled a little sadly. 'You really *are* the most tantalizing person. I don't believe you are ever going to finish our serial.'

'Shall I let you into a secret?' she said softly. 'It has progressed a little today. At least I think so.'

'That's good news. 'Bye, Lyndsey.' He touched her gently on the cheek. 'Until we meet again.'

Lyndsey wanted very much to be on her own for a while to think but no sooner were they inside than they were besieged by some of their cabin mates, including Ann, who all demanded to know what had happened. The questions came thick and fast. Why were they back so early . . . had the car broken down . . . what did they have for lunch . . . had they fallen out . . . ?

'Fallen out?' Fay exclaimed, then added on a rapturous

note, 'I've fallen in love. Oh, he's marvellous, madly attractive, strong, bossy, sensible, intelligent – '

'The captain?' Ann queried.

'No, of course not, silly. The colonel, Lyndsey's man.'

There was a gasp at this and even Lyndsey drew in a quick breath, then Fay was laughing.

'Of course it's the captain, but I could have fallen for Colonel Warrender had he not been "spoken for". I'm not a stealer of men.'

'Are you and Lyndsey meeting them again?' asked another.

'Naturally. And the sooner the better. Can't wait for our next date. Anyone know how much leave a Wren gets for her honeymoon?'

'Married?' screamed one girl. 'Talk about a whirlwind courtship. You've only been with him twice.'

'Enough to know there's no one else I would want to spend the rest of my life with,' Fay said dreamily.

The girls then turned to Lyndsey, wanting to know if wedding bells were in the offing with her colonel. Lyndsey smiled but said firmly, 'Definitely not, we're just good friends.'

One girl said, 'Is there such a thing as friendship between male and female?' Some of the others laughed. Ann remarked in a snide way:

'If you knew the number of men Lyndsey's been out with you certainly would not accept the friendship bit because they come back for more.' This brought a silence and an exchange of uncomfortable glances.

Although Lyndsey was fuming she forced herself to smile and say calmly, 'When you know Ann better you'll find out that she says things like this but doesn't really mean them. She's my friend.'

Ann had the grace to look shamefaced but afterwards she said to Lyndsey in the wistful way she seemed to have adopted, 'I wish you could introduce me to a captain or a lieutenant colonel, and especially someone as handsome as the ones that you and Fay are dating.'

To this Lyndsey replied simply, 'I think you are quite capable of finding your own boyfriends, Ann, you've had no trouble in the past, and you certainly have plenty of choice in Portsmouth.' Ann gave a deep sigh, cast Lyndsey a look of reproach and walked away.

In bed that night Lyndsey found herself wishing that Ann had not come back into her life. Then Lyndsey thought of the odd experience she had had with Elliott in the sitting room at the captain's house, and now half regretted having told him that their 'serial' was progressing. The next time they met he would be expecting her to tell him that she would marry him, and in spite of what had happened she knew she was not ready for that. It had been strange certainly, but she felt sure she would have to feel what Fay felt about her captain, that no matter what he did or said he was the one she wanted to spend the rest of her life with.

But this did not settle Lyndsey's mind. She began to wonder if Fay had felt as though something inside her had suddenly awakened. She would ask her in the morning.

'Awakened!' Fay exclaimed. 'Something bloody well exploded.'

'Stop swearing,' Lyndsey said automatically. 'Has it happened to you before, this feeling of explosion?'

'Every time I fall in love.'

'Oh, so you could, well, fall out of love with the captain?'

Fay shook her head vigorously. 'Not on your nelly. This is for keeps.'

'But how do you *know*?' Lyndsey was beginning to feel more and more bewildered.

'I just do, so does Dominic, that's his name. Stop looking as if the end of the world was coming. You'll know when you meet the right man. Actually, I think it's Elliott and one day *you* will explode inside. And you'll say "I'm in love! Why didn't I realize it before." On the other hand, it could be Andrew. Don't worry' she added on a comforting note, 'you've time to fall in and out of love with a dozen men. In the meantime, let's get something to eat.'

Lyndsey was amazed that Fay, with all this love inside her, could even think of eating. Her own appetite had gone because of the way she felt about Elliott. But when she sat down for breakfast common sense took over. It was no use starving herself for something she did not understand. As Fay had said she would know when she was really in love.

The crew on some ships, where they delivered goods, were more hospitable than others and would invite them aboard for a coffee, which was invariably laced with a drop of rum. This was certainly welcome as the weather was bitterly cold with, at times, driving rain spiked with sleet that felt like needle stabs.

Lyndsey's nickname of 'Legs' had followed her around. Ann was spoken of affectionately as Tich and Fay as Ashey, which was the derivation of her surname Ashton.

Every member of the crews had a nickname and it was difficult to remember them all. There were a number of Nobbys, the surname of these men being Clark. All Welshmen were Taffy, the Scots Jock and the Irish Paddy. Then there were names of Hip-Hop, Badger, Beaver, Trigger, Poke, Podge, Tatters... they were endless. Lyndsey, who couldn't remember them all, would call a number of men Nobby and none ever objected.

Although all of the Boats' Crew were adept at climbing the rope ladders on the sides of ships there were times during a gale when clambering up them could be tricky. One morning when Lyndsey, caught in a gust, paused to catch her breath, one of the men shouted from the deck:

'Come on, Legs, step on it, don't want you falling into the bleeding drink this weather.'

When she reached them she said, 'And how many of you would have jumped in to pull me out if I had fallen?' To this there was a chorus of, 'We all would!'

When Ann and Fay were aboard they were taken to the

wheelhouse where there would be the usual order of 'Git yer clothes orf and sit down.'

It simply meant taking off their duffle coats while they were there or their oilskins, but it always brought guffaws of laughter in which the girls joined.

And they would sit for a while, chatting, joking, with the ships lifting and falling to the movement of the sea. At times like this Lyndsey would think she wanted no other life but this, to know the warmth and that lovely feeling of belonging to one big family.

It was only when she was on shore that she would think about Elliott and Andrew, but she had stopped worrying about her relationship with each man, sure now that everything would sort itself out in time.

But there came a day when her life was to be changed yet again. She was told to go to the office. Although Lyndsey could think of nothing she had done wrong she was prepared to be scolded for something she had not been aware of – and was surprised and delighted to see Bette sitting by the desk. She stopped, becoming aware of the sorrow in Bette's eyes.

The officer said quietly, 'Mrs Bascony has something to tell you, MacLaren, I'll leave you together.'

When the woman had gone Lyndsey said, 'It's Andrew, isn't it?'

Bette got up and took her hands in hers. 'He's missing, Lyndsey. His plane came down over Germany, but of course he could have been taken prisoner of war. We mustn't lose hope.'

'No, no, of course not. I'm off duty, we could go to the mess, there'll be a quiet corner where we can talk.'

On the way Lyndsey wondered why she felt no pain.

TWENTY-FIVE

Bette and Lyndsey talked over the news of Andrew with Bette stressing they must not give up hope, hundreds of men reported missing had been traced; and as they talked Lyndsey's first numbed shock wore off, to be replaced by a dull ache. At this stage it was his parents mainly she grieved for, *their* shock and the fact that they were so many thousands of miles away.

'Perhaps Richard or Elliott could find out something,' she said. 'I must ask them. They'll know where to enquire. Are you staying, Bette? I do have time off.'

Bette sat tugging at the tips of her gloves for a moment then she looked up. 'Actually, I want to call on Marian.'

To Lyndsey's surprised query, 'Marian?' Bette nodded. 'I had a letter from her asking me to stop seeing Richard, to stop trying to destroy their marriage.'

Lyndsey stared at her. 'But you aren't seeing him – are you?'

'No, of course not. I don't know what's got into Marian.'

'Neither do I. She must be sick. Richard told her there was nothing in it when he came to see you that one time. And I told her so too and she appeared to have accepted it. Oh, Bette, I'm sorry, you can do without all this extra worry. I think it's a good thing you'll be going away.'

'I must admit I'm not looking forward to meeting Richard's wife, but I feel I must to clear the air. She told me in her letter she would be at home for the next three days.'

Bette got up. 'I must go now, Lyndsey, I want to get this interview over, it's like a dead weight pressing on my chest. I'll let you know how I get on.'

Lyndsey said she would phone Bette that evening.

Later she was telling Fay about Andrew when Ann, who had suddenly appeared, said, 'Missing? Well you can say goodbye to *him*.'

What was so awful to Lyndsey was the gloating look that had come into Ann's eyes. Fay exclaimed, 'You stupid bitch! How insensitive can you get?' and at this Ann was full of abject apology.

'Oh, I'm sorry, I just wasn't thinking. My aim was for Lyndsey not to raise her hopes, there are so many men you see who – '

'Bugger off,' Fay said, 'and don't come back.' Ann, with a hurt look, drifted away and Fay glared at her retreating back. 'One of these days I, or somebody else, will push her overboard. She's a menace, I don't know anyone who likes her, except her two pals.'

'Men like her,' Lyndsey said.

'I know, and they must want their brains examined! I heard one bloke call her his little kitten the other day. Kitten! One with the claws of a tigress. Beware of her she's acid honey.'

At any other time Lyndsey might have worried about Ann's behaviour, but Andrew dominated her thoughts. The pictures in her mind made her ache. She saw him perhaps coming down in the plane and becoming a fugitive from the enemy, hungry, cold. And then she would see him being marched to a prisoner of war camp, being interrogated . . .

At nine o'clock that evening she rang Bette to find out how she had fared with Marian.

'Well,' Bette said, 'we got on fairly well after I had behaved like a street brawler. I got so mad when she told me she didn't believe that there was nothing between

357

Richard and myself. She said he had mentioned my name in his sleep. This was when I started shouting.'

Lyndsey laughed. 'I can't imagine you shouting at anyone.'

'She got a shock. I don't think anyone had shouted at her before. I told her if her husband had mentioned my name it was her fault not mine. If she stopped being jealous and showed him a bit of love instead he might not be mentioning another woman's name in his sleep. I also made it quite clear that he had visited me alone *once* only, but if she was not careful he might come again for a bit of peace and quiet. I added that it was obvious she was a nagger.'

'So what happened then?'

'At this she burst into tears and then I was so sorry for her I found myself comforting her and making tea. Before I left she vowed she would change but whether she does or not is in the lap of the gods.'

They talked for a while on the complexities of human nature, but not about Andrew. The only time that subject was hinted at was before they rang off when Bette said, 'We'll hope for better news on *all* fronts. Take care of yourself, love, and don't worry. Ring me again when you can.'

Although nothing conclusive came out of their talk Lyndsey felt a little more settled. She would, as Bette had stressed, keep on being hopeful.

Bette had told her that Richard was away so Lyndsey wrote to Elliott, telling him about Andrew and asking if he could help with information. Elliott wrote back by return of post to say he would be seeing the captain on the Friday evening and if she was free on the Saturday they could meet. Would she leave a message with the captain.

Lyndsey *was* free and Fay delivered the message.

Saturday morning was sunny and windless and although there was a sharp nip in the air it was invigorating. He had said he would pick her up at ten o'clock and he arrived promptly in the staff car but driving himself. After greeting her he asked where she would like to spend the day. Lyndsey suggested the Isle of Wight and he agreed. It was not until they were on the ferry to cross to the island that Elliott broached the question of Andrew.

'I was sorry to hear of it, Lyndsey. It's bad luck. I don't think I would be able to get any more information but if it would make Bette feel any better she could write to the British Legion at Geneva. I must warn her, however, that it won't speed anything up, all reports have to go through the usual channels and this, as you can imagine, takes time.'

Lyndsey was feeling a little upset at what she thought was Elliott's couldn't-care-less attitude when he went on, compassion in his voice, 'I can guess what you and Bette are suffering. It's awful to get the message "Missing", and yet it's more hopeful than to get the message saying, "Missing, believed killed in action". He could well have been taken prisoner.'

'And if he had, how long would it take before Bette would hear from the War Office?'

'Difficult to predict. Many members of the RAF have come down in forest areas in Germany and been hidden by the underground movement who have eventually helped them to escape to Switzerland. There are so many possibilities, the important thing is not to give up hope.'

'No, I won't, and thanks, Elliott.'

The boat was full, many of the people young couples and servicemen with wives and families. Lyndsey and Elliott stood at the rail and Lyndsey held her face up to the sun. There was little heat in it but there was a lovely brightness. Seagulls followed the boat, screaming and swooping down for refuse thrown from the galley. When Lyndsey looked at Elliott she found him smiling at her.

'You really are a sea girl, aren't you. It's a good job I'm planning to have my farm beside the sea.'

'Farm?' she queried. 'What's all this about?'

Elliott explained that he would like to go into farming after the war and as Captain Haltane wanted to have a small boat-building yard they thought they might combine the two businesses. It was this project they had been discussing the evening before. He went on to say that the captain was also interested in farming.

'And as I have ideas for designs of small yachts,' Elliott said, 'the project might very well work. We don't, of course, know yet whether it will work, but that is why we are doing a lot of talking now, trying to find out the snags.'

Lyndsey, speaking her thoughts aloud, said, 'It would be lovely to live close to Fay and Dominic –' Lyndsey stopped abruptly, realizing what she was implying, and Elliott took her up on it.

'Oh, so you have decided to marry me. That's good news.'

She gave him an impish smile. 'You don't miss a trick, do you? Actually, I slipped up, it was Fay I was thinking about. And although it would be nice to live near to her there would be too many snags to make such a project work.'

Elliott's eyebrows went up. 'You sound very positive. I should be interested to hear them.'

'I wasn't thinking about the farming side but the yachts. Will people have money to buy them? After the First World War men, even officers, were selling matches in the streets to try and eke out some sort of living.'

'We've progressed since then, and there will always be people with money for luxuries. And don't forget that both of us will be giving employment to ex-servicemen, in my case not only on the land but in building a farmhouse. I've designed my own and know exactly what I want. You look doubtful, Lyndsey, what's wrong?'

'It's personal. I don't like the sound of a *modern* farmhouse. To me farmhouses are old and have an atmosphere all their own, oak beams, stone kitchen floors, pegged rugs in the kitchen, rocking chairs.'

Elliott said that his house would have all these features, but there would be more modern innovations, such as windows that fitted perfectly, keeping draughts out, doors that didn't have gaps. All the farmhouses that he had been in were draughty places, freezing in winter.

Lyndsey derided his ideas, she accused him of wanting to be a gentleman farmer, just walking around his estate and watching other men working.

Elliott denied this, he would be a working farmer, and surely he had a right to build the kind of house he wanted. At this Lyndsey realized she had been thinking in terms of herself living in it. Embarrassed, the colour rising to her cheeks, she tried to make light of it.

'I'm getting bossy since joining the Wrens. Yes, of course you must build the kind of house you want.'

'I was hoping you might like my ideas too, but it seems we'll never see eye to eye.' He smiled. 'We can't even agree about the serial.'

'Now don't bring that up again,' she warned, 'or you can quite definitely get yourself another script-writer.'

'All right, all right, stop nagging. I'll keep the one I've got. Change of subject, what do you think of Haltane and Fay getting together? He's really gone overboard, I've had a job to keep him on an even keel. They're talking about marriage.'

'Would it last?' Lyndsey mused. 'You know what they say, marry in haste, repent at leisure.'

Elliott replied, solemn-faced, 'I doubt whether that is ever likely to happen in *your* case, you are much too practical.'

Lyndsey was suddenly still. Was that how he saw her, practical, without any romantic notions?

'Don't look so tense,' he teased. 'A farmer's wife *has* to be practical.' Elliott paused then added softly, 'As well as being warm and loving and wanting lots of strong healthy sons to take over the farm.'

'And daughters too.'

Elliott gave her one of what she thought of as his special smiles when talking about children. 'But of course, lots of little girls too. That goes without saying.' He looked over the rail into the water then straightened. 'And I had better stop right there or I shall have you nagging at me again. Oh, will you do one thing for me? Would you look at the plans of the house some time that I've designed?'

'I should like to but we shall probably disagree over them.'

'Now that is *very* possible, but I shall tell you what an old aunt of mine told me about her marriage. She said, "It's disagreeing that keeps us lively and therefore happy." '

Lyndsey then told him she would repeat a saying of her mother's that "a bit of sweet talk kept a wife happy", which had Elliott asking if her father had "sweet-talked" her mother.

Lyndsey thought about it for a moment then replied, 'Not in public but he must have done when they were alone because it was a lovely marriage, so happy.' Then she added, 'But that was *my* parents, I should imagine every marriage is different.' She grinned. 'I think I tend to like your aunt's maxim that a bit of disagreeing keeps things lively.'

Elliott nodded. 'I thought you might.' He held out an arm. 'Shall we take a stroll, ma'am?'

During the next ten minutes the weather changed, the sun went in and the island was shrouded in mist. To Lyndsey's murmur of annoyance Elliott told her not to worry, it was just a morning mist, it would turn out fine later. She smiled at him, 'So among your other qualifications you are a weather forecaster?'

'Not really, but I did spend my summer vacations with farming people when I was young. Incidentally, why did you especially choose to come to Ryde today?'

She told him to see Osborne House and when Elliott dismissed it with a shrug as being just a house Lyndsey bridled.

'It's not just *any* house. It was Queen Victoria and Prince Albert's special retreat away from all the worries of politics. It was where they could relax – and love. They were so very much in love. It must have devastated the Queen when Albert died. I can understand her shutting herself away from the world.'

'I'm afraid I can't, Lyndsey. She was the Queen, she had responsibilities.'

'Oh, you don't understand, it was a very deep love they had for one another. She was bereft. Her husband was her whole life. She lived only for him.'

'Then she ought not to have done.' There was disapproval in Elliott's voice. 'She had children, she had subjects, many of them living in poverty. She could have done something about it instead of indulging in wasted years of grieving.'

Lyndsey stopped. 'Do you know you are spoiling my day?'

He turned to her. 'Lyndsey, I'm sorry. Forgive me. We shall go to Osborne House and I won't say another word about the Queen's behaviour. After all, who am I to judge? Forgiven?'

'There's nothing to forgive. You have a right to your opinion as I have to mine.' She asked him if there was any particular place that he would like to visit.

He said, 'Now you mention it, yes there is. I should like to visit a small boat-builder's yard and have a chat with the proprietor. That is, of course, if you won't be bored.'

'Not at all, I would be most interested.'

When they disembarked they joined the other passengers who boarded the train that would take them along the pier to the promenade and on arrival they walked along the promenade then branched off to go into the town. Lyndsey said, 'I think there are buses which go round the island; if so I should like to go to Alum Bay, I was told there are twelve different colours in the sand. I was also told that you can buy small tubes or bottles to put some in.'

'For what reason?' Elliott asked.

Lyndsey gave an exasperated sigh. 'Oh, really, Elliott, you have no imagination. I would regard it as something of interest to, well, show my children. Each colour in the sand represents a different stratum in history.' Lyndsey paused then went on, 'I would tell them I had collected the sand one day when I went to the Isle of Wight with a very unromantic lieutenant colonel.'

'You wouldn't, you know.' Elliott's expression was bland. 'You would tell them that their Daddy took you before we were married.'

'Marry you? Ha. I would need my brains examined if I did.' Elliott began to laugh and soon Lyndsey was laughing with him. 'Well, I would, wouldn't I? We don't seem to agree on a single thing.'

'Yes, we do, we agreed to spend the day here and that is what we are going to do. And we are going to enjoy it.' He cupped a hand firmly under her elbow. 'And right now let's see about buses.'

After some discussion they decided to go by bus to Osborne House, from there to Cowes and after that go on to Alum Bay. They were warned that they might have a long wait for buses in between but Elliott said there was no hurry, they had the whole day ahead of them.

But by the time they were on the bus Lyndsey decided she no longer wanted to go to Osborne House, not because she was feeling peeved at Elliott's previous remarks, but because she became interested in visiting Cowes.

And it was a delight to both of them, Elliott finding the proprietor of a small ship-building firm to talk to and Lyndsey seeing in her imagination the yachts congregating for the start of the big races. What a sight it must be, sails unfurling, billowing in the wind. There were yachts in the harbour now but they were all commandeered for the duration of the war by the navy.

When they were ready to leave, an elderly man in the boatyard offered them a lift to Alum Bay. It was a rewarding ride. He was a retired seaman with a love of geology and after he had talked about the geology of Alum Bay Elliott said with a smile to Lyndsey, 'What a lot we shall have to tell the children, darling, won't we?'

'You two married then?' enquired their driver.

'Going to be,' Elliott said, an imp of mischief in his eyes.

Lyndsey gave him a sharp dig in the ribs and grimaced at him. The old man mentioned that they would be seeing the sand at the best time because after rain it intensified the colours.

And he was right. There were shadings of green, of blue, red, yellow, orange . . . Lyndsey was transfixed at the sight, feeling a sense of timelessness, and hardly noticed when Elliott excused himself. She was shading her eyes against the brightness of the vast expanse of ocean when Elliott returned. He held out a small paper-wrapped parcel.

Wondering, Lyndsey opened it and found a glass paper-weight with all the colours of the sand arranged in a pattern. Her first reaction was one of disappointment because she had wanted to collect the colours herself, but then Elliott said softly, 'Do you think the children will like it?' and the disappointment died.

She said, 'Oh, Elliott, how unpredictable you are,' then because she was still not willing to commit herself she added, 'Thanks, I'm sure it's something any child would be interested in.'

He said, a little sadly, 'Well, at least it has saved the stiff climb back from the bay. Are you ready for something to eat, there's a café over there?'

Afterwards Lyndsey came to realize how the day out had helped to ease the ache of Andrew. But she also realized she could have been more forthcoming in her thanks to Elliott; could have behaved more warmly towards him when he kissed her on parting. But she had been afraid to let herself go and knew deep down it was because of a feeling of still being committed to Andrew.

Two days later she had a note from Elliott saying,

'Thank you again for our day together. It is one more lovely memory to store. Perhaps we can have another day out soon . . .'

She replied but heard no more and life went on with its daily routine. Fay went on seeing her captain whenever she could but although Lyndsey had been asked to dinner twice and she enjoyed the food and the conversation it was not the same without Elliott being there.

She had not wanted to be involved again with Ann, had taken care to avoid her when off duty, but once when Ann overheard her telling Fay she was going to London on her next day off to see Richard and Marian, Ann asked if she might travel with her. Lyndsey hesitated then seeing Ann's look of loneliness, agreed. Ann then told her about having to meet an old boyfriend at St Pancras. He was on his way to Devon but was breaking his journey to see her. He had told her it was important.

'I didn't really want to meet him, Lyndsey, but he's kept writing. He's still in love with me but I'm not in love with him any more. Would you come with me? I don't feel I want to meet him on my own.'

Lyndsey did make the excuse then of having to see Richard and Marian but Ann persisted. Her meeting with Danny would not be until early evening, and they could see him and then get the train back to Portsmouth. Ann became so full of pleading that at last Lyndsey, reluctantly, agreed.

They set off early the next morning to catch the train but it was as crowded with servicemen going on leave and returning as at any other time. Ann was in her element and before long had become friendly with a curly-headed young man who had several hours to look around London before going to his base.

Lyndsey hoped she might get out of going with Ann to meet her old boyfriend but the last thing Ann said to her before they parted was, 'See you at St Pancras at five o'clock,' and Lyndsey sighed and went on her way.

Richard and Marian seemed to be on quite good terms and Lyndsey hoped that perhaps Bette's talk with Marian had started a softening-up process.

Marian asked how she was getting on in her job and Lyndsey talked about it then mentioned Andrew. They both commiserated with her and Richard said, 'Poor Bette, it will hit her hard.' Marian showed no response at Bette's name, which seemed to Lyndsey to be another good sign.

But it was not long before she realized that she had been wrong and all was not well between them. She told them about the invitation to Captain Haltane's house, how Fay and the captain had fallen in love at first sight, then followed it immediately by mentioning Elliott's visit.

Marian said wryly, 'Is there such a thing as love at first sight? I used to think there was but I don't believe it any more.'

Richard's face took on a stony look then he questioned Lyndsey about Elliott, saying he hoped he was not pestering her.

She bridled. 'Pestering me? Of course not.'

Marian told Lyndsey not to take any notice of Richard, that he couldn't bear for anyone to enjoy themselves. Elliott Warrender was a charming man, caring, dependable, and Lyndsey could do a lot worse for herself.

At this Richard looked thunderous and warned Marian not to interfere, he was Lyndsey's guardian and had her interests at heart. Elliott Warrender was in his mid-thirties and too old for her.

Lyndsey, in the hope of preventing what could turn into a monstrous row, said, 'Forget it! You don't have to fall out over Elliott and me. We're good friends, nothing more.' She added, 'I don't want to create any more problems, I have enough to do to cope with the problems of other people.'

Richard and Marian had obviously taken this personally because they both looked shame-faced, and Lyndsey told them quickly about Ann and having to meet her at St

Pancras. Richard said with a slightly forced smile, 'Well, don't get too involved.'

Although the tension did ease a little after this Lyndsey found herself glad to have an excuse of meeting Ann, and when she left she wondered if Richard and Marian would ever make a go of their marriage.

When she arrived at St Pancras and saw ambulances lined up in the forecourt her stomach contracted. A troop train of wounded must have arrived. In the station itself there was a great deal of activity, wounded on stretchers were being attended to by Red Cross nurses and cups of tea given by the WVS.

Ann came hurrying up to Lyndsey. 'Danny's over there. I'm glad you came.' They went to where a tall, thin soldier was standing by his kit-bag. Ann introduced Lyndsey but although Danny was polite he could not disguise the fact that he was none too pleased to have her there. Lyndsey excused herself, saying she was sure they would want to be alone to have a chat. Ann gripped her arm and gave her a pleading look, but then she suddenly relinquished it as though realizing that Lyndsey was determined not to stay. 'You will wait for me?' she begged. Lyndsey nodded.

Although Lyndsey was not morbid by nature she found herself held there by the sheer tragedy of the scene. All around her were wounded men, some minus a leg or an arm, and some even minus an arm and a leg, others with their eyes bandaged and those whose whole faces were bandaged, apart from slits for eyes, for noses and mouths. Oh, God, she thought, this terrible war.

Yet all was not gloom. A perky soldier on a stretcher called out to her, 'You're a sight for sore eyes, me love. You're beautiful. I'll see you in my dreams.' He waved his right arm – his left was missing. 'I've still got one left to cuddle a little bit of fluff. Ain't I the lucky one?'

Lyndsey felt a lump come into her throat, but she managed a smile. 'You're lovely yourself,' she called, as the bearers carried him away. 'I'll dream about *you*.'

'You've made my day, darlin'!'

What courage, Lyndsey thought, and was still watching him out of view when she became aware of another stretcher being set down beside her. One of the bearers said, 'The nurse will be with you in a moment, Captain,' then they left.

The face of the wounded man was ashen. He appeared to be asleep but his slender fingers plucked at the edge of the bright red blanket covering him. On an impulse Lyndsey laid a hand gently over his. His eyes opened, then as he focused on her, a tremulous smile touched his lips.

'Carolyn, oh, my dear, you came, I knew you would.' Two bright spots of colour now burned on his cheeks.

A nurse who had come up as he spoke drew Lyndsey aside and explained in a low voice that Carolyn was his daughter who had recently been killed in an air-raid. Then she added, 'It might be kinder if you didn't disillusion him. He's *very* ill.'

Lyndsey nodded and taking the captain's hand in hers laid it against her cheek. 'You have to go to hospital now,' she said softly, 'but I shall come and see you.'

'You promise?'

'I promise.' She leaned over and kissed him on the brow. There were tears in his eyes but his whole face was suffused with happiness and he managed to give her a feeble wave as the men came to carry him to the ambulance.

At Lyndsey's request the nurse gave her the name of the hospital but warned her to phone before making the journey, a shake of the head implying it could be a fruitless one.

Lyndsey made no mention to Ann of the wounded man she had met, nor did she tell Fay until the following day after she had phoned the hospital and learned that the captain had died during the early hours.

'Well don't let it get you down,' Fay said. 'The captain did die happy thinking you were his daughter.'

'Yes, I know, and it must have been fate that I had to

be there, because I didn't want to go to the station with Ann, I nearly refused.'

Fay nodded slowly. 'I could tell you a dozen incidents where fate seemed to have taken a hand, but at the moment we had better find out what it has in store for us now. Plenty of hard work, I know that!' She got up. 'Come on, let's get going.'

TWENTY-SIX

A month went by in which there was no news of Andrew and Lyndsey saw Elliott only once and that was when he came to lunch on a day she was visiting Richard and Marian. The good part was that Richard and Marian were more amiable to one another but the disappointing part was that she and Elliott spent no time alone.

He kissed her on the cheek as he was leaving and said, 'We'll be in touch, Lyndsey,' but there was no look of love in his eyes, no warmth in his kiss. She had been aware of a distraction in him from time to time, but did not learn the reason for another week, when Fay told her she was invited to the captain's house on the Saturday and that Elliott would be there. Within ten minutes of her arriving he told her he was to be posted abroad. 'I'm sorry,' he said, 'but it's war.'

Over lunch the captain and Elliott discussed their project and to Lyndsey she sensed a feverishness in the way they talked, as if the project must all be settled, even if it never came to fruition.

Elliott had brought out the plans of the farmhouse and after lunch they all pored over it. Lyndsey had to admit that the building itself and the inside had all the features of the farmhouses she knew, with added comforts.

Fay said, teasing, 'Will there be a four-poster bed, Elliott, *and* a grandfather clock?'

'A tester bed and *two* grandfather clocks. One in the hall

and one in the kitchen. I have a weakness for them. Lyndsey, do you approve?'

Lyndsey, who had a feeling of loss, forced herself to say brightly, 'I do, I'm all in favour and in fact I don't think at this stage I can fault any of your plans.'

'Amazing.' Elliott held up his hands. 'Did you hear that? The lady agrees. I can't believe it.' He was laughing and Lyndsey watched him, feeling a terrible ache at the coming parting.

And when the captain brought out a plan of a small yacht he had designed Lyndsey's gaze was not on the plan but again on Elliott as she tried to memorize his every feature. It was a strong face, the nose straight, the jaw with a slightly pugnacious thrust, but there was the tenderness about the well-shaped mouth she had noticed on their first meeting. Lyndsey imagined herself lying beside him, pushing her fingers through his thick dark hair, and felt tremors go through her. How long would it be before they met again? Would they ever meet again? At that moment she knew that if Elliott wanted to make love to her she would agree.

But even if Elliott had wanted to there was no opportunity. The captain wanted them to see an old farmhouse and some land close to the sea that was likely to be put up for auction, so they all braved a strong wind and went tramping over fields, with the captain saying, 'It doesn't, of course, have to be this part of the world where we settle, I just thought it would give us an idea of the layout, see how we could work it all out.'

Lyndsey had hoped that at least she would get a chance to walk alone with Elliott, but she ended up walking with Fay while the men walked in front discussing with great enthusiasm the various aspects of their project.

Fay was just as enthusiastic as she discussed it with Lyndsey. 'It would be marvellous, wouldn't it, if we could all get together? It would be such fun.' Lyndsey said yes without enthusiasm and Fay took her up on it. 'Don't you like the idea? For God's sake don't put a damper on it. It's more important than ever now that Elliott's going abroad that he has something to dream on, and for Dominic too.'

'No, I'm not going to put a damper on it, Fay. It's just that I feel so terribly flat, Elliott going abroad to heaven knows where.

'I know, it's hard, but perhaps this war will soon be over.'

Later, when they all stopped on a rise, Lyndsey saw below them a derelict farmhouse and dilapidated outbuildings, which in the greyness of the afternoon, with lowering clouds over a stormy sea, looked like a scene from a spooky film. But this in no way dampened the men's spirits. Dominic swept his hand in an arc indicating the area where he could have his boat-building yard and said that if they did decide to buy he and Fay could do up the old farmhouse while Elliott could build his farmhouse to the left.

Fay said, 'Wherever I live I would want to grow flowers and I doubt whether they would flourish here.' She pointed to where a line of trees had been stunted, trunks curved landward by the prevailing winds. Lyndsey then contributed her first piece of cheerful conversation for some time.

'Don't let the trees put you off. We had the same at Echo Cove but our garden was full of colour from spring onwards.'

'Well now, that's promising,' Dominic exclaimed, then he and Elliott began to discuss this particular spot as a viable proposition for what they had in mind.

It was when each of them began to list faults, which Lyndsey would have thought easy to overcome, that she realized they had no intention of buying. It was a game with them. Dominic mentioned another piece of available land further along the coast they could look at, but although the others were all agreeable to go and see it, a sudden shower of hailstones driving at them with near gale force, had them turning their backs on it and making for home.

They ran the last hundred yards laughing. When they arrived and were divested of coats and jackets Elliott pulled out his handkerchief and after wiping Lyndsey's face kissed the tip of her nose.

'It's like a little block of ice,' he said.

'And you are lovely and warm, how do you do it?'

'I have a dynamo installed.' They both laughed, then suddenly they were silent, with Elliott holding Lyndsey's gaze.

'Oh, Elliott,' she said, 'I wish – '

Dominic called, 'Come along to the fire! It's freezing in that hall.'

When they went into the sitting room to the blaze of the fire Lyndsey felt it was her only comfort, and hoped there would be an opportunity for them to spend some time alone together.

It was about half an hour later when Fay said to Dominic, 'How about letting me help you to look for that *other* book you promised to lend me.'

He looked at her puzzled, then after a quick glance at Elliott and Lyndsey said, 'Oh, *that* one. Yes, let's go and look for it now.'

Their voices faded into the background when they went upstairs until only the patter of hailstones could be heard on the window panes. And when there was a lull for a few moments the silence was so complete Lyndsey felt that she and Elliott could have been in another world.

He got up and taking her hands in his pulled her to her feet, saying softly, 'I have to leave soon and I want to say goodbye now, Lyndsey.'

The sadness in his voice brought an unbearable ache to her throat. Would he be going into a combat area? Elliott wrapped his arms around her and drew her head to his chest, and she could feel his heartbeats, strong but steady. Her own heartbeats had quickened at contact with him. It was his very strength and virility that brought wave after wave of sensuousness to her.

She said, 'Oh, Elliott, I wish – ' but before she could say any more he had put a finger to her lips.

'You know how I feel about you, Lyndsey,' he said gently, 'but I can't ask you to wait for me. I realized how selfish I had been in asking you to complete our "serial". You're too young to be tied down, even to just promises. I have no idea how long I shall be away.'

She searched his face. 'I do love you, Elliott – '

'And I think you love Andrew too,' he said softly. 'You could hear any day that he had been taken prisoner. Don't commit yourself in any way, Lyndsey, but I would be pleased to hear from you.'

'Yes, of course, I'll write as often as I can, but – '

He kissed her then, but although the kiss was gentle his heart this time was beating as wildly as her own. She clung to him for a moment and he held her tight, but then released her.

Her eyes had filled with tears and a tear that hung on her lashes now rolled slowly down her cheek. Elliott wiped it away with his little finger and said in an anguished voice:

'Please don't cry, darling Lyndsey. I can't bear it.'

She pulled herself together, knowing how unfair it was to him. She said, a tremor in her voice, 'No more tears, I promise.'

He sat down in the chair again and taking Lyndsey's hand he got her to sit on the floor in front of him, saying, 'Let's see what little figures we can see in the fire.'

It was the right thing to say, it put a touch of lightness to the situation. Elliott, a note of teasing in his voice, said he could see a beautiful Wren on a yacht. She was drinking champagne with a very attractive commander.

'Now I wonder who that can be?' she replied, answering him in equally light vein. 'It couldn't possibly be me. The only excitement I get nowadays is when I rescue a soldier, sailor or airman who has fallen overboard from the liberty boat.'

'Ah, but that is what has gone before, pictures in the

fire are what is going to happen in the future. You have the yacht, the champagne and the attractive commander to look forward to.'

Lyndsey turned her head and smiled up at him. 'I note that you put them in the right order. The yacht appeals to me.'

He ran his fingertips down her cheek. 'You know the right thing to say, don't you? Now, tell me, what do *you* see in the fire?'

'I see – ' Lyndsey was going to make something up, but in the glowing centre of the fire a scene formed. She could see Elliott walking, see tanks, palm trees, men advancing with guns. She drew a quick breath and Elliott said, 'What is it?'

She took another quick breath and forced herself to say brightly, 'You're never going to believe this, but I could see you jitterbugging – with a girl who's definitely not me. Now, what do you say about that?'

'I'd say that for once the pictures lied. I would not be jitterbugging with any other girl but you. And *that* is definite.'

Fay, coming into the room at that moment, said, 'What is definite?'

Lyndsey told her about the picture in the fire and Fay laughed. 'If I told you all the things that I had seen in the fire in my lifetime I would have travelled the whole world. It's wishful thinking.'

Lyndsey did not reply. It was not wishful thinking on her part. She had no wish to see Elliott in the desert, in combat . . .

Dominic came in and, smiling, put his arm across Fay's shoulder. 'And we *did* find the book, didn't we?' He then added, 'These two look very cosy. I wouldn't be surprised if they don't know it's snowing.'

Both Lyndsey and Elliott glanced towards the window. Elliott got up. 'I don't think we did.' He held out a hand to pull Lyndsey to her feet. 'But snow or no snow, I must leave.' To Lyndsey he added, 'Are you going to help me on with my overcoat?' There was a sadness in his eyes and Lyndsey felt a lump come into her throat. She nodded and they went into the hall. There she said, a note of pleading in her voice, 'Elliott, will you say something to me that will help me over the next few weeks?'

'I have something I want to give you, Lyndsey.' He brought a small blue velvet-covered box from his pocket. 'It's a friendship ring and there's a story attached. It belonged to the aunt I told you about who said that disagreeing in marriage made it lively and therefore happy. It was given to her by a young man before he went to join up in the First World War. He called it a friendship ring because although he was in love with her she was not in love with him.'

Lyndsey looked at the box, looked at Elliott and when he remained silent she flicked the box open, and there on a bed of white satin lay a circlet of gold, studded with tiny rubies.

'Oh, Elliott, it's lovely.'

'My aunt was touched by the gift but not daring to wear it, knowing that her parents would not approve of it, wore it on a chain around her neck. She wore it for four years. The couple corresponded, and because my aunt was an only child and lonely she talked to the young man in her letters as she might have talked to an older brother.'

'So what happened? Was he – '

'Killed? No, he was one of the lucky ones who returned home safely and he and my aunt were married.'

Lyndsey gave a faint smile and Elliott shook his head. 'No, it's not what you are thinking. I don't expect to come back and find you ready to fall into my arms, and that is the truth, Lyndsey. To me it is purely a friendship ring and I would be most pleased if you will accept it.'

'I'll be pleased to, Elliott, although like your aunt I feel a little overwhelmed by the gift.' Lyndsey took the ring from the box. It was small and she tried it on the little finger of her left hand. It fitted. She held it out. 'There, I shall be proud to tell everyone that it's a friendship ring.' Tears were threatening and she had to wait a moment before she had them under control, then she said softly, 'Thanks, Elliott,' and reached up and kissed him.

'Thank you for accepting it, Lyndsey, and for agreeing to wear it. I can go away now feeling that there is this bond between us. But I must stress again there are no strings attached. You are a free spirit.'

He said his goodbyes to Dominic and Fay and then kissed Lyndsey briefly. It might have seemed a cold parting had it not been for the emotion in his voice when he said:

'Darling girl, take care of yourself.'

The three of them waited until he drove away and watched until the car was lost in a great flurry of snowflakes.

Then Fay gripped Lyndsey's hand and whispered, 'He'll be back, I know it . . .'

TWENTY-SEVEN

The next day the weather was bitterly cold. When Lyndsey and Fay cycled down the lanes to where the boats lay, ice on pools splintered under their wheels and their breath was a ghostly mist in the early morning darkness.

Ann had gone on ahead and Fay said as she bumped over a stone, 'I'm glad that bitch has got the message that I can't stand her. Did you see her face last night when she knew about the ring? She congratulated you for having been given such a lovely gift but her eyes were sparking flames of jealousy.'

'It no longer bothers me,' Lyndsey said, 'Not any more. Actually I feel sorry for her.'

They rounded a bend in the lane and found Ann standing beside her bicycle. Fay and Lyndsey dismounted and Fay said, 'What's up, got a puncture?'

'No, I thought I had better tell you I'm going back to put on an extra sweater. I'm shivering now. I am wearing an extra vest and would have worn another pair of passion killers if I had had the room!'

Lyndsey laughed, knowing what she meant about there being 'no room'. When she had first been issued with the thick woollen navy blue knickers she had thought she would never wear them, especially having been used to silk or satin cami-knicks, but she too was glad of the warmth of the wool.

Ann threw an end of her scarf over her shoulder and

379

mounted. 'I won't be long. I bet everything on the boat will be iced up this morning.'

It was. The pump was not working properly and they had to break the ice on the water to bale out. Fay started up the engine and the throb, as always, gave Lyndsey a feeling of excitement. The dinghies also had to be baled out but by then Ann was there to help.

These were mornings that Lyndsey really enjoyed, finding so much beauty in them. As the light brightened the ships seemed to come to life and looked as if they had moved away from their moorings. The sea was pink-tinged and so were the silver barrage balloons.

Some sailors from a nearby ship greeted them.

'Wotcher, girls.'

'Legs, are you going dancing wiv me tonight? Where's Tich? Oh, there she is . . . Ashey, 'ave you 'ad any more luverly dreams?'

Fay looked up. 'Right name, mate, wrong girl. I never dream.'

The sailor grinned. 'Shame, thought you dreamt about me every night.'

Another one said, 'Dream abaht you, Skinner? It 'ud be a nightmare!'

A man who had just come up called to Ann, who was on her knees, 'Tich, lass, you don't 'ave to kneel to us, we think you're all great.'

There was general laughter at this then the men dispersed to do their chores and the girls went to the bosun's shed for their early morning treat, a cup of steaming tea laced with rum.

Later they ferried sacks of potatoes and vegetables to a frigate, rowed some officers to a corvette, carried two VIPs at speed to a destroyer, the boat sending up spumes of rainbow-tinted spray, delivered some signals to a waiting convoy and also delivered the mail. Lyndsey also enjoyed this task, seeing the pleasure on the men's faces at getting letters from home.

When they returned later to the bosun's shed to await their next orders Lyndsey said with a contented sigh, 'Aren't we lucky, just think what we would have missed had we still been in clothing stores. It's so rewarding.'

Ann groaned. 'What rewards?'

Lyndsey looked at her in surprise. 'The beauty for one thing – '

'Beauty?' Ann declared. 'Where? Just take a look around you.'

Lyndsey loved everything about the shed, the tools of the trade, the mingled smell of hemp, tar, diesel oil, lamp oil, they were to her all a part of the sea, a part of her life. She shook her head sadly, 'You have no soul, Ann.'

'What has this lot got to do with soul?' Ann exclaimed. She waved a hand towards the window. 'Or all that vast expanse of water out there?'

Lyndsey said quietly, 'Why did you join the Wrens, Ann, why did you want to be a part of Boats' Crew?'

'For the chance of meeting handsome officers of course. Isn't that what every other girl joined for?'

'No, it isn't,' Fay snapped. 'All of us here joined because not only did we love the sea but we wanted to do our bit for our country. But that is something *you* wouldn't know about.'

Nothing more was said to Ann about her joining the Wrens.

They were kept busy all the morning, but the afternoon was slack. The three girls sat in the shed, Ann and Lyndsey making rope fenders while Fay read from one of her naval manuals. Mostly she read pieces that were informative for the kind of work they did and the boats they used. But every now and again she would read something that was concerned only with the larger ships, and today she was reading about the loading of them. It was about a Leading Block, with instructions about derricks, davits and sheers, which sounded somewhat complicated. When, after quite a lengthy piece Fay said, 'Well, that's the first purpose of it. Now I'll start on the second,' Lyndsey said, 'I wouldn't if I were you. To me, it's as clear as mud.'

At this Ann said, 'I understood it perfectly, no trouble at all.'

'Oh, *you* would,' Fay replied, her tone dry. 'Perhaps you can explain it to us in *simple* language.'

Ann did and Lyndsey had a job to keep herself from laughing at the astonished expression on Fay's face. But, to give Fay her due she did give Ann credit. 'I take my hat off to you, Ann Matley, you're a better man than I am, Gunga Din.' This brought a beaming smile from Ann.

Later Fay said, 'Aren't people surprising. Who would have thought that the nitwit Ann would have taken in all that jargon about a Leading Block.'

Ann was to spring another surprise two days later, but this time one that was to worry Lyndsey and make Fay furious.

They had taken the liberty boat to pick up the last return load of men for the evening and found a really boisterous lot. They were used to them singing at the tops of their voices, used to them shouting, but with these men there was aggression. They shook the gates, demanding for them to be opened. The able seaman in charge of the boat that evening gave them some plain speaking and after a while they calmed down. But once the gates were open they charged, pushing others aside to be first on the boat.

'Oh, God,' Fay wailed, 'what a trip we're going to have. It wouldn't be so bad if there was only a dozen who were out for a fight, but the whole seventy of them seem to be tonight.'

Fay talked to them and she didn't mince her words either and there were apologies from quite a few for their behaviour.

They cast off and it wasn't too bad at first, then two men started fighting and one went overboard. Lyndsey, who had been prepared, had the boathook ready and managed to get hold of him. Willing hands, as usual, pulled him aboard. But within another five minutes another went over and she hooked him too. By then the coxswain was shouting his head off and warning them if they didn't calm down he would take them back and get the MPs to take care of them.

This did settle them down and although some of them began to sing later the singing was quiet. Lyndsey was enjoying it when to her astonishment a marine took a dive overboard. She grabbed the boathook but missed him. Then suddenly he was no longer there. Without thought she divested herself of coat and shoes and dived in. She found him, shouted to him to keep still and with her hands under his armpits she was swimming quite strongly on her back when she became aware that someone else had jumped into the water beside her.

It was Ann's voice she heard shouting, 'I'll take him, Lyndsey.'

Lyndsey told her she could manage and was swimming on when she suddenly felt a vicious pinch first on her right arm and then her left. The second pinch caused her to relinquish her hold momentarily and before she could catch hold of the marine again someone pulled her by the feet and she went under.

When she surfaced and rubbed the water from her eyes she saw Ann swimming with the man.

Everything had happened so quickly she felt bewildered. Two men came swimming up to her and got her back to the boat. Then it seemed that everyone was shouting at once. Once she was on board a blanket was thrown around her shoulders and several men were asking her if she was all right. Fay then took charge, telling them all to shut up. A small bottle of rum was put to Lyndsey's lips. She drank some because she was shivering, not so much from cold as from the shock of what had happened. Had Ann deliberately tried to drown her?

All three girls were still officially on duty but because of Ann and Lyndsey needing to get out of their wet clothes they were taken to their quarters, with neither Ann nor Lyndsey saying a word on the way.

Lyndsey had had a hot shower, changed into dry clothes and was drying her hair when Fay arrived. 'We've been relieved for the rest of the shift,' she said. 'We all have to report to the office.' Fay paused a moment then continued, 'Before we go in I want to know what happened in the water. Some bloody fool dropped the Aldis lamp into the water, but I wasn't the only one to know there was some monkey business going on.'

Lyndsey began towelling her hair, longing to tell Fay what had happened yet afraid to voice her fears. 'I don't know what happened, it was all so confusing.'

Fay took the towel from her. 'You know, and if you don't tell me I'll find some way of making that two-faced Ann Matley tell me, so which is it to be?'

Lyndsey gave in and told her, concluding, 'I thought at first that Ann was trying to drown me but now I feel sure she did it wanting recognition, praise for rescuing the man. But I don't want anyone else to know what happened. They don't have to.'

'Of course they have to know! Don't be a fool. The girl could put someone else in danger, someone who was perhaps not such a strong swimmer.'

Lyndsey began to plead with her. 'Don't you see, Fay, it's important to Ann to get praise. It's not to me, and it's not to you, I know, but try and understand Ann. She's had nothing in her life. Please, Fay, promise you won't say anything.'

Fay refused to promise, saying she would let things take their course. Then she added that there were others who would perhaps complain about Ann's actions.

They were then called to go to the office. When they went in Ann and the coxswain were already there. The coxswain wore a rather bewildered look. Ann looked triumphant.

The chief said she had had a rather garbled account of

the accident from Coxswain Finley, but a very clear-cut version of it from Wren Matley. She then asked Lyndsey and Fay for their accounts.

Lyndsey said she was a little unclear what had happened but thought that the marine she had tried to rescue must have hit her during his struggles and knocked her out momentarily. When she had surfaced Wren Matley was swimming with the marine towards the boat.

The chief said quietly in answer to this that, according to witnesses, the marine had remained quiescent during the whole of the rescue operation.

This took the look of triumph from Ann's face.

Fay, when questioned, said she had seen Lyndsey swimming strongly with the man until Ann had jumped into the water. Then she had seen Lyndsey go under and Ann had taken over the rescue of the marine. She added that there had been something odd about the proceedings but was unable to say what it was.

Lyndsey realized that Fay, with her strong principles of right and wrong, had been as fair to Ann as she could.

Fay, Lyndsey and the coxswain were dismissed; Ann was asked to stay, which brought some speculation from the other Wrens. Lyndsey was surprised at how various versions of the accident had gone around especially so quickly. She was also surprised at how much Ann was disliked. One girl said, 'There's something fishy about the whole thing and it'll be a good job if Matley is kicked out. I never liked her.' This was followed by a chorus of, 'Neither did I.'

Ann did not come to bed that night, which caused a great deal more speculation and a lot of whispering. Fay in the end told them all to shut up and go to sleep, talking about what had happened would get them nowhere. There was silence but Lyndsey lay wide awake, uneasy. Had Ann admitted to the officer what she had done, and was not willing to face the others? Or had she perhaps gone to complete the rest of her shift? It was the kind of thing she might do. Ann did have complete dedication to her work.

It was exhaustion that finally took over and Lyndsey did not rouse until the morning bell. Then she found that Ann's bed had not been slept in, and when she did not show up for breakfast enquiries were started. But at the end of the day they drew a blank. Ann had disappeared and then a little fear crept in. Had she perhaps done something silly?

'Not Ann Matley,' Fay declared. 'She's too cute for that. She only wants to scare everyone, get them worried. And thinks when she does turn up she'll be welcomed like a prodigal daughter. She'll be hiding out somewhere.'

'But she left all her belongings behind,' one girl protested. To this Fay pointed out that Ann had taken her duffle coat and handbag and added that if a girl was desperate enough to take her own life she would not worry about being warm or having money to spend.

Lyndsey had been called to the office when it was learned that she and Ann had been friendly before coming into the Wrens. Lyndsey told the chief what she knew of Ann, about her mother being killed in an air-raid and her unhappy childhood, but it gave no clue to Ann's whereabouts. They had already enquired and been told she was not staying with any of her close family or relatives.

Things settled down, with all of them having become convinced that Ann had simply cleared out. So it was more of a shock when a week later they learned that her body had been found, washed up on the shores of Scotland.

Lyndsey was terribly upset and Fay was upset too, saying she wished she had not opened her big mouth and said there was something odd about the accident. 'I disliked her intensely but I wouldn't wish anyone to take his or her own life.'

Although Lyndsey had done her best to exonerate Ann from any blame in the accident she worried herself sick, thinking she could have done more, been kinder to Ann, included her in outings, and might have gone on blaming herself for Ann taking her own life had it not been for a note enclosed in a letter to the chief, which Ann had posted the night she decided to take her own life. Lyndsey read the note in solitude.

Dear Lyndsey,

I have written to the chief telling her that I take full responsibility for what happened the night the marine went overboard. I did what I did because I wanted to feel important. At times I was unkind to you, even vicious in my remarks, but I loved you as a sister and valued your friendship. *You* have nothing to regret in regard to your attitude towards me. I'm taking this way out because I think it's for the best. I've never known real happiness, and I feel I never will. It's something inside me. Forgive me for any hurt I caused you. Love, Ann.

Lyndsey folded the note, big tears running slowly down her cheeks. The tragedy of it . . . A girl who had never known real happiness and felt she never would . . .

It was in the cabin that Fay found her. Wordlessly Lyndsey handed her the note. Fay read it then after a short silence handed it back. 'Thanks for letting me read it, Lyndsey. It might help me to be more tolerant towards people I don't like, or understand. The odd thing is that I can admire Ann after admitting she was the one responsible. For someone of her nature it must have taken courage.'

It was Fay's words that helped Lyndsey over Ann's death, but she knew that Ann would always remain a sad little figure.

A few days later the Boomerangs had a date for going abroad and Bette and Lyndsey arranged to meet for a day in London. When Bette arrived she was beaming all over her face.

'Guess what! I heard this morning from the War Office

that Andrew is a prisoner of war. Oh, Lyndsey, what marvellous news!'

They hugged each other and the talk for the first half hour was all of Andrew. Bette would write a letter to him and arrange for a parcel to be sent through the Red Cross. Lyndsey could do the same. They could only send a one-page letter, she said. 'So make sure your writing is very small, he'll be wanting to hear so much news, but don't say anything about the war or it will be crossed out. Letters are heavily censored.'

Richard and Marian, who were both at home that day, had invited them for lunch and when they knew about the good news Richard said, 'Well, I can tell you now, Andrew is in quite a good camp. I have a friend who is a prisoner there. I'll write to Andrew and give him his name. Dirk's a grand fellow. I think they'll get on quite well together. It's always good to meet someone who already knows the ropes.'

When Lyndsey and Bette parted late that afternoon there was a sadness, as they had no idea when they would meet again, but it was not with tears, the good news of Andrew had given them so much pleasure.

Marian had been so pleasant Lyndsey had marvelled over it and could only put it down to the fact that with Bette going out of the country she had no need to be jealous any more of Richard's interest in her. Richard had kissed Bette and held her close to him and she appeared to be near tears. Then she was saying, 'Well, I shall let you know if the mosquitoes like my blood. The wretched little midges do here and I'm plagued to death by them in the summer.'

It wasn't until the next day that Lyndsey began to realize what it would mean not to have Bette to visit, and she felt so flat that not even Fay telling her about an invitation to a dance at a big house the following evening could make her snap out of her mood.

The invitation had come from Dominic. Fay said, 'Cheer

up, it'll be a good do, and even if you don't want to dance the grub will be worth having. Pierre's in charge. There will be a running buffet. The people holding the dance are friends of Dominic who try to give young service people a good time.' For Fay's sake Lyndsey tried to put a bright face on it, but secretly hoped she might find some secluded spot where she could sit out if she felt like it.

Dominic sent the car for them the following evening and the chauffeur delivered a message saying that the captain would meet them at the house.

It loomed up menacingly in the blackout, but inside it was brightly lit and warm. From somewhere upstairs came the sound of music, mingling with the chatter of voices and small bursts of laughter.

Their middle-aged host and hostess were plump and jolly, both saying they hoped they would enjoy themselves, and after a manservant had taken their hats and gloves Lyndsey and Fay were escorted upstairs. As they went up the broad staircase Dominic came out of a room along the passage on their left and hailed them. 'Hello, so you managed to make it.' He came up and kissed each of them on both cheeks. 'I think you'll enjoy it, they're a mixed crowd but very friendly. Come along and I'll introduce you.'

The three-piece orchestra was playing soft, dreamy music. The guests stood around in small groups. The fragrant smell of cigar smoke hung on the air. The room was large, the parquet floor gleaming. On one side of the room were small tables and chairs but around the other three walls was a variety of armchairs. The men, all in uniform, appeared to be officers but were from the three services. All the girls, apart from one, were also in uniform, but most were from the ranks. There looked to be about thirty couples. Dominic took Lyndsey and Fay around introducing them and the atmosphere was certainly one of friendliness.

The two girls were standing alone for a few moments

whilst Dominic had gone to get them drinks when Lyndsey was aware of someone staring at her. He was a naval lieutenant, a big, brawny man with dark auburn hair. Recognition was mutual. He came striding over, his face alight with pleasure. 'Lyndsey MacLaren! I don't believe it.'

She laughed. 'Johnnie Wetherby. And I can't believe it's you.' She introduced Fay to him, explaining that Johnnie lived at Echo Cove and that they had known each other since childhood.

Johnnie grinned. 'We were childhood sweethearts.'

'Sweethearts we were not!' Lyndsey declared. 'He was like a great big brother, always bossing me around.'

'Don't you believe it, Fay, she adored me, followed me everywhere.'

Lyndsey was about to make further protest when Dominic came up with the drinks. Fay introduced Johnnie and explained about Lyndsey and Johnnie having known one another since they were children. Dominic said to Johnnie, smiling, 'Then I'm sure you will both have a lot of news to catch up on.' He nodded towards a door at the far end of the room. 'There's a conservatory through there, but make sure you bring Lyndsey back before the last waltz.'

'Oh, I can promise you that, sir, I want to have a few dances with her, and with Miss Ashton too. Excuse us.'

Johnnie took Lyndsey by the hand and as he pulled at her she said, 'There you go again, bossing me around, I don't think we should have left Dominic and Fay. We had only just arrived.'

'I'm not kidnapping you, but you must admit that it will be nice to have a quiet talk.' They had reached the door and he opened it and they went into a humid atmosphere, surrounded by plants of every description. When he closed the door there was a sudden silence. Johnnie led her to two cane chairs under a massive palm plant. 'How about this?'

When they were seated Johnnie sat smiling at her. 'This is great, Lyndsey. I had heard you had joined the services but I certainly didn't expect to see you. You look marvellous, more beautiful than ever.' He paused then added softly, 'Do you remember the last time we met?'

Lyndsey nodded. 'Yes, I do, it was the night of the harvest dance. It was held in Farmer Welmet's barn. And it was not until you were walking me home that you told me you were going to join the navy. I was sixteen and you had just had your nineteenth birthday.'

'That's right. And it was the first time I kissed you, properly that is.' He reached out a hand. 'I was sorry I never wrote to you as I promised and sorry to hear from Gran that you had lost your parents and grandparents. Gran told me in her letter that you went to live in London.'

'Yes, with Uncle Richard and his wife. Then I joined the Wrens and have no regrets. Are you stationed at Portsmouth?'

'For the moment. I'm with corvettes, part of convoys. That's for your ears alone, of course. Being in the Wrens you'll have had absolute secrecy drummed into you. And anyway, that was one thing I liked about you, you could keep a secret, not like some girls I knew. Is there a special man in your life?'

'One in every port,' she answered lightly.

'I could imagine that, you were never short of boys. I should be here a few days, any chance of our getting together for an evening?'

Lyndsey, feeling full of nostalgia with mention of Echo Cove, had no hesitation in answering, 'I'm on a 24-hour shift and will be free the day after tomorrow.'

'Great, that's a date.' The door opened and a couple came in, the strains of a waltz drifting in with them. Johnnie got up. 'How about it, Lyndsey? It'll be like old times.'

They went on to the floor to the tune 'Lover Come Back to Me', from *The Desert Song*. When Lyndsey was fourteen she had developed a great crush on Johnnie, and although she had never really been in love with Johnnie, it was nice to have strong arms around her and to feel the romance of the music and the atmosphere.

The party got more lively as the evening wore on. Dominic danced only twice, once with Fay and once with Lyndsey, because of his injury, but he was mixing all the time. Johnnie said once, 'I like Haltane, a nice chap, not a bit stuffy. Are he and Fay serious about one another?'

Lyndsey told him that although they were not officially engaged they had talked about marriage. Then she asked Johnnie if he was married – or did he have a special girlfriend.

'Neither,' he said. 'I did have a special girl a year ago but she found someone else. It happens. I couldn't blame her. She liked a lot of fun.' He chuckled. 'Gran didn't like her at all, thought her terribly flighty. But she was a nice lass really, just not ready to settle down.' Johnnie then asked Lyndsey if she had been back recently to Echo Cove, then added, 'No, you couldn't have been or Gran would have mentioned it, she thought the world of you. We'll have to go together sometime and give her a surprise. She'd get the flags out!'

'I'm sure she would,' Lyndsey said, remembering the wiry old lady who had brought Johnnie and his sister up when their widowed mother had died. Another wave of homesickness engulfed her.

Both Lyndsey and Fay had managed to get late passes and were due back at midnight. Johnnie had come with another young officer and he and Lyndsey said their good nights in the hall.

'It's been a marvellous evening, Lyndsey,' he said softly, 'and I shall certainly look forward to seeing you on Thursday. Where shall we meet? We could meet at the station. I have to collect a parcel from a colleague at nine o'clock. There a green-painted wooden seat in the ticket lobby.' Johnnie grinned. 'It's not the most romantic of places, it's noisy and – '

'That will be fine,' Lyndsey said. 'I'll be there at nine.'

Johnnie kissed her then and when Lyndsey felt a familiar tremor go through her she felt annoyed. Was she always to feel sexually aroused when just any man kissed her? But then Johnnie was not just *any* man.

Fay said when they were in Dominic's car, 'Nice fellar, that Johnnie, real down to earth bod. Salt of the earth, or should I say, salt of the sea! He certainly knows his Portsmouth.'

'Oh, he didn't say anything to me about it.'

'Then you have that treat in store, and I mean it. He really is interesting.'

TWENTY-EIGHT

Lyndsey soon learned about Johnnie's love for Portsmouth and how steeped he was in the history of it when they met on the Thursday morning. But he was funny too as he related certain incidents on their way towards the dockyard where, he said, he had a quick appointment.

'Why especially Portsmouth?' she asked. 'All the other ports have a history.'

'Yes, I know, but I have a pal who lives here and during one of our voyages he brought me some books on the subject. I hated history at school but these books rolled back the centuries for me, I was *there*. I could "see" Henry the Fifth waiting with his fleet to sail to France and Agincourt. There were four hundred ships and nine hundred men at arms. Can you imagine it, all those sails?'

'Yes, I can,' Lyndsey said dreamily, caught up in the imagery. 'It must have been a magnificent sight.'

'Did you know that he sailed to the music of "Pypes, trompes, nakers and clarionnes"?'

'What are nakers?'

Johnnie shook his head. 'I haven't a clue, but it all sounds grand, doesn't it? Perhaps I'll stop people and say, "Excuse me, but could you tell me what sort of an instrument a naker is?" ' Johnnie's face was suddenly alive with laughter. 'I bet I'd get some strange looks.'

Lyndsey laughed. 'You probably would. I should imagine they would take you for a spy for thinking that an acre of land was an instrument.' Johnnie eyed her for a moment, puzzled, then he said, 'Oh, I get it, yes, yes, bright girl! Incidentally, did you know that George the Third, who visited the dockyard in 1772, was rowed out to his ship, in a barge, by twelve local *ladies*?'

'No, I didn't, and I can hardly believe it. Ladies? Rowing a barge in those days?'

'According to the historians, it's true. Sometimes I can't believe that women are doing men's jobs today, welding, working on aeroplanes, dealing with engines, torpedoes, bombs, driving three-ton lorries.' Johnnie paused and added softly, 'But I'm glad they are and that you joined the Wrens, Lyndsey, otherwise I might never have met you again. It's great.'

When they reached the dockyard Lyndsey told Johnnie she would wait for him, she would just stroll around. After he was out of sight Lyndsey started to move away then came back, caught by the constant movement. In spite of considerable bomb damage there was activity everywhere, the swinging of cranes, ships being loaded, unloaded; ships under repair, the ringing sound of hammers on metal mingling with the whine of welding. And as she stood there she found herself understanding Johnnie's enthusiasm for the history of bygone days. The people of today were the history of the future. Lyndsey experienced again the fierce loyalty for her country that she had known on her first visit to the *Victory*. They must win this war, they *must*.

Johnnie was not too long away and when she saw him coming towards her, a great giant with the slight rolling gait of a man who has been to sea for several years, she felt a great warmth towards him. He had been a part of her childhood, her growing-up years.

'Well, that's that,' he said, as the gates clanged behind him. 'How about having a coffee, then we can discuss what we are going to do today?'

Over coffee they reminisced about their years together at Echo Cove but a sadness crept in when Johnnie told her about some of the young people they had known having been killed in action. But immediately afterwards he talked about a church outing they had gone on to Tynemouth, and how they all went swimming and one of the men had lost his false teeth.

'Do you remember, Lyndsey? Do you remember how we dived and groped about in the sand trying to find them and had to give up eventually?'

'Yes, I do,' she said, laughing. 'And I remember how we were all in the coach ready to go home when a woman came waddling up, panting, waving the false teeth. She had found them when the tide went out. Poor Mr Dodd, he laughed and he cried, he was so pleased to get them back.'

'Lovely, happy, wonderful days,' Johnnie mused, smiling. Then his expression suddenly sobered. 'But days that are gone forever. When I was home on leave a while ago I went to Tynemouth and felt saddened at what I saw.'

He told her how the Germans had dropped mines in the Tyne Estuary and how when the tide carried them in they blew up the ships.

'It was a terrible thing to see, Lyndsey, a line of masts above the water. I love ships and I think of them as people. They all have a character of their own, some a great dignity, and when I saw them like that I felt their humiliation.'

'Oh, no, Johnnie, I don't see them like that at all. The masts above the water line are a sort of defiance, you know, saying "you'll never kill us off!" '

A slow smile spread over Johnnie's face. 'I hadn't thought of it like that. Thanks, Lyndsey. So, what are we going to do today? Visit museums, browse around, walk?'

'Walk, it's such a lovely day.'

The weather was unusually mild for the time of year, with intermittent bursts of sun. They walked to Southsea castle, and stood for a long time just watching the sea and shipping, not talking much.

Johnnie said suddenly, 'Tell me, Lyndsey, what do you do when you're out on the water and there's a raid?'

'What? Oh, put on my tin hat and duck. It's all you can do. Sailors dice with death every day and we *are* in the navy.'

'True, but you take care of yourself, do you hear?' his voice was gruff.

Their talk after that was mainly about family and Johnnie relating funny little experiences on board ship and in ports he had been to. Lyndsey felt relaxed and comfortable with him and would not allow herself to think of later when he took her back to her quarters and might want to linger over saying good night.

They had a meal early evening and were talking about going to see a film when the sirens went. Neither took much notice, nor did anyone else in the restaurant until a bomb dropped quite close. Johnnie got up. 'Come on, I think it would be sensible to go to a shelter.'

Lyndsey had avoided going into shelters since she had been buried in the rubble of Ann's house when it was bombed. She now felt a terrible sense of claustrophobia in them. But not wanting to talk about this she agreed to leave.

The anti-aircraft guns were going at full blast and the noise was deafening. Searchlights criss-crossed the sky, with intermittent flashes of red from the guns looking like fireworks exploding. The shelter Johnnie took her to was crowded and the vibrations from guns and exploding bombs made it uncomfortable to stand. Lyndsey kept changing from one foot to the other. There were a number of young couples and their talk was lively, but there were also wailing frightened children and two dogs barked incessantly. It was, however, the smell from makeshift toilets and closely packed humanity that made Lyndsey want to leave. She felt nauseous.

At last there came a lull in the firing and bombing, and when Lyndsey suggested they leave Johnnie agreed, but delivered the ultimatum that if the bombing resumed they would have to shelter again.

When they came up to the clean tang of salty air she took a deep breath. 'Oh, lovely. I don't know how people stick it in shelters all night, but then I suppose they have their children to consider.'

Johnnie suggested they try and find a pub. They found one open inland. It too was crowded but there was a party spirit and Lyndsey and Johnnie joined in with the singing with great gusto.

When they left so that Johnnie could see Lyndsey back to her quarters he put his arm about her waist. The all clear had gone earlier and the searchlights had been switched off.

Neither of them had had much to drink but Lyndsey knew that Johnnie was feeling amorous by the way his hand crept up from her waist so that his fingers were now touching her breast. She laughed and moved his hand down and Johnnie stopped and said softly, 'I'm not asking anything of you, Lyndsey, I just want to touch you.'

When she pointed out that touching could lead to something else Johnnie refuted it. He would give her his word and, knowing Johnnie, she knew he would keep it, but what she should also have pointed out was that it might make *her* want something more.

Johnnie, obviously accepting her silence as consent, drew her into the doorway of an empty shop. There, very slowly he undid the buttons of her jacket, then the top buttons of her blouse. She stood tense, determined to try and control her feelings, but already she was sinking into the sensual feelings his touch was awakening. She tried to concentrate on the things Johnnie had described earlier, and had an image in her mind of King Henry's fleet leaving harbour, sails unfurling, but the image soon faded when Johnnie, having slipped his hand inside her blouse, touched naked flesh. He cupped her breast and she closed her eyes and drew in a quick breath as familiar emotions surged through her body.

Johnnie's breathing was ragged as he caressed her skin, then his mouth sought hers, hungrily, and she responded. Why not, why should she deny what, after all, was a natural instinct?

It was when she felt Johnnie's hand creep up her bare thigh that part of Nelson's famous prayer flashed, for some reason, into her mind. 'A great and glorious victory, and may no misconduct in anyone tarnish it . . .' She had not thought about it as having anything to do with sex, but now the word 'misconduct' seemed to apply to her. She tried to draw away but Johnnie had her in a tight embrace. His lips were on her cheek then the tip of his tongue was in her ear, tormenting her.

'Don't, Johnnie, don't,' she moaned.

'I won't harm you, Lyndsey, I promise, just touching.'

But it was the touching that was crucifying her.

When his fingers found the most sensitive part of her body and shivers of ecstasy began to run through her, she pushed him away. 'No, Johnnie, no, no, no!'

'I'm sorry, Lyndsey, I thought – ' His voice held hurt.

'And I'm sorry, Johnnie, I was foolish. It went too far. I blame myself, not you, I misled you.' She buttoned up her blouse and had started buttoning up her jacket when Johnnie took over, saying let him at least do that for her.

'And now you won't want to go out with me any more,' Johnnie said in a forlorn voice.

Lyndsey put a hand on his arm. 'I will, Johnnie, that is, if – '

'I promise to behave myself.' He grinned suddenly. 'Actually, I thought I had done.'

Then he was the Johnnie she had known, always the one to ease an atmosphere to prevent embarrassment. She said, 'As I told you, I blame myself. And now, shall we forget it?'

They walked on but although as far as Lyndsey was

concerned the whole thing was forgotten, Johnnie would not let it go. He wanted to explain his behaviour. 'I wouldn't have gone any further, I really wouldn't, I had said I only wanted to touch you and that was it, even though you're so flipping well desirable. I remember the last time we went to a dance together and coming home in agony because I had wanted to make love to you and had to be content with a good night kiss.'

'Oh, Johnnie, and I didn't know.'

'Of course you didn't. You were sweet sixteen and I had had it drummed into me by Gran that I had to treat you with respect. I knew what she meant, but it didn't prevent me from suffering. Anyway, when I leave this time I'll take away a lovely memory. Do you have a photograph you can give me?'

She told him she had a snap and stopped to take one from her shoulder bag. 'It's a recent one. Uncle Richard took it about a month ago. He and Marian think it quite good but I think I look too smug.'

Johnnie put it into his pocket. 'I'll be able to judge it better when I see it in the light. Do you know how I picture you, Lyndsey? With your tin hat on, ducking your head at the bombs as the boat speeds across the water.'

Lyndsey felt a sudden pang as she pictured Johnnie in convoy vulnerable to a menacing U-boat waiting ready to pounce. But then she thought of the corvettes, speedy, manoeuvrable, cheeky, defiant, darting here and there, protecting the mother ships, like a sheep dog herding its charges. She could only pray that Johnnie would be kept safe.

It was coming up to ten o'clock when they arrived at her quarters so there was no time to linger. Johnnie said, 'I have no idea when we'll be moving out, Lyndsey. If I'm here the day after tomorrow I'll get in touch with you. If not it'll be when we get back.'

'I'll look forward to seeing you, Johnnie, it's been a

lovely day.' It was she who kissed him and Johnnie held her close.

'For me too,' he said softly. He touched her lightly under the chin. 'Be good.'

'And you . . .' Then, as big as he was, he just seemed to melt into the blackness, leaving Lyndsey feeling as if something had been left uncompleted.

The next morning she knew by all the activity that a convoy would be leaving soon. All the Boats' Crew were kept busy delivering signals to ships, messages, extra stores, ammunition . . . By early afternoon the movement started, oil tankers, merchant ships, corvettes, all leaving to rendezvous with other shipping. Lyndsey gave a shiver. How many of them would return?

From then on she felt that her life was centred around waiting for news of Johnnie, Andrew, Elliott and Bette.

It was six weeks before she heard anything then it all came together. News of Andrew came first in a letter from Mrs Petrie. It was written to Bette and Mrs Petrie had copied it for Lyndsey. He was quite well and conditions were not too bad at all. He was with a good crowd and had met a major who was a friend of Lyndsey's Uncle Richard. They had a good football team, did physical jerks every morning to try and keep fit, played cards, read. Here he mentioned that any reading matter would be welcomed. He had had parcels from home as well as Bette's and Lyndsey's and he asked that Bette would thank Lyndsey and give her his love. He was so very grateful for them. He concluded by asking Bette if she would write to his family. It was signed, Love, Andrew.

Lyndsey felt tearful, poor Andrew, so full of life and now imprisoned, but then it was better that than being killed. She must write to him again.

The following day she had a letter from Elliott. It was short, as most of his letters were. He said he was getting acclimatized to the heat, that he had been to an ENSA show, which he had enjoyed, and he asked about Bette's party and if they were still at home. He asked after Richard and Marian, Fay and Dominic, said he hoped that Lyndsey was not working too hard and signed it, Yours Elliott.

'Well!' Lyndsey exclaimed to Fay, who was reading her own post. 'I wait weeks to hear from Elliott Warrender and what does he tell me? Damn all. I know he's somewhere hot and that's it.

Fay looked up. 'Be pleased you have at least heard from him, he's just not the gushing type.'

'Gushing? Oh, honestly –' Lyndsey threw the letter down. 'I don't care if I never hear from him again.'

'You know you don't mean that.'

Lyndsey gave a deep sigh. 'No, I don't, but isn't it frustrating? I hear about Andrew secondhand, and always will, I suppose, even if he was away for years. I believe that the number of letters prisoners can send is limited and of course his family must always come first.'

A letter from Bette, which came by the next post, lifted Lyndsey right from the doldrums. It was cheerful, and full of news, without actually stating where they were. She said that although the conditions were as she had described earlier, everyone was in a good mood. They had travelled extensively, done many concerts and had the most fantastic welcome and ovations it was possible to imagine. 'These people were so cut off, Lyndsey. One man said it was like going to his first pantomime when he was a child, and that sums up the general reaction we had.'

Bette went on to say that she longed to hear more news of Andrew, that she had not had any letters from home at all, but perhaps they would all catch up with them in time. It was being on the move that was the trouble. Lyndsey had written a number of letters to her and was disappointed that she had not received them.

Bette's letter went on to describe how everyone tried to create a party spirit and how at one time they were still partying at five o'clock in the morning when they were due to leave at seven o'clock for their next concert! 'It was

402

great, Lyndsey, great, like my music hall days, constantly on the move. I *know* that you will have written to me and as soon as I receive my first letter from you I shall write by return. Keep 'em coming. Lots of love from us all, Bette.'

'Now that is what I call a letter,' Lyndsey declared to Fay, to which Fay replied wryly, yes, but she must remember it was a woman writing it, not a tongue-tied man.

Lyndsey's next lovely surprise was hearing from Johnnie. He was in port and wanted to see her. Although Lyndsey had known he could be away for weeks there were times when she felt sure he had been torpedoed, when she did go to meet him she felt joyous as she ran to him.

He gave her a bear hug and she kept saying, 'Oh, Johnnie, I'm glad you're safe. I'm glad you're safe . . .'

It was not until they drew apart that she saw how tired he looked. 'Bad trip?' she queried. He nodded and said, 'So-so.' Then he added with his familiar grin, 'But there's good news, I have seven days' leave. I thought of going home. Any chance of you getting leave?'

'Not for seven days, but I am due for a 48-hour pass.'

'Then how about us going to London for a couple of days and living it up? I can go on from there to home.'

It was the wicked look in Johnnie's eyes that made Lyndsey cautious. 'I was going to visit my Uncle Richard and his wife. We could – stay there.'

Johnnie's expression then changed to one of gentleness. 'That might be best, great in fact, if you're sure they would want me.'

Lyndsey laughed. 'They would never turn a Geordie away. It's settled. I'll give them a ring this evening.'

Richard said yes, of course Johnnie could come, he would take them out to dinner in the West End. Although Lyndsey thought that a foursome might not be what Johnnie wanted she could not do anything else but agree.

If Johnnie was disappointed when Lyndsey told him about the foursome he didn't show it.

To Lyndsey's surprise Marian made a great fuss of both of them. How lovely that they should meet again, and so nice for them to spend some time together.

Richard said, 'Now just make yourself at home, Johnnie. We'll have a coffee and then we can hear all your news, and Lyndsey's.'

They chatted about this and that then Richard said he had booked a table at the Café de Paris for that evening and at this Johnnie sat up in his seat, his face alight with pleasure.

'The Café de Paris! Snakehips Johnstone's orchestra is playing there.'

Marian smiled at him. 'It is and we'll have Al Bowlly crooning.'

Johnnie turned to Richard. 'Thanks, sir, thanks a lot, no one could have given me a greater treat.'

Johnnie's pleasure seemed to have spread to the rest of them, and there was an air of jollity that Lyndsey had not experienced since her grandparents had lived in the house.

Marian surpassed herself in hospitality. At first Lyndsey thought it was something about Johnnie that was responsible but realized later there was a new lovingness between Marian and Richard. She would touch him on the cheek as she was passing, smile when she asked him something, a smile with a lovely warmth that Lyndsey had never seen before and she thought that perhaps at last Marian had learned how to give love.

There was an air-raid warning on when they left that evening but Marian declared they would have to go to dinner even if bombs were dropping all around them and the other three happily agreed.

The restaurant was crowded and on first appearance it seemed to be full of young officers, but on a second look around there were men and women in evening dress, bejewelled women, diamonds sparkling under the lights.

There were couples on the floor dancing to the music of the orchestra and to Al Bowlly crooning a love song.

'Smoochy, isn't it?' Marian said, smiling as a waiter ushered them to their table. They had sat down when she stood up again and held out her hands to Richard. 'Let's dance, shall we?' He got up smiling then turned to Johnnie and Lyndsey.

'How about you two?' They got up too but by then the wine waiter had come up and Richard stopped to speak to him. Marian, who had walked on ahead, stopped on the edge of the dance floor and turned to look for him. Seeing him busy she stood, her body moving to the rhythm of the music, and Lyndsey thought she had never seen Marian so happy or so sensuous.

Johnnie had just taken Lyndsey by the arm and they were moving forward when suddenly there was a great tearing sound, the building rocked and debris came crashing down. In the split second of Johnnie and Lyndsey being flung to the ground pandemonium broke out. Screaming people pushed over tables to get out. Lyndsey, who had been momentarily stunned, was lifted to her feet by Johnnie. 'Are you all right?' She nodded and then Richard came staggering up. 'Marian?'

A crowd of fear-maddened people came surging up, carrying Richard and Johnnie with them, as though caught up by an avalanche. Lyndsey, who had been pushed aside by the crowd, could see Richard and Johnnie fighting to get back but they didn't have a chance.

She stood whimpering, not knowing what to do. Then she thought of Marian and began to look for her. Some of the lights were still on but there was a choking dust everywhere. She stumbled over broken glass and crockery, wishing she could shut out the sound of the screams of the injured. When she saw Marian there was a man in evening dress bending over her. At first she thought he was trying to help her then with a feeling of horror she saw that he was trying to get the rings from her fingers. Outrage had

405

her clambering over chairs. When she reached him she shouted, 'You bastard, you bastard!' and began pummelling his back.

He turned and punched her on the arm and as he kept on punching he yelled obscenities at her. Then he struck her a blow in the face and she staggered back. When she recovered her balance she saw two officers dragging him away.

One of them came back for her. 'Come with me, miss.' She shook her head. 'My – sister-in-law – ' She dropped to her knees beside Marian, and the officer said, 'I'm sorry, miss – the lady – there's nothing anyone can do for her. You *must* come with me.'

'No, my uncle will come back for me, so will Johnnie. I know they will.' Someone called to the officer to come and help and with some reluctance he left.

Lyndsey sat rocking to and fro. Above the clamour she could hear the ringing of bells, ambulances, fire engines, police cars, but everything seemed to be happening in a dream. Bodies were strewn all over the floor, there was blood everywhere. And she watched, in a detached way, the people robbing the dead, women as well as men. From far away she heard someone call her name. She was picked up in strong arms and she felt then the pains in her back, in her arms and in her head. 'Johnnie,' she whispered, and remembered no more.

TWENTY-NINE

A month after that terrible night at the Café de Paris,
Lyndsey was back at her job, but it was six months before
the memory of it began to fade. What made it all so much
worse was Richard's behaviour. No sooner was Marian's
funeral over than he put in for a posting abroad and
Lyndsey felt betrayed, he was the only family she had left.

And it was not until six weeks after he was abroad that
he wrote, explaining his reason and begging forgiveness.

'I know now how disgracefully I behaved, Lyndsey,
clamming up, unwilling to talk about Marian or anything
connected with our life together. For the first time since
our marriage Marian and I had come to understand one
another and could love one another freely. It was also the
first time since my early twenties that I knew real happi-
ness, and then, when I lost Marian, I felt I was being
punished for all the sadness I had brought to other people.
Please, Lyndsey, write and tell me you forgive me.'

Knowing it would serve no purpose to add to his sorrow
she wrote and told him there was nothing to forgive. But
she was still left with a terrible feeling of being rootless. In
fact, had it not been for Fay and Dominic and Johnnie she
might never have got over the traumatic experience.

Fay and Dominic were now married but as Fay had
stayed on in the Wrens Lyndsey was in constant touch
with her, and was made a welcome guest in their home.

As for Johnnie, he always contacted her the minute he

was back in port. Their meeting place was the green-painted wooden seat, which they had now come to regard as their own. Once Lyndsey had had a semaphored signal 'Lyn. Green seat. Nineteen hundred hours' and several people had told her and teased her about it.

Although she and Johnnie had never actually made love they had come close to it on occasions. It was not that Lyndsey wanted to, not any longer, but she wanted to give pleasure to Johnnie for all his kindness and caring of her. He had sensed this and he was the one who would let their 'petting' go only so far. And always he would say, 'When we go the whole way, Lyndsey, it'll be because it's something *you* want more than anything in the world.'

Lyndsey doubted she ever would because Andrew and Elliott still held a close place in her heart. She wrote to each regularly and sent parcels to Andrew. Twice she had had a personal letter from Andrew and treasured them. They were loving letters, wanting to know everything she was doing. She had not told him about Marian, but had mentioned in a casual way that Richard was abroad.

Elliott's letters were still stilted until she told him about Marian's death and Richard's posting and then they changed completely. There was a concerned note in them, a tenderness. How was she managing, where did she spend her leaves? She told him with friends and sometimes she stayed at the Mayfair house; Mrs Grey kept it aired. Elliott now signed his letters, Yours, with love.

Lyndsey and Bette corresponded regularly and Lyndsey enjoyed Bette's letters because they were always so cheerful.

In early September Bette hinted that she and the Boomerangs might be coming home any day, but it was late October when they did arrive and Lyndsey, who had seven days' leave due, packed joyfully to spend it with Bette.

They met on the station and they hugged one another and they laughed and they cried. Bette was painfully thin and had a drained look, but she was still the same effervescent person Lyndsey had known. Bette, after she had wiped her eyes, said, 'Well come on, what are we standing here for soaking the platform with our tears, we have months of news to catch up on.' They linked arms and went up the road talking, and were still talking at midnight.

Bette, who had twice been ill with malaria, made light of it; she made light of the lengthy journeys they had made over appallingly rough terrain; she joked of the fact that she and George had been 'gobbled' up by mosquitoes and of the heat that made sweat pour down one's back to raise an arm. But any discomfort they had known, according to Bette, had been worth it to see the faces of the men when they gave their concerts.

Lyndsey had told Bette most of her news in letters but they discussed certain things again, such as the way Andrew kept stressing there was no need for them to worry, they were being well treated. Then Bette mentioned that Elliott had written twice to her and added:

'Both these men are still in love with you, Lyndsey. Now you talk about this Johnnie. Are you in love with him?'

Lyndsey shook her head. 'No, we're just friends. I meet plenty of men, could have dozens of dates, but all the time I feel in limbo, waiting for the war to get over for Andrew and Elliott to be back.'

'And what then?' Bette asked gently. 'Which one would you choose?'

Lyndsey gave a sign of despair. 'I don't know, Bette, I just don't know. Both are a great deal in my thoughts, in my dreams. Am I really in love with either? Will either man want *me* when they do come home? Johnnie's a lovely person, warm, thoughtful. I would let him make love to me but he won't. He says I must want him to make love to me more than anything else in the world and it's not like that.'

'But would it be different if there was no Andrew, no Elliott? Are you chasing a dream, Lyndsey?'

Lyndsey sat looking at her for a moment then she nodded

slowly. 'I could well be. I know that Johnnie would make a wonderful husband, he's not only kind and thoughtful, he's fun to be with and we always have plenty to talk about.'

'Plenty of couples have married for less reasons.'

Lyndsey picked up the poker and stirred the dying embers of the fire. 'I've been moved sexually by Johnnie and could be a lot more if I let myself go, but – ' She looked up at Bette again, 'I think it's the magic that's missing. But then, am I living in a fantasy world that only exists in fairy tales?' She laid down the poker. 'Johnnie teases me, says I'm too practical.'

'It's not a bad thing to be, Lyndsey, not in the situation that you are in. You're young, you've plenty of time. Too many go overboard and blame the war for being promiscuous, then live to regret it. How about a cup of cocoa, then you can tell me again about Fay and Dominic. I think I would like them.'

Lyndsey and Bette had had that whole day to themselves. Even Mrs Petrie had just popped in to say hello then disappeared, and Lyndsey was glad of the time together because after that people kept dropping in all the time. Not that Lyndsey didn't enjoy all the talk, she did, it made her realize how much she had been involved with the naval side of life. Now she was hearing the problems of civilians, the worry of feeding and clothing a family on the small rations, not only because of the lack of coupons but because of the shortage of money when a husband was in the Forces.

This turned out to be one of Bette's busiest days, for as one group of people left, more arrived. The last to arrive were a few of the Boomerangs, George included. And, as always, George turned it into something of a party. He joked about their visit abroad, making them all laugh as he described certain incidents. Mrs Petrie, who had called and been persuaded to stay, said admiringly, 'Well, you've all certainly done your bit cheering up the troops. Now I must do mine.'

'And what had you in mind, Mrs P? Doing a fandango with a lonely soldier?' George teased.

'Oh, nothing like that. There was an appeal on the wireless to the public earlier to save paper. You see they want to make cardboard to pack cartridges to send to the Russian front.'

'And a very good cause, Mrs P. The Russians are making a blooming good stand against Hitler's hordes, they need all the help they can get.'

'I agree, George, but it'll be a job to find any more paper. I cleared most of it out when there was an appeal a while ago. I think all I have in the attic are the love letters my husband wrote to me before we were married.'

'Send those,' George replied promptly. 'Just think of the amount of paper they could get if everybody parted with their old letters.'

Mrs Petrie protested at this. She couldn't possibly, they were precious, very precious indeed. She read them often.

There was a short silence then George said quietly, 'If you knew that your letters would help to save a young man's life, someone close to you, would you send them?'

After another silence Mrs Petrie nodded. 'Yes, I would, George, I would. After all, I know the contents of every letter by heart.'

Lyndsey felt a lump come into her throat. Love letters – material things, but so important to the owners. She had treasured Andrew's letters and Elliott's. Must they be sacrificed too?

After their company had gone Bette said, 'When I think of all the stuff that I have hoarded in the attic, old theatre programmes, bill posters, letters from hundreds of people . . . As George pointed out, it's the quantity that will make an impact.'

'But surely that kind of thing would be of great interest to future generations?' Lyndsey said.

'They probably would, but if I were to die tomorrow

someone would come in and burn the lot.' Bette shrugged. 'So –'

Every morning Bette would go early to the village in the hope of getting some extras from the shops. One morning she came back gleefully with a couple of oranges and a small tin of apricots. The following morning it was a box of matches, with Bette exclaiming how lucky she was, she had got the last box.

During that week the Boomerangs had a number of requests to do shows for the forces, including Christmas Day and Boxing Day. Bette hesitated about the last two, wanting to know what Lyndsey's plans were. Lyndsey told her to go ahead and accept, that it was more important for the forces to be entertained and added that she could be on duty over Christmas. If not she could always go to Fay and Dominic's. And so it was left at that.

There were times when Bette and Lyndsey tramped through woods, over fields, often walking in companionable silence. And, by the end of the week, Lyndsey had lost that awful rootless feeling and Bette had lost her drawn look. When they parted it was with the promise to meet in London one day and do a matinée.

When they did meet they were a threesome. Johnnie was with them. Bette seemed greatly taken with him and said he was a fine chap and obviously very much in love with Lyndsey, and teasingly added he was worth snapping up!

Lyndsey was certainly becoming more and more fond of Johnnie and on this leave was extra loving towards him. When the time came for them to part she clung to him.

Johnnie said, 'Lyndsey, does this mean you would marry me?'

She put a finger to his lips. 'Don't let's talk about it, not now.'

She thought about it while he was away, knowing how much he had come to mean in her life, how much she looked forward to his return. It would make Johnnie happy. She felt sure they would get on well together. They could rent a flat, a home, but then she would think of Andrew and Elliott and doubt and uncertainty would overwhelm her.

Lyndsey was still undecided when Johnnie came back again, and then a decision was made for her – but not in a way she expected. Johnnie was quiet when they met and Lyndsey, as always when he looked tired, said gently, 'Bad trip, Johnnie?'

'Some of it bad, some good – well, it depends on – on the way one looks at it. Oh, Lyndsey, I have something to tell you and I don't know how to say it. You see I – I met a girl.'

Lyndsey's heart began a slow, painful beating. Another girl . . . Andrew all over again. She waited and Johnnie went on:

'It was while we were abroad. She's in the ATS, a little thing with great big eyes.' Freda, Andrew's wife, had been a 'little thing, with great big eyes'. 'For both of us it was love at first sight. It was as if something electric had passed between us. Do you know what I mean?'

'No, I don't, Johnnie.' Lyndsey felt wooden. 'I haven't been lucky enough to experience such a thing. But I'm glad for you.'

'I'm sorry, Lyndsey, really sorry, because I really did think I was in love with you until I met Carol and then – You *must* believe me, I didn't *want* it to happen, it just . . . did.'

'It's all right, Johnnie. Perhaps it will happen for me too, one of these days.'

'I hope we can still remain friends.' There was an almost desperate note in Johnnie's voice. Lyndsey felt anger rise in her. Andrew's words, could they remain friends? Then suddenly her anger died. Johnnie couldn't help falling in love. There had been an instant rapport between Fay and Dominic . . . something that she might never experience. She said: 'Yes, Johnnie, we can still be friends.'

She ran her fingertips over the green-painted wooden

seat. How many couples who had sat here had married? How many had parted to become just 'good friends'? She got up. 'It's cold. I think perhaps I had better leave you.'

He begged her to stay, to spend the rest of the evening with him, pointing out that she had said they could remain friends. Lyndsey gave in, and they went for a drink. To give Johnnie his due he did not talk about Carol as Andrew had done about Freda, and in fact he managed to make her laugh at times about silly remarks from some of the men on board. But in spite of the pub being warm she could not get the feeling of chill from her body . . . and knew it was the chill of rejection.

It was not until a month later when Lyndsey had a 48-hour pass and she and Bette spent it at the Mayfair house that she told her about Johnnie.

'I've come to the conclusion that I'm not really the type that men want to marry. They think they do but when they meet a "little thing, with great big eyes", well, that's it. I shall probably end up as one of the proverbial old maids.'

'Nonsense,' Bette said. 'I'm not a little thing with great big eyes but Rupert fell in love with me. In fact, I can't think of any wives I know who answer that description. And a good job too, otherwise there would be a world of spinsters. Snap out of it, love. It just hadn't to be. It's fate. You still have Andrew and Elliott.'

'To fall back on?' Lyndsey queried wryly, and to Bette's protest at this went on, 'From now on I shall think of Andrew and Elliott as friends only and I shall accept every date offered and let every man I go out with make love to me.'

'Oh, stop it, Lyndsey, stop being a martyr! It's just not you.' Bette paused and added, more gently, 'You've had a lot of raw deals, too many, but taking this attitude won't help. Accept the offers of dates, enjoy yourself, but stay decent. If you don't there will come a day when you find you are really in love and then you will hate yourself for being a tramp.'

Lyndsey sighed. 'Yes, I suppose so.'

It was not only the fact of having nothing to look forward to that plagued Lyndsey, but the constant ache over Johnnie, so at last she began to accept dates. She went to dances with her escorts, to dinners, to shows, but although she put on a bright face and told herself she was having a good time it did nothing to relieve the dreadful ache.

Then on 7 December came the news that the Japanese had bombed Pearl Harbor. The first shock at the attack was followed by the realization that America would now be fully committed into coming into the war. There was no great jubilation, just a quiet hope among the people that with America's help the war might soon be won.

Three days later one of Britain's newest battleships was sunk, the *Prince of Wales* and also the battle cruiser *Repulse*. This was a dreadful blow and in fact at that time the only good news was from the Russian front where the Russian armies were holding back the enemy.

One day Fay said to Lyndsey, 'I see that we're both on duty on Christmas Day, but free on Boxing Day. If you haven't any special plans spend it with us.' Lyndsey was about to refuse, then, remembering Bette telling her not to be a martyr, said, 'Thanks, Fay, I'd love to.'

For Lyndsey, Christmas Day was something to be got over, yet everyone had made an effort to make it as festive as possible. The mess was decorated with evergreens and there was the traditional dinner with roast turkey, with all the trimmings, and plum pudding, with a tot of rum to follow. And, as was the custom in the navy, the ratings were served by the officers.

During the afternoon Fay and Lyndsey, with members of another Boats' Crew team, were called out to ferry a sick sailor to shore, and missed the King's speech. They heard on the nine o'clock news that Hong Kong had fallen, which put a damper on the day. Then the following morning Fay had word to say that her father was ill, and she left with Dominic to go home.

Lyndsey was feeling so flat that when the post came bringing a letter from Andrew, she held it to her, taking it to read in isolation. It began, 'My own darling Lyndsey,' and went on: 'For three nights in a row I dreamt we were married and on our honeymoon and I feel sure you must be longing for this time to come, as much as I am . . .'

At this point Lyndsey stopped, her heart beating fast. She had signed her letters to him, 'With Love, Lyndsey', but never once had she as much as hinted about marriage. She wouldn't have done, not even knowing her own true feelings about him. He must have misinterpreted something she had said, or was it wishful thinking on Andrew's part? If so, what could she say when she wrote in reply to this letter? She couldn't very well say she had no intention of marrying him, and yet it would be so wrong to let him think she would.

The rest of the letter was about activities in the camp, playing football, chess – he was becoming quite an expert at both. He made no mention of receiving Christmas parcels, so presumably he had not yet had either Bette's or her own. Lyndsey longed to talk about it to Bette, but as Bette was doing a show she had to wait until the following day.

Bette dismissed it as nothing to worry about. Men must have something to dream about and by the time he wrote again it would probably all be forgotten. Lyndsey agreed and went on to ask Bette about the show, but afterwards she went on worrying.

She had a short note from Fay to say her father had recovered and they would be returning soon. When she did come back she announced to Lyndsey she was pregnant. Lyndsey hugged her. 'Oh, Fay, I'm so glad for both of you, but I will miss you.'

'Not yet you won't, not yet. I'm certainly not going to cosset myself, in spite of Dominic wanting to wrap me in cotton wool. Come and spend the day with us tomorrow, he's dying to tell you about it.'

Lyndsey's visit coincided with the exciting news of a raid on Norway, with enemy ships sunk and industrial plants and gun emplacements destroyed. It had been done under a smokescreen and the raid completed in less time than the estimated fifteen minutes.

'This calls for a celebration!' Dominic declared and got up to pour drinks. 'Marvellous news, it's a beginning, there'll be more.'

They drank to news of the raid then to Fay's pregnancy. She was radiant and Dominic's eyes were so full of love, so full of pride when he looked at Fay, that Lyndsey felt like weeping. Would there ever come a time when a man would look at her in that way?

It was a week later when she heard from Richard. He had received the parcels, he thanked Lyndsey, said how welcome they were. He had written to Bette thanking her for hers, and added what a wonderful person Bette was, and hoped that she and Lyndsey had managed to spend Christmas together. There was nothing about what he was doing and Lyndsey found it unsatisfactory, like most of Richard's letters.

Every day after that she looked for a letter from Elliott but it was seven weeks before she heard and then, unexpectedly, the news came from Bette, who Lyndsey was phoning.

'Don't faint,' Bette said, laughing. 'But I had Ellliott here with me earlier. I was dying to tell you when I left a message for you to ring me, but – '

'Elliott?' Lyndsey interrupted, bewildered. 'I don't get it. You mean he was with you, in *your* house? I thought he was somewhere in the Far East.'

'He was, Lyndsey.' Bette spoke soberly now. 'He was wounded six weeks ago and shipped back home. He's over the worst and recuperating in a convalescent home not too far away. Coming to me was his first real outing. He's dying to see you, naturally.' There was a pause then Bette went on, 'You'll see a big change in him, Lyndsey, he's had a head operation and three bullets taken from his leg. But he *is* recovering, I give you my word. He's calling tomorrow. Can you manage to come?'

'I'll be there, Bette, we can talk then.'

Lyndsey felt unable to say more. Wounded six weeks ago . . . a head operation, he could have died and she might never have known. She felt sick. She thought of him in hospital, possibly without visitors. Why had he not let them know?

Although Bette had prepared her for the change in Elliott Lyndsey was shocked when she saw him the next day. He was like a scarecrow, with the bandage covering his head blending in with his colourless face. She went to him with an anguished, 'Oh, Elliott,' and putting her arms around him she laid her cheek against his. 'Why didn't you let us know sooner?'

He held her away from him and she caught a glimpse of the old Elliott in his smile as he said, 'I am not a pretty sight now, but I was a horrible sight weeks ago. I didn't want anyone to see me.'

Bette gave a little sniff and dabbed at her eyes. 'Well, sit down the pair of you. I've brewed some tea and I'll bring it in.'

Lyndsey, who had sat opposite to Elliott, reached out and laid a hand over his. 'Bette and I could have come and visited you. That's what friends are for. It's the bad times when you need them the most.'

Elliott nodded slowly. 'True, but I had to have a bullet removed that was close to my brain and I didn't know how I was going to turn out. I could have been an imbecile.'

Lyndsey gripped his hand. 'But you're not and now we must see that you get well as quickly as possible. Do you hear?'

Elliott gave a boyish grin then. 'Yes, Wren MacLaren. I see you're still as bossy as ever.'

'Someone has to boss you!'

'I want to know all you've been doing,' Elliott said.

Bette, who had come in with the tea, said, 'And you better tell him, Lyndsey, he was plaguing me to know everything about you the other day when he was here.' She poured the tea for both of them then said, 'I must nip to the shops, I won't be long.' Lyndsey, who knew that Bette wanted to give them a chance to be alone for a while, said to Elliott when she had gone:

'Elliott, will you marry me?'

She was surprised to hear herself saying it, but Elliott showed no surprise.

'Why, Lyndsey? Is it because you want to help make me "better"? I want you to be honest with me.'

'No, that's only part of the reason, Elliott. I feel rootless and I have always had the feeling that you feel the same way too, but I could be wrong.'

'No, you're right, but there has to be a stronger reason than that to make a marriage. Let me ask you one thing. If Andrew had returned and had suffered the same injuries as I, would you have made the same offer to him? The truth now.'

Lyndsey looked at the floor then raised her head. 'I can't tell you that, I just don't know what my reactions would be. You are two different people, different natures. I only know at this moment that I want, more than anything else, for us to share our lives.' When he was silent, looking at her in the solemn way he had at times, she went on, speaking earnestly, 'Don't you see, Elliott, we're both without an anchor, drifting. I need someone to care for, to love, to share a home, have children.'

He gave a sigh of despair. 'Oh, Lyndsey, stop tempting me, I want to, I want to very much, but I can't say yes knowing that Andrew could come home and you would suddenly realize it was he you were really in love with. And anyway,' he gave a wry smile and touched her cheek, 'I'm in no condition at the moment to give any girl a child.'

Lyndsey wanted to tell him she would wait, it didn't matter, but she really had gone far enough, too far really. She said:

'I wonder if any other girl has proposed marriage and been talked out of it?' There was a break in her voice and Elliott, looking concerned, took both her hands in his.

'Never regret it, Lyndsey. I feel honoured that you did. It took courage and I admired you tremendously for your honesty. When you think about it later I'm sure you'll realize that we are doing the right thing.'

It was Elliott's use of the word *we*, sharing the responsibility of the proposal, that allowed Lyndsey to keep a sense of dignity.

He then began to question her about her work, asked after Fay and Dominic, Richard, and when Bette returned they were deep in conversation about the various areas of war. Bette scolded them and said this was a time when they could forget the war for once. They both agreed.

By the time the staff car came to collect Elliott a faint colour had come into his cheeks and he looked much brighter. He said he felt better for seeing them both and Lyndsey promised to come to Bette's as often as she could.

For Lyndsey the visits were something to look forward to, the anchor she needed, and she wondered what the outcome would be when Elliott was on the road to recovery.

To her dismay, a month after her first meeting with him at Bette's, she had a temporary posting to Scotland. 'I don't want to go,' she said, 'it's too far away, I won't be able to see you. I'll be there a month or six weeks. It's not fair.'

Elliott, who was beginning to put on weight and to look more like his old self, took her in his arms and rocked her to and fro. 'There's nothing fair about war, my love. Men in the services can't say they don't want to go to the battlefront, or that they don't feel like flying that particular day, or decide they don't want to go to sea. You're in the navy and you signed on for the duration.'

'Yes, I know. It's just that – '

'Anyway,' Elliott went on, 'I shall probably be posted soon, possibly abroad.'

Lyndsey drew away and stared at him. 'Posted? You're not fit to go anywhere yet, much less go abroad.'

'Lyndsey' – he spoke patiently – 'if they were allowed to send men without an arm to the front they would do so. Every man is needed and I certainly don't want to sit at home twiddling my thumbs.'

Fay, when told, said, 'I'm sure they won't send him abroad, Lyndsey.' Dominic, who thought they would, was proved right. When Lyndsey returned from Scotland after five weeks she found that Elliott had left the day before, and she wept bitter tears that fate could be so unkind.

THIRTY

During the next two years Lyndsey had so many different postings that Dominic jokingly referred to her as the 'spare part'. Lyndsey had had no objections to the moves, she needed the variety, needed to meet different people while she waited for the war to be over.

The people at home, in spite of great support from America with food and other commodities, suffered from shortages of every kind. Some people considered it a hardship when asked by the government to use no more than five inches of water in their baths. To others who had been bombed out of their homes this would have been a luxury. 'A bath?' one woman exclaimed, 'I've been washing in a cup of water for the last two weeks!'

One of Lyndsey's greatest pleasures was to spend a day, or the odd weekend, with Fay and Dominic and their sixteen-month-old son Ben. He was a sturdy, fair-haired child with a wide smile and an infectious chuckle that endeared him to everyone. Often when Lyndsey would feel his chubby arms around her neck a lump would come into her throat. If only she had a child of her own to love.

Dominic would always go up to bed first to leave the 'girls' to have a chat. Once, when Lyndsey told Fay she envied her, Fay confessed that although she enjoyed her role as wife and mother she missed her job in the Wrens. 'It was the activity, Lyndsey,' she said, 'meeting so many different characters. Do you know what I mean?'

Lyndsey did, but she felt that such things still did not compensate her for not having someone to love and be loved by. Although Johnnie had asked her to remain friends she had only seen him once since they broke up and then he was rushing to catch a train. There was only time for him to say he was getting married in a month's time and for Lyndsey to wish them luck, then he was away.

On this present visit Fay asked her how Richard and Bette were getting along. The two of them had been corresponding regularly and, in fact, more often than not it was through Bette that Lyndsey had news of her uncle.

'Splendidly,' she said now. 'At least it seems that way and I'm glad. I would like nothing better than to see them married. I feel that Bette is doing too much. She's constantly away doing concerts and she's beginning to show the strain, but knowing Bette she won't give up.'

'And Andrew and Elliott?' Fay queried. 'What news from them?'

'Well, what news I get about Andrew is also invariably through Bette. He's still sending his love, but no longer seems to expect that I shall be waiting to rush into marriage the moment he comes home.' Lyndsey sighed. 'As for Elliott's letters, they're so cryptic you need a code book. I took it from the last one that he was no longer in the Middle East but in France. He talked about little Leo and little Elliott no longer being able to make sand castles and went on to ask me to give his regards to Aunt Simone. Leo is a fellow officer and Aunt Simone is an elderly lady he knew in France. He does send his love to me but he never says anything tender, such as I miss you so much.'

'Elliott wouldn't, would he? He's not that kind of man.'

'No,' Lyndsey said.

The mention of France had them discussing the possibility of invasion. There was a lot of extra activity at a number of ports and it seemed as if the possibility of invasion was closer than ever. Lyndsey was now stationed at Southampton, where the river Hamble was full of rows of the craft known as 'trots', of tank, infantry and assault landing craft. And where once naval uniforms had predominated in the town, now army uniforms outnumbered them, mostly American. There was animosity from the British troops because the Yanks, being better paid, could not only give the girls a better time but could offer them gifts of nylons (a scarce commodity in England) and chocolates, or candies, as they called them.

More and more ships arrived, small flotillas, large merchant ships, destroyers, Polish and Greek corvettes as well as British, making the tasks of Boats' Crew more difficult when men had to be delivered to certain ships and landing craft in the blackout. Added to this was a spell of bad weather, gales and torrential rain.

The Wrens now constantly had lectures on the necessity for security. In fact, it had been so drummed into them that Lyndsey said once to Fay, 'I found myself afraid the other day to talk to a soldier on the train because I felt there was something strange about his manner. As it turned out he was all right, his parents met him at the station – quiet, rather homely people.' Lyndsey laughed. 'But then, of course, that means nothing, they could all have been spies. But how can you be sure of any person?'

'By instinct, or sheer amateurism on the part of the spy,' Fay said, and gave an instance of a German giving the Nazi salute when a Home Guard, suspicious of him, greeted him with a 'Heil Hitler!'

As activities increased and men went out on practice runs on landing craft, speculation was rife. Where would they land on the day? The Americans seemed to favour Calais because although it was known to be the most heavily defended area on the seaboard it was the most direct route to Germany. Others plumped for Normandy, reckoning that although its defences were weaker, if the bridges over the Loire and the Seine were destroyed it would cut the enemy off from the rest of Europe. There were stories of Field Marshal Rommel, who favoured

Normandy for the landings, building fortifications at great speed along the Atlantic seaboard, while Field Marshal von Runstedt concentrated on building up reserves in the Calais area.

There were other stories of huge dummy camps and dummy fleets of landing craft being assembled in the area of Dover. Lyndsey only knew that more and more ships were arriving and more and more troops, and that the Boats' Crew were kept so busy that when they were off duty all they wanted to do was sleep. They no longer worked only with their regular crews but went on boats where they were needed.

Although there were no longer heavy raids they always had to be prepared for lone raiders; then the barrage balloon boats would nip in and out among the ships to try and prevent the planes from swooping low over them.

As soon as the air-raid sirens went the Boats' Crew donned their tin helmets. Several times bombs had dropped close to Lyndsey's boat almost lifting it out of the water. It took all the expertise of the coxswain to hold the boat on course to a slow ahead.

For a time the weather was foul with gales screaming through the riggings and waves crashing over the boat like waterfalls. Often, when the crew were on constant call, they would be in soaked clothes all day and more often than not at these times had little chance of having anything to eat.

And yet Lyndsey knew she would not have wanted to do any other job. There was so much she felt that compensated: a sentry on the pier handing them steaming mugs of cocoa; beautiful dawns when wraiths of mist hovered over the water; evenings when the sea was magical with phosphorescence; the feeling of mysticism on foggy nights when the bells of buoys and anchors were 'playing a tune'; and most moving of all on a dark night was when a few men would start singing; others would join in, perhaps with a haunting Irish lullaby, and soon it would seem there was a choir of a hundred voices that sent shivers of pleasure up and down one's spine.

More and more ships kept coming in, and more and more troops. As one girl said, the place would soon burst at the seams. Another made the remark that the invasion was bound to take place at any time now, which made Lyndsey realize that they would then be more or less prisoners for security reasons. Although she felt that she could sleep the clock around on her off-duty day she decided to go and see Fay and Dominic and little Ben.

To her disappointment Dominic had taken Ben to a friend's house to stay for the afternoon because Fay had had a stomach upset. 'And I feel a fraud now,' she said to Lyndsey, 'because the pain has gone. But how lovely to see you. Let's have a drink and a long natter.'

They discussed the coming invasion at some length then Fay said, with a thoughtful look at Lyndsey, 'I haven't once heard you say that you are worried about Elliott.'

Lyndsey was silent for a long time, then she looked up. 'I've been able to close my mind to it, just as I did with Uncle Richard when I guessed he was in the Middle East. I think that both men are their own people and are not really deeply concerned about me.'

'Oh, come on, Lyndsey, how can you say such a thing. Both of them – '

'Fay, I'm not saying this in a martyred way, I just feel it's the truth. I love Uncle Richard, love him for so many things, all his kindness to me, but he admits to running away from things when he was younger and he ran away after Marian died. I needed him, I was ill with shock after the raid at the Café de Paris. He is my only living relative. I didn't want him to feel I was tied to him, but if he had only stayed a while before applying for a post abroad. Two or three months.'

'And Elliott? Do you regard him as a coward too, running away from things. Running away from you?'

'In a way, yes. I asked him to marry me and he refused.'

'For your own good.'

'But was it? Couldn't he have made it an excuse? As far as loving someone now is concerned I feel there's something dead inside me. I think that both Uncle Richard and Elliott will return, they're survivors. Elliott has been wounded twice and gone back to fight again.'

'Don't tempt fate, Lyndsey. There's always a third time.'

Lyndsey sat unmoved. 'Possibly. Then it will be fate, won't it? Whatever happens we can't get away from fate.'

Fay said with feeling, 'Lyndsey, I don't like to hear you speaking in this way. You're a warm, loving person.'

'War changes people. I would never have thought I would have matched seamen's language, but I do. I accept dates and I'll let a man kiss me good night, but that's all, and they accept it. They seem to know what to expect. Perhaps I have a name for being cold, I don't know.'

'Lyndsey, people don't change fundamentally. There will come a time when you will come to life again – with a man. How do you feel about Andrew?'

'I'm very fond of him. But shall we change the subject? Tell me about my little Ben, what mischief has he been up to lately?'

Fay said, 'You can't kid me you're dead inside. Mention of Ben makes you glow with love.' She paused then went on, 'He was a complete angel for a couple of days but yesterday, well! he was into everything . . .'

Lyndsey hoarded up in her mind all the things about Ben that Fay had told her but would not let herself dwell for a moment on either Richard, Andrew or Elliott.

After another lecture on the importance of security, the following day the Boats' Crew were told there would be no more shore leave and that from now on they would all be confined to barracks at the end of the Royal Pier. They were also told that phone calls were forbidden and it would be useless writing letters as there would be no postal service in the military zone.

A buzz of chatter broke out after these announcements

but they were told to get on with the job of transferring what they needed from their shore quarters to the barracks. They had two hours.

'Lord,' someone said, 'the invasion must be starting tonight!'

It didn't. The weather, which had been quite good at the end of May, changed again at the beginning of June to heavy rain and in this gloom the Boats' Crew worked day and night, delivering goods and urgent signals to ships – with small tugs helping them on the ammunition runs.

Most of the landing craft by then had their quota of soldiers, tanks, guns and armoured cars and were considered to be sealed ships. No one knew the exact time the invasion fleet would move out but they did assume the weather would have to be reasonable for the success of the operation.

By grapevine they heard that the weather forecast was bad with high winds and poor visibility predicted, and people said poor Eisenhower, who was in charge of the whole operation, and had to make a decision. It was said there were over a quarter of a million men and their equipment cooped up aboard landing craft and other transport and where men had left camps to go abroad, other men had taken their places and were sitting in misery under camouflage nets.

A strange expectant silence hung in the air, not disturbed by the screaming of gulls and the wind howling in the riggings of hundreds of ships. There was a general feeling that the invasion would not take place, but, on a day when the weather was still not good the whole place suddenly burst into life. There was activity everywhere, men shouting orders, heavy boots clattering along iron decks; later engines began to throb.

It was not until the hour before dawn that the great armada began to move out, phantom ships leaving to join the other ships that had converged near the Isle of Wight.

The morning was bitterly cold and it seemed that the fleet of ships moving out would never end. Many of them carried barrage balloons and as the morning lightened they became things of beauty, silver tinged with pink.

Lyndsey suddenly felt choked, wondering how many men out of this great armada would return.

It was strange the next day to see the harbour empty apart from the mooring buoys bobbing on the water. Lyndsey, with the rest of the crew, scrubbed and polished their boat and did maintenance jobs on the engine. The trouble was that after the big build-up, the constant work, the lack of sleep and snatched meals, none of them could whip up any enthusiasm for the job.

The waiting for the result of the operation seemed endless. Their first news was three days later when an armed merchant ship arrived and disembarked several hundred German prisoners. When it was first realized who they were there were some boos and catcalls, but these soon tailed off as they saw not arrogant, defiant Nazis, but youths in tattered uniforms who looked ill-fed and despairing. Many of them were wounded and the strongest of them carried stretcher cases. In the sudden silence the only sound was the shuffling of the feet of these boys and Lyndsey wept inwardly for them. Their mothers, like those of any other race, would be praying for their safe return.

The next day and on subsequent days ships kept arriving to unload their cargoes of Allied troops, and the names Utah, Gold, Juno, Omaha, and Sword, which were the code names of five beaches strung along the coast of Normandy, were suddenly on the lips of everyone.

Word of the result of the operation began to trickle through. The American 4th Division had landed on Utah beach with comparatively few losses, but on Omaha beach there had been heavy casualties.

The British and Canadians, whose task it had been to capture the towns of Bayeux and Caen and the road that linked them, failed at first, but by midnight the bridgehead into Europe had at last been won and the battle of the beaches over. But this was just the beginning. There was some hard and bitter fighting before Caen fell. And while the Allied Expeditionary Force continued to advance towards Paris lorry loads of American troops arrived every day to fill the landing craft that would take them to Normandy.

Lyndsey was not quite sure when the change started, but she began to long to have word of Elliott. She worried about him, imagining him in the thick of the fighting, or perhaps lying wounded in some hospital. And she would not get to know because she was not next of kin, nor did she know who was.

Then one day she heard someone saying there was talk of an exchange of prisoners of war and she knew then that although she would be delighted to see Andrew again, it was Elliott who was important to her, knew that her life would be completely empty if she never saw him again. She told Fay about it on her next visit.

'I know there are people like you and Dominic and Bette and her husband who fell in love at first sight, but there must be other people like me where love comes slowly. It did for my mother, so Ivy told me, and my parents had a very deep love for one another.'

Lyndsey paused then added on a note of despair, 'Oh, Fay, supposing Elliott has been killed, or is lying maimed in some hospital.'

'Don't contemplate such a thing. You said you thought of your uncle Richard and Elliott as being survivors; well, keep on thinking in that way. Incidentally, I think it's time you had some leave. Dominic thinks so too, you look all in. You were working all hours God sends before the invasion and the human body can only stand so much.'

Lyndsey gave a wan smile. 'I'm trying to be a survivor too. Actually, I'm all right. All I want is to see or hear from Elliott.'

By the end of that month most of the trots were full

again and all Boats' Crew were constantly ferrying men, stores and messages to ships' masters. All the crew were feeling the strain and were at times almost asleep on their feet when they came off duty.

Lyndsey had not heard from Bette for some time and when a message was left for her to phone her she went right away.

'I'm home for a few months, love,' Bette said. 'Had to give up the travelling, but the Boomerangs are carrying on. I had a few bouts of malaria. Any chance of you coming to see me? If not I'll come to see you.'

Lyndsey, joyful, said she would come to Kent and later went to the office to ask for leave. The officer said, 'There are three of you down for ten days' leave. You would have heard this afternoon.'

Lyndsey felt she was swaying on her feet. 'Thanks, ma'am.'

Ten days, without having any scrubbing and polishing to do, or going out in all weathers and at all hours. It seemed like heaven.

Bette met her at the station and after they had hugged and shed a few tears each she said, 'Oh, it is good to have you here, love. We have so much news to catch up on. Let's get home and have a cup of tea, then we can talk ourselves to death!'

They talked practically non-stop for two hours then Bette said, 'I had a very special gift today from an old lady. She said she had been hoarding it but wanted me to have it.'

It was a large tablet of sandalwood soap and Bette and Lyndsey gloated over it. Later they each had a bath, but taking only the regulation five inches of water.

For the first two nights they went to bed early and slept late the mornings following, and on the third morning Lyndsey said, 'I feel ready to chop down a tree and saw it up!' Bette echoed this, then added, 'It's a treat to see you out of uniform and wearing a dress. You look really lovely,

Lyndsey. If Elliott were to arrive now I'm sure he would sweep you off your feet.'

'And I would be willing to be swept off,' Lyndsey said quietly. 'But I mustn't indulge in wishful thinking. What are we going to do today?'

'I'll tell you what you can do for me while I'm tidying up. Nip down to the village and see if anything is going. Mr Moore said they might have some currants in, and while you're there bring a tin of dried egg and we can have a spam omelette, I can only get a couple of new-laid eggs from the farm now and then.'

Lyndsey didn't manage to get currants but Mr Moore pushed a small packet of dried apricots into her basket saying, 'A little something special for you, my dear. I know what a rough time you've been having.' His wife added a small bar of chocolate and Lyndsey came back dying to tell Bette of her little bit of luck.

But news of Lyndsey's 'little extras' was lost in Bette's exciting news when she arrived. Andrew had phoned, he had been repatriated. 'He's in London,' Bette exclaimed, 'and coming here. Isn't it great?'

'Oh, Bette, that's marvellous! When is he coming, what time will he be here?'

'As soon as he can get a train. I'll have to make up a bed and dust the room. What can I give him to eat?'

'Bette, calm down, I don't think that Andrew would notice if the place was hanging with cobwebs.'

'You're right, of course, but I must make up the bed, he might be tired and want to go to bed right away. Come up and help me and we can talk.'

They speculated about the changes they might find in Andrew. Lyndsey said, 'He hasn't mentioned about us getting married for some time, so I don't think he'll expect me to, well, greet him lovingly.'

'I don't think so. He knew you went to dances, had dates with other men, knows you like Elliott.'

Lyndsey shook out the folds of the sheet. 'But he doesn't

know how deeply I am in love with Elliott.' She flung the sheet over the bed. 'But I can't tell him the minute he's back.'

'Stop worrying, I'm sure there'll be no need to. He'll have all sorts of things to talk about. What shall I give him to eat? Look, if you finish making the bed I'll nip up to the farm and see if I can beg a few slices of bacon. I'll be back soon.'

It was three hours later when Andrew arrived and Bette was out. She had suddenly become worried that they might not have enough bread and decided she would nip into Mrs Petrie's and see if she could borrow some until the next day.

Hardly had Bette gone when Andrew arrived. With a wide grin he picked Lyndsey up and swung her around. When he set her down he held her at arms' length. 'Do you know something, Lyndsey MacLaren, you are more beautiful than ever.'

She gave a breathless laugh. 'And you are just as exuberant, as cheeky, and as teasing as ever.'

'But he's much thinner,' Bette said as she came hurrying into the kitchen. Then she was laughing and crying as Andrew swung her off her feet.

Bette said, 'I can't believe you're here! Do you want to go to bed?'

Andrew threw back his head and laughed. 'What an invitation!'

She punched him on the shoulder. 'Oh, stop it, you know what I mean. Are you tired, are you hungry, shall I get you a meal?'

'I'm not tired, my lovely Bette, and I'm not hungry.' He walked to the window and spread his arms. 'All this lovely countryside. I want to walk, enjoy the glorious freedom.' He turned to face them. 'You've no idea what it was like coming back to London, to see girls, hundreds of them.' He grinned. 'We were love-starved.'

Then he sobered and began to talk about the prison

camp, about everything he had done, about his buddies, how good it had been in some ways, how bad in others, the lack of privacy. Then he ran his hand through his hair and apologized. 'I'm sorry, it was something I had to get out of my system.' He then told them he wanted to know about all that they had been doing.

'You, Bette, when did *you* get back? You must certainly have had some adventures in the Far East.'

It was not until later when Bette insisted on getting a meal ready that Andrew asked Lyndsey about her life.

'How about all your boyfriends? Are you serious about any particular one?'

Lyndsey thought it obvious by his question that he had not expected her to wait for him coming home, but although he had spoken lightly she was aware that he was watching her closely.

'No, I'm not serious about anyone. I don't think it's wise in wartime.'

'Oh, come on,' he said with a laugh. 'It wouldn't do if all girls thought the same, or there would be no one getting married.' After a pause he added, his tone now casual, 'Did I tell you that the sister of one of my pals in the camp had been writing to me?'

'No, I don't think so.'

'Her name's Janet, she's working in London, for the Ministry. She seems a very nice girl, writes chatty letters. I promised to look her up sometime.'

'It'll be nice for you to meet her.'

'Do you hear anything from Elliott?' Again Andrew spoke in a casual way and again she was conscious of him watching her.

'Yes, I hear now and again. He seems all right, but makes no mention of getting home.'

Bette came in then to say the meal was ready and Lyndsey was glad of the interruption. Although she knew it was a good thing that Andrew was interested in another girl she had an odd feeling of being rejected yet again.

Possibly because Andrew had been so much a part of her life for so long. Later, she realized that her attitude had been a selfish one, and having accepted it she was completely at ease with him that afternoon when the three of them went for a walk.

In the evening Andrew had his wish and they went to the local pub where they had drinks and a sing-song around the piano. Everyone made a great fuss of him and he was so full of boyish high spirits that Lyndsey felt moved by it. It was the freedom he was enjoying.

The next morning at breakfast he suggested they all go to London, take in a show, live it up. But both Bette and Lyndsey suggested he went on his own, with Bette adding, 'I've been away for so long I have a lot to catch up on and Lyndsey really needs a rest. We've both had a pretty gruelling time.'

'Yes, of course. But don't you worry, I'll be back.'

When he was ready to leave he thanked them quietly for what they had both done for him.

'You've no idea what it meant to me to have your letters, your parcels. Getting parcels was like Christmas every time. Any news was a godsend. I'll just never forget that.'

The next moment he was teasing them again. 'Keep the bed aired, I'll be back in a couple of days. I'll see what I can scrounge in the way of food while I'm away.'

He kissed them both and left and they watched him striding down the road, waving to people who called to him. When he was out of sight Bette and Lyndsey came inside. Bette said, 'It was best he went on his own.' She began to clear away the breakfast pots. 'After we've washed up we'll go to the shops, okay?'

Andrew did not come back while Lyndsey was there, but he did phone to say he had looked up Janet. She was a fine-looking girl and a great sport, and there was a group of them going round together having a whale of a time.

Lyndsey felt a small ache, remembering the good times

435

she had had with Andrew. She said to Bette, 'And I'm enjoying the peace and the quiet. It's what I needed.'

'And me too,' Bette declared.

By the end of Lyndsey's leave they had both lost their look of strain.

Lyndsey returned to London to Hitler's new weapon, flying bombs. They were causing casualties and a great deal of damage. Although the RAF had found their launching ramps and bombed them they still came. They were a terrible weapon that filled people with fear. They fell at once when the engine cut out and if you heard it stop you were lucky if you had time to dive for shelter.

They became known as doodlebugs and as their number increased many people became immune to them, just as they had with the heavy bombing earlier. But it was a shock to all when figures were announced that over four thousand people had been killed between June and July, seven thousand houses destroyed and over eight hundred thousand damaged.

Although the news was good on other fronts Lyndsey became depressed as time went by and she had no word from Elliott. All news she had of Andrew came from Bette. He was flying again and seeing Janet whenever he could.

Every opportunity Bette and Lyndsey had they spent together. Lyndsey would go to Kent to stay perhaps only overnight and at other times Bette came to London and stayed with Lyndsey. When Mrs Grey knew they would be there she lit fires to warm the house.

Once when Bette arrived she was quiet and when Lyndsey asked what was wrong she said, a little tentatively, 'Richard has asked me to marry him and I didn't know how you would feel about it.'

Lyndsey jumped up and hugged her. 'How I'd feel about it? I think it's great! Oh, Bette, it's the best thing that could happen. Richard was always a different person when he was with you. When's the wedding?'

'As soon as he can get leave.'

They talked about the wedding with Bette now getting as excited as Lyndsey. When Lyndsey asked where they were planning to live, Kent or London, Bette said, 'Richard prefers London, for convenience. We will, of course, have to go into it more thoroughly, but wherever we live you will of course be with us.' Bette smiled. 'That is, until *you* get married. And I'm sure that will be when Elliott comes home.'

'I doubt it, I haven't even heard from him.'

'You will, I know. He's very much in love with you and he did ask you to marry him.'

'So did Andrew and so did Bill.' There was a desolate note in Lyndsey's voice. 'And look what happened.'

'But Elliott is made of different stuff,' Bette said quietly. 'I feel sure he's a one-woman man.'

'Is there such a person?' Lyndsey shook her head. 'I doubt it.'

'Just you wait, you'll see.'

The weeks slipped by and still there was no word from Elliott. At the beginning of November when Lyndsey had a 48-hour pass it was arranged that Bette would come to London for the weekend.

She had said she would arrive about eleven o'clock on the Saturday morning and when the front door bell rang Lyndsey ran to answer it. Then she stood motionless, the smile of greeting dying as she saw the khaki-clad figure standing there.

'Elliott – ' Her body suddenly felt numb.

'Hello, Lyndsey.' He was as solemn-faced as if he had come for a funeral. 'How are you? I phoned Bette earlier and she told me to tell you that she would be delayed. Apparently George, one of the concert party, had arrived home ill and she wanted to visit him.'

Feeling was beginning to return to Lyndsey's limbs.

'Come in. It was a bit of a shock seeing you, I haven't heard from you for ages.'

'You haven't?' He took off his cap and stepped into the

hall. 'I wrote to you, several times, told you I was hoping to get some leave. I can't understand you not receiving any of my letters.'

'Well, I didn't. Come into the kitchen, it's warmer. I'll make some coffee. Bette brought me some. It's getting scarce. So is fuel, so is everything. Sit down.'

Heavens, Lyndsey thought, this is crazy, I'll be talking about the weather next. She asked when he had got back to England and he told her three days ago.

Three? He had not exactly rushed to contact her. He explained there had been certain formalities to be dealt with and she said, yes, of course, but thought that a phone call would have taken no more than minutes.

The next few minutes seemed an age to Lyndsey with their conversation being as formal as that between strangers on a train. They discussed all the areas of war, the flying bombs, the casualties and the devastation they had caused. He then asked about Fay and Dominic and little Ben, said that Bette had sounded just like her old self on the phone and added what a good job of work the concert party had done.

He then went on, 'Bette told me that Andrew had been repatriated and that he had been to see her when you were there. How did you find him?'

'Oh, fine, a lot thinner, but full of life, enjoying his new-found freedom, which was understandable. It must have been terrible to be restricted for so long. Caged, as it were.'

Elliott nodded. 'I agree.'

Lyndsey went on talking about Andrew, almost in a feverish way to keep the conversation going. She told him how he had enjoyed his first walk in Kent and about going to the local pub and having a sing-song, how everyone had made a fuss of him. But then Andrew had always been popular, he had this charisma. Lyndsey might have gone on talking about him had she not become aware of Elliott studying her in a thoughtful way.

Flustered she said, 'More coffee, Elliott?' It was when

she got up to take his mug that she caught sight of her reflection in the mirror. Her cheeks were flushed, her eyes bright . . . like a love-sick adolescent.

She wanted to tell him that Andrew had someone else in his life but knew it was impossible. It would be like telling him she was available and there could be someone else in Elliott's life. He had not behaved like a man still in love with her. He had not even kissed her when he arrived.

Elliott finished his coffee, said he must go and got up.

'Oh, must you? Can't you wait until Bette comes?'

'I should like to but I do have an appointment.' He paused. 'Would you mind very much if I came back after lunch, I really would like to see her.'

For the first time Elliott was smiling and for the first time it occurred to Lyndsey that it might be Bette he was in love with. They had always got on well together. It was Bette he had contacted when he was recovering from his wounds; Bette he had phoned earlier. But Bette would be marrying Richard. Lyndsey was about to tell him so when Elliott said, 'Well, thanks for the coffee, Lyndsey, I'll see you between half past two and three. 'Bye for now.'

She closed the door and stood, her back to it, a bleakness in her soul. She walked slowly back to the kitchen and sat in front of the fire. Was this the end to all the waiting, all the longing to see him?

It was not until later that she began to see the situation from Elliott's viewpoint. She had not been exactly forthcoming with *her* welcome. She had said something like, 'It was a shock, seeing you,' instead of greeting him with pleasure, with warmth. After all he had been away a long time – fighting. Perhaps when he came back after lunch – but then if it was really Bette he wanted to see . . . The phone rang.

Bette said, 'Lyndsey, I won't be able to get to London until after lunch. George is so low and he asked me if I would stay and have a meal with him. But I will get to

439

you. How are you getting on with Elliott?' There was a note of excitement now in Bette's voice. 'Wasn't it a marvellous surprise? I couldn't believe it when I heard his voice.'

Lyndsey tried to put some life into her own voice as she explained about him having to keep an appointment. 'But he is coming back after lunch. He wants to see you, Bette.' And then, because Lyndsey did not want to go into all that had happened, she added brightly, 'You'll hear all the other news when you arrive.'

'Lovely, and I know it will be good.' After a pause Bette said, 'Look, love, I've just been thinking. If I don't get to you by three o'clock I won't come until tomorrow. But I'll come early, okay?'

It was about half past two when Elliott returned and when he asked about Bette Lyndsey passed on her message. Elliott said,

'Actually, I'm glad she's not here yet. I wanted to have a talk with you, Lyndsey. I avoided it earlier because it was something that I didn't want to rush.' Lyndsey's heartbeats quickened as she led the way into the kitchen, not sure what it was he had to say.

She made no attempt to sit down and neither did he.

'Lyndsey, I once asked you to marry me.'

All the hurt, the humiliation of her rejections welled up.

'Yes, you did, Elliott. So did Andrew, but he married Freda instead. Then Johnnie asked me to marry him too. Did I tell you about Johnnie? He wanted us to set up a little house and do you know what? He suddenly fell in love with someone else.' Her voice broke and she turned away from him.

'Lyndsey – '

'And I asked you to marry me and *you* turned me down too.' This time the words ended on a sob.

'Oh, Lyndsey, my darling girl.' He took her by the shoulders and turned her to face him. Tears hung on her lashes and he wiped them away. 'I thought it was for your own good. I thought it was possible you were still in love with Andrew, and earlier, when you talked about him – '

'He's in love with someone else,' she blurted out.

'Yes, I know, Bette told me.'

Lyndsey looked up. 'Yet you asked me how I felt about him.'

'You could still have been in love with Andrew. And I know the terrible ache of loving someone and thinking she might care for someone else. Oh, Lyndsey, how I've longed to hold you. At times it's been a torment.'

The stern lines of his face had softened and there was a tenderness about his mouth.

'Elliott, why didn't you tell me all this? It would have meant so much to me. At times I've felt so alone.'

He wrapped strong arms around her and held her close, talking gently, 'There will be partings in the future. I have to leave in a few days' time, but we shall always be together in thought. We'll get married. I'll make arrangements.'

She looked up at him. 'Married? But I may not be able to get any more leave.'

'You won't need it. We'll get married on your next off-duty day. Even if we only have an hour together.'

'An hour!' she exclaimed.

A wicked gleam came into his eyes. 'A great lot of loving can be achieved in an hour.'

In spite of his teasing she could feel the wild beating of his heart. Her body responded to it and not wanting to show the strength of her emotions she drew away.

The grandfather clock in the hall began to chime. Elliott looked up and she was aware of a tension in him. Was he remembering that three o'clock was the deadline for Bette to arrive? In the seconds before the third chime came it was as though everything in the room was holding breath.

Elliott's gaze held hers and to the questioning in his eyes she said, a tremor in her voice:

441

'Shall we wait? Who knows what could happen tomorrow?'

He reached for her again and as she saw his expression she knew that all the waiting had been worthwhile. She had reached the haven she had yearned for . . . where love was all-enduring.

Bestselling Romantic Fiction

☐ The Lilac Bus	Maeve Binchy	£2.99
☐ The Sisters	Pat Booth	£3.50
☐ The Princess	Jude Deveraux	£3.50
☐ A World Apart	Marie Joseph	£3.50
☐ Erin's Child	Sheelagh Kelly	£3.99
☐ Satisfaction	Rae Lawrence	£3.50
☐ The Ladies of Missalonghi	Colleen McCullough	£2.50
☐ Lily Golightly	Pamela Oldfield	£3.50
☐ Women & War	Janet Tanner	£3.50

Prices and other details are liable to change

ARROW BOOKS, BOOKSERVICE BY POST, PO BOX 29, DOUGLAS, ISLE
OF MAN, BRITISH ISLES

NAME..

ADDRESS ....

....

....

Please enclose a cheque or postal order made out to Arrow Books Ltd. for the amount
due and allow the following for postage and packing.

U.K. CUSTOMERS: Please allow 22p per book to a maximum of £3.00.

B.F.P.O. & EIRE: Please allow 22p per book to a maximum of £3.00.

OVERSEAS CUSTOMERS: Please allow 22p per book.

Whilst every effort is made to keep prices low it is sometimes necessary to increase cover
prices at short notice. Arrow Books reserve the right to show new retail prices on covers
which may differ from those previously advertised in the text or elsewhere.

Bestselling General Fiction

☐ No Enemy But Time	Evelyn Anthony	£2.95
☐ Skydancer	Geoffrey Archer	£3.50
☐ The Sisters	Pat Booth	£3.50
☐ Captives of Time	Malcolm Bosse	£2.99
☐ Saudi	Laurie Devine	£2.95
☐ Duncton Wood	William Horwood	£4.50
☐ Aztec	Gary Jennings	£3.95
☐ A World Apart	Marie Joseph	£3.50
☐ The Ladies of Missalonghi	Colleen McCullough	£2.50
☐ Lily Golightly	Pamela Oldfield	£3.50
☐ Sarum	Edward Rutherfurd	£4.99
☐ Communion	Whitley Strieber	£3.99

Prices and other details are liable to change

ARROW BOOKS, BOOKSERVICE BY POST, PO BOX 29, DOUGLAS, ISLE
OF MAN, BRITISH ISLES

NAME..

ADDRESS...

....

....

Please enclose a cheque or postal order made out to Arrow Books Ltd. for the amount
due and allow the following for postage and packing.

U.K. CUSTOMERS: Please allow 22p per book to a maximum of £3.00.

B.F.P.O. & EIRE: Please allow 22p per book to a maximum of £3.00.

OVERSEAS CUSTOMERS: Please allow 22p per book.

Whilst every effort is made to keep prices low it is sometimes necessary to increase cover
prices at short notice. Arrow Books reserve the right to show new retail prices on covers
which may differ from those previously advertised in the text or elsewhere.